FROM COMMUNICATION TO PRESENCE

Emerging Communication

Studies in New Technologies and Practices in Communication

Emerging Communication publishes state-of-the-art papers that examine a broad range of issues in communication technology, theories, research, practices and applications.

It presents the latest development in the field of traditional and computer-mediated communication with emphasis on novel technologies and theoretical work in this multidisciplinary area of pure and applied research.

Since Emerging Communication seeks to be a general forum for advanced communication scholarship, it is especially interested in research whose significance crosses disciplinary and sub-field boundaries.

Editors-in-Chief

Giuseppe Riva, Applied Technology for Neuro-Psychology Lab., Istituto Auxologico Italiano, Milan, Italy

Fabrizio Davide, TELECOM ITALIA Learning Services S.p.A., Rome, Italy

Editorial Board

Luigi Anolli, University of Milan-Bicocca, Milan, Italy
Cristina Botella, Universitat Jaume I, Castellon, Spain
Martin Holmberg, Linköping University, Linköping, Sweden
Ingemar Lundström, Linköping University, Linköping, Sweden
Salvatore Nicosia, University of Tor Vergata, Rome, Italy
Brenda K. Wiederhold, Interactive Media Institute, San Diego, CA, USA
Luciano Gamberini, State University of Padua, Padua, Italy

Volume 9

Previously published in this series:

ISSN 1566-7677

From Communication to Presence

Cognition, Emotions and Culture Towards the Ultimate
Communicative Experience

Festschrift in honor of Luigi Anolli

Edited by

Giuseppe Riva
Catholic University of Milan, Milan, Italy

M. Teresa Anguera
University of Barcelona, Barcelona, Spain

Brenda K. Wiederhold
Interactive Media Institute, San Diego, California, USA

and

Fabrizia Mantovani
University of Milan-Bicocca, Milan, Italy

IOS
P r e s s

Amsterdam • Berlin • Oxford • Tokyo • Washington, DC

ISBN 1-58603-662-9
Library of Congress Control Number: 2006932506

Publisher
IOS Press
Nieuwe Hemweg 6B
1013 BG Amsterdam
Netherlands
fax: +31 20 687 0019
e-mail: order@iospress.nl

Distributor in the UK and Ireland
Gazelle Books Services Ltd.
White Cross Mills
Hightown
Lancaster LA1 4XS
United Kingdom
fax: +44 1524 63232
e-mail: sales@gazellebooks.co.uk

Distributor in the USA and Canada
IOS Press, Inc.
4502 Rachael Manor Drive
Fairfax, VA 22032
USA
fax: +1 703 323 3668
e-mail: iosbooks@iospress.com

Preface

> By nature, meaning design is not a homogeneous and univocal representation of reality but has an intrinsically composite character. Such hybrid theory of meaning entails that many aspects of meaning should be explained resorting to different layers and components of communication involving cognitive principles, knowledge factors, subjective experiences, and interactional principles, and no doubt much besides. Grice was essentially correct in thinking of meaning as a composite notion. The full meaning of an utterance may only be captured by considering different kinds of content: what is said, what is conventionally implicated, and what is presupposed.
>
> Anolli, 2000

If there is one prerequisite that is critical for education, it is the need to communicate clearly and effectively. Communication is the core activity for an educator, conveying and sharing information from one person to another, from one organisation to another – or a combination of both. Professor Luigi Anolli has been one of the most distinguished leaders in the field of communication psychology in the past three decades through his contributions and his deep influence on many researchers and colleagues. Throughout his long career, he has made fundamental and profound contributions to various areas of psychology, including communication, emotion and culture psychology.

Luigi is one of the pioneers in the psychological study of miscommunication. Overcoming the traditional concept of miscommunication as a lack, fault and violation of rules, he has advanced modern communication psychology in a unique and far reaching manner. In this perspective, detailed in his *Miscommunication as CHance Theory* (MaCHT), communication sets up a unique and global category, which definitely includes miscommunication phenomena as important objects of investigation. Luigi also had a significant impact on defining and applying advanced techniques to understand and analyze a broad range of communicative and emotional phenomena – from Irony and Deception to Shame – throughout the physiological parameters, vocal nonverbal features, facial expression and posture emerging within a communicative interaction.

Luigi's work has been seminal in a broad spectrum of psychological research; not only has he settled a long list of critical questions but he has also opened new directions of research which have inspired students and colleagues throughout the world. His most recent contributions are related to the psychology of culture, described as the "natural" horizon of communication. Luigi's research as well as the one of his colleagues over the years have highlighted the importance of culture in understanding human behavior. Increasingly intrigued by culture, over a decade ago he started to review the cross-cultural literature in all areas of psychology. Soon he realized that culture played an important role for understanding communication, gradually recognizing its pervasive and profound influence on psychological processes in all areas of functioning.

The method, context, structure, language, knowledge and an understanding of the needs of the recipients to whom the information is being transmitted are vital in understanding the importance of communication in a culture. Without a proper understanding of the complex and dynamic process of meaning co-construction and sharing, the communication between different cultures will be very difficult.

Like many other colleagues, I have benefited from his presence and from his generous help. In the summer of 2004, Luigi Anolli joined my Faculty at the *University of Milan-Bicocca* where he founded the Centre for Studies in Communication Science (CESCOM).

The chapters in this book are authored by colleagues and friends of Luigi and the topics covered are closely related to Luigi's research. In fact, the contributions included in this *festschrift* encompass a series of topics in communication psychology to which he contributed directly, exhibited an abiding interest, and/or supported indirectly through his role as Director of the CESCOM.

I am very grateful to all the authors who have contributed their excellent theoretical and research chapters to this book. At this occasion, I would like to express my deepest friendship and gratitude to Luigi Anolli and to wish him many more happy and productive years ahead.

Prof. Susanna Mantovani
Dean of the Science Education Faculty
University of Milan-Bicocca
Milan, Italy

Foreword

We want to overcome the Gricean distinction between "what is said" and "what is meant (or implicated)". The essential thing is "what is communicated", and this cannot be conceived simply as the sum of "what is said" plus "what is meant". What is communicated subsumes both what is said and what is meant, but it is also more than that and different from that. We ought to overcome the distinction between sentence-meaning and utterance-meaning, since meaning, in any case, is a unitary totality of what is communicated, though it is neither monolithic nor rigid, but composite and flexibly organized within itself.

Anolli, 2003

It is our pleasure to present this work, entitled *From Communication to Presence. Cognition, Emotions and Culture towards the Ultimate Communicative Experience*, which is published by IOS Press as part of its prestigious *Emerging Communication* series.

In the first place, we praise the initiative for being a publication made in honour of the eminent professor Luigi Anolli, Full Professor in Communication Psychology at the University of Milan-Bicocca. To Luigi Anolli, an exceptional human being, for decades a teacher among teachers, the author of over 150 publications, and an international reference in the field of communication psychology (to which he has dedicated so much of his life, sharing this interest with other fields, such as visual perception or, more recently, emotion psychology), we offer our warmest regards and dedication together with our gratitude for having shared with us his wisdom and friendship, and express our desire to continue doing so.

The thematic area of communication, ancient in its origin, yet always emerging in its treatment from new perspectives, reveals to us in this work interesting aspects that converge upon each other, based on a comprehensive conception of human communication: a complex phenomenon that is apparently inherent to human beings, but which is often empty, without content and of which only its appearance or formal structure is maintained. Its potential is immeasurable and it would really be difficult for us to imagine a society, or a human group, in which its members systematically displayed cognitive, emotional or cultural shortcomings.

Methodologically speaking, human communication presents unquestionable difficulties, which basically originate from the complexity that accompanies expressive subtlety, multimodality, interpretative issues, the establishment of conventional units in a communicative situation, or even, the setting of appropriately delimited scientific objectives, considering the communicative act as a whole. Such difficulties are maximised during the delicate phase of obtaining data, given the inevitable need to present objectively and without simplification a multilevel reality that we capture in systems of codes. With regard to data analysis, a whole host of possible options has emerged, and the detection of temporal patterns such as *T-Patterns*, towards which numerous research projects have been channelled, offers us the possibility of taking decisions around the critical interval, allows us to navigate through the temporal patterns obtained, establishing the filters considered most appropriate, while making it possible for us to interpret each dendogram obtained. Undoubtedly, the multidimensional nature of the communication phenomenon requires a careful and precise procedural treatment.

The work is well structured and offers an overall perspective of communication in which the different areas are interconnected in order to provide a broad understanding of communication through its link with "presence". It starts out discussing the possible route from media presence to inner presence. Then goes on to study the approach of the triad made up of emotion, culture and cognition in communication, and concludes with a section about communication and presence in practice.

In conclusion, the reading has an extremely rich and interesting approach, and we hope that the reader will positively value its content. In particular, the chapters will allow the reader to flourish in personal contributions and new advances in an area as fertile as communication. The task of developing skills in this field is not complete, and this work represents, in its own way, a new stimulus we positively value and encourage.

M. Teresa Anguera, Ph.D.
Faculty of Psychology
University of Barcelona
Barcelona, Spain

Magnus S. Magnusson, Ph.D.
Human Behavior Laboratory
University of Iceland
Reykiavik, Iceland

Introduction

Meaning is a marvellous and dreadful matter, as it is neither totally intelligible nor totally unintelligible. It cannot be considered as a univocal, closed and fixed entity, atomic in nature, universally shared and invariable in time. Rather, meaning has a complex design, composed by different facets: a referential, an inferential, and a differential one. This standpoint, which overcomes the truth-conditional semantics as well as the structural one, entails that meaning is patterned in nature, based on the encyclopaedic knowledge and connected with mental concepts.

Anolli, 2005

The contributions collected in this book are a Festschrift in honor of Luigi Anolli, a great scholar and communication researcher. Luigi Anolli has had, and continues to have, a remarkable career, one in which his commitment to interdisciplinary study stands out.

His ties to the psychological research date back as far as 1977, when he was appointed external professor of Applied Psychology at the Catholic University of Milan. At that time, his research activity focused on visual perception. Nine years later, in 1986, he was awarded a Social Psychology chair at Milan University. Here he deepened the analysis of social influence both at an interpersonal level and at a group one, especially with regard to the devices connected with uniformity and social acquiescence and the processes connected with mass media and new media.

Since the Nineties, his scientific interests have been focused on communication and emotion psychology. Continuing his involvement in new approaches to establishing interdisciplinary connections, he particularly deepened deception and irony in communication. In the former he proposed the Deceptive Miscommunication Theory (DeMiT) as a new model for the analysis of deceptive communication. In the latter, starting from the distinction between kind and sarcastic irony, Luigi Anolli advanced the so-called "fencing game" model as a specific way of irony in communication.

Within communication domain, he gave special attention to nonverbal communication (vocal, facial expression, gestures and body posture) as well as to new devices for non-verbal behavior analysis. Main results of his work in this area are the concepts of "modal meaning" and semantic and pragmatic tuning.

The development of communication study led him to identify the psychology of culture as "natural" horizon of communication, overcoming the dichotomized distinction between nature and nurture (gene-culture). In particular, Luigi Anolli proposed a new perspective of culture, as a domain-general device both internal (in the minds) and external (out of the minds) able to manage every specific-domain of life.

His most recent topics of interest concern on one side, the analysis of optimism as a cross point between positive emotions and subjective well-being, on the other side the concept of multicultural mind.

The book draws from the work of Luigi Anolli the criticism towards the nature/nurture distinction. It has been thought that any outcome of the development of individuals (personality, intelligence, physical appearance, etc.) is caused mostly, if not entirely, by either inheritance (genes) or learning (environment). Even if this distinction is now fairly widely known to be faulty, the critical part is to understand how nature and nurture interact. The writings of Prof. Anolli suggest four interdependent levels of analysis: genetic activity, neural activity, behavior, and environmental influences. In particular, he claims that in the communicative and cultural processes these levels are coactive and bidirectional; that is, in communication all levels mutually influence each other.

For this reason, the study of communication is a special setting for understanding how these processes interact. Specifically, Prof. Anolli underlined the critical role played by non-verbal communication: it subsumes several categories of human expressiveness such as facial displays (including eye contact and gaze behavior), gesture and body movement, posture and body orientation, touch, proxemics and territorial behavior, and vocal and paralinguistic behavior. Through their analysis it is possible to investigate three key dimensions of interpersonal relationships: immediacy (how positive or close individuals feel toward others), status (whether individuals have higher, equal, or lower standing with respect to others), and responsiveness (how active and focused an individual's communication is).

The emergence of new media made this analysis even more complex. In the latest media – high definition TV, computer games and, especially, Virtual Reality – the user is no more a passive receiver but fully experiences the media content: he *is present* in it.

The book, accepting the difficult challenge taken by Luigi Anolli, tries to outline a unitary theory of interpersonal relationship where communication and presence are simply the two faces of the same coin: intersubjective experience. In particular, the main message of the book is the following: the cooperative activities are created and governed by a reciprocal intentional game between the communicators regulated by the level of presence experienced by the interactants: the display and ostension of a given intention by the speaker ("intentionalization" process) and the ascription and attribution of a certain intention to him/her by the addressee ("re-intentionalization" process).

As suggested by Prof. Anolli, Miscommunication has a central role in these processes. This is why this book tries to provide the reader with worthwhile options for a vast array of specific communicative contexts – leisure, learning and therapy – and discusses the theories and methods needed to understand them. After completing this text, the reader should thus be better equipped to make more reasoned and more effective communication decisions. We have put a great deal of thought and effort into the definition of the structure of the book and the sequence of the contributions, so that those in search of a specific reading path will be rewarded. To this end we have divided the book into four main Sections comprising 14 chapters overall:

The starting point of the book is the assumption that a viable theory of interpersonal relationship has also to explain the link between communication and presence – *the feeling of being there*. Following this perspective, in *Section I – Communication and Presence: Their Relationship* – the Chapter 1 by Mantovani and colleagues opens a discussion on the links and reciprocal contributions between communication and presence, by arguing that they might be identified and analyzed at three levels: theoretical, methodological and applicative.

In *Section II – From Presence to Communication: Inner Presence vs. Media Presence* the attention of the authors moves to the analysis of what presence is and how it can be used to better understand our personal and interpersonal activities.

Coelho and colleagues in *Chapter 2* analyze the two different but coexisting visions of presence found in literature: the rationalist and the psychological/ecological points of view. The rationalist point of view considers a VR system as a collection of specific machines with the necessity of the inclusion of the concept of presence. The researchers agreeing with this approach describe the sense of presence as a function of the experience of a given medium (*Media Presence*). At the other extreme, there is the psychological or ecological perspective (*Inner Presence*). Specifically, this perspective considers presence as a neuropsychological phenomenon, evolved from the interplay of our biological and cultural inheritance, whose goal is the control of the human activity.

Riva in *Chapter 3* focuses on the ecological perspective. He argues that different visions from social and cognitive sciences – *Situated Cognition, Embodied Cognition, Enactive Approach, Situated Simulation, Covert Imitation* – and discoveries from neuroscience – *Mirror and Canonical Neurons* – suggest that our conceptual system dynamically produces contextualized representations (simulations) that support grounded action in different situations. In this picture the role of presence and social presence is to allow the process of self-identification through the separation between "self" and "other," and between "internal" and "external".

Chapter 4 by Waterworth and Waterworth, expands on the general notion of presence as a dimension of communication, and describes how this perspective can inform an understanding of designed variations in presence as a function of use, context, and individual psychological factors. The chapter underlines that the presence required in a communicative situation depends on many factors, including the communication devices available, the intended use and the context of use. In addition, differences between individuals, such as personality, as well as physical and psychological state, will affect how readily presence is invoked and also its impact on the individual concerned.

Moller and Barbera, in *Chapter 5* suggest that dreaming consciousness may be considered the most archetypal form of media technology, and discuss dreams as a useful metaphor for virtual reality. They argue that presence can be equally compelling whether experienced via self-generated simulation during the process of dreaming, or through an externally generated media simulation. A speculative therapeutic approach, "dream simulation therapy", is discussed as a future possible area of study.

Section III – From Communication to Presence: Emotion, Cognition and Culture presents a framework for the analysis of Communication in terms of the main cognitive, emotional and cultural processes.

Magnusson, in *Chapter 6* underlines how patterns in behavior are frequently hidden from the consciousness of those who perform them, as well as to unaided observers. Considering this as a fact, the chapter presents a method – *t-system* – for defining and discovering repeated temporal patterns – *t-pattern* – in behavior with a special focus on interactive behavior.

Chapter 7 by Ciceri and Biassoni, considers the vocal interaction in a multicomponential perspective, both as a multilayered phenomenon in itself and as one component in wider interactive patterns. Starting from this perspective the authors present an analysis model that handles both the complexity of the vocal act and its *being-in-context* in the interactive flow. Two different vocal interactions are then examined using it: a human face-to-face interaction, and another one between an Embodied Conversational Agent and its user.

Li and Roloff in *Chapter 8* present an overview of the actual research on emotion in negotiation that integrates cognitive, affective, and cultural aspects of the field. The chapter addressed the following issues: the effects of mood and emotion on negotiator cognition and performance and the potential of emotion as a negotiation strategy; individual differences in emotional expression and individual traits, such as self-monitoring and emotional intelligence, that impact on the use of strategic emotion; and cultural influences on negotiation and on emotional experience and expression.

Jonsson discusses in *Chapter 9* the idea that face-to-face interaction can be construed as having a definite organization or structure, just as language is understood in terms of its grammar. In particular he suggests that the structure of interaction is related to the personality traits of the subject. This position is tested through the analysis of real-time patterns in twenty-four dyadic interactions between male students.

Chapter 10 by Anguera and Izquierdo, presents an overview of different methodological process whose aim is the objective observation of perceivable communicative behavior. Specifically the authors suggest how the methodological options available within scientific observation, both qualitative and quantitative, can be used to approach a number of problems in the field of human communication research.

Deepening this topic, Agliati and colleagues present in *Chapter 11* a methodology for the analysis of the interaction with Embodied Conversational Agents. The proposed approach considers the hidden temporal organization underlying communicative interaction and provides a specific methodology for the structural analysis of the interactive flow.

The final section, *Section IV – Communication and Presence in Practice: Leisure, Therapy and Learning,* is devoted to the analysis of the interaction between Communication and Presence within three different contexts: leisure, therapy and learning.

Chapter 12 by Thon, describes multiplayer first-person-shooter games as a form of computer-mediated communication (CMC). Within this general context, the chapter examines these games showing that it is possible to understand the large amounts of social-emotionally oriented communication happening in them as a form of miscommunication.

Wiederhold and Wiederhold discuss in *Chapter 13* how virtual reality driving simulators may be used as an aid to traditional cognitive-behavioral therapy in the treatment of a variety of driving-related disorders. Clinical applications include specific driving phobias, driving phobias related to panic and agoraphobia, and posttraumatic stress disorder (PTSD) as a result of motor vehicle accidents. Another presented application is the neurorehabilitation for individuals who have sustained various brain injuries.

Chapter 14 by Realdon and colleagues, details how communication skills could be learned through computer-based interactive simulations. First, a definition of communication skills is proposed. Second, a framework for building interactive simulations is presented. Finally, a road map for building e-learning simulations specifically targeted at the training of communication skills is sketched out, focusing on the development of a narrative structure that adequately reduplicates the flow of the communicative interaction.

The fourteen contributions selected are among the first scientific attempts to take a serious look at the interaction between communication and presence. However, the authors did not start from scratch but draw from the vision coming out from both Prof. Anolli writings and the ones from his disciples.

For this reason, through this book we thank Luigi Anolli for his years of generous, wise advice, to us and to his many other students and colleagues. No effort shall be made here to evaluate and praise his many merits as a teacher and researcher in communication, emotion, culture and other fields. We only wish to express our gratitude for both the friendship and generous support offered to those who have known him for a long time, and his kind and open manner towards those who have joined this research area more recently.

His deep knowledge and understanding of what communication is and what it should be will remain a major source of inspiration to all those who take a genuine interest in the field. *Grazie* Luigi.

Fabrizia Mantovani, Ph.D.
CESCOM
University of Milan-Bicocca
Milan, Italy

Giuseppe Riva, Ph.D.
Faculty of Psychology
Catholic University of Sacred Heart
Milan, Italy

Contributors

Alessia AGLIATI, Ph.D.
Senior Researcher
CESCOM, Centre for Studies in Communication Science, University of Milan-Bicocca
Milan, Italy

M. Teresa ANGUERA, Ph.D.
Professor of Methodology of Behavioral Sciences
Faculty of Psychology, University of Barcelona
Barcelona, Spain

Joseph BARBERA, M.D.
Staff Psychiatrist/Sleep Specialist
Sleep and Alertness Clinic
University of Toronto
Toronto, Canada

Federica BIASSONI, M.S.
Senior Lecturer
Communication Psychology Lab., Catholic University of Sacred Hearth
Milan, Italy

Rita CICERI, Ph.D.
Associate Professor of General Psychology
Communication Psychology Lab., Catholic University of Sacred Hearth
Milan, Italy

Carlos COELHO, Ph.D.
Invited Assistant Professor
School of Psychology and Human Studies, University of Madeira
Funchal, Portugal

Linda CONFALONIERI, M.S.
Junior Researcher
CESCOM, Centre for Studies in Communication Science, University of Milan-Bicocca
Milan, Italy

Trevor J. HINE, Ph.D.
Senior Lecturer
School of Psychology, Griffith University
Brisbane, Australia

Conrad IZQUIERDO, Ph.D.
Associate Professor of Developmental Psychology
Faculty of Psychology, Autonomous University of Barcelona
Bellaterra (Barcelona), Spain

Gudberg K. JONSSON, Ph.D.
Human Behavior Laboratory, University of Iceland
Reykjavik, Iceland
Department of Psychology, University of Aberdeen
Aberdeen, United Kingdom

Shu LI, Ph.D.
Assistant Professor
Department of Communication, University of Memphis
Memphis, TN, USA

Magnus S. MAGNUSSON, Ph.D.
Research Professor
Human Behavior Laboratory, University of Iceland
Reykjavik, Iceland

Fabrizia MANTOVANI, Ph.D.
Research Professor
CESCOM, Centre for Studies in Communication Science, University of Milan-Bicocca
Milan, Italy

Senior Researcher
ATN-P Lab., Istituto Auxologico Italiano
Milan, Italy

Henry J. MOLLER, M.D.
Lecturer in Psychiatry
Neuropsychiatry Division, Department of Psychiatry
University Health Network, University of Toronto
Toronto, Canada

Medical Science Research Affiliate
Knowledge Media Design Institute
Toronto, Canada

Marcello MORTILLARO, M.S.
Junior Researcher
CESCOM, Centre for Studies in Communication Science, University of Milan-Bicocca
Milan, Italy

Olivia REALDON, M.S.
Senior Researcher
CESCOM, Centre for Studies in Communication Science, University of Milan-Bicocca
Milan, Italy

Giuseppe RIVA, Ph.D.
Associate Professor of Communication Psychology
ICE NET Lab., Catholic University of Sacred Hearth
Milan, Italy

Head Researcher
ATN-P Lab., Istituto Auxologico Italiano
Milan, Italy

Michael E. ROLOFF, Ph.D.
Professor
Department of Communication Studies, Northwestern University
Evanston, IL, USA

Jan-Noël THON, M.A.
University of Hamburg
Hamburg, Germany

Jennifer G. TICHON, Ph.D.
Senior Research Fellow
School of Human Movement Studies, The University of Queensland
Brisbane, Australia

Antonietta VESCOVO, M.S.
Junior Researcher
CESCOM, Centre for Studies in Communication Science, University of Milan-Bicocca
Milan, Italy

Guy M. WALLIS, Ph.D.
Senior Research Fellow
School of Human Movement Studies, The University of Queensland
Brisbane, Australia

Eva L. WATERWORTH, Ph.D.
Senior Lecturer
Department of Informatics, Umeå University
Umeå, Sweden

John A. WATERWORTH, Ph.D.
Professor
Department of Informatics, Umeå University
Umeå, Sweden

Brenda K. WIEDERHOLD, Ph.D.
Executive Director
The Virtual Reality Medical Center (VRMC)
San Diego, CA, USA

Chief Executive Officer
Interactive Media Institute
San Diego, CA, USA

Mark WIEDERHOLD, M.D., Ph.D.
President
The Virtual Reality Medical Center (VRMC)
San Diego, CA, USA

Valentino ZURLONI, Ph.D.
Senior Researcher
CESCOM, Centre for Studies in Communication Science, University of Milan-Bicocca
Milan, Italy

Contents

Section IV. Communication and Presence in Practice: Leisure, Therapy and Learning

SECTION I

COMMUNICATION AND PRESENCE: THEIR RELATIONSHIP

Meaning is a marvellous and dreadful matter, as it is neither totally intelligible nor totally unintelligible. It cannot be considered as an univocal, closed and fixed entity, atomic in nature, universally shared and invariable in time.

Rather, meaning has a complex design, composed by different facets: a referential, an inferential, and a differential one.

The meaning dilemma between variability and stability is crucial for every semantic theory, as meaning flexibility, grounded on the daily experience, displays a large range of linguistic phenomena like the defeasibility of semantic traits, fuzzy boundaries, radial categorization, semantic gradualness and polysemy, the interconnection between the literal and non-literal semantic domain as well as the context dependence.

Anolli, 2005

From Communication to Presence
G. Riva et al. (Eds.)
IOS Press, 2006

1 Communication – Presence Roundtrip: Travelling along Theoretical, Methodological and Applicative Connections

Fabrizia MANTOVANI, Alessia AGLIATI, Marcello MORTILLARO,
Antonietta VESCOVO, Valentino ZURLONI

Abstract: The convergence between telecommunication, virtual reality and artificial intelligence technologies resulted in a dramatical increase and modification of the opportunities to experience the physical and social world. Their diffusion and integration into multi-user and multi-agent virtual worlds highlighted the relevance of addressing from a common psychological perspective the domain of communication and the domain of presence. New theoretical and practical questions are emerging, in the double intent to explain phenomena at the interplay between mind and technology and to design effective technological applications. This chapter has the goal to start an exploration of the links and reciprocal contributions between communication and presence, analyzed at theoretical, methodological and applicative level.

Contents

1.1 Communication, Presence and Emerging Technologies: The Need for an Integrated Psychological Perspective

1.1.1 Background

Main goal of this chapter is a first exploration of the links between communication and presence.

Communication and presence are two processes of great importance in the psychological dimension of the individual. Recently, a potential converging trend of these two domains emerged with the development of new technological applications [1, 2].

We are, in fact, in front of the convergence between two types of technology: on the one hand, *telecommunication* technology, allowing for computer-mediated communication or CMC; on the other hand, Virtual Reality (VR) *simulation* and Artificial Intelligence (AI) technology, allowing for simulation and (re-)production of 3D environments and agents.

In their respective domain, these are specific technological applications, developed along the last 30-40 years, through which we have now opportunities to: communicate with each other over distance (that is, with someone who is not physically present, like in CMC) and do this as if we were physically co-present; communicate and interact with autonomous agents who are not human but electronic (like Intelligent Virtual Agents-IVAs) and do this relating to them as we do to human people; try the experience of feeling present in a place which is different from the one where our body is (like in Virtual Environments or in telepresence situations), and doing this having the sense that we are really "there".

Applications of these technologies can be found in the most various domains, from health-care (telemedicine, e-therapy, VR therapy) to learning and training (VR training environments, collaborative e-learning), from entertainment (developing interpersonal relationships through meeting and social networking sites, multi-user online gaming) to business and commerce (computer-supported collaborative work, e-commerce), etc. [3-8].

Moreover, advances in the last ten years resulted in the development of hybrid forms, combining the features and applications of telecommunication and simulation technologies described above: it was the birth of multi-user multi-agent 3D worlds, simulated graphic worlds where real people interact and communicate with other people over distance and/or with autonomous agents while they are represented in the simulated world by a 3D character, also called avatar [7, 9]. These most advanced forms combine immersiveness and multimodal input/output typical of VR technology with possibilities of mediated social interaction (with human and/or electronic autonomous agents), leading to a dramatic increase and modification of the possibility of experience of the physical and social world. We are in front of what might be defined *"experiential technology"* [10-12], a technology able to provide a more and more compelling "illusion of nonmediation" to the user [13], who finds herself/himself actively immersed and involved in a world of experience.

This potential for changing and enhancing the very nature of the processes involved in interpersonal communication and in our sense of being-in-the-world with other people (be them real human beings or autonomous artificial agents) favored the birth of *new questions* [14-16], both theoretical (in terms of explaining emergent phenomena) and practical (in terms of providing a framework for design and evaluation of effective applications) .

As for practical, *application-relevant questions,* they focus on identifying guidelines for designing effective applications, with issues like [14]: how to design successful CMC (video conference, chats, etc.) applications? How to design effective IVAs? What characteristics do they need to possess in order to be considered believable conversational partners and to elicit a sense of social presence? How to design virtual environments able to elicit a sense of *"being there"* and an *"illusion of non-mediation"* in the user?

The implicit assumption of application developers has been for a long time characterized by a fidelity approach consisting of a sort of technological equation saying *"the more sophisticated (tech), the better"*. Initially, in fact, CMC, AI, and VR developers relied on the hypothesis that a perfect and complete reproduction of reality in technological applications and mediated experiences would ensure their efficacy [17-23]. In most cases the goal of designers was to replicate as precisely and richly as possible the non-mediated processes: for CMC this meant including as many channels as possible, like in videoconference, for VR it meant integrating sophisticated multimodal input and output devices, in order to replicate as well as possible the flow of sensorial inputs and action possibilities.

However, following theoretical reflections and empirical work gradually modified this perspective [24-35; see also Coelho *et al.* in this volume for an overview], due to the acknowledgement of two important issues.

First, the goal of reproducing reality as richly as possible generally requires an effort that is beyond the reach either of technological developments and/or developer's possibility (time and/or costs).

Second, growing anecdotal and research evidence suggests that this "technological equation" approach does not always hold [28-32], in the sense that high-tech systems do not forcedly result in higher levels of social presence and better success as compared to simpler systems. As an example, phenomena such as the explosion of online relationships established and maintained through text-based CMC challenged media-richness theory and reduced-social-cues theory assumptions [36], according to which text-based chats were not likely to support the development interpersonal relationships due to their lack of nonverbal features (and consequently assumed poverty of socio-emotional communication). In general, it was highlighted that communication, as well as presence, are processes with a complex psychology behind. Since what we need is to make the final process more effective for the user (be it therapy, entertainment, work, etc.) we need to consider the use [29] that the individual makes and her/his psychology (i.e. the psychological features of her/his subjective experience).

Moreover, like a boomerang, experience with -and reflection on- these technologies did not limit to raise application-related issues, but often challenged assumptions in classical theories and elicited questions on the nature of the psychological processes involved [14]: how is it possible that we relate to agents and computer interfaces in a social way, as if they were human, despite the fact that we generally are explicitly aware of the fact they are not human? How is it possible that low graphic realism but high opportunity for action and significance for the individual elicit high sense of presence?

In some cases these questions even led to open up a systematic investigation of the very foundation of these processes [24, 31, 37] independently from technology (e.g. trying to understand the basis of our sense of presence-as-"being in the world" and sense of social presence-as-"being with others").

In particular, as discussed in the following section, the questions elicited by the advent of new technologies had a different impact on communication psychology as compared to presence psychology (considered as domains of study): for the first, they entailed adaptation and broadening of classical theoretical framework originally developed for face-to-face [38], for the second they led to the actual identification of presence as a domain for psychological investigation.

1.1.2 Communication and Presence between Technology and Psychology

As a general premise, it should be noticed in fact that communication psychology and presence psychology were in a very different scientific situation at the time when digital technologies started so radically to modify and alter the way we communicate and experience the physical and social world. Technology had therefore a different impact on the development of a psychological approach to these two domains.

The interest for communication as a specific domain of psychological inquiry existed well before the advent of Computer-Mediated Communication: *communication psychology* had developed, by the means of a process of theoretical evolution that took from cybernetic/mathematical approaches [39], from linguistics [40] and pragmatics [41, 42], as well as from sociological and relational perspectives [43, 44] in order to account for face-to-face communicative interaction. Along the last two decades we can say that a specific psychological tradition developed, through a gradual identification of defining features of the psychological processes involved in communication, with emphasis on issues such as: nonverbal behavior and multimodal communication; the role of inferential processes, representations and mental models in the production and comprehension of communicative acts (with cognitive semantics and pragmatics); the notion of intentionality and communicative intention [45, 46]; the detection of "hidden" behavioral patterns [47]; miscommunication and intentional opacity [48, 49].

On the opposite, while communication psychology existed before the emergence of CMC technologies and had developed pretty much for the study of face-to-face communication, it was VR technology that played a key role for the birth of presence as a separate domain of psychological investigation (although, as noticed by Revonsuo [50], the notion of presence did not "inhabit a philosophical vacuum" [51]; see also the analysis of Heideggerian *"Dasein"* in the chapter by Riva in this volume). The term 'presence' was coined in 1992 by Sheridan and Furness [21] when they used it in the title of the new journal dedicated to the study of virtual reality systems and teleoperations: Presence, Teleoperators and Virtual Environments.

While, therefore, communication psychology was born for the study of non mediated communicative interaction and had to adapt its own categories to the mediated one, presence psychology was born and developed from the study of the experiences in mediated contexts and just more recently evaluated the possibility of addressing presence as a process and phenomenon that is worth investigating also prescinding from technological mediation [52].

In general, we might say that the psychological inquiry of communication and that of presence developed quite independently up to very recently. As pointed out above, however, the convergence of new technologies defined an interesting area of study, at the intersection between these two domains, highlighting the need for an integrated psychological perspective on communication, presence and technology.

So, these are the *general questions* that this book aims at answering and that we tried to partially anticipate in this chapter: what are the points of contacts between communication and presence? What is the added value of studying them together, from a common perspective and with a psychological approach? What kind of reciprocal contributions can the world of communication and the world of presence offer each other?

Two background assumptions will drive us along this way towards an integrated perspective.

The first one refers to the existence of a common background for the analysis of technologically-mediated and non technologically-mediated phenomena: processes mediated and non mediated by technology should not be seen as separated, in a radical dichotomy. Cultural psychology [53, 54] (and the concept of mediation and artifacts developed within it) helps us in blurring this distinction: we are never, even in our "real world" in a process of non mediation. It would be, in fact, highly questionable the idea that technologies introduce ways of functioning which are completely different, since technology (meant as an artifact) is nothing but a further mediation beyond natural perception systems and other artifacts such as tools and language that are inherently part of our so-called "natural world". Therefore, mediated and non-mediated phenomena should be addressed as much as possible within a common theoretical and methodological framework.

The second assumption refers to the idea that communication and presence as psychological phenomena are strongly related and intertwined, both in technological and natural experiences. We argue that this link lies in the concepts of action and experience, and in the framing of communication and presence in a psychology of action [55]: communication on the one hand is considered, since the contribution of pragmatics, an action; presence on the other hand was recently connected to the perception of opportunities and constraints [29, 56] for the user's interaction (see the chapter by Riva in this volume for a more in-depth analysis of this point).

Within this volume and within this chapter, we argue that considering communication and presence together might offer a number of advantages, at different levels.

The overall goal is to start from the identification of the links between the world of communication and the world of presence in order to define a specifically psychological approach, with a particular focus on the role of new technologies.

We will try to follow this path through an analysis of some of the connections and the reciprocal contributions between communication and presence, which, we argue, might be identified *at three levels*:

- *theoretical level*, with the aim of fostering comprehension of concepts and phenomena in the two domains;
- *methodological/research* level, with the aim of empowering research on communication and on presence;
- *applicative level*, with the aim of enhancing technological applications and processes in the domains of presence and communication.

1.2 A First Look at the Theoretical Connections between Communication and Presence

Main goal of this paragraph is to discuss some of the links between communication and presence at a theoretical level, with focus on their common inclusion within a framework of psychology of action, as well as on the relevance of the concepts of embodiment and embeddedness for communication psychology.

At a general level we might say that on one side physical/environmental presence and social presence are a requisite for communication, in that communication is rooted in the phenomenal experience of being-in-the-world and being-with-others. Our sense of being in the physical and social world defines a set of opportunities and constraints for communicative exchange. On the other side communication and social interaction are the basis for the construction of this being-in-the-world experience from a developmental point of view, as well as in adult life they represent a tool for negotiating and restructuring it continuously; thanks to communication and social interaction, in fact, we have the opportunity to manage the process of meaning attribution to the world, its objects/people and events and to negotiate the "position" we occupy relatively to them.

Specifically, the link is given by our bodily experience: we are present in a body located in space and ready to act and inter-act, multimodally with other people.

This suggests that is possible to frame both communication and presence within a *psychology of action*, as briefly anticipated in the previous section: on one side, communication is an act (or, better, a "situated inter-act"); on the other side, presence is an evolutionary mechanism to control action. Experience is where these two processes meet. In fact, pragmatics highlighted how communicating is always doing something within a given context, and in order to obtain specific goals [57]. On the other hand Riva and colleagues identified in presence the mechanism deputed to regulating/controlling action through supporting progressive differentiation between self-and non-self [37]. These authors view it as an evolutionary process (relevant both in mediated and nonmediated settings), whose aim is to separate the internal from the external and to define, dynamically and continuously, the opportunities and constraints for action (see the chapters by Riva and by Waterworth and Waterworth in this book).

This vision of communication, presence and action is consistent with recent trends on cognitive sciences (see chapter by Riva in this volume, for a more comprehensive account of these issues): the theory of situated action [58], the activity theory [59, 60] and the Embedded Cognition approach [61-63]. All these visions highlighted the role of body and context and the inadequacy of the idea that cognition is primarily a matter of performing formal operations on abstract symbols. Specifically the *Embodied Cognition* approach underlines the central role of body in shaping the mind [61, 64-69] suggesting that presence has to be understood in the context of its relationship to a physical body that interacts with the world.

The acknowledgement of the key role played by embodiment and by situativeness/embeddedness compliments well the importance of regarding and investigating communicative acts *multimodally* and *in context* [46, 70; see also Ciceri & Biassoni in this volume]. On one side, in fact, meaning is not connected with a unique and exclusive signaling system, but is generated by the network of semantic and pragmatic connections between different signaling systems, from face to gestures, from voice to proxemics, etc. In any communicative exchange, interlocutors hence must be able to arrange and tune a set of different signaling systems to communicate and share their communicative intentions [46]. Moreover, meaning is never a fully evident datum, but exhibits an intrinsic opacity insofar as it is the semantic expression of each interlocutor's experience, which does not only generate what is said, but also points out and indexes how to intend what is said. This requires interlocutors to resort to active, inferential processes and to strongly rely on information from the context in which they are 'present'.

Within communication theory, we assisted to a growing acknowledgement of the importance of context and to a progressive modification and broadening of the very notion of 'context'. This modification was characterized by three shifts: from an additive to an interdependent vision of the relationship between 'text' and 'context'; from a definition of context simply indicating spatial-temporal characteristics of the interaction to a notion encompassing many other aspects, such as the relational, social and cultural ones; finally, from an idea of context as a collection of fixed and objective conditions to an idea of context as the result of a choice made –implicitly or explicitly- by the interlocutor(s) within a multiplicity of possible definitions that are available to her/him [71]. As Mc Neill [70] points out, "while context reflects the physical, social and linguistic environment, it is also a mental phenomenon". Social neuroscience has recently shown how neural processes and representations are context-sensitive and can change dynamically with goals and motivations and experience [72, 73], and McIntosh [74] suggested this might come to constitute an intrinsic neural context which complements the extrinsic one.

In synthesis, when we say that *communication* is a situated, multimodal act, we acknowledge the potential interest of deepening the relationship with the inherently human features of embodiment and situativeness implied by the notion of *presence*.

1.3. Methodological Connections: How to Empower Research on Presence and Communication by Reciprocal Contributions

When getting to the methodological level, questions are focused on the contribution of communication to the study of presence and *vice versa*. Within this section we will analyze on the one hand the use of methodologies and corroborative measures coming from communication psychology for the analysis of sense of presence (and in particular social presence in mediated contexts); on the other hand, we will see how technologies able to elicit mediated environmental and social presence could provide useful and innovative experimental test-beds for a systematic investigation of communication processes.

1.3.1 Communication for Presence: Using Input from Communication Psychology to Enhance Social Presence Measurement

Although questionnaires are still the most used measurement tools of presence, in the last ten years we have assisted to a growing interest into the development of different sets of measures (e.g. physiological, behavioral and social responses), to provide corroborative information to self-reports measures [75-82]. Within this framework, it is possible to envisage the use of measures and instruments developed in the domain of communication psychology to integrate and enrich the analysis and measure of sense of presence: facial expressions, vocal nonverbal features, gesture and posture, proxemics, etc.

These measures can be considered part of the so-called *behavioral correlates* of presence, and might prove most useful for studying mediated social presence. As pointed out by Biocca [83]: "Behavioral measures are common in studies of face-to-face interactions. Some of the verbal markers or non-verbal indicators such as facial expression may be indicative of social presence. More commonly non verbal behaviors such as *proximity* to the other are used as dependent variables or independent variables in studies of social interaction" (p.10). Moreover, Bente and colleagues [84](p.132) highlighted how "research from the last two decades has significantly advanced methodological knowledge in the definition of adequate descriptive methods of movement analysis in the context of nonverbal communication [85]. A series of transcription procedures and coding strategies have been developed that provide detailed and accurate protocols for both facial behavior and body movement [86, 87]".

In general, this opens the path to an investigation of social presence in terms of the social and communicative (verbal and nonverbal) responses to embodied avatars and agents [88], with underlying questions such as: is the agent/avatar able to elicit them? And if so, are they consistent with literature on non-mediated (face-to-face) interactions?

A few studies have investigated the social presence elicited by an autonomous agent by verifying whether users displayed similar reactions to those they would with a human partner, in terms of different nonverbal behaviors.

Bailenson and colleagues [89] used *proxemics/interpersonal distance* (minimum distance and reversal count) as a behavioral measure of copresence: building on previous work [81, 90-92], the authors proposed this approach based on the idea that "copresence would be positively related to hesitation in approaching an embodied agent, interpersonal distance, and maintenance of interpersonal distance" (p.6). In a different study [75] they used interpersonal distance as an explicit compliment to self-report measures of social presence, obtaining results that highlighted the sensitivity of proxemic indexes and confirmed the importance of an integrated approach to social presence measurement.

In two other studies [76, 93], user's *eye-gaze* in videoconferencing and virtual meetings was measured, given its importance in detecting user's attentive focus and communicative interaction management; both studies reported satisfying results to integrate self-report scales of copresence and social presence.

Moreover, although not specifically addressing the issue of measuring social presence, several authors (see below) measured a number of nonverbal indicators in the analysis of user interactions with Embodied Conversational Agents (or ECAs, sophisticated versions of IVAs that can converse with the user by one or more of the natural modalities of human-human communication [4]). It might be interesting to explicitly include and investigate them within social presence domain.

In their work of search for new parameters and metrics to evaluate multimodal dialogue systems with ECAs, Cerrato and Ekelint [94] showed how user's *vocal nonverbal features,* such as prosodic variation, and other nonverbal communicative behaviors, such as *head movements* and *facial expressions*, can give an indication of their attitude and overall evaluation of the interaction with the agent.

In order to move towards more comprehensive and sophisticated ways to analyze user social and communicative responses to virtual agents, two promising directions concern on the one hand multimodality and on the other hand interactivity and accommodation measures. The chapter by Ciceri and Biassoni (in this volume) suggests the need to focus on co-occurrence and synergy between different channels and systems, as well as on joined and coordinated action between various subjects; the authors discuss how theories and studies from human-human communication can be integrated with observations and research in human-machine interaction in a common framework of analysis. As far as interaction synchrony within communication exchange is concerned, Agliati and colleagues (see chapter in this volume) describe a methodology for the detection of emotional and relational involvement with virtual agents through an analysis of human-agent behavioral patterns. This kind of indicator might represent an interesting measure of the third level of social presence outlined by Biocca [83], the level of *behavioral engagement,* meant as an "interdependent multichannel exchange of behaviors" [95].

In synthesis, for each of the above-mentioned measures, communication psychology might provide both the rationale for its use and specific coding and analysis tools. Its contribution might thus consist both in providing theoretical and empirical accounts for the use of different verbal and nonverbal behaviors as corroborative measures of social presence and in offering standardized and reliable tools for coding and analysis of the selected behavior(s) (e.g. Facial Action Coding System [86] for facial expression coding, Bernese Coding System [87] for movement coding, CSL/Praat for vocal acoustic measurement, Observer for supporting computer-supported frame-by-frame coding and analysis ANVIL [97] and Theme [47] software for multimodal coding and analysis, etc.)

1.3.2 Presence for Communication: Using Presence Technologies and Mediated Social Presence to Enhance Research on Communication Processes

Simulation and immersive technology, given their potential to elicit mediated physical and social presence might represent an innovative methodology for the study of psychological processes involved in human-human communication and social interaction. The combination of virtual reality environments and embodied conversational agents, in fact, can provide controlled experimental settings for a systematic analysis of communication processes and can therefore offer a test-bed for classical theories. In virtue of their potential for embodiment and embeddedness, these technologies (virtual agents and environments) allow for systematic manipulation of multimodal and contextual features: on the whole, they might represent an extremely powerful research tool, offering significant advantages in terms of systematicity, standardization, controllability and repeatability of multimodal behaviors and contextual/situational variables.

This might be fruitful in many domains, from more general social interaction issues (broader issues underlying any communicative interaction) to more specific interpersonal communication domains (e.g. testing relationships between communication and attentional workload hypothesis, person perception processing starting from combination of different multimodal features, etc.)

Blascovich and colleagues [77] suggested the use of IVET (Immersive Virtual Environment Technology) for experimental research in *social psychology,* highlighting its remarkable potential in addressing three methodological problems that have traditionally affected research in this domain: 1. the experimental control/mundane realism trade-off; 2. lack of replication; 3. unrepresentative sampling. Blascovich's research team obtained extremely promising results by using IVET in studies designed and modeled after classic social influence experiments (to carry out replications of classical studies) on social facilitation/inhibition, conformity and social comparison paradigms [98, 99].

Schilbach and colleagues [100] have shown the potential of using interaction with 3D agents in virtual environments for *social neuroscience*, for the investigation of "the neural processes underlying our ability to understand other minds" (p.718). In particular, they investigated the so-called *second-person phenomena* (i.e. aspects of the dynamic interplay of being personally involved in social interactions) in mentalizing function by manipulating two variables: the fact of being personally involved in social interaction as opposed to being a passive observer of social interaction between others; the processing of socially relevant facial expressions as opposed to arbitrary facial movements.

Restricting the field, it is possible to hypothesize the use of embodied agents and VR environments to study the various domains specifically related to *communication*. As pointed out by Ruttkay and colleagues [101], "the introduction of ECAs has motivated research in human-human communication, by posing new, succinctly formulated questions, some of which could be answered only by using ECAs as controllable mediums that exhibit the effects to be tested" (p.49).

A domain where ECAs have undoubtfully provided today new stimuli is research on nonverbal communication systems [4, 84, 102]: 3D agent technology (computer graphics and synthesized speech) offers in fact a unique opportunity to manipulate the specific modality feature(s) of interest (e.g. facial action units, gestures, vocal features, etc.) while controlling all other modalities and/or additional cues concerning for example physical appearance (e.g. specific skin color, physiognomy, attractiveness, etc.). Bente and colleagues [84], for example, proposed a method for the 3D computer animation of *body movement* as a new tool for nonverbal communication research, endowed with a broad range of simulated behavior and with realism of the computer animation (realistic 3D-poligon-models with skeleton and skin-like envelope). In a similar fashion, Wehrle an colleagues [103] used 3D synthetic images of *facial expression* (manipulated through a dedicated software tool called FACE) to investigate the influence of changes in the patterning of facial expressive features over time on emotion inferences by judges.

Several researchers have also begun to use agents and VR technologies virtual environments and virtual humans as a tool to investigate *proxemics* and personal space [81, 90-92, 104], by testing classical research hypotheses such as those related multimodal nonverbal compensation effects (e.g. dynamic relationship between mutual gaze and interpersonal distance [105, 106].

As examples of studies that explicitly investigate issues related to *multimodality* in communication by using virtual agents, Krahmer and colleagues [107] investigated the role of pitch and eyebrows in the perception of focus and prominence through systematic manipulation of a 3D ECA features; in a following study [108] they broadened their work by investigating cross-cultural difference in these multimodal characteristics, comparing Italian and Dutch participants.

Overall, these works demonstrate the potential held by new social and environmental presence technologies for the study of human-human communication and social interaction. Although their advantages are undoubtful, their use needs to address an important issue: is it possible, as a general assumption, to hypothesize that people respond to virtual agents as they would respond to real people? An affirmative answer to this question is a fundamental prerequisite to be able to use virtual reality and embodied agent technology in research settings [84, 100].

A growing amount of literature seems to confirm this hypothesis [81]. The study by Bente and colleagues [84] yielded evidence for a remarkable correspondence between person perception effects of video recorded dyadic nonverbal interactions and the 3D computer animation based on the transcripts of the same interaction behaviors.

Other studies were able to show important similarities between social reactions to virtual agents and findings in traditional social and communication psychology literature describing social responses to human people in specific situations. For example, in their study on emotional reactions in public speaking virtual environments Pertaub and colleagues [109] found that participants reported higher anxiety levels in front of negative audiences as compared to static or positive ones, despite participant's awareness that the agents were computer-generated and that there were no real people in the audience. Results from a study by Bailenson and colleagues [90] showed that consistent gazing lead to more interpersonal distance, coherently with Argyle's intimacy equilibrium theory [110]. Garau and colleagues [88] found that participants characterized by higher levels of social anxiety were significantly more likely to avoid disturbing virtual humans in a VR library, confirming the fact that participants responded to virtual humans as social actors.

These findings in general show that people tend to respond to virtual agents as they would respond to real people and seem to confirm the validity of this approach for communication research; however, a reliable answer to this question should include the development of more complex models able to explain and predict under which conditions this equivalence holds. Blascovich and his colleagues [77], for example, started developing a "threshold model of social influence within immersive virtual environments" with the aim of identifying the relative impact of different factors (such as behavioral realism and belief of being in front of a veritable human being behind the avatar/agent) and moderating variables (self-relevance and user's target response system) on the occurrence of social influence phenomena in virtual environments.

Altogether, these reflections should raise remarkable interest on these technologies as research tools in human communication processes, while at the same time stimulate empirical studies for the development of virtual agents and environments validated *ad hoc* for experimental communication studies.

1.4 Applicative Connections: Design Guidelines from Communication Theory and Empowerment of Interpersonal Communication through Mediated Presence Technology

At an applicative level, the exploration of the links and interdependencies between communication and presence leads us to focus on two main ideas: first, communication psychology might provide a relevant contribution to designing technological applications (in particular embodied agents and avatars) able to elicit high levels of mediated presence and social presence; second, application technologies endowed with physical and social presence affordances might provide an experiential setting to train and empower interpersonal communication processes (also in non-mediated contexts).

1.4.1 Towards the Definition of Psychologically Sounded Design Empowering Technological Applications

As we have seen, considerable research efforts are to date devoted to developing humanoid software agents that use speech, gaze, gesture, intonation and other signaling systems in the way humans use them in the communication process as conversational partner, leading to the development of so-called Embodied Conversational Agents [4, 111, 112].

Within this framework, communication psychology might offer guidelines and design principles (coming from theoretical reflections and/or empirical studies on human-human communication) for the design and evaluation of technological applications able to support the emergence of a sense of social presence in the user [112]. As pointed out by Garau and colleagues [113], in fact, simple presence of avatars/agents in a 3D shared space is not enough, what is really critical is that they are *expressive*, in order to contribute meaningfully to the communication process; there is a significant difference between simple liveliness and communicative meaningful expressiveness, which is fundamental for the agent/avatar to be perceived as a conversational partner. Its achievement requires the ability to employ different signaling systems in a synchronic way in order to convey meaning within the communicative exchange [4].

As a support to this effort, communication psychology provides an important basis in the literature sources on human communication [114]: within this section, we will focus specifically on the relevance of *multimodality, accommodation and interaction synchrony*.

Meaning design is quite complex, since it is not connected with a unique and exclusive signaling system, but comes out of the network of semantic and pragmatic connections between different signaling systems (multimodal configurations). As, among others, Anolli [45, 46, 48] pointed out, besides language, there are several other communicational devices to show interactants' own communicative design, like the paralinguistic (or supra-segmental), the face and gestures system, the gaze, the proxemics and the haptics, as well as the chronemics. Each of these communicative systems bears its contribution and participates in defining the meaning of a communicative act in an autonomous way. However, the generative capacity of each signaling system must be connected to produce a global and unitary communicative action, with a more or less high consistency degree. Such a consistency degree involves both the horizontal dimension in the use of each signaling system (i.e., for non verbal signaling systems, consistency among different behaviors within the same system) and the vertical dimension, regarding the convergence in meaning generation between several and different signaling systems (principle of semantic synthony, [46]; see also the chapter by Ciceri & Biassoni in this volume).

Examples of design with specific focus on a multimodal communicative architecture can be found in some recent studies and applications [113-115]. Garau and colleagues [113] focused on multimodal synchrony between speech and eye-gaze. The authors based on social psychology research on the differences in gaze patterns while speaking and while listening in face-to-face interactions, in order to build avatars with *informed eye-gaze* (related to the conversation), and found out that this provides a marked improvement as compared to an avatar that merely exhibits liveliness. Buisine and colleagues [115] implemented different multimodal strategies used for combining speech and gestures in the design of a presentation ECA and looked at their effects on user's subjective ratings and recall performance.

Besides the issue of coordination of multimodal signals within the individual interlocutor/agent, an emerging issue concerns the setting of these multimodal configurations within the complexity of interaction with the conversational partner [106; see also the chapters by Ciceri & Biassoni, and Agliati *et al.* in this volume]. Multimodal configurations aimed at meaning generation and negotiation are in fact acted and carried out in *hic et nunc* communicative exchanges, which require participation from both interlocutors, and develop over time. Therefore, considering the multimodal configurations jointly acted by interlocutors (be it human-human or human-agent) over time entails relevant conceptual connections with the issue of interaction synchrony, as related to the convergence of non verbal behaviors in temporal processes of interaction (even exhibiting exactly the same behaviors, as in the case of mirroring phenomena) [106, 116]. According to Burgoon [106], when people communicate, they have to "adapt their interaction styles to one another. For example, they may match each other's behavior, synchronize the timing behavior, or behave in opposite ways". Indeed, it is widely acknowledged in common observations as well as in the scientific field that participants in communicative interaction are usually engaged in a common rhythm [117].

A first application of these concepts to human-computer interaction was recently proposed by Bailenson and Nick [118]. In their study, assuming the theoretical paradigm of the chameleon effect [117], participants interacted with a virtual agent in an immersive virtual reality environment. The agent either mimicked the participant's head movements (which were tracked and recorded through specific sensors) at 4-second delay or utilized prerecorded movements of another participant as it verbally presented an argument. Mimicking agents were perceived as more persuasive and received more positive trait ratings that nonmimickers, despite participant's inability to explicitly detect the mimicry.

The works described up to this point suggest the valid potential of endowing synthetic characters with increasing embodiment and multimodal affordances in order to increase their social presence; however, this consideration should not result automatically in design trends claiming "the more modalities, the better".

It seems, in fact, that achieving consistency in the design and implementation of multimodal behavior might be more important than endowing agents with animation and control of all communicative signals humans use. Multimodality should be exploited according to principle of semantic synthony and synchrony [46], where the attunement of all the communication signals involved prevails on the number and richness.

Consistently with this perspective, the above cited study by Garau and colleagues [113] showed that also very limited, though consistent manipulations can be effective: a surprising result was, in fact, that the inferred eye gaze avatar led to significantly better results than the avatar simply exhibiting liveliness, but was not significantly different from the video condition (full and accurate nonverbal feedback from the face). This, according to the authors, suggested that "an avatar can begin to make a significant contribution to the positive perception of communication even without detailed facial expression". Moreover, the authors pointed out that the salience and role of a specific nonverbal behavior can change according to the task (e.g. eyegaze when performing equivocal tasks that have no "correct" outcome and require negotiation). The relative importance of the representation/inclusion of different behaviors should be weighted on the application and related user tasks.

Finally, the idea that multimodal animation of the agent should be settled within the interactive flow with the human user and the importance of dynamic adaptation between the interlocutors highlight the possible relevance to endow agents and avatars with "perceptual" capabilities, allowing them a form of sensing and monitoring of user input [101]; as far as this effort is concerned, research carried out within the affective computing domain [119-121] might offer an interesting integration.

1.4.2 Presence Simulation Technologies to Enhance Interpersonal Communication

Technological applications allowing for virtual co-presence and sense of social presence have the potential to empower interpersonal communication processes, by offering tools to simulate a number of professional and interpersonal contexts and situations. Within this section, we will focus on the use of 3D interactive simulations to train communication skills and of VR worlds to enhance therapeutic communication process.

As a first example, we consider the development of interactive simulations for the training of communication and emotional skills for different professional contexts, e.g. health-care, commercial, etc. [122, 123; see also Realdon *et al.* in this volume]. In these simulations trainees find themselves "immersed" in a virtual world populated by 3D characters that engage them in communicative exchanges, modeled after protypical complex situation found in their actual context (e.g. a physician breaking bad news to a patient, a bank-teller dealing with an angry and polemic customer). This allows trainees to practice communication and relational skills, experiencing the effects of different communication strategies in an experiential, realistic (though "safe") setting. A careful crafting of the simulation to ensure that the situations and communicative interactions with virtual agents elicit a sense of physical and social presence in the trainee can turn the fact of "playing" the simulation into an involving life experience, fostering the transfer of learning to her/his actual professional contexts.

On the clinical side, a similar rationale underlies the use of VR environments, for the treatment of social phobia and fear of public speaking [109, 124, 125]: in these applications, used in psychotherapeutic settings, the patient faces a number of difficult situations, from meeting new people to speaking in front of a large audience, and gradually learns how to manage related emotions, beliefs and behaviors.

Apart from VR environments specifically devoted to these disorders, we might say more generally that the use of VR-based applications in the therapy of most various disorders, such as eating disorders, phobias and anxiety disorders, might represent a powerful device to enhance communication processes in patient-psychotherapist interaction [126]. Communication is a key feature of therapy, and participation, shared re-attribution of meaning to the experience of the patient play an important role in it. Technologies able to elicit sense of presence might be functional to this process. Within psychotherapeutic process, in fact, exchange and communication between patient and therapist are used to re-evoking worlds, to build new meanings, new mental representations of the situations and of the opportunities for action of the patient: the use of virtual presence technologies might support this process by providing a reification of a common context towards which the attention of both patient and therapist is directed.

1.5 Conclusions

Along this chapter, we tried to open an exploration of the complex and manifold relationships between the domains of communication and presence.

This exploration was stimulated by how digital technologies are changing the ways we communicate and we make physical and social experiences in natural and mediated worlds. Phenomena and questions raised by advanced technologies have defined interesting challenges at different levels, whose implications went well beyond practical/application-related issues and resulted in stimulating inquiries on the very foundations of communication and presence as psychological phenomena. A possible approach to address this challenge is identifying an integrated theoretical and methodological platform within which addressing these issues in a coherent and systematic fashion.

As a first step to outline this framework we started by looking at some of the links between the two domains, which we identified at three different levels:

- *theoretical*, with the settling of communication and presence within a psychology of action, as well as the acknowledgment of importance of embodiment and context;
- *methodological*, with the use of communication psychology to define integrative measures of social presence and the use of technologies eliciting high levels of mediated presence as a tool for research on human-human communication processes;
- *applicative*, with discussion of how communication theory might provide insights for the design of embodied virtual agents and of how virtual reality and virtual agents might constitute an experiential setting for the training and fostering of interpersonal communication skills.

Our goal was to provide some initial stimuli for reflection, rather than exhaustive treatment of the topic. Although we are aware that the coverage of the links is far from being complete, nevertheless we hope this work will stimulate further integration and exploration of this passionating domain at the intersection between communication and presence, psychology and technology.

Of course the road ahead is still very long, and the next part of the journey unfolds along the pages of the other chapters in this volume. So… we wish you to be curious, active and "present" readers … and to enjoy the journey.

1.6 References

[1]   G. Riva, From technology to communication: Psycho-social issues in developing virtual environments. *Journal of Visual Languages and Computing,* (1999), 10, 87-97.
[2]   F. Biocca and M.R. Levy, Virtual reality as a communication system. In: *Communication in the age of virtual reality.* Edited by Biocca F and Levy MR. Hillsdale, NJ: Lawrence Erlbaum Associates; 15-31, 1995.
[3]   G.C. Burdea, Virtual rehabilitation--benefits and challenges. *Methods of Information in Medicine,* (2003), 42(5), 519-523.

[4]   J. Cassell, J. Sullivan, S. Prevost and E. Churchill (eds.), Embodied Conversational Agents. Cambridge, MA: MIT Press; 2000.
[5]   T. Kling-Petersen, R. Pascher and M. Rydmark, Virtual reality on the Web: the potentials of different methodologies and visualisation techniques for scientific research and education. *Studies in Health Technology and Informatics,* (1999), 62, 181-186.
[6]   R.M. Satava, Surgical education and surgical simulation. *World J Surg,* (2001), 25(11), 1484-1489.
[7]   R. Schroeder, The Social Life of Avatars: Presence and Interaction in Shared Virtual Environments. London: Springer-Verlag; 2002.
[8]   G. Székely and R.M. Satava, Virtual reality in medicine. *Bmj,* (1999), 319(7220), 1305.
[9]   J.N. Bailenson, K. Swinth, C. Hoyt, S. Persky, A. Dimov and J. Blascovich, The Independent and Interactive Effects of Embodied-Agent Appearance and Behavior on Self-Report, Cognitive, and Behavioral Markers of Copresence in Immersive Virtual Environments. *Presence: Teleoperators and Virtual Environments,* (2005), 14(4), 379-393.
[10]   A. Carassa, F. Morganti and M. Tirassa, A situated cognition perspective on presence. In: *XXVII Annual Conference of the Cognitive Science Society: 2005; Stresa, Italy*: Sheridan Printing; 384-389,2005.
[11]   W.A. IJsselsteijn and G. Riva, Being There: The experience of presence in mediated environments. In: *Being There: Concepts, effects and measurements of user presence in synthetic environments.* Edited by Riva G, Davide F and IJsselsteijn WA. Amsterdam: Ios Press. Online: http://www.emergingcommunication.com/volume5.html; 3-16, 2003.
[12]   A. Spagnolli and L. Gamberini, A Place for Presence. Understanding the Human Involvement in Mediated Interactive Environments. *PsychNology Journal,* (2005), 3(1), 6-15. On-line: http://www.psychnology.org/pnj13(11)_spagnolli_gamberini_abstract.htm.
[13]   M. Lombard and T. Ditton, At the heart of it all: The concept of presence. *Journal of Computer Mediated-Communication   [On-line],*   (1997),   3(2),   Available: http://www.ascusc.org/jcmc/vol3/issue2/lombard.html.
[14]   F. Biocca, C. Harms and J.K. Burgoon, Toward a more robust theory and measure of social presence: Review and suggested criteria. *Presence: Teleoperators, and Virtual Environments,* (2003), 12(5), 456-480.
[15]   F. Biocca, The Cyborg's Dilemma: Progressive embodiment in virtual environments. *Journal of Computer   Mediated-Communication   [On-line],*   (1997),   3(2),   Available: http://www.ascusc.org/jcmc/vol3/issue2/biocca2.html.
[16]   F. Biocca, Communication within virtual reality: Creating a space for research. *Journal of Communication,* (1992), 42(4), 5-22.
[17]   S.R. Ellis, Virtual environments and environmental instruments. In: *Simulated and virtual realities: Elements of perception.* Edited by Karen Carr RE: Taylor & Francis, London, England; 11-51, 1995.
[18]   D. Schloerb, A Quantitative Measure of Telepresence. *Presence: Teleoperators, and Virtual Environments,* (1995), 4(1), 64-80.
[19]   W.J. Sadowski and K.M. Stanney, Measuring and managing presence in virtual environments. In: *Handbook of Virtual Environments Technology.* Edited by Stanney KM. Mahwah, NJ: Lawrence Erlbaum Associates, 2002.
[20]   J.M. Loomis, Distal attribution and presence. *Presence, Teleoperators, and Virtual Environments,* (1992), 1(1), 113-118.
[21]   T.B. Sheridan, Musing on telepresence and virtual presence. *Presence, Teleoperators, and Virtual Environments,* (1992), 1, 120-125.
[22]   T.B. Sheridan, Further musing on the psychophysics of presence. *Presence, Teleoperators, and Virtual Environments,* (1996), 5, 241-246.
[23]   T. Marsh, P. Wright and S. Smith, Evaluation for the design of experience in virtual environments: modeling breakdown of interaction and illusion. *Cyberpsychology & Behavior,* (2001), 4(2), 225-238.
[24]   G. Riva, F. Davide and W.A. IJsselsteijn (eds.), Being There: Concepts, effects and measurements of user presence in synthetic environments. Amsterdam: Ios Press. Online: http://www.emergingcommunication.com/volume5.html; 2003.
[25]   K. Moore, B.K. Wiederhold, M.D. Wiederhold and G. Riva, Panic and agoraphobia in a virtual world. *Cyberpsychology & Behavior,* (2002), 5(3), 197-202.
[26]   J.A. Waterworth and E.L. Waterworth, Focus, Locus, and Sensus: The three dimensions of virtual experience. *Cyberpsychology and Behavior,* (2001), 4(2), 203-213.
[27]   G. Mantovani and G. Riva, "Real" presence: How different ontologies generate different criteria for presence, telepresence, and virtual presence. *Presence, Teleoperators, and Virtual Environments,* (1999), 8(5), 538-548.

[28]   T. Schubert, F. Friedman and H. Regenbrecht, The experience of presence: Factor analytic insights. *Presence: Teleoperators, and Virtual Environments,* (2001), 10(3), 266-281.

[29]   P. Zahoric and R.L. Jenison, Presence as being-in-the-world. *Presence, Teleoperators, and Virtual Environments,* (1998), 7(1), 78-89.

[30]   G. Riva and F. Davide (eds.), Communications through Virtual Technologies: Identity, Community and Technology in the Communication Age. Amsterdam: Ios Press. Online: http://www.emergingcommunication.com/volume1.html; 2001.

[31]   J.A. Waterworth and E.L. Waterworth, The meaning of presence. *Presence-Connect,* (2003), 3(2), Online: http://presence.cs.ucl.ac.uk/presenceconnect/articles/Feb2003/jwworthFeb1020031217/jwworthFeb1020031217.html.

[32]   R.M. Baños, C. Botella, A. García-Palacios, H. Villa, C. Perpiñá and M. Alcañiz, Presence and Reality Judgment in virtual environments: A unitary construct? *Cyberpsychology & Behavior,* (2000), 3(3), 327-355.

[33]   R.M. Baños, C. Botella and C. Perpiña, Virtual Reality and Psychopathology. *CyberPsychology & Behavior,* (1999), 2(4), 283-292.

[34]   A. Spagnolli, L. Gamberini and D. Gasparini, Breakdown analysis in Virtual Reality usability evaluation. *PsychNology Journal,* (2003), 1(1), Online: http://www.psychnology.org/pnj1(1)_spagnolli_gamberini_gasparini_abstract.htm.

[35]   A. Spagnolli and L. Gamberini, Immersion/Emersion: Presence in hybrid environments. In: *Presence 2002: Fifth Annual International Workshop: 9-11 October 2002; Porto, Portugal:* Universidade Ferdinando Pessoa; 421-434,2002.

[36]   M.J. Culnan and M.L. Markus, Information technologies. In: *Handbook of organizational communication: An interdisciplinary perspective.* Edited by Jablin FM, Putnam LL, Roberts KH and Porter LW. Newbury Park, CA: Sage; 420-443, 1987.

[37]   G. Riva, J.A. Waterworth and E.L. Waterworth, The Layers of Presence: a bio-cultural approach to understanding presence in natural and mediated environments. *Cyberpsychology & Behavior,* (2004), 7(4), 405-419.

[38]   F. Mantovani, Cyber-attraction: The emergence of computer-mediated communication in the development of interpersonal relationships. In: *Say not to say: New perspectives on miscommunication.* Edited by Anolli L, Ciceri R and Riva G. Amsterdam: IOS Press, 2002.

[39]   C.E. Shannon and W. Weaver, The mathematical theory of communication. Urbana: University of Illinois Press; 1949.

[40]   F. de Saussure, Cours de linguistique générale. Paris: Payot; 1916.

[41]   J.L. Austin, How to do things with words. Oxford: Clarendon Press; 1962.

[42]   H.P. Grice, Meaning. In: *Semantics: An interdisciplinary reader.* Edited by Steinberg DD and Jakobovits LA. Oxford: Oxford University Press; 53-59, 1971.

[43]   G. Bateson, Steps to an ecology of mind. New York: Chandler; 1972.

[44]   E. Goffman, Behavior in public place. Glencoe, ILL: The Free Press; 1963.

[45]   L. Anolli (ed.), Psicologia della Comunicazione. Bologna: Il Mulino; 2002.

[46]   L. Anolli, MaCHT – Miscommunication as CHance Theory: Toward a unitary theory of communication and miscommunication. In: *Say not to say New perspectives on miscommunication.* Edited by Anolli L, Ciceri R and Riva G. Amsterdam: IOS Press; 3-43, 2002.

[47]   L. Anolli, S.J. Duncan, M. Magnusson and G. Riva (eds.), The hidden structure of interaction: From neurons to culture patterns. Amsterdam: IOS Press; 2005.

[48]   L. Anolli, R. Ciceri and G. Riva (eds.), Say not to Say: New persectives on miscommunication. Amsterdam: Ios Press. Online: http://www.emergingcommunication.com/volume3.html; 2002.

[49]   C.D. Mortensen, Miscommunication. Thousand Oaks, London: Sage Publications; 1997.

[50]   A. Revonsuo, Inner Presence, Consciousness as a Biological Phenomenon. Cambridge, MA: MIT Press; 2006.

[51]   W. James, The principles of psychology. New York: Holt; 1890.

[52]   M.V. Sanchez-Vives and M. Slater, From presence to consciousness through virtual reality. *Nature Review Neuroscience,* (2005), 6(4), 332-339.

[53]   L. Anolli, Psicologia della Cultura. Bologna: Il Mulino; 2004.

[54]   M. Cole, Cultural psychology: A once and future discipline. Cambridge, MA: Harvard University Press; 1996.

[55]   A. Noë, Action in perception. Cambridge, MA: MIT Press; 2004.

[56]   T. Marsh, Staying there: an activity-based approach to narrative design and evaluation as an antidote to virtual corpsing. In: *Being There: Concepts, effects and measurements of user presence in synthetic environments.* Edited by Riva G, Davide F and IJsselsteijn WA. Amsterdam: IOS Press; 85-96, 2003.

[57]   C.S. Levinson, Pragmatics. Cambridge, MA: Cambridge University Press; 1983.
[58]   L. Suchman, Plans and situated action. Cambridge, UK: Cambridge University Press; 1987.
[59]   G. Mantovani and A. Spagnolli, Imagination and culture: What is it like being in the cyberspace? *Mind, Culture, & Activity,* (2000), 7(3), 217-226.
[60]   B. Nardi (ed.), Context and consciousness: Activity theory and Human-Computer Interaction. Cambridge, MA: MIT Press; 1996.
[61]   A. Clark, Reasons, robots and the extended mind. *Mind & Language,* (2001), 16(2), 121-145.
[62]   J. Haugeland, Having Thought: Essays in the Metaphisics of Mind. Cambridge, MA: Harvard University Press; 1998.
[63]   A. Clark, Being There: Putting Brain Body and World Together Again. Cambridge, MA: MIT Press; 1997.
[64]   A. Clark, Natural Born Cyborgs: Minds, technologies, and the future of human intelligence. Oxford: Oxford University Press; 2003.
[65]   T. Ziemke, What's that thing called embodiment. In: *Annual Meeting of the Cognitive Science Society: 2003; Boston, MA, USA*; 1305-1310,2003.
[66]   G. Lakoff and M. Johnson, Metaphors we live by. Chicago, IL: University of Chicago Press; 1980.
[67]   F. Garbarini and M. Adenzato, At the root of embodied cognition: Cognitive science meets neurophysiology. *Brain And Cognition,* (2004), 56(1), 100-106.
[68]   V. Gallese and G. Lakoff, The brain's concept: The role of the sensory-motor system in reason and language. *Cognitive Neuropsychology,* (2005), 22, 455-479.
[69]   S. Gallagher, How the Body Shapes the Mind. Oxford; 2005.
[70]   D. McNeil, Gesture and Thought. Chicago: The University of Chicago Press; 2006.
[71]   D. Sperber and D. Wilson, Mutual knowledge and relevance in theories of comprehension. In: *Mutual knowledge.* Edited by Smith N. London: Academic Press; 61-87, 1982.
[72]   W.J. Freeman, Neurodynamic models of brain in psychiatry. *Neuropsychopharmacology,* (2003), 28, S54-S63.
[73]   H.C. Nusbaum and S.L. Small, Investigating Cortical Mechanisms of Language Processing in Social Context. In: *Social Neuroscience: People Thinking about Thinking People.* Edited by Cacioppo JT, Visser PS and Pickett CL: MIT Press; 131-152, 2005.
[74]   A.R. McIntosh, Towards a network theory of cognition. *Neural Networks,* (2000), 13, 861-870.
[75]   J.N. Bailenson, E. Aharoni, A.C. Beall, R.E. Guadagno, A. Dimov and J. Blascovich, Comparing Behavioral and Self-Report Measures of Embodied Agents' Social Presence in Immersive Virtual Environments. In: *7th Annual International Workshop on PRESENCE: 2004; Valencia, Spain,*2004.
[76]   A.C. Beall, J.N. Bailenson, J. Loomis, J. Blascovich and C. Rex, Non-zero-sum mutual gaze in immersive virtual environments. In: *Proceedings of HCI International.* vol. 1: Lawrence Erlbaum Associates; 1108-1112, 2003.
[77]   J. Blascovich, J. Loomis, A. Beall, K.H. Swinth, C. and J.N. Bailenson, Immersive virtual environment technology as a methodological tool for social psychology. *Psychological Inquiry,* (2002), 13, 103-124.
[78]   W.A. IJsselsteijn, H. de Ridder, J. Freeman and S.E. Avons, Presence: Concept, determinants and measurement. In: *Human Vision and Electronic Imaging V: 2000; San Jose, USA*; 3959,2000.
[79]   B.E. Insko, Measuring presence: Subjective, behavioral and physiological methods. In: *Being There: Concepts, effects and measurement of user presence in synthetic environments.* Edited by Riva G, Davide F and IJsselsteijn WA. Amsterdam: IOS Press, 2003.
[80]   M. Meehan, B. Insko, M. Whitton and F.P. Brooks Jr., Physiological Measures of Presence in Stressful Virtual Environments. *ACM Transactions on Graphics,* (2002), 21(3), 645-652.
[81]   B. Reeves and C. Nass, The Media Equation: Cambridge University Press; 1996.
[82]   M. Slater, A. Brogni and A. Steed, Physiological responses to breaks in presence: A pilot study. In: *The 6th Annual International Workshop on Presence: 2003,*2003.
[83]   F. Biocca, J. Burgoon, C. Harms and M. Stoner: Criteria and scope conditions for a theory and measure of social presence. In. E. Lansing: Media Interface and Network Design (M.I.N.D.) Lab; 1-19, 2001.
[84]   G. Bente, N.C. Kraemer, A. Petersen and J.P. de Ruiter, Computer animated movement and person perception: Methodological advances in nonverbal behavior research. *Journal of Nonverbal Behavior,* (2001), 25(3), 151-166.
[85]   W.C. Donaghy, Nonverbal communication measurement. In: *Measurement of communication behavior.* Edited by Emmert P and Barker L. White Plains, NY: Longman; 296-332, 1989.
[86]   P. Ekman and W.V. Friesen, The facial action coding system. Palo Alto, CA: Consulting Psychology Press; 1978.
[87]   S. Frey, H.P. Hirsbrunner, A. Florin, W. Daw and R. Crawford, A unified approach to the investigation of nonverbal and verbal behavior in communication research. In: *Current issues in*

European social psychology. Edited by Doise W and Moscovici S. Cambridge: Cambridge University Press, 1983.

[88] M. Garau, M. Slater, D.-P. Pertaub and S. Razzaque, The Response of People to Avatars in an Immersive Environment. *Presence: Teleoperators & Virtual Environments,* (2005), 14(1), 104-116.

[89] J.B. Bailenson, K.R. Swinth, C.L. Hoyt, S. Persky, A. Dimov and J. Blascovich, The independent and interactive effects of embodied agent appearance and behavior on self-report, cognitive, and behavioral markers of copresence in Immersive Virtual Environments. *PRESENCE: Teleoperators and Virtual Environments,* (2005), 14(4), 379-393.

[90] J.N. Bailenson, J. Blascovich, A.C. Beall and J.M. Loomis, Equilibrium revisited: Mutual gaze and personal space in virtual environments. *Presence: Teleoperators & Virtual Environments,* (2001), 10, 583-598.

[91] J.N. Bailenson, J. Blascovich, A.C. Beall and J.M. Loomis, Interpersonal distance in immersive virtual environments. *Personality and Social Psychology Bulletin,* (2003), 29, 1-15.

[92] D.H. Krikorian, J.S. Leee, T.K. Chock and C. Harms, Isn't that spatial? Distance and communication in a 2-D virtual environment. *Journal of Computer Mediated Communication,* (2000), 5(4), On-line: http://www.ascusc.org/jcmc/vol5/issue4/krikorian.html.

[93] J.N. Bailenson, A.C. Beall. and J. Blascovich, Mutual gaze and task performance in shared virtual environments. *Journal of Visualization and Computer Animation,* (2002), 13, 1-8.

[94] L. Cerrato and S. Ekeklint, Evaluating users reactions to human-like interfaces: Prosodic and paralinguistic features as new evaluation measures for users' satisfaction. In: *From Brows to Trust: Evaluating Embodied Conversational Agents.* Edited by Ruttkay Z and Pelachaud C. Dordrecht, The Netherlands: Kluwer Academic Publishers; 101-124, 2004.

[95] M. Palmer, Interpersonal communication in virtual reality: Mediating interpersonal relationships. In: *Communication in the age of virtual reality.* Edited by Biocca FL. Hillsdale, NJ: Lawrence Erlbaum Press; 277-302, 1995.

[96] J.N. Bailenson, N. Yee, D. Merget and R. Schroeder, The Effect of Behavioral Realism and Form Realism of Real-Time Avatar Faces on Verbal Disclosure, Nonverbal Disclosure, Emotion Recognition, and Copresence in Dyadic Interaction. *Presence: Teleoperators & Virtual Environments,* (2006, in press).

[97] M. Kipp, Anvil - A Generic Annotation Tool for Multimodal Dialogue. In: *Eurospeech2001: 2001,*2001.

[98] C.L. Hoyt, J. Blascovich and K.R. Swinth, Social inhibition in immersive virtual environments. *PRESENCE: Teleoperators and Virtual Environments,* (2003), 12(2), 183-195.

[99] K.R. Swinth and J. Blascovich, Perceiving and responding to others: Human-human and human-computer social interaction in collaborative virtual environments. In: *5th Annual International Workshop on PRESENCE: 2002; Porto, Portugal,*2002.

[100] L. Schilbach, A.M. Wohlschlaeger, N.C. Kraemer, A. Newenh, N.J. Shah, G.R. Fink and K. Vogeley, Being with virtual others: Neural correlates of social interaction. *Neuropsychologia,* (2006), 44, 718-730.

[101] Z. Ruttkay, C. Dormann and H. Noot, Embodied Conversational Agents on a common ground: A framework for design and evaluation. In: *From Brows to Trust: Evaluating Embodied Conversational Agents.* Edited by Ruttkay Z and Pelachaud C. Dordrecht: Kluwer Academic Publishers, 2004.

[102] C. Pelachaud and I. Poggi, Multimodal Communication and context in embodied agents. In: *Workshop W7, 5th International Conference on Autonomous Agents: 29 May 2001 2001; Montreal, Canada,*2001.

[103] T. Wehrle, S. Kaiser, S. Schmidt and K. Scherer, Studying the dynamics of emotional expression using synthesized facial muscle movements. *Journal of Personality and Social Psychology,* (2000), 78(1), 105-119.

[104] J.N. Bailenson, A.C. Beall, J. Blascovich, M. Raimundo and M. Weisbuch, Intelligent Agents Who Wear Your Face: Users Reactions to the Virtual Self. In: *Third International Workshop Intelligent Virtual Agents, IVA 2001: 2001; Madrid, Spain*: Springer; 86-99,2001.

[105] M. Argyle and J. Dean, Eye-contact, distance and affiliation. *Sociometry,* (1965), 28(289-304).

[106] J.K. Burgoon, L.A. Stern and L. Dillman, Interpersonal adaptation: Dyadic interaction patterns. New York: Cambridge University Press; 1995.

[107] E. Krahmer, Z. Ruttkay, M. Swerts and W. Wesselink, Pitch, Eyebrows and the Perception of Focus. In: *Speech Prosody 2002: 2002; Aix en Province, France,*2002.

[108] E. Krahmer and M. Swerts, More about brows: A cross-linguistic study via analysis-by-synthesis. In: *From Brows to Trust: Evaluating Embodied Conversational Agents.* Edited by Ruttkay Z and Pelachaud C. Dordrecht: Kluwer Academic Publishers; 191-216, 2004.

[109] D.P. Pertaub, M. Slater and C. Barker, An experiment on fear of public speaking in virtual reality. *Studies in Health Technology and Informatics,* (2001), 81, 372-378.

[110] M. Argyle, Bodily Communication, 2nd ed. edn. London: Methuen; 1988.

[111] C. Pelachaud, E. Magno Caldognetto, C. Zmarich and P. Cosi, Modelling an Italian Talking Head. In: *AVSP 2001: 2001; Aalborg, Denmark,*2001.

[112] Z. Ruttkay and C. Pelachaud (eds.), From Brows to Trust: Evaluating Embodied Conversational Agents. Dordrecht: Kluwer Academic Publishers; 2004.

[113] M. Garau, M. Slater, S. Bee and M.A. Sasse, The impact of eye gaze on communication using humanoid avatars. In: *SIG-CHI Conference on Human factors in computing systems: 2001; Seattle, WA;* 309-316,2001.

[114] Z. Ruttkay, C. Pelachaud, I. Poggi and H. Noot, Excercises of Style for Virtual Humans. In: *Animating Expressive Characters for Social Interactions.* Edited by Canamero L and Aylett R: John Benjamins Publishing Co., 2004.

[115] S. Buisine, S. Abrilian and J.-C. Martin, Evaluation of multimodal behaviour of embodied agents. In: *From Brows to Trust: Evaluating Embodied Conversational Agents.* Edited by Ruttkay Z and Pelachaud C. Dordrecht: Kluwer Academic Publishers; 217-238, 2004.

[116] L. Anolli, The detection of the hidden design of meaning. In: *The hidden structure of interaction: From neurons to culture patterns.* Edited by Anolli L, Duncan SJ, Magnusson M and Riva G. Amsterdam: IOS Press; 23-50, 2005.

[117] T.L. Chartrand and J.A. Bargh, The chameleon effect: The perception-behavior link and social interaction. *Journal of Personality and Social Psychology,* (1999), 76, 893-910.

[118] J.N. Bailenson and N. Yee, Digital Chameleons: Automatic assimilation of nonverbal gestures in immersive virtual environments. *Psychological Science,* (2005), 16, 814-819.

[119] M. Pantic and L.J.M. Rothkrantz, Toward an affect sensitive multimodal human-computer interaction. *Proceedings of the IEEE,* (2003), 91(9), 1370-1390.

[120] R.W. Picard, Affective Computing. Cambridge, MA: The MIT Press; 1997.

[121] H. Prendinger, H. Dohi, H. Wang, S. Mayer and M. Ishizuka, Empathic embodied interfaces: addressing users' affective state. In: *Tutorial and Research Workshop on Affective Dialogue Systems: 2004; Kloster Irsee, Germany;* 53-64,2004.

[122] C. Aldrich, Simulations and the future of learning: An innovative (and perhaps revolutionary) approach to e-learning. San Francisco: Jossey-Bass/Pfeiffer; 2003.

[123] L. Anolli, F. Mantovani, M. Balestra, A. Agliati, O. Realdon, V. Zurloni, M. Mortillaro, A. Vescovo and L. Confalonieri, The Potential of Affective Computing in E-Learning: MYSELF project experience. In: *Workshop on "eLearning and Human-Computer Interaction: Exploring Design Synergies for more Effective Learning Experiences", part of INTERACT 2005 Conference: 2005; Rome, Italy,*2005.

[124] C. Botella, S. Quero, R.M. Banos, C. Perpina, A. Garcia Palacios and G. Riva, Virtual reality and psychotherapy. *Stud Health Technol Inform,* (2004), 99, 37-54.

[125] B.O. Rothbaum, L. Hodges and R. Kooper, Virtual reality exposure therapy. *J Psychother Pract Res,* (1997), 6(3), 219-226.

[126] G. Riva, Virtual reality in psychotherapy: review. *CyberPsychology & Behavior,* (2005), 8(3), 220-230; discussion 231-240.

SECTION II

FROM PRESENCE TO COMMUNICATION: INNER PRESENCE VS. MEDIA PRESENCE

Meaning seems to have the same disease of being: as soon as you grasp a meaning of something, it changes and fades away to leave room for new meanings. Consequently, meaning appears to be struggled between contingency and fixedness.

From time to time, the meaning's pendulum swings to contingency and variability to turn back to stability and steadiness, and vice versa.

This twofold nature of meaning makes it a theoretical and empirical challenge for scholars belonging to different disciplines. At the same time, it is graspable and ungraspable, as in any case we can grasp it only partially.

Anolli, 2005

From Communication to Presence
G. Riva et al. (Eds.)
IOS Press, 2006

2 Media Presence and Inner Presence: The Sense of Presence in Virtual Reality Technologies

Carlos COELHO, Jennifer TICHON, Trevor J. HINE
Guy WALLIS, Giuseppe RIVA

Abstract. Presence is widely accepted as the key concept to be considered in any research involving human interaction with Virtual Reality (VR). Since its original description, the concept of presence has developed over the past decade to be considered by many researchers as the essence of any experience in a virtual environment.

The VR generating systems comprise two main parts: a technological component and a psychological experience. The different relevance given to them produced two different but coexisting visions of presence: the rationalist and the psychological/ecological points of view. The rationalist point of view considers a VR system as a collection of specific machines with the necessity of the inclusion of the concept of presence. The researchers agreeing with this approach describe the sense of presence as a function of the experience of a given medium (Media Presence). The main result of this approach is the definition of presence as the perceptual illusion of non-mediation produced by means of the disappearance of the medium from the conscious attention of the subject. At the other extreme, there is the psychological or ecological perspective (Inner Presence). Specifically, this perspective considers presence as a neuropsychological phenomenon, evolved from the interplay of our biological and cultural inheritance, whose goal is the control of the human activity.

Given its key role and the rate at which new approaches to understanding and examining presence are appearing, this chapter draws together current research on presence to provide an up to date overview of the most widely accepted approaches to its understanding and measurement.

Contents

2.1 Introduction

Up until the twentieth century, one of the driving forces behind western art was the quest for faithful and compelling reproduction – a virtual rendering of another place, frozen in time. During the twentieth century new technologies such as still cameras and cinematography replaced the canvas and provided a faithful and even dynamic historical record [1]. As the twenty-first century begins a wealth of new technologies have been developed to replace those of cinema and aim to provide an even richer sensory experience. This chapter considers how far technology has come and the potential for new technologies to create not a rendering of a place in time but of that place here and now. The chapter goes on to discuss the means by which one can attempt to quantify the fidelity of a virtual rendering of a real environment as a means of improving current technology and gauging its effectiveness as a training tool.

When it first arrived, image motion was a major leap forward in purveying a sense of virtual realism. Rumour has it that when, in 1895, the Lumière brothers showed the first movie - depicting a train approaching a station - it had people screaming and running for cover. But today's more sophisticated audiences are less unlikely to be convinced by a grainy, black and white, two-dimensional image. Fortunately, technology has improved. One important aspect of this improvement is in the use of man-machine interfaces. Whereas an audience was once restricted to the role of mere passive observer or to the use of an external devices such as a mouse or keyboard, technological developments that have occurred since the 60's have allowed the production of more natural and compelling man-machine interaction systems.

This is nowhere better represented than in the area of haptic control devices. There has been a series of ever more sophisticated devices developed which successfully transmit a feeling of being within the perceptive world created by the machine. Visual display devices have also developed enormously, providing higher resolution, stereoscopy, a larger field of view and devices, which respond almost immediately to the human body's natural movements. For the observer, these developments create a stronger feeling of being a part of the virtual environment. The person while physically located in the real world, through sensory stimulation is manipulated to develop a feeling that the objects surrounding them are actually present in the same environment as the individual [2].

2.2 Origin of the Term "Presence"

The term "*telepresence*" was coined by Marvin Minsky in 1980 and refers to the phenomenon that a human operator develops a sense of being physically present at a remote location through interaction with the system's human interface [1]: through the user's actions and the subsequent perceptual feedback he/she receives via the appropriate teleoperation.

Teleoperations are a specific type of VR that allow the individual to operate in a distant environment (e.g., in space, in the depths of the sea or harmful locations). The user is given the opportunity to command a machine with an anthropomorphic design, which moves according to the user's movements and gives both auditory and visual feedback [5]. Such sensory feedback is of sufficient quality and quantity to maintain the operator's feeling of presence in the remote workplace [6]. The operator perceives two separate environments simultaneously: the physical environment where he or she actually is, and the environment, which is being presented via the technology. The term "telepresence" is used when the virtual experience dominates the real world experience. So it describes the feeling of being in the environment generated by the technology, rather than the surrounding physical environment [4].

However, the term *"presence"* entered in the wide scientific debate in 1992 when Sheridan and Furness used it in the title of a new journal dedicated to the study of virtual reality systems and teleoperations: *Presence, Teleoperators and Virtual Environments*. In the first issue, Sheridan [3] refers to presence elicited by a virtual environment as "virtual presence", whereas he uses "telepresence"only for the cases involving teleoperations [4].

Nowadays, most new VR devices are not used to operate at a distance. Rather, these systems generate a virtual environment in which the user can participate: not by altering an external real world, but by altering a virtual world generated by the computer. The participant ceases to think of himself as interacting with a computer and starts to interact directly with the three dimensional environment.

2.3 The Two Sides of the Same Coin: Media Presence and Inner Presence

An electronic Forum "Presence-L Listserv" established in July 1999 by the *Information Systems Division* of the *International Communication Association*, hosted a discussion of presence in 2000. A tentative definition of the concept of presence resulted from this: "Presence is a psychological state or a subjective perception in which the participant, although working with an instrument, fails to understand the role of technology in his experience. Although the subject might assert (except in extreme cases) that he is using technology, up to a certain point, or a certain degree, the subject gets involved in the task, in objects, entities and event perception, as if technology was not present"[7]. Although quite comprehensive, this is not the last word on the debate of the term's meaning. Presence entails some emotional involvement and is related to different levels of realism [8]. Many different definitions and descriptions of media presence exist, although it is almost always defined as a feeling of being present in a virtual environment [9]. The objective for most researchers is to develop an operational definition of media presence, with objective measures that may determine adequate levels of presence for the accomplishment of certain tasks. Bearing in mind these aspects, a definition of presence would allow standardization of its evaluation as a valid and reliable measure.

The VR generating systems comprise two main parts: a technological component and a psychological experience. Following this, there will be a dichotomy of the definitions and explanations of the feeling of presence: the rationalist and the psychological point of view.

The rationalist point of view considers a VR system as a collection of specific machines with the necessity of the inclusion of the concept of presence. The researchers agreeing with this approach describe the sense of presence as a function of our experience of a given medium (*Media Presence*). The main result of this approach is the definition of presence as the *perceptual illusion of non-mediation* produced by means of the disappearance of the medium from the conscious attention of the subject.

However, the technologic definitions of VR do not deny existence of the psychological component offered by the VR systems, it is simply not included in the definition. At the other extreme there is the psychological or ecological perspective (*Inner Presence*). As we will see in the next two chapters by Riva and by Waterworth *et al.*, the feeling of presence is seen as an experience common among different types of human experiences independent of any technology. Specifically, these researchers consider presence as a neuropsychological phenomenon, evolved from the interplay of our biological and cultural inheritance, whose goal is the control of the human activity [10-11].

The logical extension of this definition, as discussed in the final chapter of this Section by Moller and Barbera, is that dreams too are virtual experiences involving presence.

2.4 Media Presence in Virtual Reality

VR from a rationalist perspective is typically defined in terms of a collection of technological hardware (computers, helmets and gloves) normally involving a means to communicate [11]. Thus, according to this point of view, a system is VR if it comprises a minimal set of machines. In other words it is a set of diverse technologies placed together. An analogy would be multimedia (MM) applications based on the integration of multiple media like audio, text, video and image. The main difference between VR and MM systems is that the former allows interactive environments.

VR offers a new paradigm in which the users are active participants in a computer generated three-dimensional virtual world [3]. VR is characterized by the illusion of participating in a synthetic world instead of the external observation of that environment through an immersive and multi-sensorial experience [12]. Machover and Tice's [13] definition of presence emphasizes the interactive and immersive components. According to Pimentel and Teixeira: "through visualizing stereoscopic images, hearing binaural sound and manipulating three-dimensional objects in real time in a computer generated world, the subject can overcome the barrier represented by the computer screen and experience new realities" [14]. In functional terms VR is a simulator in which computer-generated graphics respond to the user's command.

Existing sensory stimulation devices allow the users to enter three-dimensional worlds where they can see, hear, touch, move and explore. The virtual space immerses the user and he has an egocentric position similar to the real world. The diversity and quality of these impressions determine the level of immersion, creating a feeling of presence. A technologically ideal system should allow the stimulation of all sensory systems, having trackers for the torso and limbs that would be used to provide precise and instantaneous stimulation feedback to the user [15].

Mazuryk and Gervautz [6] group VR systems according to the different levels of immersion offered to the user. They consider VR immersive systems those which put the user completely inside the world generated by computer, with the help of a

HMD which supports a stereoscopic vision of the scene according to the positioning of the user and the use of audio and haptic man-machine interfaces. The more VR stimulation and the less external stimulation, the more immersive is the virtual environment.

Some researchers consider immersion as the description of a technology [16, 2, 17]. Total immersion requires, for example, that the participant be able to see 360°, in other words, immersion refers to the physical extent of the sensorial information. To these authors, immersion is purely technological and the feeling of presence is, mostly, determined by the insertion of the subject in the system. This way, immersion depends on technology and the world is presented from the user's point of view such that each time the user moves his head new images are generated according to new viewing geometry. Immersion increases with isolation from the physical environment, inclusion in the virtual situation, the possibility of a natural interaction with the environment and control over it, as well as the existence of stimuli that support the perception of self-motion [18].

According to this perspective, the higher the sensorial immersion, the higher the feeling of non-mediation, offering a feeling of 'being there'. The main purpose of VR is, therefore, to induce the feeling of reality through the development of an immersive synthetic system, in which the subject can interact with computer generated objects and people [19]. It is, therefore, basically, about 'misleading' the senses.

Thus, what differentiates VR from other systems and ways of communicating (e.g., cinema, television) is the bringing together of immersive stimulation (which is the capacity of the system to decrease stimulation due to the real world and increase stimulation from the synthetic world) mostly conveyed by the HMD, and the active participation in the environment, mostly conveyed by the tracker. The sensorial stimulation and the participation in a world generated by a computer seem to be the main factors which lead participants to feel, when immersed in one of these systems, what researchers of this field call presence.

2.5 Inner Presence in Virtual Reality

According to Steuer [6], presence is a component with such importance to VR that it can be seen as part of its definition, and virtual reality should not be defined solely in terms of hardware. He offers an alternative definition for VR as a particular type of experience instead of a technology. Presence can be evoked in writing (e.g, letter, journal), through hearing (e.g., telephone calls, music records) and in a composed process (e.g., movies, videogames). Thus, without referring to any type of hardware, Steuer defines VR as a real or simulated environment in which the participant experiences telepresence [6]. The author does not deny, however, that although many factors contribute to generate the feeling of presence, the quality of the sensorial input and the interactivity of the participant are important in its existence.

According to this point of view, the interaction with the synthetic world offers the subject a feeling of immersion and the world of the computer becomes the world of the user. However this immersion is a result of the interaction between man and environment and not a technological component of VR [6]. Because immersion promotes the feeling of 'being there', in the virtual environment, presence is considered a property that emerged from immersion [17], and 'being there' is enhanced by the possibility of 'acting there' [20].

In order to understand this point of view it is useful to contrast it with Loomis' [21]. Loomis considers that the understanding of synthetic experiences should begin by recognizing that its phenomenology is continuous with the normal experience. The perceptual world is created by our senses and nervous system and interaction with the physical world is mediated by such processes. Loomis reminds us of our naïve realism in which we often assume that our vision of the world is equivalent to the world itself. In particular Loomis states that: "The physical world, including our nervous system, is not given to us directly through experience but is inferred through observation and critical reasoning. Given the separation between these two domains, it is useful to recognize the 'normal' division between 'self' or internal phenomenon and 'non self', or external phenomenon". According to these authors and these perspectives, normal experience is therefore mediated. What we experience is a construction, elaborated from our senses and nervous system, as functional as the representation of reality, which makes us act upon the representation as if it was the reality; yet, the real world can merely be inferred [8].

Alternatively, the ecological perceptionist J.J. Gibson believed that the environment can be directly understood, without the need for mediation through cognitive processes [22]. Based on Gibson's ecological theory, Zahorik and Jenison [23] define presence as actions successively afforded by the environment. They maintain that the feeling of presence results from the efficacy of the match between perception and action; in this case, between the user and the virtual environment. The authors suggest that a change in perspective from the rationalist tradition to a Heidggerian vision might be useful for the study of presence (see for more details the next chapter by Riva). The rationalist tradition is the metaphysical position underlying most current theories, and theories regarding VR systems are no exception [23]. Opposed to empiricism, rationalism theorizes that knowledge acquisition is based on reason. This orientation separates the individual world into the mental and physical domains.

Heidegger was a German philosopher who worked mainly on the question of the meaning of 'being'. In order to explore this subject, Heidegger explains we are thrown towards the situations in which we should continuously act and interpret, labelling this 'throwness'. In this way: "...given that we are continuously interpreting, we cannot (in normal circumstances) represent in a detached and analytical way the situation we live in" [23]. Along with Heidegger's proposal of a form of existence, he also argues that when a person is working such as using an object with intention, there is no stable representation of the object, the tool or the equipment [23]. The equipment is conceived according to the use it has to the task. Through action, the equipment becomes transparent to the user and the stable representation of the instrument disappears. Hand gives an interesting example of the power of the use of an instrument to the accomplishment of a task: "When we look at a mirror we are not concerned with the fact that the image presented is not us, but we use it as if it was, because it serves the execution of a task which without the mirror would become much harder" [25].

It seems that Gibson's [24] perspective is quite similar to Heiddeger's in this regard. His theory states that, in perception, the environment is closely related to the observer. Perceptions support successful actions in the environment capturing its opportunities, permissions or affordances. For example, the ground permits walking and a hole permits falling, an apple permits being eaten and a tiger permits us getting eaten [26]. Each possibility or permission depends on the environment and the animal. There is, therefore, a perception-action in which the organism understands the environment according to what it allows it to do. Gibson's ontology is one of reciprocity between perceiver and environment. Both reject distinctions between subject and object. The instruments become, according to Heidegger, 'ready-to-hand', unconscious, when the user is not more conscious of the tool itself but only on its use for the task he is performing [26]. Both authors agree that the objects of perception should be understood in terms of possible actions with the perceiver. Given that the VR system is presented in a concrete way, the interaction with it is not accomplished in a symbolic form of textual language, as in books. The user experiences VR through the same perceptive processes with which he interacts with the real world [27].

The fact that the virtual environment allows the perceptive, cognitive and psychomotor capacities of humans to be projected into distant, dangerous or simulated environments [28], allows presence to simply be a consequence of a supported and successful action in the environment. When the response is seen as commensurate with the response that would be given usually in the real world, within the parameters of evolution of the organism and the perceptive system, then it is an action that supports expectations. It can be assumed that the user understands the VR equipment in terms of what can be done with it, resulting in invisibility of the VR (*ready-to-hand*) technology to the user [26]. In fact, when an individual is immersed, his self-perception is inseparable from the perceived environment [17]. The feeling of presence occurs when the subject mentally represents the possibility of acting upon the virtual world. The real cause of the feeling of presence is the interactions [29, 4]. Therefore, presence in a virtual environment is an active suppression process of the real world and the construction of a set of action patterns based on the immediate stimulus.

Following this approach, Riva and Waterworth [10, 11, the next two chapters] defined presence as an evolved neuropsychological process whose goal is the control of the activity of the subject. This is achieved by filtering and organizing the streams of sensory data: the more this process differentiates the self from the external world, the more is the level of presence experienced by the subject. Within this vision, they suggest that the ability to feel "present" in a virtual reality system – an artifact - basically does not differ from the ability to feel "present" in the real world.

A final point expressed by the psychological approach is the link between presence and its evolutionary role [10-11]. Even if presence is a unitary feeling, recent neuropsychological research has shown that, on the process side, it can be divided in three different layers/subprocesses, phylogenetically different, and strictly related to the evolution of self:

- *proto presence* (self vs. non self);
- *core presence* (self vs. present external world);
- and *extended presence* (self relative to present external world).

The existence of three different layers underlying presence suggests that in the real world, the sense of presence is not the same in all the situations but can be different in relation to the characteristics of the social and cultural space the subject is in. For instance, if I'm attending a presentation in a conference, my level of presence in it can be lower or higher in relation to the interest I have in the topic discussed. If the presentation is totally boring I may become absent (totally internal). As will by discussed in the fothcoming chapter by Waterworth and Waterwoth, the role of absence is critical for the survival of the subject, because it is in absence that the subject defines plans and organizes future behaviors.

2.6 Variables that Influence the Feeling of Presence

Much research has been devoted to discovering the range of variables, which might contribute to an enhanced sense of presence in VR. In general, two categories of variables can determine a user's presence: (i) user characteristics, and (ii) media characteristics [12]. Moreover, it is possible to divide the characteristics of the medium into media *form* and media *content* variables. The following sections reports how each of these characteristics either support or erode this experience.

2.6.1 User Characteristics

Although the VR technology used will highly influence the level of immersion achieved, the individual user also plays an active part with respect to his interest in the material presented [19]. There are several psychological variables that can impact presence including: concentration, previous experience with VR, previous experience with required tasks, expectations regarding the mediated experience and susceptibility to motion sickness. Although simulator sickness is a form of motion sickness induced by discrepancies between visual and vestibular information in a VE, some individuals can also have an increased predisposition to succumb to the sickness. Each of these variables influence the extent to which the user becomes involved in any task required of them in the VE.

According to Heeter [30], VR can benefit from lessons learned in cinema direction and the resultant capacity to suspend audience disbelief, thereby creating a feeling of presence. Some authors report that users need to be willing to suspend disbelief to participate in a VR environment and experience the feeling of presence [31]. This willingness appears to be related to what is commonly referred to as absorption (the ability to "get lost in the task at hand") and dissociation (disruption in the normally integrated functions of consciousness, memory, identity, or perception of the environment), as defined by Murray, Fox and Pettifer [32]. So, there appears to be a commitment between man and machine in the experience of presence where the machine's task is to mislead man's senses while man himself must allow himself to be misled in order to be immersed in the VE.

Hoffman, Prothero, Wells and Groen [33] demonstrated that chess players experienced increased presence when chess pieces were distributed in significant positions, compared to random positions. The authors also suggested that the more the users focused their attention on virtual environment stimuli, the more they were involved in the experience, resulting in higher degrees of presence [18]. Thus, the feeling of presence also depends on the meaning the user gives to the stimuli that are presented to him. The notion of presence is therefore inseparable from attentional factors [34, 18].

According to Witmer and Singer [18], involvement is a psychological state resulting from the focus of energy and attention to a coherent group of significantly related stimuli and activities. The level of involvement achieved depends on the degree of importance attached and meaning given to the event by individual users. It is also influenced by the level of intent a user is capable of directing toward the virtual environment. The participant's ability and will to focus on the task can increase their feeling of presence since it requires the individual to not only concentrate on the task and virtual environment but also to ignore external distractions [18].

VR seems to facilitate, through technological immersion, selective attention regarding the mediated environment. Selective attention is the tendency to focus on significant information of particular interest to the individual [18]. Usually, attention is divided among one or more components of the physical and mental world of memories and planned activities. Darken, Bernatovich, Lawson and Peterson [35] consider that in order to be present in an alternative world, it is necessary to be focused on that world and not the real one. Thus, the extension of presence might depend not only on the quality and extension of the sensorial information, but also in the interest evoked by the presented scene. If the user is worried about personal issues or focused on activities that are occurring outside the virtual environment they will naturally be distracted and therefore less involved [18].

Due to the range of influential user variables a VR experience is ultimately a personal one. It is an experience that becomes inexplicably tied to personal aspects of the user and how they construct an explanation of their experience. Even with the identical technology in use, therefore, it is unlikely any two users would experience the identical level of presence. As discussed in a later section on presence measurement this becomes highly problematic for self-report measures.

2.6.2 Media Characteristics: Media Form

Technological or system characteristics can play an important role in the experience of presence. Although systematic research regarding the causes of presence is ongoing, a considerable number of variables have been identified. Several causal factors have been investigated and a growing number of possible determinants of presence have been empirically tested. The majority of these studies have tried through manipulation of system characteristics to increase the user immersion in the VR system and thereby increase the feeling of being present in the virtual world [36]. Among the topics studied are latency of response [37]; audio system [35]; stereoscopic presentation [38]; head tracker [39]; visual field [40] and the control process [29, 42].

For further discussion the findings of this research have been grouped under the following variables of influence: sensorial channels; pictorial realism; media content; system response time; control; vision field; isolation; body representation and the presence of other subjects in the VR environment.

2.6.2.1 Number of Sensorial Channels

According to Steuer [4], the sensorial input quality refers to the capacity of the technology to produce an environment of sensorial richness, with information for all the senses. This potential depends on the variety of sensorial stimulation achievable and the level of 'resolution' for each of these types of stimuli.

In a study with 322 subjects, Dinh; Walker; Song, Kobayashi and Hodges, [43] assessed the impact of a variety of sensorial inputs upon the feeling of presence and object memory. Results indicated that when enhancing the sensorial input modes in the virtual environment, there was an increase not only in the feeling of presence but also on object memory in that environment. Data indicates that it is particularly useful adding tactile clues (e.g., heat from a lamp when the subject approaches the balcony); olfactory clues (e.g., coffee aroma near a coffee machine) and auditory clues (e.g., volume variations when approaching a copy machine).

Several authors report that any stimulation increase that creates sensorial redundancy (e.g., seeing and touching an object) contributes to the feeling of presence [30; 3; 18], for instance, the inclusion of dynamic shadows [44]. It is however important that there is consistency among different presentations [45]; if not, both the absence of redundant cues and the conflict between cues can have a negative effect on the experiment [15]. Therefore, the quantity of sensorial information must be presented in a way that is consistent with the user's senses.

It has also been asserted that the introduction of sound is very useful for the induction of feelings of presence [35; 46]. One study tested participants divided into groups of different audio conditions: no sound, low fidelity sound (typical AM quality) and high fidelity sound (typical CD quality). Each virtual location was allocated a distinct sound. Results revealed a higher feeling of presence and capacity to recall objects among participants who were exposed to sound, independent of its quality [46]. Additionally, adults who have become suddenly deaf frequently complain of feeling disconnected from the surrounding environment [15]. Auditory cues can be incorporated in lower-end technology, allowing an increase in presence without introducing computational delays in the system that pictorial realism can generate (see below) [42].

2.6.2.2 Pictorial Realism

Pictorial realism increases presence in a virtual environment [42, 18]. Part and parcel of the issue of pictorial realism is the rendering of visual depth. Several authors have found a positive relation between sense of depth and presence. Indeed, the use of stereoscopic clues has been described as an important factor in enhancing presence [38, 39, 48]. However, such glasses have previously been linked with an increase in simulator or 'cybersickness' – a form of motion sickness [26].

2.6.2.3 System Response Time

System response time is the time adjustment between the user's actions and the perceived effects of those actions on the environment [49]. Response time becomes a crucial issue when wearing an HMD for example, since it affects the responsiveness of the HMD to head movements. The latency of visual feedback, in other words, the time existent between the user's action and the system's response, was seen as responsible for the degradation of presence when it generated significant time intervals between action and its results [37, 45, 42]. In order to preserve the illusion of interactive instantaneous control, the intervals should be no longer than 0.1s [50].

According to Durlach & Mavor [50], there should be a display of more than 8 to 10 images per second in order to offer a continuous illusion of movement, although this figure will vary to some extent with the speed of head movements. It has been shown that presence decreases abruptly under 15-20 images a second [51]. It is therefore suggested that response velocity of the system increases the feeling of control from the user upon his actions in VR, increasing presence [3, 18].

2.6.2.4 Control

According to some authors, presence occurs when the subject mentally represents the possibility of acting upon the virtual world [29]. Presence can be increased, for example, if the participant perceives his own movement inside the virtual environment [18], or when the subject has more capacity to change the environment he is in. One study reports presence was higher in users that had control over their actions in VR, as opposed to passive observers [43]. It is likely then that subjects would experience more presence if they were capable of anticipating what would happen next [45].

2.6.2.5 Field of vision

Field of vision is important in two different ways. First, a large field of view provides larger and more compelling visual motion cues. Second, by restricting vision of the real-world environmental, less distraction/conflict occurs with images from the virtual world. In other words, devices which isolate users from their physical environment can increase presence in VR environments, facilitating immersion. Use of a mask, in order to limit the field of vision close to the eyes, has been shown to reduce the referred quantity of presence [41]. Additionally, a HMD, which isolates the participant from the real world, might increase presence in the virtual environment compared with a regular screen [52, 53, 18]. HMDs, however, cause cybersickness which can be experienced by up to 95% of HMD users [54]. Cybersickness has been shown to reduce one's sense of presence by diverting attention away from the VE and there is a negative correlation between simulator sickness and presence measured by the Presence Questionnaire [18].

2.6.3 Media Characteristics: Media Content

Irrespective of whether the system uses is a high-end or low-end VR interface, the content of media experienced by the user has been reported to influence the level of presence. A study by Banos, Botella, Alcaniz, Liano, Guerrero and Rey [55] compared three immersive systems (a PC monitor, a rear projected video wall, and a head-mounted display). Their aim was to test the role of immersion and media content on the sense of presence and to determine if presence could be enhanced in less immersive VEs by using emotional content. They found that presence could be enhanced in less immersive virtual environments by using emotional content.

This result is coherent with the cultural approach to presence [12]. As suggested by Riva and colleagues, to be "present" in the context offered by a symbolic system, the user has to be aware of its meaning. Only "making sense there", the user really experiences a full sense of presence.

According to this vision, researchers have to study presence by analyzing the user/s interaction with and within the media experience, including all the different aspects that converge on it: the relevance of the content, the social relationships established, the physical and symbolic resources exploited and the cultural competence used.

2.6.3.1 Body Representation

The participant's body representation in the virtual space is important to the sense of presence [15]. Other researchers agree with the key role of possible interactions, however, they stress that action is essentially social. Thus, the presence experience will depend on the accordance between the virtual environment and our cultural expectations. Slater and Usoh [15] emphasize the body and the way it can be perceived and represented in the virtual environment. The body works as an interaction, communication and self identification system. Thus, in order for the VR system to function ideally, it is necessary to offer proprioceptive information which will offer a mental model of our body and of the disposition of its limbs [17].

2.6.3.2 Presence of Others

There is a growing interest in presence generated by the existence of virtual actors in VR systems [4; 30]. The differentiation and experience of the self can be enhanced if other people exist in the virtual world and seem to recognize the existence of the participant [30]. One might choose to refer to this sensation as *social presence* (see also the next chapters of the book). This concept has its basis on the premise that if other people are in a virtual world it is more likely that it exists. In this way it justifies a sub-type of presence called social presence [42]. The hypothesis is that presence can increase with the existence of other individuals in the virtual environment and with the number of interactions between the participant and the virtual actors. Heeter [30] also takes into consideration environmental presence where the environment seems to 'know' we are there and reacts to our presence, e.g., lights turning on when the subject enters a room.

Recently, Biocca and colleagues [56] analyzed in a comprehensive review the concept of social presence. In the paper they indicated different factors influencing the experience of "being together with another" (pp. 462-465):

-   *Sensory awareness of the embodied other*: The representation of the other triggers a sensory impression of the other that exists of a continuum from the minimal to the intense.
-   *Mutual awareness*: The user is aware of the mediated other, and the other is aware of the user.
-   *Sense of access to intelligence*: Social presence is activated when the user believes that an entity in the environment displays some minimal intelligence in its reactions to the environment and the user.
-   *Salience of the interpersonal relationship:* It affects the "apparent distance" of the other and the level of social presence.

- *Intimacy and immediacy:* They describe a cognitive state in which individuals feel more or less directly "present" in the interaction and in the process by which relationships are being created.
- *Mutual understanding:* The definition of social presence emphasizes the ability to project a sense of self through the limitations of a medium.
- *Behavioral engagement*: Social presence implies the effective negotiation of a relationship through an interdependent, multi-channel exchange of behaviors.

These variables suggest that the *continual awareness* of others in a shared media is required to flexibly adapt the behavior in social situations (e.g., a user heading across the room towards another, probably indicates an interest in beginning an interaction). This implies, for example, that the virtual environment has to allow changes in the way in which both the user is represented and he/she monitors what is going on in the environment.

2.7 Presence Measurement

As a consequence of the casual relationship evident between presence and the perceived realism of VR, much research has also undertaken the task of determining possibilities for reliable measurement of the concept. While many questionnaires and surveys are available to attempt to measure presence via underlying causal factors and determining variables such as those identified in earlier sections of the chapter, only a small number of these have gained widespread use.
Presence measurements must be reliable. They can achieve this through designs which are dependent only on the considered characteristics, and ensuring validity through measuring only what they are intended to measure [18]. Approaching the concept from different perspectives researchers have as a consequence developed different methods of measuring presence. These attempts are discussed here under the two major types: subjective self-reports, and objective measures.

2.7.1 Subjective Measurements of Presence

As described earlier, under considerations of user characteristics, even if users have the same experience in a VE it is unlikely they would report the identical experience. It is for this reason that Slater [57] claims self-report is not appropriate for measuring presence. Subjective self-reports are by nature inexplicably tied to personal aspects of the user. For example, Nisbett and Wilson [58] argue that introspective reports do not function as memories of mental process, but rather, that they are a process of the subject constructing an explanation of their behaviour based on personal theories of behaviour.

Subjective measurements of presence, however, are essential in order to collect the user's personal opinion [2, 3]. In addition, the majority of methods developed to measure presence to date have relied on subjective measurements using self-report [26, 59]. Subjective measures of presence include distinct forms of evaluation: scales (e.g., from 1 to 10, what level of being there did this virtual environment offer?); paired comparative method (e.g., which system offered more presence?); and comparative method by similarities among distinct modes (e.g., put this light as bright as the strength of presence you have experimented in this VR system). In utilizing any self-report measure of presence, however, it must be borne in mind that results can be tied to the personal aspects of the user.

2.7.1.1 Scales

Subjective evaluation scales have been used extensively to assess presence in virtual environments [63]. As data collection during the exposure could influence negatively the experience of presence it is recommended it be done immediately after the exposure [2]. Commencing with a theoretical body of work, essentially based on Sheridan [3], Held and Durlach's [45] work, and on a number of empirical studies, Witmer, Jerome and Singer [60] developed and validated the *Presence Questionnaire* (PQ), including 32 items measured through a 7 point Likert scale, that measures presence after using a VR system via causal factors. The questionnaire has gained a significant level of acceptance and has been tested across a number of studies [61; 62]. The PQ has four sub-scales: a) involvement; b) sensory fidelity; c) adaptation/immersion and d) interface quality. All four sub-scales measure user's perception of display system features.

Another well-known scale is the ITC-Sense of Presence Inventory (ITC-SOPI). It is a state questionnaire measure that focuses on users' experiences of media, with no reference to objective system parameters [64]. It has been translated in many languages and used in studies covering a wide range of media.

The ITC-SOPI, including 44 items measured through a 5 point Likert scale, has four factors:

- *Sense of Physical Space*, 19 items: a sense of being located in a physical space depicted by the media system
- *Engagement,* 13 items: a sense of involvement with the narrative/content of the mediated environment
- *Ecological Validity*, 5 items: a sense of naturalness and believability of the depiction of the environment itself and events within the environment;
- *Negative Effects*, 6 items: the negative experiences associated to an immersive media, such as eye-strain, headache, sickness.

Other widely used questionnaires are (for the full list of the available questionnaires see the Presence Research web site: http://www.presence-research.org): the UCL Presence [65] questionnaire (3 items), the Reality Judgement Presence [66] questionnaire (18 items) and the Igroup Presence [67] questionnaire (14 items).

However, it must be considered that by measuring presence using subjective self-report, a conflict is created between a user's feelings or emotions and their knowledge. For example, the user knows he is in a virtual world and remembers how he entered this new situation yet the investigator is asking him to respond to questions relating to the extent to which he feels present in this artificially entered situation [59].

2.7.1.2 Comparative

Presence has been divided into subjective and objective aspects [68]. The first is the likelihood of the person perceiving himself as being physically present in the virtual environment; the second, the feasibility of a task being completed successfully. We would suggest that the subjects be asked to compare the virtual environment with reality in order to measure presence. Because it is still very unlikely that someone would mistake the real world for the virtual presentation, Schloerb [68] suggests a degradation of the real scene through the use of filters, in order to confuse the real and virtual environments. However, this measure might become an assessment of the discrimination ability between two images, instead of the evaluation of presence [1], and "in similarity limit, the answers between the systems would be equivalent" [59].

With current technology it is hard for the participant to confuse the two worlds, and the level of degradation needed can be used as a measure of presence. It is natural that the subject is more sensitive to the degradation of a particular stimulus (e.g., frame rate of image presentation) than another (e.g., sound). It will also be difficult to deteriorate aspects of the real scene in order to fit the virtual scene. One of the advantages of this method would be the lack of need to question the participants about presence directly.

A variant of this method is the "Break in Presence" approach [69]. This approach is based on the idea that a participant experiencing virtual reality technology interprets the stimuli coming from the environment as belonging either to the virtual or to the real world. Slater & Steed suggested that the participant switches between the two interpretations throughout the experience, and that a measure of presence could be obtained if the amount of time that the participant spent interpreting the stimuli as coming from the virtual could be estimated. They proposed to do this estimation by looking for "breaks" those times when the participant realised they were in the real world. The main limitation of this approach is its oversimplification: it does not address the full complexity of mediated experience. For example, it does not account for mixed perceptions where the participant simultaneously holds and even partially responds to both (real and virtual) interpretations, as noted by Spagnolli and Gamberini [70, 71].

2.7.1.3 Similarities between Distinct Modes

In order to assess presence, one can also ask the participant to compare magnitudes in different modes. Pressure and luminance are sometimes used as an example. In this case, the participant presses a button with the strength he believes is correspondent to the level of brilliance of the light. Another possibility is sound and presence: the subject elevates the amplitude of a sound to the level of presence he felt in the VR environment. Although this method has many methodological difficulties it is considered to be an adequate quantitative measure of presence [72].

In order to continuously evaluate presence, Ijsselsteijn and collaborators [1] used an instrument to continuously evaluate image quality in television screens. It consisted of a small sliding part (*hand-held slider*), that the subject moved forward or backwards, according to the degree of presence they felt. A possible criticism of this measure is that the participant will be dividing his attention between the virtual task and the measure of presence. These authors defend their method by stating that the participants are aware of being in a laboratory, making it unlikely that they would believe they were in fact in the scene presented on screen. Instead, according to the authors, they refer to a feeling of being in the environment similar to the one they would feel if they actually were there.

2.7.2 Objective Presence Measurements

Objective performance measures have the advantage of not interfering with the task. However, presence has no physical manifestation objectively measurable [2]. The objective methods to measure presence have mostly used neurophysiologic measures, performance evaluation and postural response evaluation. Each of these forms of evaluation will now be briefly considered.

2.7.2.1 Physiological Measures

The use of a high number of neurophysiologic responses like cardiac frequency, skin's electric conductance (GSR), reflex motor behaviours and VR event evoked cortical responses were suggested as objective measures corroborative of presence. However, available research is still scarce [1]. Authors consider that physiologic reactions should be similar to those observed in a real environment. In a study by Dillon, Keogh, Freeman and Davidoff [38], it was observed that cardiac frequency was higher during the presentation of rally sequences as compared with calm boat sequences.

However, a critical issue for using neurophysiologic responses for presence measurement is the understanding of the link between emotion and presence. In particular its critical to identify what is an emotional response and what is a presence response. As noted by Baños and colleagues [55] within the activity of the "EMMA" European funded research project (http://alemania.did.upv.es/~juansoler/emma/), there are significant differences between emotional and neutral environments in presence measurements. On one side, the emotional environment seems to be more engaging, natural, believable and real to users than the neutral environment. On the other side, the influence of immersion on presence was higher in non-emotional environments than in emotional ones.

Recently "PRESENCIA" (http://www.cs.ucl.ac.uk/presencia), another European funded research project, has tried to identify a neural and physiological characterization of presence. Specifically the project is carrying out different psycho-physiological and brain imaging studies to identify the physiological and neuronal signatures associated with switches between different presence states. The key goal is to implement fMRI experiments, using event-related designs, where the presence state (or switches in state of presence) is indexed by (i) phenomenological report from subjects (ii) a change in bodily state indexed by independent psycho-physiological markers.

2.7.2.2 Performance Measures

It is frequently suggested that increased presence will produce better task performance and better skill transfer to the real world [72]. In order for these constructs to have validity, they should first allow the empirical establishment of equivalent classes [73]. This demonstration asks for a registration of performance variation when the factors which influence the construct vary. This also requires that a variation which does not change the construct also does not influence the performance the construct it is supposed to explain. Thus, equivalent classes are of use for the evaluation of change in presence. However, the relationship between presence and performance is unclear, given that performance can actually improve with a decrease in presence [73].

2.7.2.3 Postural Responses

According to Steuer [4], immersion is a function of system and user. However it seems likely that one can be physically immersed in a VR system but not 'be there', that is, feel presence. In other words, participation in a VR system does not guarantee presence. Immersion is created for a user when they give their attention and commitment to their closest physical environment [4]. Thus, it is the level of commitment to the environment which determines the level of immersion.

According to Usoh, Alberto and Slater [17], an increase in presence raises the similarity between behaviour in virtual environment and usual behaviour in a real environment. The measure of these differences should therefore provide a means of measuring presence. The adjustment of the observer's posture as a possible corroborative measure of presence has also been explored. It is a distinct and promising measure of presence assessment that consists of postural response evaluation to stimuli presented. Referred to as *behavioural realism,* the basic principle of this form of assessment is that the more similar the virtual environment is to the one it mimics, the more similar the observer's response to the virtual presentation will be [59].

These measures are potentially useful for two reasons. First, the observers are not normally conscious of their postural responses, and so their responses are less likely to be affected by subjective assessments [30]. Second, because postural measures have the capacity of producing different levels of responses, they do not simply generate binary results such as yes and no. Instead, it is possible to assess degrees of response and relate them to different degrees of presence [59]. The implicit theory in this form of assessment is that postural changes only occur if the subject is extremely present in the virtual environment. The advantage of this approach is in the evaluation of observable phenomena. Its weakness is lies in a lack of sensitivity to and exclusion of subtle aspects of presence [74].

2.8 Conclusions

The rationalist (*Media Presence*) and psychological/ecological (*Inner Presence*) points of view of presence reflect a remarkable epistemological difference between them. It seems evident, however, that the use of multiple sensory channels (particularly vision, hearing and feeling); immersion (through the exclusion of external stimuli to the ones offered by the virtual environment); egocentric location (offered specially by the HMD which provides images in accordance with the head's location) and the possibility of action in the environment (provided by an environment's response to our movements), seem to be the main determinant factors in presence.

Other systems and means of communication offer similar feelings, but VR ameliorates that feeling in a way never before achieved. In the case of VR, instead of the device being unconsciously used as a function of its operation in a task, it is the environment that becomes 'invisible' by turning into and becoming part of the task. While reading a book, watching television or talking on the phone might create a certain level of presence because VR is capable of high levels of immersion and interaction, these effects are multiplied.

The division existent among researchers regarding the definition of presence seems to mirror their adherence to the rationalist or ecological perspective of presence. The rationalist point of view does not consider presence necessary in order to define a VR system but rather presence is considered an epiphenomenon of the immersive stimulation allowed by VR, in other words its physical properties. In contrast, the psychological point of view defines presence as a possible experience outside a VR system. In the next chapters of this Section this position will be discussed in depth by Riva, Waterworth and Waterworth, and Moller and Barbera.

Despite the controversy regarding its definition, there is greater consensus on the variables which influence presence. Technological variables are numerous. The number of sensorial channels stimulated increases not only presence but also the memory of objects in that environment. Sound is a particularly important cue because of its large impact without costly investment demands. However, when adding cues, it should be taken into account that consistency is needed between different presentations, given that the conflict among different cues can have a negative effect on the overall experience. Consistency between the user's movements and the system's feedback presentation should also be preserved. In terms of measuring presence much work still needs to be done, but a combined strategy based on objective and subjective measures seems preferable since each brings with it specific advantages and disadvantages.

2.9 References

[1]   W. A. Ijsselsteijn, H. Ridder, J. Freeman, & S. E. Avons, Presence: concept, determinants and measurement. *Proceedings of SPIE, Human Vision and Electronic Imaging.* San Jose, CA, 2000.
[2]   R. S. Kalawsky, S. T. Bee, & S. P. Nee, Human factors evaluation techniques to aid understanding of virtual interfaces. *BT Technology Journal*, 17, 128-141, 1999.
[3]   T. B. Sheridan, Musings on telepresence and virtual presence. *Presence: Teleoperators and Virtual Environments*, 1, 120-126, 1992.
[4]   J. S. Steuer, Defining virtual reality: dimensions determining telepresence. *Journal of Communucation*, 4, 73-93, 1992.
[5]   J. M.   Loomis, Distal attribution and presence. *Presence: Teleoperators and Virtual Environments*, 1, 113-119, 1992a.
[6]   T. Mazuryk, & M.   Gervautz, Virtual reality. *History, applications, technology and future.* Technical Report. TR-186-2-96-06. Institute of Computer Graphics. Technical University of Vienna, 1992.
[7]   M. Lombard, *Resources for the study of presence: Presence explication*, 2000. Online: http://nimbus.temple.edu/~mlombard/presence/explicat.htm.
[8]   J. M. Loomis, Understanding synthetic experience must begin with the analysis of ordinary perceptual experience. *Proceedings on Research Frontiers in Virtual Reality* (pp. 54-57). California: IEEE Computer Society Press, 1993.
[9]   M. Huang, & N. Alessi, Presence as an emotional experience. In J.D. Hoffman, H.M. Robb & D. Stredney (Eds), *Medicine meets virtual reality: The Convergence of Physical and Informational Technologies Options for a New Era in Healthcare.* Amsterdam: IOS Press, 1999.
[10]   G. Riva and J.A. Waterworth, Presence and the Self: A cognitive neuroscience approach. *Presence-Connect,* (2003), 3(1). Online: http://presence.cs.ucl.ac.uk/presenceconnect/articles/Apr2003/jwworthApr72003114532/jwworth Apr72003114532.html.
[11]   G. Riva, J.A. Waterworth, and E.L. Waterworth, The Layers of Presence: a bio-cultural approach to understanding presence in natural and mediated environments. *Cyberpsychology & Behavior*, 7(4): p. 405-419, 2004.

[12] G. Riva, F. Davide, and W.A. IJsselsteijn, eds. *Being There: Concepts, effects and measurements of user presence in synthetic environments.* Emerging Communication: Studies on New Technologies and Practices in Communication, ed. G. Riva and F. Davide. Ios Press: Amsterdam, 2003. Online: http://www.emergingcommunication.com/volume5.html:

[13] Machover, C., & Tice, S.E. (1994). Virtual Reality. *IEEE Computer Applications and Graphics*, 14, 15-16, 1993.

[14] K. Pimentel, & K. Teixeira, *Virtual Reality. Through the New Looking Glass.* New York: Windcrest/McGraw-Hill, 1993.

[15] M. Slater & M. Usoh, Representations systems, perceptual position, and presence in immersive virtual environments. *Presence: Teleoperators and Virtual Environments*, 2, 221-23, 1993.

[16] R. S. Kalawsky, The validity of presence as a reliable human performance metric in immersive environments. *Proceedings of the 3rd International Workshop on Presence*, Delft, Netherlands, 2000.

[17] M. Usoh, C. Alberto, & M. Slater, *Presence: experiments in the psychology of virtual environments.* 1996. Online: http://www.cs.ucl.ac.uk/external/M.Usoh/vrpubs.html,

[18] B. G. Witmer, & M. J. Singer, Measuring presence in virtual environments: a presence questionnaire. *Presence: Teleoperators and Virtual Environments*, 7, 225-240, 1998.

[19] R. S. Kalawsky, A comprehensive virtual environment laboratory facility. In R.A. Earnshaw, M.A. Gigante & H. Jones (Eds.), *Virtual Reality Sistems*, (pp.77-89). San Diego: Academic Press, 1993.

[20] M. Usoh, E. Catena, S. Arman, & M. Slater, Presence questionnaires in reality, *Presence: Teleoperators and Virtual Environments*, 9, 497-503, 2000.

[21] J.M. Loomis, Presence and distal attribution: phenomenology, determinants, and assessment. *Human vision, visual processing, and digital display III*, 1666, 590-594, 1992b.

[22] V. Bruce, & P. R. Green, *Visual perception physiology, psychology and ecology.* Lawrence Erlbaum Associates, London, 1985.

[23] P. Zahorik, & R. L. Jenison, Presence as being-in-the-world. *Presence: Teleoperators and Virtual Environments*, 7, 78-89, 1998.

[24] J. J. Gibson, *The ecological approach to visual perception.* Boston: Houghton Mifflin, 1979.

[25] C. Hand, Other faces of virtual reality. *Proceedings of the east-west international conference on multimedia, hypermadia and virtual reality* (69-74). Moscow, Russia, 1994b.

[26] M. J. Schuemie, P. van der Straaten, M. Krijn, & C.A.P.G. van der Mast, Research on presence in VR: a survey. *Cyberpsychology and behavior*, 4, 183-201 2001.

[27] J. A. Waterworth, & E. L. Waterworth, The meaning of presence. *Presence-Connect*, 3, 3, 2003.

[28] J. V. Draper, D. B. Kaber, & J. M. Usher, Speculations on the value of telepresence. *Cyberpsychology & Behavior*. 2, 349-362, 1999.

[29] Schubert, T., Friedmann, F., & H. Regenbrecht, Embodied presence in virtual environments. In R. Paton & I. Neilson (Eds.), *Visual representations and interpretations*, pp. 268-278. London: Springer-Verlag, 1999.

[30] C. Heeter, Being there: the subjective experience of presence. *Presence: Teleoperators and Virtual Environments*, 1, 262-271, 1992.

[31] C. Hand, From dreams to reality. *Proceedings of the 1st UK VR-SIG Conference*, Nottingham University, UK, 1994 march.

[32] C. D. Murray, J. Fox, & S. Pettifer, Absorption, dissociation, locus of control and presence in virtual reality. *Computers in Human Behavior*, in press.

[33] H. G. Hoffman, J. Prothero, M. J. Wells, & J. Groen, Virtual chess: meaning enhances user's sense of presence in virtual environments. International. *Journal of Human-Computer Interaction*. 10, 251-263, 1998.

[34] W. Barfield, S. Weghorst, The sense of presence within virtual environments: a conceptual framework. In G. Salvendy & M. Smith (Eds.), *Human computer interaction: aplications and case studies,* pp. 699-704, Amsterdam: Elsevier, 1993.

[35] R. P. Darken, D. Bernatovich, J. P. Lawson, & B. Peterson, Quantitative Measures of Presence in Virtual Environments: The roles of Attention and Spatial Comprehension. Workshop on Presence. *CyberPsychology & Behavior*. 2, 337-347, 1999.

[36] H. G. Hoffman, S. R. Sharar, B. Coda, J. J. Everett, M. Ciol, T. Richards & D. R. Patterson, Manipulating presence influences the magnitude of virtual reality analgesia. *Pain*, 111, 162-168, 2004.

[37] S. R. Ellis, N.S. Dorighi, B. M. Menges, B. D. Adelstein, & R. H. Jacoby, In search of equivalence classes in subjective scales of reality. In M. J. Smith, G. Salvendy & R. J. Koubek (Eds.), *Design of computing systems: social and ergonomic considerations*, 873-876. Amsterdam: Elsevier, 1997

[38]   C. Dillon, E. Keogh, J. Freeman & J. B. Davidoff, Presence: is your heart in it? *Proceedings of the 4th Annual International Workshop on Presence*, 21-23, Temple University, Philadelphia, 2001 May.

[39]   C. Hendrix, & W. Barfield, Presence within virtual environments as a function of visual display parameters. *Presence: Teleoperators and Virtual Environments*, 5, 274-289, 1996.

[40]   T. Hatada, H. Sakata, H. Kusaka, Psychophysical analysis of the "sensation of reality" induced by a visual wide-field display. *SMPTE Journal*, 89, 560-569, 1980.

[41]   J. Prothero & H. Hoffman *Widening the field of view increases the sense of presence*. HITLab Technical Report R-95-5, 1995.

[42]   R. B. Welch, T. T. Blackmon, A. Liu, B. A. Mellers & L. W. Stark The effects of pictorial realism, delay of visual feedback and observer interactivity on the subjective sense of presence. *Presence: Teleoperators and Virtual Environments*, 5, 263-273, 1996.

[43]   H. Q. Dinh, N. Walker, C. Song, A. Kobayashi and L. F. Hodges, Evaluating the Importance of Multi-sensory Input on Memory and the Sense of Presence in Virtual Environments. *Proceedings of the IEEE Virtual Reality '99,*222—22, 1999.

[44]   M. Slater, M. Usoh & Y. Crysanthou, The influence of dynamic shadows on presence in immersive virtual environments. In M. Goebel (Ed.), *Virtual environments '95*, 8-21, Springer Computer Science, 1995.

[45]   R. M. Held & N. I. Durlach, Telepresence. *Presence: Teleoperators and Virtual Environments*, 1, 109-112, 1992.

[46]   E. T. Davis, K. Scott, J. Pair, L. F. Hodges & J. Oliverio, *Can audio enhance visual perception and performance in a virtual environment?* Technical Report: GIT-GVU- 99-28, 1999.

[47]   R. Cook, L. Carpenter & E. Catmul, The Reyes Image Rendering Architecture. Proceedings of SIGGRAPH, *Computer Graphics*, 4, 95-1021987, July.

[48]   S. C. Nichols, C. Haldane, J. R. Wilson, Measurement of presence and its consequences in virtual environments. *International Journal of Human-Computer Studies*. 52, 471-491, 2000.

[49]   J. Freeman, J. Lessiter & W. Ijsselsteijn, *An introduction to presence: A sense of being there in a mediated environment*, 2002. Online: http://homepages.gold.ac.uk/immediate/immersivetv/futuretv-psychol.pdf

[50]   N. I. Durlach & A. S. Mavor, *Virtual reality. Scientific and technological challenges*. Washington, DC: National Academy Press, 1995.

[51]   W. Barfield, K. M. Baird & O. J. Bjorneseth, Presence in virtual environments as a function of type of input device and display update rate, *Displays*, 19, 91-98, 1998.

[52]   W. Sadowski & K. Stanney, Presence in virtual environments. In K. M. Stanney (Ed.), *Handbook of virtual environments: Design, implementation and application*, 791-806 New Jersey: Lawrence Erlbaum Associates, 2002.

[53]   G. Riva & F. Vincelli, Virtual reality as an advanced imaginal system: A new experiential approach for counseling and therapy. *The International Journal of Action Methods, 54* (2), 51-65, 2001.

[54]   K. Mania & A. Chalmers, The effects of levels of immersion on memory and presence in virtual environments: A reality centered approach. *CyberPsychology and Behavior, 4* (2), 247- 264, 2001.

[55]   R. M. Banos, C. Botella, M. Alcaniz, B. A. Liano, B. Guerrero & B. Rey, Immersion and emotion: Their impact on the sense of presence. *Cyberpsychology & Behavior*. 7:734-740, 2004.

[56]   F. Biocca, C. Harms, and J.K. Burgoon, Toward a more robust theory and measure of social presence: Review and suggested criteria. *Presence: Teleoperators, and Virtual Environments*, 12(5), 456-480, 2001.

[57]   M. Slater, Measuring presence: a response to the Witmer and Singer presence questionnaire. *Presence: Teleoperators & Virtual Environments*. 8:560-565, 1999.

[58]   R. E. Nisbett & T. D. Wilson, Telling more than we know: Verbal reports on mental processes. *Psychological Review*. 84:231-259, 1977.

[59]   J. Freeman, S. E. Avons, R. Meddis, D. E. Pearson & W. A. Ijsselsteijn, Using behavioral realism to estimate presence: a study of the utility of postural responses to motion stimuli. *Presence: teleoperators and virtual environments*, 9, 149-164, 2000.

[60]   B. G. Witmer, C. J. Jerome & M. J. Singer, The factor structure of the Presence Questionnaire. *Presence: Teleoperators & Virtual Environments*. 14:298-312, 2005.

[61]   P. Renaud, J. Rouleau, L. Granger, et al., Measuring sexual preferences in virtual reality: A pilot study. *Cyberpsychology & Behavior*. 5:1-9, 2002

[62]   K. M. Stanney, K. S. Kingdon, D. Graeber, et al, Human performance in immersive virtual environments:Effects of exposure duration, user control, and scene complexity. *Human Performance*. 15:339-366, 2002.

[63] D. Freeman, J. Lessiter, E. Keogh, K. Chapman, and M. Alcañiz, *Emma Project Technical Report 1: Functional description of the measurement protocol.* European Project "Engaging Media for Mental Health Applications" - EMMA (IST-2001-39192): Valencia, Spain, 2003. On-line: http://alemania.did.upv.es/~juansoler/emma/pdf/TR1.pdf.

[64] J. Lessiter, J. Freeman, E. Keogh, and J. Davidoff, A Cross-Media Presence Questionnaire: The ITC-Sense of Presence Inventory. *Presence: Teleoperators, and Virtual Environments*, 10(3): p. 282-297, 2001.

[65] M. Slater, M. Usoh, and A. Steed, Depth of presence in virtual environments. *Presence: Teleoperators and Virtual Environments*, 1(3): p. 130-144, 1994,.

[66] R.M. Baños, C. Botella, A. García-Palacios, H. Villa, C. Perpiñá, and M. Alcañiz, Presence and Reality Judgment in virtual environments: A unitary construct? *Cyberpsychology & Behavior*, 3(3): p. 327-355, 2000.

[67] T. Schubert, F. Friedman, and H. Regenbrecht, The experience of presence: Factor analytic insights. *Presence: Teleoperators, and Virtual Environments*, 10(3): p. 266-281, 2001.

[68] D. Schloerb, A quantitative measure of telepresence. *Presence: Teleoperators and Virtual Environments*, 4, 64-80, 1995.

[69] M. Slater and A. Steed, A Virtual Presence counter. *Presence: Teleoperators, and Virtual Environments*, 9(5): p. 413-434, 2000.

[70] A. Spagnolli and L. Gamberini, A Place for Presence. Understanding the Human Involvement in Mediated Interactive Environments. *PsychNology Journal*, 3(1), 2005.
On-line: http://www.psychology.org/pnj3(1)_spagnolli_gamberini_abstract.htm.

[71] A. Spagnolli, L. Gamberini, and D. Gasparini, Breakdown analysis in Virtual Reality usability evaluation. *PsychNology Journal*, 1(1), 2003.
Online: http://www.psychology.org/pnj1(1)_spagnolli_gamberini_gasparini_abstract.htm.

[72] K. M. Stanney Stanney, G. Salvendy, J. Deisigner, P. DiZio, S. Ellis, E. Ellison, G. Fogleman, J. Gallimore, L. Hettinger, R Kennedy, J. Lackner, B. Lawson, J. Maida, A. Mead, M. Mon-Williams, D. Newman, T. Piantanida, L. Reeves, O Riedel, M. Singer, T. Stoffregen, J. Wann, R. Welch, J. Wilson, B. Witmer, Aftereffects and sense of presence in virtual environments: Formulation of a research and development agenda. Report sponsored by the Life Sciences Division at NASA Headquarters. *International Journal of Human-Computer Interaction*, 10, 135-187, 1998.

[73] S. R. Ellis, Presence of mind: a reaction to Thomas Sheridan's Further musings on the psychophysics of presence. *Presence: Teleoperators and Virtual Environments* 5, 247-259, 1996.

[74] D. Nunez & E. H. Blake, *Cognitive presence as a unified concept of virtual reality effectiveness.* UCT Technical Report CS01-11-00, 2001.

From Communication to Presence
G. Riva et al. (Eds.)
IOS Press, 2006

3 Being-in-the-world-with: Presence Meets Social And Cognitive Neuroscience

Giuseppe RIVA

Abstract: In this chapter we will discuss the concepts of "presence" (Inner Presence) and "social presence" (Co-presence) within a cognitive and ecological perspective. Specifically, we claim that the concepts of "presence" and "social presence" are the possible links between self, action, communication and culture. In the first section we will provide a capsule view of Heidegger's work by examining the two main features of the Heideggerian concept of "being": spatiality and "being with". We argue that different visions from social and cognitive sciences – *Situated Cognition, Embodied Cognition, Enactive Approach, Situated Simulation, Covert Imitation* - and discoveries from neuroscience – *Mirror and Canonical Neurons* - have many contact points with this view. In particular, these data suggest that our conceptual system dynamically produces contextualized representations (simulations) that support grounded action in different situations. This is allowed by a common coding – the motor code – shared by perception, action and concepts. This common coding also allows the subject for natively recognizing actions done by other selves within the phenomenological contents. In this picture we argue that the role of presence and social presence is to allow the process of self-identification through the separation between "self" and "other," and between "internal" and "external". Finally, implications of this position for communication and media studies are discussed by way of conclusion.

Contents

3.1 Introduction

In this chapter we will discuss the concepts of "presence" (Inner Presence) and "social presence" (Co-presence) within a cognitive and ecological perspective. Specifically, we claim that the concepts of "presence" and "social presence" are the possible links between self, action, communication and culture.

To support this vision, in the first section of the chapter we will provide a capsule view of Heidegger's work by examining the two main features of the Heideggerian concept of "being": spatiality and being with. We argue that different visions from social and cognitive sciences – *Situated Cognition, Embodied Cognition, Enactive Approach, Situated Simulation, Covert Imitation* - and discoveries from neuroscience – *Mirror and Canonical Neurons* - have many contact points with this view.

These data suggest that our conceptual system dynamically produces contextualized representations (simulations) that support grounded action in different situations. This is allowed by a common coding – the motor code – shared by perception, action and concepts. This common coding also allows the subject for natively recognizing actions done by other beings within the phenomenological contents.

However, this picture has some holes in it: if perception, action and concepts share the same language how can we differentiate between them. In particular how can we distinguish between a perceived action, a planned or an executed one?

More, even if imitation has frequently been proposed as the central mechanism mediating the reproduction, spread, intergenerational transmission and stabilization of human cultural forms, our imitation is selective. How and why do we imitate? Finally, developmental psychology clearly shows that our simulative abilities are not the same in the different phases of our life. How and why do they evolve?

In this chapter we suggest that a psychology of presence is a possible answer to these questions. In our vision "Presence" and "Social Presence" have a simple but critical role in our everyday experience: the control of agency and social interaction through the unconscious separation of both "internal" and "external", and "self" and "other". Finally, implications of this position for communication and cultural studies are discussed by way of conclusion.

3.2 "Being-in-the-world-with": the Vision of Heidegger

The German philosopher Martin Heidegger, (born Sept. 26, 1889; dead May 26, 1976) was one of the most significant thinkers of the 20th century. His main interest was to analyze the issue of "being" [Dasein], that is, to make sense of our capacity to make sense of things [1].

In colloquial German "Dasein" ("there" [Da] + "Being" [Sein]) means "everyday human existence." Using this expression Heidegger underlines that a human being cannot be taken into account except as being an existent in the middle of a world amongst other things and other beings [2]. Specifically, in the book "*Being and Time*" Heidegger underlines the following structural (ontological) features of the being [1]:

- *Spatiality*: the space is not around us but within us;
- *Being with*: we exist not on our own terms, but only in reference to others.

The first assumption is that spatiality is the mode of our existence. In this vision, humans are not "*in*" space, but they do exist in some spatially salient manner. So, the world is mainly a "space-of-action": the human beings are thrown into situations in which they must continually act and interpret [3].

Heidegger identifies three main features of this space-of-action [4]: "de-severance" [*Ent-fernung*], "directionality" [*Ausrichtung*] and "regions" [*Zuhanden*]. De-severance describes the non contemplative nature of being: it exists through concretely acting in the world, by reaching for things and going to places. In this view the being is the result of a process of spatial self-determination, "making things available" to him/herself. As noted by Arisaka [4]:

"When I walk from my desk area into the kitchen, I am not simply changing locations from point A to B in an arena-like space, but I am 'taking in space' as I move, continuously making the 'farness' of the kitchen 'vanish,' as the shifting spatial perspectives are opened up as I go along." (p. 37).

This process is always "directional" [4]: aimed toward something or in a certain direction. The direction is determined by our concern and by specific "regions". In fact regions - the office, the park, the kitchen, etc. - are functional for organizing our activities and contextualizing tools and other beings. Regions are not neutral, container-like space, but are inherently organized by activities, which determine the center of action[3]: our spatial activities determine a "here" related to the objects/beings we deal with. Following this view, "existence" is the main feature of being: a temporally-structured making intelligible of the place in which we find ourselves. As delineated by Heidegger [1]:

"[I]t follows that Being-in is not a 'property' which Dasein sometimes has and sometimes does not have, and without which it could just be just as well as it could be with it. It is not the case that man 'is' and then has, by way of an extra, a relationship-of-Being towards the 'world'--a world with which he provides himself occasionally." (p. 84).

To describe this feature of being, Heidegger introduced the concept of "throwness" [*Geworfenheit*]: he claims that we are limited, and determined to some extent, by conditions and circumstances beyond our control. During the life each human being is "thrown" into existence, into situations in which he/she must continually act and interpret. In this process a critical role is played by moods, described as a unique and primary way of disclosing the being-in-the-world, that is prior to the "cognitive" disclosure [5]. In fact, is not "reason" that gives us our basic access to being, but moods [1]:

"The disclosure-possibilities of cognition fall very short when compared with the primordial disclosure that belongs to moods." (p. 134).

The interaction with objects follows a similar path: when the being is engaged in purposeful actions, "cognitive" representations of objects as tools or equipment do not exist. This means that objects are conceived of according to their usefulness in whatever task is currently being performed. This situation is described by Heidegger [1] as "readiness-to-hand" [*Zuhandenheit*]:

"The kind of Being which equipment possesses - in which it manifests itself in its own right – we call "readiness-to-hand"… If we look at Things just 'theoretically', we can get along without understanding readiness-to-hand. But when we deal with them by using them and manipulating them, this activity is not a blind one; it has its own kind of sight, by which our manipulation is guided and from which it acquires its specific Thingly character. Dealings with equipment subordinate themselves to the manifold assignments of the 'in-order-to'. And the sight with which they thus accommodate themselves is circumspection." (pp. 97-98).

In contrast, we may also encounter objects as purely bare "presence-at-hand," [*Vorhanden*], simply alongside us in the world. Typically, this happens in "breakdown" situations. In them the object ceases to be "ready-to-hand" and becomes "present-at-hand," that is, non transparent to the user. As noted by Winograd and Flores [6]:

"[In Heidegger] objects and properties are not inherent in the world, but arise only in an event of breaking down in which they become present-at-hand. One simple example he gives is that of a hammer being used by someone engaged in driving a nail. To the person doing the hammering, the hammer as such does not exist. It is a part of the background of readiness-to-hand that is taken for granted without explicit recognition or identification as an object. It is part of the hammerer's world, but is not present any more than are the tendons of the hammerer's arm." (p. 36).

In the example of hammering, it is only during a breakdown - when the hammer breaks or misses the nail - that the properties of the hammer are revealed and become "present-at-hand." In this process, the being comes across entities [*Seiende*] like himself. It is important to underline that "being-with" [*Mitsein*] is a mode of our existence, too [7]: as the being is never without a world so, too, it is never without others. Heidegger clearly underlines this point:

"Thus in characterizing the encountering of Others, one is again still oriented by that Dasein which is in each case one's own… [Others] are rather those from whom, for the most part, one does not distinguish oneself—those among whom one is too… The world of Dasein is a with-world. Being-in it Being-with Others." (pp. 154-155).

For this reason, the character of being towards others is different from the character of being towards entities ready-to-hand and present-at-hand. This new character is defined "solicitude" [*Fursorge*]: attentive care and protectiveness.

The fourth chapter of "Being and Time" introduces two forms of solicitude [3]: "leaping in" [*Einspringen*] and "leaping ahead" [*Vorspringen*]. "Leaping in" is an inauthentic form of solicitude: in it the being relieves other beings of responsibility, but with the result that they may become dominated by or dependent upon him. Apparently, in "leaping in" the being consider the other being like an object, an extension of him/her. In "leaping ahead" - the authentic form of solicitude - the being helps other beings to become transparent to them. Using transparency only, the being is able to see the truth of his or her condition and become free.

In summary, in "being-with" we have the possibility of comprehending that we cannot be selves unless it is within our possibilities to relate in a unique way to other human beings: we exist not on our own terms, but only in reference to others [7].

3.3. The "Being-in-the-world" for Cognitive Neuroscience

In our capsule view of Heidegger's work, we discussed the two faces of his concept of being. On one side, the main features of "being-in-the-world" are spatiality and throwness. On the other side, the "being-in-the-world-with" is characterized by the reference to others and solicitude. Further, both sides are ontologically connected in our existence.

Even if this is a philosophical vision, there are strict links with the more recent outcomes of cognitive science. In the next paragraphs we will try to outline these links, starting from the "being-in-the-world".

3.3.1 Embedded Cognition

A critical part within Heidegger's reflection is the concept of "throwness", as original state in which the being must continually act and interpret.

However, for a long time cognitive science considered action, perception, and interpretation as separate activities. As provocatively outlined by Prinz [8]:

"We had perception on one side, which is in the business of representing inputs from the external world. Then we had action, on the other side, which controls an organism's outputs, or behavior. Nestled between these "peripheral systems" when had central systems, which were presumed be the main engines of "cognition" or "thinking." Each of these systems was supposed to work independently, like separate committees in a great corporation, only vaguely away of what the others are up to. In cogsci lingo, each system was supposed to use proprietary rules and representations." (p. 19).

A recent trend in cognitive science is instead seeing cognition as *embedded*, or *situational*. This is a rethinking of the idea that cognition is primarily a matter of performing formal operations on abstract symbols and has little or nothing to do with the environment in which it occurs [9]. Countering it, *Embedded Cognition* takes as its starting point the idea that cognition occurs in specific environments, and for specific ends [10-12]. The main approaches related to this trend are *Situated Cognition, Distributed Cognition* and *Embodied Cognition*.

3.3.1.1 Situated and Distributed Cognition

The *Situative* perspective shifts the focus of analysis from individual activity to larger systems that include behaving subjects interacting with each other and with other subsystems in the environment [13].
Within it, the *Situated Cognition* approach includes a family of research efforts [14-17] explaining cognition - including problem solving, sense making, understanding, transfer of learning, creativity, etc. - in terms of the *relationship between subjects (agents) and the properties of specific environments (affordances/constrains)*. This is

possible, because the inside/outside relationship between subject and environment is replaced by a part/whole relationship [18]. As noted by Clancey [19]:

"Situated activity is not a kind of action, but the nature of animal interaction at all times, in contrast with most machines we know. This is not merely a claim that context is important, but what constitutes the context, how you categorize the world, arises together with processes that are coordinating physical activity. To be perceiving the world is to be acting in it - not in a linear input-output relation (act>observe>change) -but dialectically, so that what I am perceiving and how I am moving co-determine each other." (p. 88).

The final outcome of this view is that action is highly dependent upon its material and social circumstances. As noted by Norman [20], any activity is "intrinsically" connected to the particular setting in which the subject acts. Its course is influenced by the physical, social and cultural space (context) in which it happens (situation).

In particular it depends on the natural and contextual characteristics (*affordances* and *constrains)* of the situation. It is important to note that the characteristics of the situation may be perceived or not by the subject. For the action of the subject, *the only relevant characteristics are the ones he/she is able to identify*.

Strictly related to this approach is the one of *Distributed Cognition*. As for Situated Cognition, the analysis is moved from the subject to the his/her relationship with the environment [18]. However, it focuses mainly on three kinds of distributed cognitive processes:
- *Social processes*: across the members of a social group;
- *Processes related to material environment*: across internal and external (material or environmental) structures;
- *Distributed cognition in time*: how the products of earlier events can transform the nature of later events.

3.3.1.2 Embodied Cognition

Within the paradigm of *Embedded Cognition*, the *Embodied Cognition* approach underlines the central role of body in shaping the mind [10, 21-26]. Specifically, the mind has to be understood in the context of its relationship to a physical body that interacts with the world. Hence human cognition, rather than being centralized, abstract, and sharply distinct from peripheral input and output modules, has instead deep roots in sensorimotor processing.

Although this broad claim is enjoying increasingly support, there is in fact a great deal of diversity in the subclaims involved and the degree of controversy they attract. Wilson [27] recently identified six different definitions of *Embodied Cognition*, of which, however, only one explicitly addresses the role of the body (p. 626):

1. *Cognition is situated.* As in *Situated and Distributed Cognition*, the cognitive activity takes place in the context of a real-world environment;
2. *Cognition is time pressured.* As in *Situated Cognition*, the cognitive activity is constrained by the pressures of real-time interaction with the environment;
3. *We off-load cognitive work onto the environment.* As in *Distributed Cognition*, the limits in our information-processing abilities (e.g., limits on working memory) forces us in exploiting the environment to reduce the cognitive

workload;
4.   *The environment is part of the cognitive system.* As in *Distributed Cognition*, the mind alone is not a meaningful unit of analysis;
5.   *Cognition is for action.* As in *Situated and Distributed Cognition*, the main function of the mind is to guide action;
6.   *Off-line cognition is body based.* The activity of the mind is grounded in mechanisms that evolved for interaction with the environment.

One of the first authors to address the last point was George Lakoff [23, 25, 28]. Since the publication of *Metaphors We Live By* [23] he has suggested that almost all of human cognition depends on the sensorimotor system. Particularly he underlined the role of metaphors in the development of thought and their link with spatial relationships.
    To explain this point Anderson used the metaphorical mapping "Purposes are Destinations," [29]:

"We imagine a goal as being at some place ahead of us, and employ strategies for attaining it analogous to those we might use on a journey to a place. We plan a route, imagine obstacles, and set landmarks to track our progress. In this way, our thinking about purposes (and about time, and states, and change, and many other things besides) is rooted in our thinking about space. It should come as no surprise to anyone that our concepts of space—up, down, forward, back, on, in—are deeply tied to our bodily orientation to, and our physical movement in, the world." (p. 105).

This example underlines two points. First, metaphors allow the understanding of a conceptual domain in terms of another one through a process of *mapping*: to know a conceptual metaphor is to know the mappings that applies to a given source-target pairing. Second, at the core of this process there are some pre-linguistic schemas concerning space, time, moving, controlling, and other core elements of our bodily experience. These reflections pushed different researchers to better explore the *link between body and experience*. If we look at the features of the phenomenal level - the level of description in science which deals with immediate experience – it is possible to distinguish [30] between four ones (pp. 33-34):
1.   *Location*: all the experience have a spatial location within the sphere of our subjective experiences;
2.   *Duration*: An experience comes into existence at some point in time and it ceases to exist at some later point;
3.   *Intensity*: Experiences vary along a dimension of strength;
4.   *Quality*: Any experience has a qualitative feature that makes it the kind of experience it is.

Nevertheless, even if it is possible to decompose the features of the phenomenal level, our phenomenal experience is just one. What does it unify the phenomenal level as a whole? The answer suggested by many cognitive researchers and philosophers of mind is surprisingly similar to the Heidegger's one: *phenomenal space* is the basic unifying feature of human consciousness.
    To support this point Metzinger [31] underlines how, in human beings, sensory and motor systems are physically integrated within the body of a single organism:

"This singular 'embodiment constraint' closely locates all our sensors and effectors in a very small region of physical space, simultaneously establishing dense causal coupling... The persistent functional link just mentioned has many theoretically relevant aspects. One of them is that it firmly ties all activities of the organism (be cognitive, attentional, or behavioral) into an internal context." (p. 161).

Recent studies suggest that proprioceptive awareness is the very first kind of consciousness to emerge in the nervous system [32, 33]: it exists prenatally and is sufficiently developed at birth for neonate imitation [34]. As underlined by Gallagher [26]:

"Conscious experience is normally of an intermodally seamless spatial system... One of the important functions of the body in the context of perception and action is to provide the basis for an egocentric [body-centered] spatial frame of reference. Indeed, this egocentric framework is required for the very possibility of action, and for the general structure of perceptual experience. The fact that perception and action are perspectivally spatial (for example, the book appears to my right or to my left, or in the center of my perceptual field), is a fact that depends precisely on the spatiality of the perceiving and acting body." (p. 59).

Supporting this position, Revonsuo suggests [30]:

"Each distinct phenomenal coordinate system defines a different subject: the global bundles of phenomenal features synchronously present within each coordinate system are the momentary phenomenal contents of one subject... Empirically based phenomenology should be built on a model that takes the spatiality and centeredness of consciousness as its fundamental structural and organizational property. The phenomenal level is based on an egocentric, bounded coordinate system whose regions can instantiate qualitative features." (pp. 178-179).

It is important to underline that - as predicted by Heidegger - the phenomenal space is different from the "real" and "physical" space that surrounds us: phenomenal spatiality is directly present in experience whereas the "physical" space is an abstraction, not experienced directly.

3.3.2 Action in perception

An emerging trend within embodied cognition is the *analysis of the link between action and perception*. According to it, action and perception are more closely linked than has traditionally been assumed. This view is strongly influenced by (and in many respects, very similar to) a number of earlier proposals. Both Husserl, Merleau-Ponty, and Poincaré suggested that spatial content may be acquired from knowledge of possible movements. In psychology of perception, the *ecological approach* presented by Gibson [35, 36] shares many similarities to this vision.

Gibson introduced a shift of focus in perception: from how the visual system actually detect the forms, to the invariants - optical flow, texture gradient, and affordances - that visual systems detect in the dynamic optical array.

This approach underlines that perception requires an *active* organism. On one side, the act of perception depends upon an interaction between the organism and the environment. On the other side, perceptions are made in reference to body position and functions: *the awareness of the environment derives from how it reacts to our movements*. In his own words [35]:

"Locomotion and manipulation… are controlled not by the brain but by information… Control lies in the animal-environment system… The rules that govern behavior are not like laws enforced by an authority or decisions made by a commander; behavior is regular without being regulated." (p. 225).

In the next two paragraphs we will discuss the two positions – the *Enactive View* and the *Theory of Event Coding* – that are a step towards the understanding of the link between action and perception. Further, we will focus on the outcomes of different neuroscience researches that investigated the functioning of the motor system.

3.3.2.1 Enactive view

According to the *Enactive Approach*, the human mind is embodied in our entire organism and embedded in the world, and hence is not reducible to structures inside the head. Specifically, Thompson defines any autonomous and self-determining organism as an *autopoietic* system [37, 38]: a system whose component processes must recursively depend on each other for their generation and their realization as a system, so that they constitute the system as a unity in whatever domain they exist.

Any such system, in defining itself as a unity, also defines (*enacts*) its environment as a domain of meaning, and defines things in its environment as meaningful within that domain (in the way that, for instance, sugar is meaningful for bacteria). This process involves three permanent and intertwined modes of bodily activity – self-regulation, sensorimotor coupling, and intersubjective interaction [38]. As noted by Varela [39]:

"Cognition is not the representation of a pre-given world by a pre-given mind but is rather the enactment of a world and a mind on the basis of a history of the variety of actions that a being in the world performs" (p. 9).

Within this general approach, the *Enactive View's* main claim is that *perceptual experience depends on the acquisition and exercise of sensorimotor knowledge*. This knowledge include different elements, some having to do with the expected effects of our own movement on the input, others concerning the way some external conditions, like sun or wind, will affect the input.

As provided by Noë in his book "Action in Perception" [40]:

"The main idea… is that perceiving is a way of acting. Perception is not something that happens to us, or in us. It is something we do… Perceptual experience acquires content thanks to our possession of bodily skills. What we perceive is determined by what we do (or what we know how to do); it is determined by what we are ready to do. In ways I try to make precise, we enact our perceptual experience; we act it out." (p. 1).

In this view, bodily skills are intrinsically tied to perception: *to perceive is to understand how sensory stimulation varies as we act.*

The *Enactive View* has different corollaries.

-   *The differences in our perceptual experience correspond to differences in the sensorimotor expectations associated with certain objects or properties*: Two objects are perceived differently, because in encountering them we bring to bear different sets of sensorimotor expectations.
-   *The very same real property (e.g. shape) may be apprehended differently – e.g. by touch or vision*: the mode of sampling varies dramatically, and with it the associated sensorimotor contingencies.
-   *Despite specific differences, many objects will share large parts of the sensorimotor signatures*: It is these commonalities that make the experiences sensorially characterized: visual rather than, auditory or tactile.

Even if the *Enactive View* is a promising theoretical approach, the actual formulation is not immune to criticisms [8, 41, 42]. As underlined by Clark:

"I have raised three challenges for Noë-style sensorimotor contingency theory. The first challenge is to find a safe haven between two unsatisfactory readings of the central claim that perceptual experience is conditioned by expectancies concerning sensory stimulation. One reading looks circular, since it depicts the expectancies as already operating in the realm of experience… The second challenge is to fix the intended force of the central claim. Is the claim that there is a conceptual connection between sensorimotor knowing and the contents of perceptual experience?... The third, and perhaps most serious, challenge is to accommodate (or give principled reasons to reject) the fairly extensive empirical data suggesting that the contents of conscious visual experience are optimized for selection, choice and reason rather than the fine guidance of action." (p.8).

3.3.2.2 The Theory of Event Coding

The *Theory of Event Coding* [43], is a broad framework for understanding relationships between perception, cognition, and action planning that shares many similarities with the *Enactive View*.

According to the *Theory of Event Coding* [43] the cognitive representations for perceived events (*perception*) and intended or to-be generated events (*action*) are formed by a common representational domain.

From this broad position it is possible to identify three different corollaries (pp. 860-861):

-   *Common coding of perceptual content and action goals*: perceiving and action planning are functionally equivalent, inasmuch as they are merely alternative ways of doing the same thing: internally representing external events;
-   *Feature-based coding of perceived and produced events*: If actions are represented in a way that is at least very similar to how visual objects are represented, the principles underlying the organization of perceptual and action-related information should be comparable;
-   *Distal coding of event features*. The cognitive codes that represent perceptual objects are identical to those representing action plans because both kinds of code refer to external (distal) events.

This position, too, has raised many concerns. In particular, as underlined by the same authors, the theory does not consider the complex machinery of the 'early' sensory processes that lead to them. Thus, the *Theory of Event Coding* is meant to provide a framework for understanding linkages between (late) perception and (early) action, or action planning, only.

However, within the *Theory of Event Coding,* the most important part for our discussion is the one related to the common coding (*Common Coding Theory*): *actions are coded in terms of the perceivable effects they should generate.* More in detail, when an effect is intended, the movement that produces this effect as perceptual input is automatically activated, because actions and their effects are stored in a common representational domain. As underlined by Prinz [44]:

"Under conditions where stimuli share some features with planned actions, these stimuli tend, by virtue of similarity, either to induce those actions or interfere with them, depending on the structure of the task at hand. This implies that there are certain products of perception on the one hand and certain antecedents of action on the other that share a common representational domain. This is the common coding principle. The second conclusion is that actions are planned and controlled in terms of their effects; that is, that representations of action effects play an important role in the planning and the control of these actions." (p. 152).

The *Common Coding Theory* may be considered a variation of the *Ideomotor Principle* introduced by William James [45]. According to James, imagining an action creates a tendency to its execution, if no antagonistic mental images are simultaneously present. Prinz [44], suggests that the role of mental images is instead taken by the distal perceptual events that an action should generate. When the activation of a common code exceeds a certain threshold, the corresponding motor codes are automatically triggered.

Further, the *Common Coding Theory* extends this approach to the domain of event perception, action perception, and imitation. The underlying process is the following [46]: first, common event representations become activated by the perceptual input; then, there is an automatic activation of the motor codes attached to these event representations; finally, the activation of the motor codes results in a prediction of the action results in terms of expected perceptual events on the common coding level. We will discuss more in depth this "simulative" process later.

3.3.2.3 The Converged Zone and Situated Simulation Theories

The motor system was considered to play a very specific role within our cognitive processes: the control of movement. However, recent neurophysiological findings convey a totally different picture: the motor system controls *actions*.

As we will see below, recent data showed that cortical premotor areas contain neurons that respond to visual, somatosensory, and auditory stimuli. Further, posterior parietal areas, turned out to play a major role in motor control. Finally, the premotor and parietal areas, rather than having separate and independent functions, are neurally integrated not only to control action, but also to serve the function of building an integrated representation. In particular, as underlined by Gallese [47] *"the so-called 'motor functions' of the nervous system not only provide the means to control and execute action but also to represent it." (p. 23).*

This conclusion - that is very close to the claims of both the *Enactive View* and the *Theory of Event Coding* - is the outcome of a long series of experiments of single-neuron recordings in the premotor cortex of behaving monkeys [48, 49]. In particular, Rizzolatti and colleagues discovered that a functional cluster of premotor neurons (F5ab-AIP) contains "*canonical neurons*", a class of neurons that are selectively activated by the presentation of an object in function of its shape, size, and spatial orientation [50-52]. Specifically, these neurons fire during the observation of objects whose features - such as size and shape - are strictly related to the type of action that the very same neurons motorically code.

Further, the *canonical neurons* are activated not only observing the same object, but also observing a group of objects that have the same characteristics, in terms of the type of interaction they allow.

Two aspects of these neurons are important [25, 53]. On one side, what correlates to their discharge is not simply a movement (e.g. opening the mouth), but an action, that is, a movement executed to achieve a purpose (e.g. tear apart an object, bring it to the mouth). Second, the critical feature for the discharge is the purpose of the action, and not some dynamic details defining it, like force, or movement direction.

In a different cluster (F4-VIP) Rizzolatti and colleagues [50, 54] identified a class of neurons that are selectively activated when the monkey heard or saw stimuli being moved in its peri-personal space. The same neurons discharge when the monkey turns its head toward a given location in peri-personal space.

A possibility to explain the dual activation is that these neurons simulate the action (head-turning) in presence of a possible target of action seen or heard at the same location [25]:

"We maintain that what integrates these sensory modalities is action simulation. Because sound and action are parts of an integrated system, the sight of an object at a given location, or the sound it produces, automatically triggers a "plan" for a specific action directed toward that location. What is a "plan" to act? We claim that it is a simulated potential action." (p. 460).

The existence of these functional clusters of neurons suggests, as predicted by Heidegger, that a constitutive part of the representation of an object is the type of interaction that is established with the object itself (*readiness-to-hand*). In other words, different objects can be represented in function of the same type of interaction allowed by them. As underlined by Gallese [47]:

"If this interpretation is correct, objects are not merely identified and recognized by virtue of their physical 'appearance', but in relation to the effects of the interaction with an agent. In such a context, the object acquires a meaningful value by means of its dynamic relation with the agent of this relation. This dynamic relation is multiple, as multiple are the ways in which we can interact with the world by acting within it. The object-representation ceases to exist by itself. The object phenomenally exists to the extent it represents the target of an action." (p.31).

These experimental data match well with the *Converged Zone Theory* proposed by Damasio [55]. This theory has two main claims. First, when a physical entity is experienced, it activates feature detectors in the relevant sensory-motor areas. During visual processing of an apple, for example, neurons fire for edges and planar surfaces, whereas others fire for color, configural properties, and movement. Similar patterns of activation in feature maps on other modalities represent how the entity might sound and feel, and also the actions performed on it.

Second, when a pattern becomes active in a feature system, clusters of conjunctive neurons (*convergence zones*) in association areas capture the pattern for later cognitive use. As shown also by the data collected by Rizzolatti, cluster of conjunctive neurons codes the pattern, with each individual neuron participating in the coding of many different patterns.

Damasio assumes the existence of different convergence zones at multiple hierarchical levels, ranging from posterior to anterior in the brain. At a lower level, convergence zones near the visual system capture patterns there, whereas convergence zones near the auditory system capture patterns there. Further, downstream, higher-level association areas in more anterior areas, such as the temporal and frontal lobes conjoin patterns of activation *across* modalities.

A critical feature of convergence zones underlined by Simmons and Barsalou is *modality-specific re-enactments* [56, 57]: once a convergence zone captures a feature pattern, the zone can later activate the pattern in the absence of bottom-up stimulation. In particular, the conjunctive neurons play the important role of reactivating patterns (*re-enactment*) in feature maps during imagery, conceptual processing, and other cognitive tasks. For instance, when retrieving the memory of an apple, conjunctive neurons partially reactivate the visual state active during its earlier perception. Similarly, when retrieving an action performed on the apple, conjunctive neurons partially reactivate the motor state that produced it. This process has two main features:

- *It is similar, but never constitutes a complete reinstatement of the original modality-specific state*: even if some semblance of the original state is reactivated, a re-enactment is always partial and potentially inaccurate.
- *It is not necessarily conscious*: Although conscious re-enactment is viewed widely as the process that underlies mental imagery, re-enactments need not always reach awareness.

The process of re-enactment is at the core of the *Situated Simulation Theory* proposed by Barsalou [56]. For this author, conceptual representations are contextualized and dynamical multimodal simulations (re-enactments) distributed across modality-specific systems. As suggested by Barsalou [56]:

"A concept is not a single abstracted representation for a category but is instead a skill for constructing idiosyncratic representations tailored to the current needs of a situated action... More than the focal category is represented in a given simulation. Additional information as background settings, goal directed actions and introspective states are also typically included in these simulations, making them highly contextualized." (p. 521).

According to this view, a fully functional conceptual system can be built on reenactment mechanisms. As shown by Barsalou and his group [56, 58, 59] using these mechanisms, it is possible to implement the type-token distinction, categorical inference, productivity, propositions, and abstract concepts.

The *Situated Simulation Theory* fits well with the *Common Coding Theory*: first, modality-specific sensorimotor areas become activated by the perceptual input (an apple) producing patterns of activation in feature maps; then, clusters of conjunctive neurons (convergence zones) identify and capture the patterns (the apple is red, has a catching size, etc.); later the convergence zone fire to partially reactivate the earlier sensory representation (I want to take a different apple); finally this representation reactivate a pattern of activation in feature maps similar, but not identical, to the original one (re-enactment) allowing the subject to predict the action results.

The final outcome of this vision is the idea of a spatial-temporal framework of virtual objects directly present to the subject: *an inner world simulation in the brain*. As described by Barsalou [59]:

"In representing a concept, it is as people were being there with one of its instances. Rather than representing a concept in detached isolated manner, people construct a multimodal simulation of themselves interacting with an instance of the concept. To represent the concept they prepare for situated action with one of its instances." (p. 9).

3.4 The "Being-in-the-world-with" for Social and Cognitive Neuroscience

In the picture described by Heidegger the second ontological features of the being is "being-with", the being is always a "being with others". In this paragraph we will discuss this assumption in the view of the results coming from social and cognitive neuroscience.

3.4.1 Mirror Neurons in Social Neuroscience

Recently, research in the neurosciences has focused its attention to understand social cognition. With the term *"social cognition"* is usually defined the information-processing system that enables us to engage in social behavior. Specifically, social neuroscience is interested to understand whether the processes that give rise to social cognition are a subset of more general cognitive processes or whether specific social-cognitive processes exist [60].

In responding to this question, social neuroscience has three assumptions [61]:
- the mechanisms underlying mind and behavior will not be fully explicable by a biological or a social approach alone;
- a multi-level integrative analysis may be required;
- a common scientific language, grounded in the structure and function of the brain, can contribute to this endpoint.

A significant step towards this common language comes from the *Common Coding* and *Situated Simulation* theories. Specifically, a consequence of the link between perception and action is that *observing actions or action effects produced by another individual may also activate a representation of one's own actions*.

This assumption, too, has been recently confirmed from the outcome of single-neuron recordings in the premotor cortex of behaving monkeys [48, 49]. Specifically, Rizzolatti and colleagues discovered that a functional cluster of premotor neurons (F5c-PF) contains *"mirror neurons"*, a class of neurons that are activated both during the execution of purposeful, goal-related hand actions, and during the observation of similar actions performed by another individual [48, 62, 63]. Different brain-imaging experiments demonstrated in humans the existence of a mirror system in the premotor and parietal areas - similar to that observed in monkeys - matching action observation and execution [64-66].

Further, a recent study showed that a similar process happens with emotions [67]. In the experiment, a group of male subjects observed video clips showing the emotional facial expression of disgust. Both observing such faces, and feeling disgust, activated the same sites in the anterior insula and to a lesser extent in the anterior cingulate cortex.

Finally, the results of three studies by Keyser and colleagues [68] showed that the first-person subjective experience of being touched on one's body activates the same neural networks in the secondary somatosensory cortices activated by observing the body of someone else being touched.

3.4.2 Embodied Simulation

The general framework, outlined by the above results, suggests the sensory-motor integration supported by the mirror matching system instantiates simulations of transitive actions utilized not only to generate and control goal-related behaviors, but also to map the goals and purposes of others' actions, by means of their simulation [25, 52, 56, 69].

This process, as predicted by Heidegger, establishes a direct link between the being and the other beings, in that both are mapped in a neutral fashion: the observer uses her/his own resources to directly experience the world of the other by means of an unconscious process of motor simulation. To summarize, *action observation constitutes a form of embodied simulation of action [69]*. As suggested by Gallese [52]:

"First, the same neural structures modeling the functions of our body in the world also contribute to our awareness of our lived body in the world and of the objects that the world contains. Embodied simulation constitutes the functional mechanism at the basis of this dual property of the same neural circuits... Second, there are neural mechanisms mediating between the multi level personal background experience we entertain of our lived body, and the implicit certainties we simultaneously hold about others. Such personal body-related experience enables us to understand the actions performed by others, and to directly decode the emotions and sensations they experience." (p. 42).

However, the *Embodied Simulation* approach, at least in this broad formulation raised a critical concern (for a detailed description see the full text of the interdisciplinary conference *"What do mirror neurons means"*, available online at the address: http://www.interdisciplines.org/mirror/papers/1): the activity of mirror neurons alone is not enough to provide the richness required for representing a subject's social intention. Jacob and Jeannerod [70] clearly detailed this point:

"The firing of MNs is a social cognitive process only in a very weak sense. When MNs fire in the brain of a monkey during action execution, the discharge is not a social cognitive process at all. When MNs fire in the brain of a monkey watching another grasp a fruit, the discharge is a weakly social process: the two monkeys are not involved in any kind of non-verbal intentional communication. The agent intends

to grasp a fruit, not to impart some information to his conspecific. Nor does the observer's understanding of the action require him to understand the agent's communicative intention (because the agent has none)." (pp. 22-23).

Another criticism related to this approach is the limited role of imitation in our interpersonal relationships [71]: imitation is not a very common response to watching other people. Indeed, Baldissera and colleagues [72] found evidence of spinal "inverted mirror" behavior: structures in the spinal cord specifically inhibit undesired imitative action.

3.4.3 Imitation in Social Cognition

As we have seen, one of the main criticisms to the *Embodied Simulation* approach is that mirror neurons alone are not enough to provide the richness required for representing a subject's social intention. But what are the main features of human social cognition?

According to Tomasello and colleagues [73, 74] it is possible to identify three different levels of social understanding:

- *Perception of the behavior of animate beings*: this level allow the subject to predict the consequences of the observed behavior. In particular this level allows for both *Motor Empathy* - the tendency to automatically mimic and synchronize facial expressions, vocalizations, postures, and movements with those of another person – and *Emotional Empathy* – the response to the emotional displays of others [75];
- *Understanding that others' behavior is goal-directed*: on this level, other individuals are conceived of as intentional agents whose behavior and attention are purposive.
- *Theory of Mind (ToM)*: on this level, other individuals are conceived of as agents whose thoughts and beliefs may differ from those directly inferred from their perceived behavior. This level allows *Cognitive Empathy*, the ability to represent the mental states of others, i.e., their thoughts, desires, beliefs, intentions, and knowledge.

Apparently, mirror neurons have a critical role in the first level only. So, what is missing is an explanation for how a neural mirror system begets a theory of mind. According to Meltzoff and colleagues [76-80], the starting point for such an explanation is the imitation process.

Meltzoff, in his thirty-year-long research about infant imitation, found that newborns – even only 42 minutes old - demonstrate successful facial imitation. Moreover he found that 12–21-day-old infants can imitate four different adult gestures: lip protrusion, mouth opening, tongue protrusion and finger movement. Interestingly, the newborns' first response to seeing a facial gesture is the activation of the corresponding body part [77]: apparently young infants isolate *what* part of their body to move before understanding *how* to move it (*organ identification*).

The developmental work shows that infants not only imitate but also know when they are being imitated by others (recognition of goal-directed behavior). However, data show an important difference between the younger and the older infants [78]: younger infants increase the particular gesture being imitated, but do not switch to mismatching gestures to see if they will be copied. Specifically, older infants both recognize the difference between them and the other, and seem to be exploring the sense of agency involved—exploring who is controlling whom.

Decety and colleagues [80] investigated using a PET the brain regions involved in this process. The data showed the involvement of the inferior parietal cortex. In particular, the right superior temporal gyrus was involved in visual analysis of the other's actions, while its homologous region in the left region was concerned with analysis of the other's actions in relation to actions performed by the self.

Meltzoff investigated, too, the earliest developmental roots of decoding the goals and intentions of others [78]. His research showed that 18-month-old infants distinguish between what an adult means to do and what he actually does. The infants linked goals to human acts inferring the goal even when it was not attained. The infants in these experiments were already exhibiting a fundamental aspect of our adult framework: the acts of persons (but not the motions of objects) are based on goals and intentions.

To explore the neural correlates of this ability, Chaminade, Decety and Meltzoff [81] designed a functional neuroimaging experiment. The results show that, when subjects imitated either the goal or the means to achieve it, overlapping activity was found in the right dorsolateral prefrontal area and in the cerebellum. Moreover, on one side, imitating the goal was associated with increased activity in the left premotor cortex. On the other side, the imitation of the means was associated to specific activity in the medial prefrontal cortex that is known to have a role in inferring others' intentions and is involved in mentalizing tasks.

This activation of the medial frontal region suggests that observing the means used by an actor prompts the observer to construct/infer the goals whereto this human agent is aiming [78]. This inference is consistent with the proposal by Moses [82] that ToM is intimately bound with the advances of the children in executive functioning: the skills and processes implicated in the monitoring and control of action.

3.4.4 The Covert Imitation Theory

Given the critical role of imitative abilities in the development of social skills, Wilson and Knoblich [71, 83] introduced a different simulation theory based on imitation: the *Covert Imitation Theory*. For these authors *covert imitation* functions as *an automatic action emulator*, tracking the behavior of other subjects in real time to generate perceptual predictions. As explained by Wilson and Knoblich:

"The various brain areas involved in translating perceived human movement into corresponding motor programs collectively act as an emulator, internally simulating the ongoing perceived movement. This emulator bypasses the delay of sensory transmission to provide immediate information about the ongoing course of the observed action as well as its probable immediate future. Such internal modeling allows the perceiver to rapidly interpret the perceptual signal, to react quickly, to disambiguate in situations of uncertainty, and to perceptually complete movements that are not perceived in their entirety." (p. 468).

This theory can be considered a social extension of the *Situated Simulation* and *Common Coding* theories. Earlier we presented the construct of re-enactment as the underlying mechanism behind them. However, this simple construct is not sufficient alone to implement *covert imitation*. As suggested by Barsalou and colleagues [58] *covert imitation* may involve two further mechanisms: *selective attention* and *memory integration*.

First, the capture process does not operate on entire perceptual states but only on components of them. On viewing someone catching an apple, for example, the brain does not capture the entire scene. Instead, as attention focuses on the specific action, such the moving hand, an associative area captures the neural state that represents it.

Second, once attention selects a component of experience, a memory of the component becomes integrated with memories of similar components, via content addressable memory. When focusing attention on the moving hand, for example, the active neural state in the visual system becomes integrated with similar visual patterns captured previously.

In this occasion, a subset of mirror neurons produces one particular simulation in the visual system. The content of the simulation depends on which subsets of stored information become active. Possible outcomes are a given instance, an average of several instances, or a variety of other possibilities. Moreover, re-enactments typically occur on multiple modalities simultaneously, producing a multimodal simulation of the action including not only sensory states but also motor and mental states. In this view a simulator is a "distributed collection of modality-specific memories captured across a category's instances" [58].

Neuro-physiological evidences support the *Covert Imitation Theory*. On one side, the mirror neurons within the F5c-PF functional cluster of premotor neurons already discharge in early phases of the movement [84]. Moreover, the pre-motor cortex, the posterior parietal cortex, and the cerebellum are activated during action generation, action imagination, and action observation [66, 85].

There is a main criticism to this view coming from Gergely and Csibra [86, 87]. Gergely and colleagues showed that a novel response – illuminating a box by touching it with the head - imitatively learned from the demonstration of a human model is retained by infants in spite of the availability and production of more readily accessible and rational response alternatives – the use of the hands - that also produce the same effect [88]. This suggests that imitative learning of novel actions is a qualitatively different process in humans than the imitative copying of new and reinforcing behavior of observed conspecifics that has been demonstrated in several other animal species. Specifically, it suggests the existence of some specific processes selecting what to imitate.

Another issue is raised by Lyons and colleagues [89]. They note that macaque monkeys, who have mirror neurons, simply do not imitate. So, what are mirror neurons for in monkeys? In their opinion, their mirror neuron system is tuned to extract the goal structure of observed action, as opposed to the lower-level kinematic features of the action. In other words, "mirror neurons enable non-human primates to infer the intentions of other agents" (p 231).

The difference between humans and primates appears to be related to the level of intentional granularity: the human mirror system is capable of extracting not only high-level goals (*do x*) but also more subtle, subsidiary goals (*do x in manner y*). This could account for human ability to reproduce not only the overall results of observed actions but also the specific means that were used to achieve them.

3.5 The Missing Links: Presence and Social Presence

After this long analysis of the recent outcomes of the social and cognitive neuroscience it is possible to underline an overall scenario: our conceptual system dynamically produces contextualized representations (simulations) that support situated action in different situations. This is allowed by a common coding – the motor code – shared by perception, action and concepts.

On one side, the vision of an object immediately activates the appropriate hand shape for using it: seeing a red apple activates a precision grip for grasping and turning. On the other side, thinking an apple produces the simulation of an action related to the apple in a specific context of use.

This common coding also allows the subject for natively recognizing actions done by other beings within the phenomenological contents. Further, the subject predicts the outcome of the identified action using the same simulation mechanism described above: seeing someone grasping an apple produces a contextualized simulation of the full course of the action.

However, this picture has some holes in it: if perception, action and concepts share the same language how can we differentiate between them. In particular how can we distinguish between a perceived action, a planned or an executed one?

More, even if imitation has frequently been proposed as the central mechanism mediating the reproduction, spread, intergenerational transmission and stabilization of human cultural forms, our imitation is selective. How and why do we imitate? Finally, developmental psychology clearly shows that our simulative abilities are not the same in the different phases of our life. How and why do they evolve?

In this chapter we suggest that a psychology of presence is a possible answer to these questions. In our vision "Presence" and "Social Presence" have a simple but critical role in our everyday experience: the control of agency and social interaction through the unconscious separation of both "internal" and "external", and "self" and "other".

Below are summarized the key ideas behind this vision that will be deepened in the next paragraphs:

o We claim that human beings at birth have *"naked intentionality"*: they have the direct ability of recognizing intentions but lack self-identification. As suggested by Jeannerod and Pacherie [90] in this condition intentions are "naked", unattributed: *the infant recognizes an intention without being aware of whose intention it is.* Different neurological disorders - like the *echopraxia*, or the *anarchic hand* - support the existence of *naked intentionality* [30, 90].

o The need for self-identification and attribution requires a specific neuropsychological process (presence-as-process) embedding sensory-referred properties into an internal functional space [91]. This is achieved by separating both "self" and "other," and "internal" and "external" within different kinds of afferent and efferent motor codes. The presence-as-process can be divided in three different layers/subprocesses phylogenetically different, and strictly related to the evolution of self: *proto presence (self vs. non self), core presence (self vs. present external world)*, and *extended presence (self relative to present external world)*.

o   The outcome of this process is the *presence-as-feeling*: the non mediated perception that an intention is being enacted successfully. This feeling is experienced indirectly (prereflexively) by the self through the characteristics of action and experience. In fact the self perceives directly only the *variations* in the level of presence-as-feeling: breakdowns and optimal experiences (flow).

o   The development of the self allowed by presence leads to the recognition of the "other" as "another intentional self". This requires a specific neuropsychological process (social-presence-as-process) tracking the behavior of the other to understand the characteristics (content and motive) of his/her intentions. This process is based on *covert imitation*: an automatic action emulator, tracking the behavior of other subjects in real time to generate perceptual predictions [71, 83]. The social-presence-as-process can be divided in three different layers/subprocesses phylogenetically different, but mutually inclusive: *proto social presence (the intention of the other is toward the self)*, *joint social presence (the self and the other have the same intentional focus)*, *shared social presence (the self and the other share the same intention)*.

o   The outcome of this process is the *social-presence-as-feeling*: *the non mediated perception of other's intentions*. It is not separated by the experience of the subject but it is related to the quality of his/her social interactions. In fact, a higher level of social-presence-as-feeling is experienced prereflexively as empathy and communicative synchrony. The self experiences reflexively the *social-presence-as-feeling* only when the quality of his experience is modified during a social interaction. More in detail, the self perceives directly only the variations of *social-presence-as-feeling*: intentional opacity and attunement/empathy.

o   Presence and social presence converge within the social and cooperative activities. Specifically, these activities are created and governed by a reciprocal intentional game between the communicators regulated by the level of presence and social presence experienced by the interactants [92]: the display and ostension of a given intention by the speaker ("intentionalization" process) and the ascription and attribution of a certain intention to him/her by the addressee ("re-intentionalization" process).

o   Another important role of presence and social presence is related to the processes of internalization and externalization. As suggested by Vygotsky [93, 94], on one side external activity transforms internal cognitive processes (internalization). On the other side, knowledge structures and moments of internal activity organize and regulate external social processes (externalization). We claim that the processes of internalization and externalization are influenced by the experienced presence and social presence in actions and interactions: *the more is the presence and social presence, the more is the possibility that the contents of the action/interaction will be internalized/externalized.*

3.5.1 Naked Intentionality in Infants

The starting point of the Presence theory is the situation of infants at birth. There is a large body of evidence underlying that infants, even in the first months of life, show a special sensitivity to communication and participate in emotional sharing with the caregivers [95].

To explain these processes, different authors underlined the innate ability of infants to identify with conspecifics. As we have just seen, Meltzoff [76-79] suggested the existence of a biological mechanism allowing infants to perceive others "like them" at birth. Specifically, Meltzoff and Brooks suggest [96]:

"Evidently, infants construe human acts in goal-directed ways. But when does it start? We favor the hypothesis that it begins at birth... The hypothesis is not that neonates represent goal directedness in the same way as adults do. In fact, neonates probably begin by coding the goals of pure body acts and only later enrich the notion of goals to encompass object directed acts." (p. 188).

Trevarthen [97, 98] goes further, arguing that the infant is conscious, since birth, of the others' subjectivity: he is conscious of other's mental states and react in communicative, emotional ways so to link each other's subjectivity. Extending this vision, Tirassa and colleagues [99] suggest that infants are in a particular state that they define "sharedness": the infant's capability to take it for granted that the caregiver is aware of her mental states and will act accordingly. In this vision the infant considers his own mental states as mutually and overtly known to the caregiver.

Here we take a related but different position. We believe that infants have a direct ability – "naked" intentionality – of recognizing intentional behaviors in their phenomenological contents. We define *"naked" intentionality* as a primitive and innate mental state type which can be characterized in the following terms: *to be able to recognize an intention without being aware of whose intention it is*. Following this point we claim that in humans, *intentionality* – the ability to recognize purposeful actions – appears before *intention* – the agent's mental state that represents such actions. Specifically, is the need to separate between "internal" and "external" intentions forcing the nervous system to identify a "self".

Naked intentionality is allowed by the activity of *"mirror neurons"*, the functional cluster of premotor neurons (F5c-PF) that, as we have just seen, are activated both during the execution of purposeful, goal-related actions, and during the observation of similar actions performed by another individual [48, 62, 63].

Apparently, the concept of *naked intentionality* is counterintuitive. However, it includes - and can be considered the *precursor* of - the two different definitions of intention found in literature [100]:

  a) intention as a *property of all mental states*. In such a perspective any subjective, conscious experience – no matter how minimal – is an experience *of* something.

  b) intention as an *act concerning and directed at some state of affairs in the world*. In this sense, individuals deliberately perform an action in order to reach a goal.

Further, the existence of *naked intentionality* is supported by the recent outcomes of neuroscience research. As underlined by Jeannerod and Pacherie [90]:

"Our contention is that this [premotor] cortical network provides the basis for the conscious experience of goal-directedness – the primary awareness of intentions – but does not by itself provide us with a conscious experience of self- or other- agency." (p.140).

Finally, different neurological disorders suggest the existence of *naked intentions* [30, 90]. For instance, in *anarchic hand*, patients seem to be aware of the actions of their anarchic hand but do not attribute to themselves its intentional behavior: the complex movements of one hand are apparently directed towards a goal and are smoothly executed, yet are unintended [101]. This condition seems to demonstrate that the recognition of an intentional action can be separated from the awareness of its authorship: the patients affected are aware of the intentional actions of their anarchic hand, which they know to be their hand, yet they disown them.

In another disturbance – *echopraxia* - found in demented patient, the subject has an impulsive or automatic imitation of other's people gestures. The imitation is performed immediately - irrespective of the meaning or the nature of the gesture - with abruptness and speed of a reflex action. This condition suggests that the patient, who recognized an intentional action in the other, mistakenly attributed it to himself.

It is also important to note that *naked intentionality* allows a simple form of imitation found in newborns, *resonance behavior*: the tendency to reproduce, immediately or with some delay, movements, gestures or actions made by another individual.

3.5.2 From Naked Intentionality to Presence

If intentionality in neonates is naked, they require a specific mechanism to differentiate between internal and external intentions, between their actions and the other's ones: *(Inner) Presence.*

Presence is described here as a defining feature of self allowing the nervous system to solve a key problem for its survival: *how to differentiate between internal and external* (see also the next chapter by Waterworth and Waterworth). In other words, is presence that transforms *intentionality* – the ability to recognize purposeful actions – in the ability of producing an *intention* – the agent's mental state that drives such actions.

In this vision it is critical to distinguish between presence-as-process and presence-as-feeling. The presence-as-process is the continuous activity of the brain in separating "internal" and "external" within different kinds of afferent and efferent signals. So, presence-as-process can be described as a sophisticated form of monitoring of action and experience, transparent to the self but critical for its existence. As clarified by Russell [102]:

"Action-monitoring is a subpersonal process that enables the subjects to discriminate between self-determined and world-determined changes in input. It can give rise to a mode of experience (the experience of being the cause of altered inputs and the experience of being in control) but it is not itself a mode of experience." (p.263).

For this reason, the presence-as-feeling – the non mediated (prereflexive) perception that an intention is being enacted successfully - is not separated by the experience of the subject but *it is related to the quality of our actions*. It corresponds to what Heidegger [1] defined "the interrupted moment of our habitual standard, comfortable *being-in-the-world*". In fact, a higher level of presence-as-feeling is experienced by the self as a better quality of action and experience [103, 104].

Further, the self becomes aware of the presence-as-feeling separated by our *being-in-the-world* when its level is modified. More in detail, the self perceives directly only *the variations* in the level of presence-as-feeling: *breakdowns* and *optimal experiences.*

On one side we have optimal experiences. According to Csikszentmihalyi [105, 106], individuals preferentially engage in opportunities for action associated with a positive, complex and rewarding state of consciousness, defined *"optimal experience"* or *"flow"*. Here we argue that flow is the result of the link *between the highest level of presence-as-feeling, with a positive emotional state*. In fact, it is also possible to experience high levels of presence in negative emotional states: e.g. in the battlefield during an attack from the enemy.

On the other side we have breakdowns. Winograd and Flores [6] refer to presence disruptions as *breakdowns:* when, during an action, an object or an environment becomes part of our consciousness then a *breakdown* has occurred. Why do we experience these breakdowns? Our hypothesis is that breakdowns are a sophisticated evolutionary tool used to control the quality of experience: the more the breakdown, the less is the level of presence-as-feeling, the less is the quality of experience, and the less is the possibility of surviving in the environment.

At this point we can argue that is the *feeling of presence that provides to the self a feedback about the status of its activity*: the self perceives the variations in the feeling of presence and tunes its activity accordingly. Specifically, the self tries to overcome any breakdown in its activity and searches for engaging and rewarding activities (optimal experiences).

3.5.2.1 The Layers of Presence

Even if presence is a unitary feeling, the recent neuropsychological research has shown that, on the process side, it can be divided in three different layers/subprocesses (for a broader and more in-depth description see [91] and the next chapter by Waterworth and Waterworth), phylogenetically different, and strictly related to the evolution of self [107]:
- *proto presence* (self vs. non self);
- *core presence* (self vs. present external world);
- and *extended presence* (self relative to present external world).

More precisely we can define *"proto presence"* the process of internal/external separation *related to the level of perception-action coupling (self vs. non-self)*. The more the organism is able to couple correctly perceptions and movements, the more it differentiates itself from the external world, thus increasing its probability of surviving.

"Core presence" can be described as *the activity of selective attention made by the self on perceptions (self vs. present external world)*: the more the organism is able to focus on its sensorial experience by leaving in the background the remaining neural

processes, the more it is able to identify the present moment and its current tasks, increasing its probability of surviving.

Finally, the role of *"extended presence"* is to *verify the significance to the self of experienced events in the external world (self relative to the present external world)*. The more the self is present in significant experiences, the more it will be able to reach its goals, increasing the possibility of surviving. Extended presence requires emotionally or culturally significant content.

3.5.3 From Presence to Social Presence

The development of the self also leads to the recognition of the "other" as "another intentional self". This requires a specific neuropsychological process (social-presence-as-process) tracking the behavior of the other to understand his intentions. In fact, *naked intentionality* allows infants to detect *intentionality* – they recognize that an intention is being enacted – but neither to detect the *content* of the other's intention – they do not recognize which specific intention, or set of intentions is being enacted – nor to identify the *motives* of such content – they do not recognize why the specific intention, or set of intentions is being enacted.

So, *social presence* is described here as a defining feature of self *allowing the detection of the content and motives of other's intentions*. Without the emergence of the sense of social presence it is impossible for the self to develop a theory of mind allowing the comprehension, explanation, and prediction of behavior and, in general, the management of the social interactions.

As for Presence, we distinguish between *social-presence-as-process* and *social-presence-as-feeling*. The *social-presence-as-process* is the continuous activity of the brain in identifying intentions within the perceptual field. So, it can be described as a sophisticated form of monitoring of the others' actions transparent to the self but critical for its social abilities. As we have seen previously, this process is based on *covert imitation*: an automatic action emulator, tracking the behavior of other subjects in real time to generate perceptual predictions [71, 83].

Social-presence-as-feeling is instead *the non mediated perception of other's intentions*. The concept of social-presence-as-feeling is similar to the concept of *"intentional attuning"* suggested by Gallese [69, 108]: our capacity to prereflexively identify with others. In fact the social-presence-as-feeling is not separated by the experience of the subject but it is related to the quality of our social interactions. In fact, a higher level of social-presence-as-feeling is experienced prereflexively as empathy and communicative synchrony.

The self experiences reflexively the *social-presence-as-feeling* only when the quality of his experience is modified during a social interaction. More in detail, the self perceives directly only the variations of *social-presence-as-feeling*.

As underlined by Anolli [92] intention does not constitute by itself an "on–off" process, but it is characterized by an articulated graduation and differentiation within itself:

"First of all, in everyday life, intentionality is regulated by continuous variations of intensity and precision. This intentional gradability allows communicators to manage the focusing of different communicative acts during everyday life...Moreover, a single communicative act can be governed by a plurality of intentions, embedded in each other and hierarchically organized. Such a choice and

continuous gradation of communicative intentions make the communicative act particularly complex, since, on the one hand, it needs a precise cognitive and emotional direction; on the other, it can give rise to communicative uncertainties and difficulties." (pp. 36-37).

So according to the level of social presence experienced by the subjects, they will experience *intentional opacity* on one side, and *communicative attuning and synchrony* on the other side [109].

3.5.3.1 The layers of Social Presence

The study of infants and the analysis of their ability of understanding and interacting with people suggest that social-presence-as-process includes three different layers/subprocesses phylogenetically different, but mutually inclusive [110]:
   - *proto social presence* (the intention of the other is toward the self);
   - *joint social presence* (the self and the other have the same intentional focus).
   - *shared social presence* (the self and the other share the same intention).

As we have seen, presence allows the identification of other intentional selves in the phenomenological world (there is an other intentional self). From an evolutionary viewpoint, the more the self is able to understand other selves, the more it is the possibility of starting an interaction, thus increasing its probability of surviving.
   Within this context *"Proto Social Presence"* can be described as the process allowing the identification of an interactive intention in other selves (the intention of the other is toward the self). The more the self is able to identify a communicative intention in other selves, the more it is the possibility of starting an interaction, thus increasing its probability of surviving.
   As suggested by Reddy [110] infants are aware of the directedness of others' attention in the first months of life:

"I will argue that mutual attention in the first months of life already involves an awareness of the directedness of attention. The self is experienced as the first object of this directedness followed by gradually more distal 'objects'. This view explains early infant affective self-consciousness within mutual attention as emotionally meaningful, rather than as bearing only a spurious similarity to that in the second and third years of life. Such engagements precede and must inform, rather than derive from, conceptual representations of self and other, and can be better described as self–other conscious affects." (p. 397).

The role of *"joint social presence"* is to allow the identification of a common intentional focus in other selves (the self and the other have the same intentional focus). The more the self is able to recognize a common intentional focus in other selves, the more it is the possibility of having an interaction, thus increasing its probability of surviving.
   The first expression of joint social presence appears at the end of the first year of age as infants are beginning to engage with caregivers in activities that are triadic in the sense that they involve child, adult, and some outside entity – *joint attention* - toward which they both direct their actions. By 12 to 14 months of age, then, the triadic interactions of child and adult around external entities appear more

coordinated since the child can do such things as reverse roles and help the adult in her role if needed – both necessary for engaging in joint actions embodying joint intentions [111].

Finally, the role of *shared social presence* (the self and the other share the same intention) is to identify "others that are *like* the self", sharing intentions and emotions (*intentional attunement*). The more the self is able to identify intentional attunement in other selves, the more it is the possibility of successfully conducting an interaction, thus increasing its probability of surviving.

3.5.4 From Presence and Social Presence to Communication

Till now we considered presence and social presence separately. However, they converge and interact within the social and cooperative activities. In particular, is *through their interaction that the self improves his intentional action and interaction*: the higher is the level of presence and social presence experienced by the self, the higher is the complexity of the expressed and recognized intentions.

In naked intentionality the structure of the intention includes *action* and *goal* only. When the self experiences full presence and social presence he is able to express and recognize complex intentions including *subject, action, goal, way of doing* and *motive*.

According to Bratman [112] joint cooperative activities have three critical features that distinguish them from social interaction in general: (1) the interactants are mutually responsive to one another, (2) there is a shared goal in the sense that each participant has the goal that we (in mutual knowledge) do X together, and (3) the participants coordinate their plans of action and intentions some way down the hierarchy – which requires that both participants understand both roles of the interaction (*role reversal*) and so can at least potentially help the other with his role if needed.

To achieve it, the self need to separate himself from the other (proto presence), to differentiate between his action and his planned action (core presence), to recognize the communicative intention of the other (proto social presence), to share with him the intentional focus (joint social presence), to identify intentional attunement (shared social presence) and to evaluate it as significant for himself (extended presence).

In this way the social and communicative exchange is created and governed by a reciprocal intentional game between the communicators regulated by the level of presence and social presence experienced by the interactants [92, 113]: the display and ostension of a given intention by the speaker ("intentionalization" process) and the ascription and attribution of a certain intention to him/her by the addressee ("re-intentionalization" process).

For instance, when self perceives a reduction in the extended presence – e.g. the communication is no more interesting - he can activate a new behavior – e.g. asking for a new question – to improve it. At the same way, the self can use his perception of other's intentions to tune the communication. A similar mechanism is probably behind the imitation process: without an elevated level of presence and social presence the infant does not imitate.

The interaction between the lowest levels of presence and social presence also allows the identification of the *enemy/stranger*: the other who is not a self [114]. According to Karl Schmitt the specific political distinction to which political actions and motives can be reduced is the one between friend (*amicus*) and enemy (*hostis*). In fact the *hostis* is, in a specially intense way, existentially something different and alien so that, in the extreme case, conflicts with him are possible.

Finally, another important role of presence and social presence is probably related to the processes of internalization and externalization. Vygotsky [93, 94] states that internalization and externalization are the dialectical mechanisms that allow an individual to construct higher psychological structures. On one side external activity transforms internal cognitive processes (*internalization*). On the other side, knowledge structures and moments of internal activity organize and regulate external social processes (*externalization*).

According to Vygotsky [93], internalization is social by its very nature: is not just copying but rather a transformation or reorganization of incoming social information and mental structures based on the individual's characteristics and existing knowledge. The opposite process of internalization is externalization. Mental processes manifest themselves in external actions performed by a person, so they can be verified and corrected, if necessary. This dialectical process also leads to the production of new tools.

Here we suggest that the processes of internalization and externalization are influenced by the experienced presence and social presence in actions and interactions:

o   *the more is the presence and social presence experienced during an interaction, the more is the possibility that the contents of the interaction will be internalized;*

o   *the more is the level of presence experienced during an activity, the more is the possibility that the content of the activity will be externalized.*

3.5.5 From Inner Presence to Media Presence

As discussed in detail in the previous chapter by Coelho and colleagues the research work on virtual reality produced two coexisting visions of presence: the rationalist and the psychological/ecological points of view. The researchers agreeing with the rationalist approach describe the sense of presence as a function of the experience of a given medium (*Media Presence*). The main outcome of this vision is the definition of presence as the *perceptual illusion of non-mediation* [115], produced by means of the disappearance of the medium from the conscious attention of the subject. The main advantage of this approach is its predictive value: the level of presence is reduced by the experience of mediation during the action. The main limitation of this vision is what is not said. What is presence for? What is not mediated?

In contrast, the psychological/ecological point of view presented in this chapter considers presence as a neuropsychological phenomenon, evolved from the interplay of our biological and cultural inheritance, whose goal is the expression and recognition of self/other intentionality (*Inner Presence*).

However, the difference between *Inner Presence* and *Media Presence* is not so much: rationalists define the feeling of presence as the "perceptual illusion of nonmediation" [115]; we defined it as the "non-mediated (prereflexive) perception that an intention is being enacted successfully". Where is the difference?

Apparently the main difference is in what is "non-mediated" by presence. In this paper we clearly indicated successful intentions as the non-mediated content. Lombard and Ditton suggest that a person is present when his/her response to the medium is not mediated:

"An illusion of nonmediation occurs when a person fails to perceive or acknowledge the existence of a medium in his/her communication environment and responds as he/she would if the medium were not there. ... Presence in this view can not occur unless a person is using a medium."
(online: http://jcmc.indiana.edu/vol3/issue2/lombard.html).

Are these positions so far? According to Searle the answer maybe no. For this author [116], an action is "a causal and Intentional transaction between mind and the world" (p. 88). Specifically, any action is composed of two parts: an intention, and a movement. When the action is premeditated, it is caused by a "prior intention": an intention to act formed in advance of the action itself.

However, in most everyday actions there is not a prior intention. These actions are caused by an "intention-in-action": an intention not formed in advance of the action. The basic intentional content of the intention-in-action is self-referential causality: its success or satisfaction can come about only if it (and not some other force) is the cause of the movement whose mental component it is. In short, intentions-in-action drive the movement prereflexively, without the need of a prior intention.

This is possible because, as suggested by the *Common Coding Theory*, actions are coded in terms of the perceivable effects they should generate. More in detail, when an effect is intended (intention-is-action), the movement that produces this effect as perceptual input is automatically activated, because actions and their effects are stored in a common representational domain [44].

This is the typical case of synchronous mediated communication when the user masters the medium: the fingers of an expert chatter or the hands of a Doom III cooperative player are driven by intentions-in-action. Following Heidegger [1], the medium is "ready-to-hand". Only when there is a breakdown, a problem - the keyboard is no more responsive or the screen disappears – the user needs to plan a new action (prior-intention) to solve the problem.

For Lombard and Ditton the Doom cooperative players are present in the game "if this does not draw attention to itself reminding them that they are having a mediated experience". For us, the players are present in the virtual environment if they are able to drive successfully and prereflexively their interaction. If we substitute in our definition of presence the word "intention" with the one "intention-in-action" we have an almost perfect match with the Lombard and Ditton's position: *the non mediated (prereflexive) perception of successful intentions-in action.* The main difference is that this definition works for experiences not related to media, too.

To make this concept clearer two examples may help. A stroke patient with a left hemiplegia is no more "present" in the left part of his body: using his left hand he is not able to translate an intention-in-action in a purposeful behavior.

But it is not only, or not mainly, the body to be not "present" – or not "ready-to-hand" - to the self. I'm in a restaurant for a formal dinner with my boss and some colleagues, but I don't know how to directly use (intention-in-action) the many different strange forks I have around my dish. In this situation I'm physically there, but the lack of knowledge puts me outside, at least partially, from the social and cultural space of the "formal dinner". The result is a reduced presence and a limitation in my agency: I don't use the forks to avoid mistakes. These examples show clearly how both physical boundaries (body, wall, obstacles, etc.) and social and cultural boundaries have a strong influence on the possibility of action and the experienced presence of the subject.

In this context, *a breakdown* occurs when, during our activity, we are forced to stop the use of intentions-in-action. To illustrate, imagine sitting in a balcony engrossed in reading a book on a pleasant evening. As the sun sets and the light diminishes one continues reading (intention-in-action), engrossed in the story until one becomes aware that the light is no longer suitable for reading. In such conditions, before any overt change in behavior, what we experience is a breakdown in reading and a shift of attention from the book to the light illuminating the book. At that stage we are not present anymore in the reading and we have to reflexively plan an action (prior intention) to switch on the light on the balcony.

This vision has two important suggestions for media developers:

o   it is also "external" to the subject what is not related to his/her activities, interests and values.

o   to be more "present" in the situation (social and cultural space) defined by a symbolic system, the user has to be aware of its meaning. Only "making sense there", the user really experiences a full sense of presence [104, 117].

3.6 Conclusions

The German philosopher Martin Heidegger, underlined in his writings the following structural (ontological) features of the being:

-   *Spatiality*: the space is not around us but within us;
-   *Being with*: we exist not on our own terms, but only in reference to others.

As we have discussed in the chapter, the recent outcomes of cognitive science support this vision. In particular we showed how different theories from social and cognitive sciences – *Situated Cognition, Embodied Cognition, Enactive Approach, Situated Simulation, Covert Imitation* - and discoveries from neuroscience – *Mirror and Canonical Neurons* - have many contact points with this view.

The overall picture we depicted is different from the traditional view of cognition. Cognition is no more the simple performance of formal operations on abstract symbols, but has instead deep roots in sensorimotor processing.

Specifically, our conceptual system dynamically produces contextualized representations (simulations) that support grounded action in different situations. These simulations include not only sensory states but also motor and mental states. This is allowed by a common coding – the motor code – shared by perception, action and concepts. On one side, the vision of an object immediately activates the appropriate hand shape for using it: seeing a red apple activates a precision grip for grasping and turning. On the other side, thinking an apple produces the simulation of an action related to the apple in a specific context of use.

This common coding also allows the subject for natively recognizing actions done by other beings within the phenomenological contents. Specifically, the subject predicts the outcome of the identified action using the same simulation mechanism described above: seeing someone grasping an apple produces a contextualized simulation of the full course of the action. This covert imitation functions as an automatic action emulator, tracking the behavior of other subjects in real time to generate perceptual predictions.

However, this picture has some holes in it: if perception, action and concepts share the same language how can we differentiate between them. In particular how can we distinguish between a perceived action, a planned or an executed one?

More, even if imitation has frequently been proposed as the central mechanism mediating the reproduction, spread, intergenerational transmission and stabilization of human cultural forms, our imitation is selective. How and why do we imitate? Finally, developmental psychology clearly shows that our simulative abilities are not the same in the different phases of our life. How and why do they evolve?

In the chapter we suggested that a psychology of presence is a possible answer to these questions. In our vision "Presence" and "Social Presence" have a simple but critical role in our everyday experience: the control of agency and social interaction through the unconscious separation of both "internal" and "external", and "self" and "other". Specifically, Presence allows the recognition of the intentions of the self and Social Presence allows the recognition of the intentions of the other.

For this reason, Presence and Social Presence converge within the social and cooperative activities. Particularly, these activities are created and governed by a reciprocal intentional game between the communicators regulated by the level of presence and social presence experienced by the interactants [92]: the display and ostension of a given intention by the speaker ("intentionalization" process) and the ascription and attribution of a certain intention to him/her by the addressee ("re-intentionalization" process). For instance, when self perceives a reduction in the extended presence – e.g. the communication is no more interesting - he can activate a new behavior – e.g. asking for a new question – to improve it. At the same way, the self can use his perception of other's intentions to tune the communication. A similar mechanism is probably behind the imitation process: without an elevated level of presence and social presence the infant does not imitate.

Another important role of presence and social presence is related to the processes of internalization and externalization. As suggested by Vygotsky [93, 94], on one side external activity transform internal cognitive processes (internalization). On the other side, knowledge structures and moments of internal activity organize and regulate external social processes (externalization).

We suggest that the processes of internalization and externalization are influenced by the experienced presence and social presence in actions and interactions: the more is the presence and social presence, the more is the possibility that the contents of the action/interaction will be internalized/externalized.

Obviously, this chapter has its limitations: the psychology of presence here introduced is still in progress and some of the claims presented require an empirical confirmation and additional theoretical work. Specifically, given space limitation – as well as the preliminary state of the model in my mind – further details of the psychology of presence remain to be specified elsewhere.

More, no clear indications are provided about how to measure presence. Related to this point, some suggestions may come from the chapters by Magnusson, and Agliati and colleagues in this book (see also [118]). Finally, additional studies are needed to understand the links between presence and classical cognitive processes like attention, emotions or memory. Nevertheless, quite independently of the intricacies of terminology and conceptualizations, we hope that the model presented here will help to disentangle the large variety of claims, notions and theories that currently characterizes research in this area.

3.7 References

[1]   M. Heidegger, Being and Time. New York: Harper & Row, 1962.
[2]   M. Warnock, Existentialism. Oxford: Oxford University Press, 1970.
[3]   H. Dreyfus, Being-in-the-world: A commentary on Heidegger's Being and Time. Cambridge, MA, 1991.
[4]   Y. Arisaka, Spatiality, temporality, and the problem of foundation in Being and Time. *Philosophy Today,* (1996), 40(1), 36-46.
[5]   Q. Smith, On Heidegger's theory of moods. *The Modern Schoolman: A Quarterly Journal in Philosophy,* (1981), LVII(4), 56-61.
[6]   T. Winograd and F. Flores, Understanding Computers and Cognition: A New Foundation for Design. Norwood, NJ: Ablex Publishing Corporation, 1986.
[7]   G. Steiner, Heidegger. Sussex: The Harvester Press Limited, 1978.
[8]   J. Prinz, Putting the brakes on Enactive Perception. *PSYCHE,* (2006), 12(1), 1-12; online: http://psyche.cs.monash.edu.au.
[9]   W.J. Freeman and R. Núñez, Restoring to cognition the forgotten primacy of action, intention and emotion. *Journal of Consciousness Studies,* (1999), 11-12, ix-xix.
[10]   A. Clark, Reasons, robots and the extended mind. *Mind & Language,* (2001), 16(2), 121-145.
[11]   J. Haugeland, Having Thought: Essays in the Metaphisics of Mind. Cambridge, MA: Harvard University Press, 1998.
[12]   A. Clark, Being There: Putting Brain Body and World Together Again. Cambridge, MA: MIT Press, 1997.
[13]   J.G. Greeno, The situativity of knowing, learning, and research. *American Psychologist,* (1998), 53(1), 5-26.
[14]   L. Suchman, Plans and situated action. Cambridge, UK: Cambridge University Press, 1987.
[15]   W.J. Clancey, Situated cognition: On human knowledge and computer representation. Cambridge: Cambridge University Press, 1997.
[16]   L.A. Stein, Imagination and situated cognition. In: *Android epistemology.* Edited by Kenneth M, Ford CN, Glymour P and Hayes J: American Association for Artificial Intelligence, Menlo Park, CA, US; 167-182, 1995.
[17]   J. Lave and E. Wenger, Situated Learning: Legitimate Peripheral Participation. Cambridge, MA: Cambridge University Press, 1991.
[18]   E. Hutchins, Cognitions in the wild. Cambridge, MA: MIT Press, 1995.
[19]   W.J. Clancey, Situated action: A neuropsychological interpretation (Response to Vera and Simon). *Cognitive Science,* (1993), 17(1), 87-107.
[20]   D.A. Norman, Affordance, Conventions and Design. *Interactions,* (1999)(5), 38-43.
[21]   A. Clark, Natural Born Cyborgs: Minds, technologies, and the future of human intelligence. Oxford: Oxford University Press, 2003.
[22]   T. Ziemke, What's that thing called embodiment. In: *Annual Meeting of the Cognitive Science Society: 2003; Boston, MA, USA*; 1305-1310,2003.
[23]   G. Lakoff and M. Johnson, Metaphors we live by. Chicago, IL: University of Chicago Press, 1980.
[24]   F. Garbarini and M. Adenzato, At the root of embodied cognition: Cognitive science meets neurophysiology. *Brain And Cognition,* (2004), 56(1), 100-106.
[25]   V. Gallese and G. Lakoff, The brain's concept: The role of the sensory-motor system in reason and language. *Cognitive Neuropsychology,* (2005), 22, 455-479.
[26]   S. Gallagher, How the Body Shapes the Mind. Oxford, 2005.
[27]   M. Wilson, Six Views of Embodied Cognition. *Psychonomic Bulletin & Review,* (2002), 9(4), 625-636.
[28]   G. Lakoff and M. Johnson, Philosophy in the flesh: The embodied mind and its challenge to Western thought. New York: Basic Books, 1999.
[29]   M.L. Anderson, Embodied Cognition: A field guide. *Artificial Intelligence,* (2003), 149, 91-130.
[30]   A. Revonsuo, Inner Presence, Consciousness as a Biological Phenomenon. Cambridge, MA: MIT Press, 2006.
[31]   T. Metzinger, Being no one. Cambridge, MA: MIT Press, 2004.
[32]   G. Butterworth and L. Hicks, Visual proprioception and postural stability in infancy. A developmental study. *Perception,* (1977), 6(3), 255-262.
[33]   G. Butterworth, Origins of Self-Perception in Infancy. *Psychological Inquiry,* (1992), 3(2), 103-111.
[34]   S. Gallagher, Bodily self-awareness and object perception. *Theoria et Historia Scientiarum: International Journal for Interdisciplinary Studies,* (2003), 7(1), online: http://www2.canisius.edu/~gallaghr/theoria03.html.
[35]   J.J. Gibson, The ecological approach to visual perception. Hillsdale, NJ: Erlbaum, 1979.

[36]   J.J. Gibson, The senses considered as perceptual systems. Boston: Houghton Mifflin, 1966.
[37]   H.R. Maturana and F.J. Varela, Autopoiesis and cognition. The realization of the living. Dordecht, The Netherlands: D. Reidel Publishing, 1980.
[38]   E. Thompson, Sensorimotor subjectivity and the enactive approach to experience. *Phenomenology and the Cognitive Sciences,* (2005), 4, 407-427.
[39]   F.J. Varela, E. Thompson and E. Rosch, The embodied mind: Cognitive science and human experience. Cambridge, MA: MIT Press, 1991.
[40]   A. Noë, Action in perception. Cambridge, MA: MIT Press, 2004.
[41]   A. Clark, Vision as dance? *PSYCHE,* (2006), 12(1), 1-10; online: http://psyche.cs.monash.edu.au.
[42]   P. Jacob, Why visual experience is likely to resist being enacted. *PSYCHE,* (2006), 12(1), 1-12; online: http://psyche.cs.monash.edu.au.
[43]   B. Hommel, J. Müsseler, G. Aschersleben and W. Prinz, The Theory of Event Coding (TEC): A framework for perception and action planning. *Behavioral and Brain Sciences,* (2001), 24(5), 849-937.
[44]   W. Prinz, Perception and action planning. *European Journal of Cognitive Psychology,* (1997), 9(2), 129-154.
[45]   W. James, The principles of psychology. New York: Holt, 1890.
[46]   G. Knoblich and R. Flach, Action identity: Evidence from self-recognition, prediction, and coordination. *Consciousness and Cognition,* (2003), 12, 620-632.
[47]   V. Gallese, The inner sense of action: Agency and motor representations. *Journal of Consciousness Studies,* (2000), 7(10), 23-40.
[48]   G. Rizzolatti, L. Fadiga, V. Gallese and F. L., Premotor cortex and the recognition of motor actions. *Cognitive Brain Research,* (1996), 3, 131-141.
[49]   G. Rizzolatti, G. Luppino and M. Matelli, The organization of the cortical motor system: new concepts. *Electroencephalography and Clinical Neurophysiology,* (1998), 106, 283-296.
[50]   G. Rizzolatti, L. Fadiga, L. Fogassi and V. Gallese, The space around us. *Science,* (1997)(277), 190-191.
[51]   V. Gallese, The brain and the self: Reviewing the neuroscientific evidence. *Psycoloquy,* (2000), 11(34), Online: http://www.cogsci.ecs.soton.ac.uk/cgi/psyc/newpsy?11.034.
[52]   V. Gallese, Embodied simulation: From neurons to phenomenal experience. *Phenomenology and the Cognitive Sciences,* (2005)(4), 23-48.
[53]   G. Rizzolatti, L. Fogassi and V. Gallese, Cortical mechanisms subserving object grasping and action recognition: A new view on the cortical functions. In: *The cognitive neurosciences, 2nd Edition.* Edited by Gazzaniga MS. Cambridge, MA: MIT Press; 539-552, 2000.
[54]   L. Fogassi, V. Gallese, L. Fadiga, G. Luppino, M. Matelli and G. Rizzolatti, Coding of peripersonal space in inferior premotor cortex (area F4). *Journal of Neurophysiology,* (1996), 76(1), 141-157.
[55]   A.R. Damasio, Time-locked multiregional retroactivation: a systems-level proposal for the neural substrates of recall and recognition. *Cognition,* (1989), 33, 25-62.
[56]   L.W. Barsalou, Situated simulation in the human conceptual system. *Language and Cognitive Processes,* (2003), 18, 513-562.
[57]   K.W. Simmons and L.W. Barsalou, The similarity-in-topography principle: reconciling theories of conceptual deficits. *Cognitive Neuropsychology,* (2003), 20, 451-486.
[58]   L.W. Barsalou, K.W. Simmons, A.K. Barbey and C.D. Wilson, Grounding conceptual knowledge in modality-specific systems. *Trends in Cognitive Sciences,* (2003), 7(2), 84-91.
[59]   L.W. Barsalou, Being there conceptually: Simulating categories in preparation for situated action. In: *Representation, memory and development: Essays in honor of Jean Mandler.* Edited by Stein NL, Bauer PJ and Rabinowitz M. Mahwah, NJ: Erlbaum; 1-15, 2002.
[60]   R. Adolphs, Social cognition and the human brain. *Trends in Cognitive Sciences,* (1999), 3(12), 469-479.
[61]   J.T. Cacioppo, P.S. Visser and C.L. Pickett (eds.), Social Neuroscience: People thinking about thinking people. Cambridge, MA: MIT Press, 2006.
[62]   V. Gallese, L. Fadiga, L. Fogassi and G. Rizzolatti, Action recognition in the premotor cortex. *Brain,* (1996), 119(593-609).
[63]   G. Rizzolatti and M.A. Arbib, Language within our grasp. *Trends in Neuroscience,* (1998), 21, 188-194.
[64]   M. Iacoboni, R.P. Woods, M. Brass, H. Bekkering, J.C. Mazziotta and G. Rizzolatti, Cortical mechanisms of human imitation. *Science,* (1999), 286, 2526-2528.
[65]   G. Buccino, F. Binkofski, G.R. Fink, L. Fadiga, L. Fogassi, V. Gallese, R.J. Seitz, K. Zilles, G. Rizzolatti and H.-J. Freund, Action observation activates premotor and parietal areas in somatotopic manner: An fMRI study. *European Journal of Neuroscience,* (2001), 13, 400-404.

[66]   J. Decety and J. Grèzes, Neural mechanisms subserving the perception of human actions. *Trends in Cognitive Sciences,* (1999), 3, 172-178.
[67]   J.E. Wickham, Minimally invasive surgery. Future developments. *Bmj,* (1994), 308(6922), 193-196.
[68]   C. Keysers, B. Wicker, V. Gazzola, J.-L. Anton, L. Fogassi and V. Gallese, A touching sight: SII/PV activation during the observation and experience of touch. *Neuron,* (2004), 42(22), 1-20.
[69]   V. Gallese, Intentional Attunement: The mirror system and its role in interpersonal relations. *Interdisciplines,* (2004), 1, Online: http://www.interdisciplines.org/mirror/papers/1.
[70]   P. Jacob and M. Jeannerod, The motor theory of social cognition: A critique. *Trends in Cognitive Sciences,* (2005), 9, 21-25.
[71]   M. Wilson and G. Knoblich, The case for motor involvement in perceiving conspecifics. *Psychological Bulletin,* (2005), 131(3), 460-473.
[72]   F. Baldissera, P. Cavallari, L. Craighero and L. Fadiga, Modulation of spinal excitability during observation of hand actions in humans. *European Journal of Neuroscience,* (2001), 13(1), 190-194.
[73]   M. Tomasello, A. Kruger and H.H. Ratner, Cultural learning. *Behavioral and Brain Sciences,* (1993), 16, 495-552.
[74]   M. Tomasello, The cultural origins of human cognition. Cambridge, MA: Harvard University Press, 1999.
[75]   R.J.R. Blair, Responding to the emotions of others: Dissociating forms of empathy through the study of typical and psychiatric populations. *Consciousness and Cognition,* (2005), 14, 698-718.
[76]   A.N. Meltzoff, W. Prinz, G. Butterworth, G. Hatano, K.W. Fischer, P.M. Greenfield, P. Harris and D. Stern (eds.), The imitative mind: Development, evolution, and brain bases. Cambridge: Cambridge University Press, 2002.
[77]   A.N. Meltzoff and M.K. Moore, Imitation of facial and manual gestures by human neonates. *Science,* (1977), 198, 702-709.
[78]   A.N. Meltzoff and J. Decety, What imitation tells us about social cognition: a rapprochement between developmental psychology and cognitive neuroscience. *Philosophical Transactions of the Royal Society,* (2003), 358, 491-500.
[79]   A.N. Meltzoff, Origins of theory of mind, cognition and communication. *Journal of Communicative Disorders,* (1999), 32, 251-269.
[80]   J. Decety, T. Chaminade, J. Grèzes and A. Meltzoff, A PET exploration of the neural mechanisms involved in reciprocal imitaton. *Neuroimage,* (2002), 15, 265-272.
[81]   T. Chaminade, A.N. Meltzoff and J. Decety, Does the end justify the means? A PET exploration of the mechanisms involved in human imitation. *Neuroimage,* (2002), 15, 318-328.
[82]   L.J. Moses, Executive functioning and children's theories of mind. In: *Other Minds: How humans bridge the divide between self and others.* Edited by Malle BF and Hodges SD. New York: The Guilford Press; 11-25, 2005.
[83]   G. Knoblich, I. Thornton, M. Grosjean and M. Shiffrar (eds.), Human Body Perception from the Inside Out. New York: Oxford University Press, 2005.
[84]   M.A. Umiltà, E. Kohler, V. Gallese, L. Fogassi, L. Fadiga, C. Keysers and G. Rizzolatti, I know what you are doing: A neurophysiological study. *Neuron,* (2001), 31, 155-165.
[85]   J. Decety and T. Chaminade, When the self represents the others: A new cognitive neuroscience view on psychological identification. *Consciousness and Cognition,* (2003), 12, 577-596.
[86]   G. Gergely and G. Csibra, The social construction of the cultural mind: Imitative learning as a mechanism of human pedagogy. *Interaction Studies,* (2005), 6, 463-481.
[87]   G. Csibra and G. Gergely, Social learning and social cognition: The case for pedagogy. In: *Process of change in brain and cognitive development Attention and performance XXI.* Edited by Munakata Y and Johnson MH. Oxford: Oxford University Press; 249-274, 2006.
[88]   G. Gergely, H. Bekkering and I. Kiraly, Rational imitation in preverbal infants. *Nature,* (2002), 415(6873), 755.
[89]   D.E. Lyons, L.R. Santos and F.C. Keil, Reflections of other minds: How primate social cognition can inform the function of mirror neurons. *Current Opinion in Neurobiology,* (2006), 16(2), 230-234.
[90]   M. Jeannerod and E. Pacherie, Agency, simulation and self-identification. *Mind & Language,* (2004), 19(2), 113-146.
[91]   G. Riva, J.A. Waterworth and E.L. Waterworth, The Layers of Presence: a bio-cultural approach to understanding presence in natural and mediated environments. *Cyberpsychology & Behavior,* (2004), 7(4), 405-419.
[92]   L. Anolli, MaCHT -Miscommunication as CHance Theory: Toward a unitary theory of communication and miscommunication. In: *Say not to say: New perspectives on miscommunication.* Edited by Anolli L, Ciceri R and Riva G. Amsterdam: IOS Press; 3-42, 2002.

[93]   L.S. Vygotsky, Mind in society: The development of higher psychological processes, vol. Harvard University Press: Cambridge, MA, 1978.

[94]   L.S. Vygotsky, Thought and language. Cambridge, MA: MIT Press, 1965.

[95]   M. Legerstee, Infants' sense of people: Precursors to a Theory of Mind. Cambridge: Cambridge University Press, 2005.

[96]   A.N. Meltzoff and R. Brooks, "Like me" as a building block for understanding other minds: Bodily acts, attention and intention. In: *Intentions and Intentionality: Foundation of social cognition.* Edited by Malle BF, Moses LJ and D.A. B. Cambridge, MA: MIT Press; 171-191, 2001.

[97]   C. Trevarthen, The neurobiology of early communication: Intersubjective regulations in human brain development. In: *Handbook on brain and behavior in human development.* Edited by Kalverboer AF and Gramsbergen A. Dordrecht, The Netherlands: Klewer Academic Publisher, 2001.

[98]   C. Trevarthen and K. Aitken, Infant intersubjectivity: Research, theory and clinical applications. *Journal of Psychological Psychiatry,* (2001), 42, 3-48.

[99]   M. Tirassa, F.M. Bosco and L. Colle, Rethinking the ontogeny of mindreading. *Consciousness and Cognition,* (2006), 15, 197-217.

[100] B.F. Malle, L.J. Moses and B. D.A. (eds.), Intentions and Intentionality: Foundation of social cognition. Cambridge, MA: MIT Press, 2001.

[101] S. Della Sala, The anarchic hand. *The Psychologist,* (2006), 8(18), 606-609.

[102] J.A. Russell, Agency: Its role in mental development. Hove: Erlbaum, 1996.

[103] P. Zahoric and R.L. Jenison, Presence as being-in-the-world. *Presence, Teleoperators, and Virtual Environments,* (1998), 7(1), 78-89.

[104] T. Marsh, Staying there: an activity-based approach to narrative design and evaluation as an antidote to virtual corpsing. In: *Being There: Concepts, effects and measurements of user presence in synthetic environments.* Edited by Riva G, Davide F and IJsselsteijn WA. Amsterdam: IOS Press; 85-96, 2003.

[105] M. Csikszentmihalyi, Beyond Boredom and Anxiety. San Francisco: Jossey-Bass, 1975.

[106] M. Csikszentmihalyi, Flow: The psychology of optimal experience. New York: HarperCollins, 1990.

[107] A. Damasio, The Feeling of What Happens: Body, Emotion and the Making of Consciousness. San Diego, CA: Harcourt Brace and Co, Inc., 1999.

[108] V. Gallese, The roots of empathy. The shared mainfold hypothesis and the neural basis of intersubjectivity. *Psychopathology,* (2003)(36), 171-180.

[109] L. Anolli, R. Ciceri and G. Riva (eds.), Say not to Say: New persectives on miscommunication. Amsterdam: Ios Press. Online: http://www.emergingcommunication.com/volume3.html, 2002.

[110] V. Reddy, On being the object of attention: implications for self-other consciousness. *Trends in Cognitive Sciences,* (2003), 7(397-402).

[111] M. Tomasello, M. Carpenter, J. Call, T. Behne and H. Moll, Understanding and sharing intentions: The origins of cultural cognition. *Behavior and Brain Sciences,* (2005), 28(5), 675-691.

[112] M.E. Bratman, Shared cooperative activity. *Philosophical Review,* (1992), 101, 327-341.

[113] L. Anolli, The detection of the hidden design of meaning. In: *The hidden structure of interaction: From neurons to culture patterns.* Edited by Anolli L, Duncan SJ, Magnusson M and Riva G. Amsterdam: IOS Press; 23-50, 2005.

[114] C. Schmitt, The Concept of the Political. New Brunswick: Rutgers University Press, 1976.

[115] M. Lombard and T. Ditton, At the heart of it all: The concept of presence. *Journal of Computer Mediated-Communication   [On-line],   (1997),   3(2),   Available: http://www.ascusc.org/jcmc/vol3/issue2/lombard.html.

[116] J. Searle, Intentionality: An essay in the philosophy of mind. New York: Cambridge University Press, 1983.

[117] E. Ochs and L. Capps, Living narrative. Creating lives in everyday storytelling. Cambridge, MA: Harvard University Press, 2001.

[118] L. Anolli, S.J. Duncan, M. Magnusson and G. Riva (eds.), The hidden structure of interaction: From neurons to culture patterns. Amsterdam: IOS Press, 2005.

From Communication to Presence
G. Riva et al. (Eds.)
IOS Press, 2006

4 Presence as a Dimension of Communication: Context of Use and the Person

John WATERWORTH, Eva L. WATERWORTH

Abstract. We claim that presence is elicited most strongly when information is presented as an inhabitable, external world. Technical developments that permit this, such as the creation of interactive, immersive virtual environments herald a profound change in how people relate to sources of information, and how they communicate. This change has psychological, social and cultural effects. It has been claimed that in many ways, our relationship to information becomes that of our ancestral, pre-literate relationship to the physical world. By this view, we are heading for a post-literate future of body-based communication. But this view is too simple, since information must serve a variety of purposes, and how much presence is desirable in a communicative situation depends on many factors, including the communication devices available, the intended use and the context of use. In addition, differences between individuals, such as personality, as well as physical and psychological state, will affect how readily presence is invoked and also its impact on the individual concerned. In this chapter, we expand on the general notion of presence as a dimension of communication, and how this perspective can inform an understanding of designed variations in presence as a function of use, context, and individual psychological factors.

Contents

4.1 Introduction: Presence as Consciously Being in an External World

Our theoretical stance suggests that presence originated as the feeling of something happening to an organism from outside rather than from within (see also the chapter by Riva in this volume). In other words, it distinguishes self from other. In complex organisms such as humans, presence has evolved into the ability to distinguish external, perceived events from internal, imagined or otherwise internally-modeled events. This is still a vital distinction, because imagined events evoke the same emotional responses as external events; otherwise we would be unable to evaluate the desirability of planned actions and possible outcomes, or learn by contemplating past mistakes.

Unfortunately, terminological and other confusions about what comprises presence, and what does not, have impeded progress in the field. At the current time, no unifying theory of presence is possible, because the word "presence" is being used differently by different researchers. Perhaps we need different words for these different meanings, as Slater suggested [1].

As he suggests, what Slater means by presence could, perhaps more accurately, be labeled *pretence*. According to Websters online dictionary, this means "An artful or simulated semblance". This is consistent with his earlier [2] definition of presence as:

"the total response to being in a place, and to being in a place with other people. The 'sense of being there' is just one of many signs of presence - and to use it as a definition or a starting point is a category error: somewhat like defining humor in terms of a smile" (p. 7).

The problem with this is that it begs the questions: which place, and what response? If presence (in a virtual environment) is the total response to a simulation, as compared to the response to the physical environment being simulated, then what about fictional virtual environments? Can we not measure presence in them? And if no comparison with reality is involved, how can something as unspecific as "total response" be quantified? This view seems to boil down to the most common everyday meaning of presence, of being physically present somewhere. But in this case, one can be present while mentally elsewhere or nowhere - say, on the phone, solving a difficult cross-word puzzle, asleep, or even in a coma. This view seems to imply that presence is simple the degree of similarity with physical reality, not a thing that can be experienced in itself (*feeling* more or less present). In contrast, we view presence as a feeling.

Some researchers (e.g. [3, 4]) maintain that presence can be evoked equally well by imagining a world as by directly perceiving and acting in it (the "book problem"). But for us, presence is the feeling of "being there" in the present, the here and now of the physical or a virtual world. The feeling one gets from absorption in an internal world (a novel, a fantasy, or whatever) is quite different, which is why healthy people almost never confuse the two [5, 6]).

In an internal imagined world the person does not experience the same degree of emotion, for example reading a scary text does not usually evoke the same degree of fear as the situation would when acting in a physical or a virtual world. Imagined worlds are often not related to real time; a book can be put down, a line of thought can be suspended until later. When reading the text of a book, one can only directly perceive the abstract symbols of written language. To make sense of those symbols, the reader must construct what is represented in internal, mental space.

We suggest that *presence* must be tied to the *present*, the here and now, real time world – that is, the *perceived* world of the body and its surroundings (in which in the perceiver is able to act). Its evolutionary purpose is to enable us to distinguish what is happening around us, now, from what we may create in our imagination - the external versus the internal. The extent to which a medium invoked presence therefore depends on the extent to which the information presented is presented as a external, perceivable world. We agree with Heeter [7] that "Presence occurs during periods of time when cognition (processes such as perception, attention, learning, thought and affect ...) is closely tied to current perceptual stimuli.".

Of course, any useful definition must exclude things, and a useful definition of presence must have implications for what is not presence [8]. This has been termed "*absence*", a state of absorption in an internal world [9, 5] detached from the current perceptual flow. By introducing the concept of "absence", presence can be distinguished from other concepts with which it is sometimes confused, including engagement, attention, or even consciousness itself.

A counter argument is sometimes made [4], that we experience high presence when dreaming, when we are not perceiving or acting in the external world (the "dream state problem"). We suggest that dreaming while asleep is a special case ("dream presence"), in that our motor systems are immobilized while we dream to prevent damage to ourselves and those around us. In the rare cases that this defense fails, the results are shocking: we may wake up in a state of paralysis (failure to turn the defense mechanism off), or we may act out deeds totally against our normal waking nature (failure to turn the defense mechanism on); see for example [10]. When dreaming we do - by definition - mistake the internal for the external because, we suggest, the presence mechanism is suspended when dreaming, along with motor responses.

Organisms must be attentive to relevant perceptions of the current external world in order to carry out successful actions in that world. Action in the world requires information that is not available from imagination. At the same time, communication seems to rely on a degree of abstraction from the world; of mental reflection in relation to possible or actual action. We cannot direct our attention fully to both action in the world and communication about that action or other possible actions, and communication itself can be seen as a form of action.

We can see several common psychological problems, for example PTSD, depression, phobia, panic attacks, as examples of a maladjustment of the normal presence mechanism, which may be set too high or too low for the needs of the individual concerned. The power of presence – as we define it – in psychotherapy stems from the ability to override and reset this faulty mechanism, either by adjusting it upwards or downwards. What is too much or too little presence also depends on the individual concerned and we discuss this aspect, especially, in subsection 4.5.2.

The power of presence is that it ensures that we orient ourselves to significant external events, and we describe in more detail in the next section how this relates to its evolutionary function. The danger is that presence evoked by communication forms, by orientating us towards synthesized external events, may distract us from significant real events in the physical world in which we are located. We discuss this point further in subsection 4.5.1, on the importance of communicative contexts.

4.2 The Three Layers of Presence

Riva, Waterworth and Waterworth [6] present a model of presence as consisting of three potentially contributing layers: proto presence, core presence, and extended presence (see Figure 1), based on Damasio's neurological account of the evolution of the human psyche ([11, 12]).

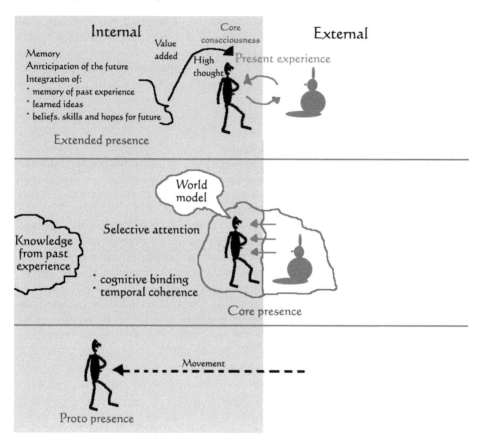

Figure 1. The three layers of presence (from [6], with permission)

Proto presence is based in embodiment, of what is the self versus what is not, and depends on the level of sensori-motor coupling. Core presence depends on the ongoing conscious perception of the current state of the world in which a person finds herself, of being in a perceived world. In contrast, extended presence depends on the cognition of relations between the current situation and past or imagined future situations, of the self in relation to what is happening in the world.

Unless core presence is invoked, the overall level of experienced presence will be relatively low. The other layers may reinforce core presence, or detract from it. Proto presence is determined only by form of information experienced, core presence by both form and content, and extended presence only by content.

It is not a simple matter to create the illusion of being in a computer-created reality, to be convincing at all three levels of the psyche. While significant progress has been made in recent years with specific kinds of virtual environment, current approaches are unlikely ever to generate a general solution to this problem.

Mimicking natural interactivity in an immersive environment involves rapid response times between a medium and its user, and often involves detailed inspectability of aspects of any displayed information. Proto presence has the most demanding technological requirements, and was the last of the three layers to be addressed through media. In a virtual world this is sometimes known as "spatial presence" and requires the tracking of body parts and appropriate updating of displays. Core presence is based largely on vividness of perceptible displays. This is equivalent to "sensory presence" (e.g., in non-immersive mediated environments) and requires good quality, preferably stereographic, graphics and other displays. The extent to which these two levels are integrated produces what is usually called degree of immersion. If proto presence is not invoked appropriately, for example with poor or slow coupling between body movements and display changes, it will detract from the overall sense of presence in a mediated experience.

Extended presence relies on working memory ([13, 14], see also [12]), which can be seen as the "active scratchpad" of mental [15]. It allows us to consider the significance and consequences of events. When this cognitive work is applied to the current external situation, presence will be reinforced; but when applied to other mental content, it will lower the overall sense of presence.

An additional factor that affects the level of presence experienced is the type and intensity of the emotions that are evoked. In tests conducted in a virtual environment called the Exploratorium [16] the results indicates that people felt much more present in the Inferno (a scary, hellish place) than in Paradiso (a relaxing heavenly place). The Exploratorium was developed as a so called mood device, and the aim is to induce different kinds of moods via technology. The intention of the Inferno is to elicit anxiety and in Paradiso the intention is to induce calm [17]. The intensity of an emotion is the level of activation or the level of arousal [18]. It seems that more intense negative emotions tend to elicit a higher degree of presence; most likely due to the instinct for self preservation. Emotions such as disgust, fear, and anger will tend to elicit a high degree of presence, whereas emotions such as tranquility, motherly feelings and grief elicit low level presence. In general, more intense positive emotions do not evoke higher levels of presence, whereas more intense negative emotions do.

According to our three-layer model, the overall presence level depends on how well integrated the cognitive system is to focus on the environment around the individual. Emotion can affect this in several different ways, for example, by creating an arousing effect that orientates the individual to attend to the environment (stimulating presence) from the bottom up. On the other hand, emotion induced at the extended layer of the psyche may increase attention to the environment or reduce it, depending on whether the content is associated with the current environment or opposed to it.

4.3 Presence and Time Perception

Variations in the ongoing experience of being-in-the-world can be seen as reflecting the changing ways in which we deal with information, from the physical world and through media. When vigilantly on the look out for the occurrence of a specific event

- say the arrival of a loved one at a pre-arranged, public meeting place - one's experience of being in the world is quite different from when one is lying on a sun bed, daydreaming, or reading a newspaper. In the first case, a large part of attention is devoted to sampling what is currently happening in the physical world; in both the second and the third cases, we pay little attention to the physical world. These differences affect how much presence we feel, and they also affect our perception of time-in-passing.

Like our varying sense of presence, our experience of time-in-passing is also a reflection of features of the information with which we are dealing. The picture is complicated by the fact that duration estimates change as a function of the time elapsed from the end of the test interval to the time the estimates are taken. A familiar example is that a period that seems slow in passing may appear very short in retrospect (vacations are a notorious case of this). Time seems to pass relatively quickly for us when working memory is heavily loaded, so that attending to information that requires significant conceptual work will tend to result in shorter duration estimates than when the ongoing memory load is lighter, other things being equal, and if the estimates are taken during or immediately after the test interval ([19]; see also [20]).

The relation between presence and experienced duration is a contentious issue. Different researchers disagree on how presence affects the subjective experience of duration. Some researchers have suggested that if the degree of experienced presence of an interval were high, then the subjective duration would tend to be short (e.g. [21, 22]). In contrast, Waterworth and Waterworth [5] found evidence that when there is a correlation it is positive, with long duration estimates corresponding to high presence judgements.

Taken together, our sense of presence and our sense of time-in-passing constitute a way of characterizing our ongoing relationship with information. When we are predominantly attending to an external world, we will tend to feel relatively high presence; and when we are mostly attending to an internal world or worlds we will tend to experience relatively low presence. We can thus envisage four paradigm cases: high presence with low working memory load, low presence with low working memory load, high presence with high working memory load, and low presence with high working memory load (see Table 1):

Table 1. Being-in-the-world: presence and time perception

	External world focus	**Internal world focus**
Low working memory load	Watching the sun set (High presence/slow time)	Daydreaming (Low presence/slow time)
High working memory load	Climbing a difficult rock face (High presence/fast time)	Solving a logical puzzle (Low presence/fast time)

If time-in-passing depends on ongoing working memory load (also referred to as "conscious processing load" or CPL), whereas presence depends only on the internal/external focus of attention, we would expect no correlation between the two. In fact, there is some evidence that subjective presence ratings and estimates of elapsed duration are correlated, but not in a simple way.

Waterworth and Waterworth [5] found that different versions of a media production elicited different levels of presence, depending on the degree of abstraction of the information presentation (see Figure 2). All versions told the same story and were isomorphic in terms of events and timings. As indicated in the figure, four media streams were used:

- a real/concrete stream (filmed events with natural soundtrack - the *Camera* stream),
- a real/abstract stream (text, sketches and spoken words describing events - the *Words* stream),
- a virtual/concrete stream (a detailed animated 3D graphics version, with synthesised sound effects - the *3D* stream),
- and the virtual/abstract stream (a wireframe 3D with text labels and stylised synthetic sound effects - the *3D Wired* stream).

In this study, we found that when the abstraction level of an experience increased, the feeling of presence decreased, and vice versa, and that when the subjective experience of presence increased, experienced duration also increased, but only under certain circumstances. Figure 3 shows the relationship between presence ratings and duration estimates over four test durations (23, 50, 77 and 104s) for one of the media streams. The two sets of data were significantly (though modestly) correlated, but this was only true for one media stream, the *3D Wired* condition.

We suggest that our three-layer model of presence (described in Section 2) can help explain this kind of situation-specific correlation. As already mentioned, the model proposes three layers of the psyche that may contribute to our overall sense of presence in a situation, only one of which relies on working memory. Variations in the contribution of this layer ("extended presence") will be correlated with changes in duration estimates, whereas variations in the contribution of other layers will not. This is indicated by the lack of variation in duration estimates across rows in Table 1, compared with the lack of variation in presence across columns.

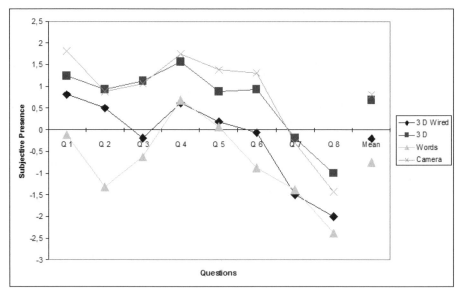

Figure 2. Subjective Presence for Different Media Forms
(from Waterworth and Waterworth, 2003)

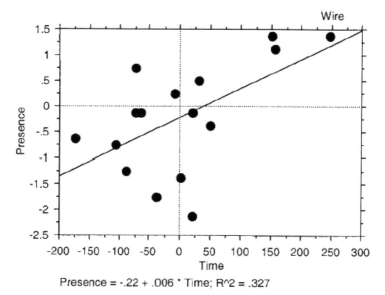

Presence = -.22 + .006 * Time; R^2 = .327

Figure 3. Scattergram, including regression (from [5], with permission)

Our interpretation of these results is that only in the *3D Wired* condition were both core and extended presence invoked. Hence, only in this condition were duration estimates and presence ratings found to be correlated.

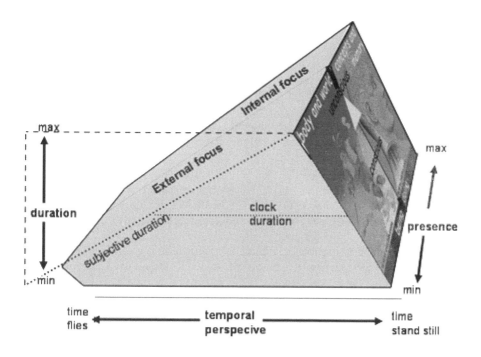

Figure 4. Presence level and temporal perspective

Various extraordinary states of consciousness can be interpreted in terms of the combination of the two dimensions depicted in Table 1 and Figure 4: presence level and temporal perspective. When experienced presence is high, and working memory is heavily loaded (so that time seems to fly) this may correspond to what has been called "the flow experience" [23]. A literally ecstatic state (out from the internal, into the external), in contrast, may refer to a combination of external focus and low memory load, when presence is high and time seems to stand still. When low presence and high working memory load are combined, a state of absent-mindedness with automatized actions prevails; attention is directed almost exclusively to the internal and time passes quickly. And when low presence is combined with low working memory load, the individual may be experiencing a trance-like state, with an internal focus, but processing only the simplest of conceptions perhaps, for example, mentally repeating a simple mantra.

4.4 Dimensions of Communication

We have suggested elsewhere, and most researchers would surely agree, that the form in which information is presented will have an effect on the level of presence experienced, with more abstract forms tending to elicit lower levels of presence. It is also generally accepted that the content of information will affect the level of experienced presence. (The usual, though not universal, view is that we will feel more presence with engaging information than with boring information, while our own position is that content that stimulates more interest in the currently-present environment will raise the level of experienced presence). Here, we suggest that the level of presence elicited by the presentation of information in a particular medium comprises a necessary dimension for understanding the cognitive effect of messages conveyed through a given medium (see also the chapters by Mantovani and Riva in this volume).

Table 2 presents a rough first attempt at tabularizing the different dimensions that might comprise an adequate characterization of a particular communication form. The first dimension is the classic Shannon and Weaver [24] formulation where information carried by a communication channel is measured in terms of the reduction of uncertainty, which is inversely related to redundancy.

The second, storytelling, refers to the fact that any communication channel can be used to convey different kinds of story, where a narrative can be specified in terms of the structure of the elements of information in a particular story (a simple example might be: introduce characters, set up scenario, present an anomaly/problem, resolve problem, present effect on characters, conclude).

A third dimension is the mood induced by the information. One characteristic of this is whether the receiver is stimulated to move away from or towards the information source, and how strongly. This dimension can perhaps be most easily measured in terms of valence (pleasant versus unpleasant) and arousal (level of activation).

We see presence level induced by a communication as a potentially useful fourth dimension. This is characterized as the level of interpretation needed cognitively to deal with information, and can be partially specified in terms of cognitive load. By our view, cognitive load will tend to be inversely related to the level of presence experienced, since it is a reflection of the abstractness of a medium. But locus of attention is another important factor.

Table 2. Four Dimensions of Communication

	Measurement	**Characteristic**
1. Information carried	Reducing uncertainty in bits	Redundancy
2. Telling a story	Structural characterization	Fictional or factual narrative
3. Mood induced	Valence and arousal	Action or inaction Attraction or repulsion
4. Presence level	Cognitive load and focus (inside-outside)	Level(s) of interpretation (internal-external focus)

While high cognitive loads will interfere more with other types of attentional task than low cognitive loads, two perceptual (potentially presence-evoking) tasks will interfere with each other even though each imposes a relatively low cognitive load. In other words, presence cannot be viewed as a simple result of redundancy. A concrete, perceptual presentation of information - say an animation that portrays a simple narrative - will interfere less with other more abstract tasks than, say, a textual description. But if the individual is already focusing her attention on the external world, as when driving, there will be a conflict between the one perceptual task and the other.

The appropriate level of mediated presence thus depends on both internal and external factors, on what the observer is thinking, but also on what she is perceiving and doing in any external world or worlds.

4.5 Communicational Context, Presence and the Person

4.5.1 Communication Forms in Relation to the Communicative Context

Communication plays an essential part in today's society, and much communication now takes place via different kinds of media, such as telephones, email, chat, text messages or traditional mail letters. The most expressive way to communicate, however, is through person to person contact, where the sender and receiver are in the same physical space. When this is the case the communication is conducted via several senses, including the words used, facial and postural expressions, the intonation and speed of the speech and so on. In most mediated communication there is a much greater potential for misunderstandings and misinterpretations due to the lack of the expressions via multiple senses. In other words, presence in communication reduces the potential for misunderstandings.

But high presence requires and demands a high level of attention. Depending on the context in which communication is taking place, this may or may not be appropriate. For example, most mobile phone applications should not demand much attention, since the user is often engaged in other activities concurrently. In contrast, when one is separated from a loved one and wants to communicate richly, the highest possible level of presence may be preferred - by, for example, including sight, sound, tactile feedback, and perhaps even aroma.

An important feature of modern communication patterns is their lack of symmetry. By this, we mean that the different partners in a communication are often in different physical situations, which may have very different characteristics. And increasingly, they may be using different types of communication device. In two completely different situations the same message could be interpreted very differently.

For example, imagine one person waiting for a flight, who receives a text message from a loved one as he is waiting. He has plenty of time to compose a heartfelt reply, but starts his message with a playfully provocative remark. As he is about to respond further, he hears an announcement to the effect that his flight is actually at a different gate, quite some way away. He realizes he will have move quickly to get to the gate in time. But he has no time to finish the SMS he is writing, nor even to explain his current urgent problem. Because he was expected to be in contact before catching the long flight, he sends the partially composed SMS and sets off for the correct gate. But the receiver, unaware of the context in which the message was composed, completely misunderstands the sender's intent and is offended by the communication.

The above problem could potentially be addressed in several ways, taking account of both presence and the potential for monitoring emotional responses. A communication medium with greater presence would make the problem less likely to arise. By definition, more presence evoked by a communication form means more information about the present situation external to a sender is being transmitted. In a phone message, for example, the sender could explain the situation more quickly, while dashing to the correct location. And perhaps more importantly, the sender would also receive indications of the sender's true state, through paralinguistic cues such as breathing style, intonation, pitch and so on, as well as acoustic information from the surroundings. When video capability is also available, this tendency will be further enhanced, through the availability of facial expressions, visual features of the surroundings, and so on.

A different approach would be to use sensor technology to monitor the sender's physiological state directly. Such information could be presented to the receiver in a variety of different forms, and transmitted as an attachment to any form of communication. Although, in this case, the text message would be the same, the attachment would convey the fact that the sender was in an agitated state at the time the message was sent.

State-sensitive communication devices seem a promising way to cater for the fact that different individuals prefer different levels of presence. This may be because of the personal characteristics of the person concerned, which we discuss further in subsection 4.5.2, below. Contextual factors will also affect a person's state, and one of the most useful ways of tracking context may be through tracking the person's state, although without also tracking physical context this is open to misinterpretation and could be potentially hazardous.

4.5.2 Communication, Presence and the Individual

Since presence is, for us, a reflection of the extent to which an individual is engaged with (and feels able to act in) an external world rather than with an internally modeled world, we would expect personality factors that are known to affect this relation to also affect experienced presence. For example, we might expect that extrovert personalities in general experience higher presence than introvert personalities. Similarly, elderly people might be expected to experience less presence in common situations than the young.

Although relatively little work has been carried out in this area, there is some evidence to support our conjectures. Laarni et al. [25] present evidence of a positive relationship between experienced presence and extraversion, impulsivity and self-transcendence. Since Eysenck's [26] characterization of the extravert was of a person who was predominantly engaged with events in the external world, rather than the internal world of thoughts and imaginings, this is to be expected from our own view of presence as a focus on action in the present, external environment. The same is true of impulsivity, since according to Laarni et al. [25] impulsive individuals are better able to shift their attention in external space. And it has been previously suggested that the highest levels of presence are associated with self-transcendence, with a loss of self consciousness (e.g. [6, 27]).

This is not to say that individual differences in imaginative skill do not predict the tendency to feel presence, to some extent, as Sas and O'Hare [28] suggested. They conclude that "the more users think, feel and act in the remote world [......] the greater the sense of presence they will experience" (page 535). And, clearly, we do not really act in imagined worlds. Indeed, the point of imagination can be seen as the testing of possible actions without carrying them out [12].

The more general concept of absorption: a characteristic of the individual that involves an openness to experience emotional and cognitive alterations across a variety of situations [29], also seems to be important in predicting the tendency to experience presence. Both presence and absence can be seen as absorption states, the former based around the current perceptual flow, the latter around imagined events and situations. This may explain the suggested relationship between the tendency to experience presence and hypnotic suggestibility [28].

In our view, hypnotic suggestibility should be related to a tendency to experience either intense presence or intense absence or, more likely, both. The absorption state underlying hypnosis can be seen as a focusing of attention on a single object (and in such a state duration seems to stretch - time "stands still"; [20, 30]). But since this single object of attention may be internal or external, the state may result in extreme presence *or* absence.

We suggest a tentative set of individual characteristics and states that we would expect to be associated with high presence, and another set associated with relatively low presence, as set out in Table 3. An important implication of these differences is that communication forms will have differing impacts on individuals with different personalities, or in differing states (and personality can to at least some extent be seen as a tendency to be in certain states).

From these differences follow a large set of possibilities for misunderstandings and miscommunications through existing communication media such as e-mails, phone calls, text messages and traditional letters. Many people are uncomfortable with phone conversations and prefer less immediate and personal forms such as e-mails. But e-mails are often misinterpreted, especially in terms of the attitude or intentions of the sender. Conversely, there is a set of people who prefer phone calls, and this is likely to be related to a preference for less abstract communication forms - and less abstract forms by our account will tend to evoke more presence. Another important factor is whether a communication form is *synchronous* or *asynchronous*, and this will also vary between individuals and also situations. When the variation is between individuals, this may reflect preferences for specific *rates* of information exchange, amongst other things. By our definition, a communication form that elicits more presence will be slower than one which elicits less.

Table 3. Presence in Relation to Personal Characteristics and States (tentative)

Low Presence	High Presence
Old	Young
Awareness of themes, stories	Awareness of perceptual details
Sensory deprivation	Rich sensory stimulation
Introversion	Extroversion
Depression	Mania
Sedatives, alcohol	Stimulants, psychedelics
High error on vigilance task	Low error on vigilance tasks
Infrequent stimulus sampling	Frequent stimulus sampling
Long reaction times	Short reaction times
Ideological bias	Experiential bias

With existing media, the form is largely fixed. And in synchronous communications this means that the rate of information exchange is also largely fixed. In the following subsection we discuss the potential for creating new types of communication technology offering adjustable degrees of presence in use.

4.5.3 Designing for Adaptable Asymmetric Presence in Interpersonal Communication

By the three-layer, evolutionary account of presence [6] discussed in Paragraph 2 a typical, unexceptional level of presence arises from a split of attentional resources between layers of differing content, with some attention being directed to the current external situation and some to a different internal concern. Minimal presence, as we have suggested, results from an almost complete lack of integration of the three layers, such as is the case when attention is mostly directed towards contents of extended consciousness unrelated to the present external environment. By the same reasoning, maximal presence arises when proto consciousness, core consciousness and extended consciousness are focused on the same external situation or activity. Maximal presence thus results from the combination of all three layers with an abnormally tight focus on the same content (see Figure 5). Different ways of designing for maximal presence are outlined in [6].

Here we are concerned with designing communication devices for *appropriate* presence, rather than maximal presence. What is appropriate may depend on several factors, including the user's personality, her current contextual situation and purpose in using the device, and perhaps her internal state. We envisage a future in which the presence level induced by a communication is selectable, either deliberately by a communicant, or automatically by the device itself.

Imagine a headset conveying information to the eyes and ears, used for a variety of communicative functions, including messaging, telephone calls and conferencing. According to user choice or system sensitivity to context, the presence level could be adjusted to take account of the wearer's external situation and internal state.

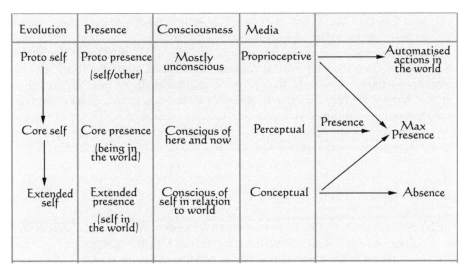

Evolution	Presence	Consciousness	Media	
Proto self	Proto presence (self/other)	Mostly unconscious	Proprioceptive	Automatised actions in the world
Core self	Core presence (being in the world)	Conscious of here and now	Perceptual	Presence → Max Presence
Extended self	Extended presence (self in the world)	Conscious of self in relation to world	Conceptual	Absence

Figure 5. Layers, media and mental states (from [6], with permission)

Adjusting the presence level would effectively amount to including more or fewer of the three layers shown in Figure 5. A mostly conceptual media form would yield low levels of presence which would permit the receiver to also attend to perceptual events in her surroundings, and to carry out actions not related to the communication. A person listening to a recorded message on a hands-free mobile phone while simultaneously selecting grocery at the local store is one example of this. At the other end of the spectrum, participating in a distributed virtual reality in which one interacts in an embodied way, via gestures, speech, and so on, would tend to demand such a high level of presence that no other activities would be possible.

Currently available, low-cost sensor technology brings the realistic possibility of a wearable system that can detect physiological (and thus emotional) state, and use this to adjust the form of the communication. Existing work on detection includes functioning systems such as Thought Technologies' Procomp family, Mindmedia's Nexus device, and BodyMedia's SenseWear system. Any such system would probably need the ability to learn the responses of its wearer to set the presence level appropriately. Low-cost interaction devices that are sensitive to breathing and body orientation also already exist, for example our own "Body Joystick" interface [16]. The trend is likely to be for more asymmetry in communication forms, with each participant likely to have a personalized way of sending and receiving communications (and these need not be the same). Level of presence needed or preferred by a particular person in a specific context is a potentially important component of this trend.

Increasing presence, though, need not always be a function of widening the communicational bandwidth. What is communicated may be abstract, but its realization could be highly concrete. Virtual realization allows the possibility for simulating a richly presence-inducing form from a highly abstract communication. We thus see two ways in which communicational presence can be adapted: by moderating bandwidth and by modifying the richness of virtual realization. This reflects the fact that presence may be enhanced by richer access to physical *or* virtual reality, even though the latter may be largely fictional. We can envisage a time when communicants may choose not only how rich a form their side of a communication may take, but also the extent to which the form reflects physical reality versus fiction.

Although presence arose as a feeling enabling the discrimination of the internal and imagined from the external and physical, new media allow the imagined to be rendered as external. Currently, the presence mechanism allows us to distinguish the physical from the virtual, because of technical limitations in virtual realization. But as the technology continues to improve, to the point that all three layers of presence are accurately addressed, we will have no psychological means to separate the physical from the virtual. A technology-based solution will then be required.

4.6 Conclusions

The level of presence invoked by, or required for understanding, a given medium is an important dimension of communicating through that medium. The presence parameter may vary according to several factors, including the available technology, the required use, and the context of such use. Individual factors such as personality will also impact on the ease with which different levels of presence can be induced, and also their desirability.

We have related these factors to what we consider to be a plausible model of the origins of the human presence mechanism and its current psychological function as a faculty for internal-external discrimination. We have also discussed possible inter-relationships between psychological, social and cultural aspects of viewing presence as a dimension of communication. Our overall aim has been to show how presence forms an essential element of our relationship with information, whether this resides - or is - the physical world or a virtual environment specifically designed for communication. Viewing presence a dimension of communication also sheds light on a variety of ways in which people may have differing experiences - of each other and of the world around them - even when apparently communicating efficiently.

4.7 References

[1]   M. Slater, Presence or pretence? Panel presentation at PRESENCE 2003, Aalborg, October 2003.
[2]   M. Slater, Siggraph 2002 Course Notes on Understanding Virtual Environments: Immersion, Presence and Performance. San Antonio, TX: ACM - Siggraph.
[3]   F. Biocca, F., Communication within virtual reality: Creating a space for research. *Journal of Communication, 42*(4), 5-22, 1992.
[4]   F. Biocca, Can we resolve the book, the physical reality, and the dream state problems? *Presentation at EU Presence Research Conference.* Venice, Italy. May 7, 2003.

[5]   J. A. Waterworth, & E. L. Waterworth, Being and Time: Judged Presence and Duration as a Function of Media Form. *Presence: Teleoperators and Virtual Environments*, 12 (5), 495-511, 2003.

[6]   G. Riva, J.A Waterworth & E. L. Waterworth, The Layers of Presence: a bio-cultural approach to understanding presence in natural and mediated environments. *Cyberpsychology and Behavior*, 7 (4) 402-416, 2004.

[7]   C. Heeter, Reflections on Real Presence by a Virtual Person. *Presence: Teleoperators and Virtual Environments*, 12(4), 335-345, 2003.

[8]   L. Floridi, Exploring the informational nature of presence. *Opening invited keynote address at* 7th Annual International Workshop on Presence 2004. Polytechnic University of Valencia, Spain, 13-14-15 October 2004.

[9]   E. L. Waterworth & J. A. Waterworth, Focus, Locus, and Sensus: The three dimensions of virtual experience. *Cyberpsychology and Behavior*, 4 (2), 203-213, 2001.

[10]   M. M. Ohayon, J. Zulley, C. Guilleminault and S. Smirne, Prevalence and pathologic associations of sleep paralysis in the general population. *Neurology 52*: 1194, 1999.

[11]   A. Damasio, *Descartes' Error: Emotion, Reason and the Human Brain.* New York, USA: Penguin Putnam, 1994.

[12]   A. Damasio, *The Feeling of What Happens: Body, Emotion and the Making of Consciousness.* San Diego, CA: Harcourt Brace and Co, Inc, 1999.

[13]   G. J. Hitch & A. Baddeley, Verbal reasoning and working memory. *Quarterly Journal of Experimental Psychology*, 28, 603-631, 1976.

[14]   A. Baddeley, *Working Memory.* Oxford: Oxford University Press, 1986.

[15]   B. J. Baars, *A Cognitive Theory of Consciousness.* New York: Cambridge University Press, 1988.

[16]   E. L. Waterworth, M. Häggkvist, K. Jalkanen, S. Olsson, J. A. Waterworth and H. Wimelius, The Exploratorium: An Environment To Explore Your Feelings. *Psychnology*, 1 (3), 189-201, 2003.

[17]   S. Olsson and E. L. Waterworth, Does the Exploratorium Evoke Emotion? *Proceedings of Design and Emotion 2004*, Ankara, Turkey, July 2004.

[18]   R. Plutchik, A general psychoevolutionary theory of emotion. In R- Plutchik & H. Kellerman (Eds.), *Emotion: Theory, research and experience: Vol 1. Theories of emotion*, New York: Academic, 1980.

[19]   J. A. Waterworth, *The Influence of Variations in Cognitive Processing on the Perception of Time.* PhD thesis, University of Hertfordshire, UK. Available through the British Lending Library (Accession no. D50267/84), 1984.

[20]   M. G. Flaherty, *A Watched Pot: How we experience time.* New York: New York Univerity Press, 1999.

[21]   W. A. Ijsselsteijn, I. Bierhoff and Y. Slangen-de Kort, Duration Estimation and Presence. *Paper presented at Presence 2001*, Philadelphia, May 21-23 2001.

[22]   M. Lombard, *Presence Measurement*, 2000; Online: http://nimbus.temple.edu/~mlombard/Presence/measure.htm

[23]   M. Csikszentmihalyi, *Flow: The psychology of optimal experience.* New York: HarperCollins, 1990.

[24]   C. E. Shannon & W. Weaver, *A Mathematical Model of Communication.* Urbana, IL: University of Illinois Press, 1949.

[25]   J. Laarni, N. Ravaja, T. Saari & Hartmann, Personality-related differences in subjective presence. Proceedings of Presence 2004. Valencia, Spain, October 2004.

[26]   H. J. Eysenck, *The biological basis of personality.* Springfield, IL, USA: Charles C. Thomas, 1967.

[27]   J. A. Waterworth, E. L. Waterworth and J. Westling, Presence as Performance: the mystique of digital participation. Proceedings of Presence 2002. Porto, Portugal, October 9-11, 2002.

[28]   C. Sas & G. M. P. O'Hare, Presence Equation: An Investigation into Cognitive Factors Underlying Presence, *Presence: Teleoperators and Virtual Environments*, 12 (5), October 2003.

[29]   M. SM. Roche & K. M. McConkey, Absorption: Nature, assessment and correlates. *Journal of Personality & Social Psychology*, 59(1), 91-101, 1990.

[30]   G. Quarrick, *Our sweetest hours: Recreation and the mental state of absorption.* Jefferson, USA: McFarland, 1989.

From Communication to Presence
J. Riva et al. (Eds.)
IOS Press, 2006

5   Media Presence, Consciousness and Dreaming

Henry J. MOLLER, Joseph BARBERA

Abstract: Advances in media and communication technology have opened up new avenues for understanding consciousness through observation of behaviour in virtual environments. A convergence of progress in cognitive neuroscience and computer science should consider the powerful role of conscious and unconscious states as an interface between self and virtual worlds. In this chapter, we review the premise of presence as a dimension of consciousness from both a phenomenological and neuroscientific perspective. Working from a model in which dreaming consciousness is considered the most archetypal form of media technology, dreams are discussed as a useful metaphor for virtual reality. We argue that presence can be equally compelling whether experienced via self-generated simulation during the process of dreaming, or through an externally generated media simulation. Attempts to use media technology in a therapeutic context need to consider clinical aspects of mechanisms involved in both normal and clinical/pathological aspects of consciousness. A speculative therapeutic approach, "dream simulation therapy", is discussed as a future possible area of study. Dreaming consciousness reminds us that the key factor in approaching an ultimate technology-mediated presence experience is the sum rather than its parts: a subjective/affective state of being.

Contents

5.1 Introduction

Advances in media and communication technology have opened up new avenues for understanding consciousness through observation of behaviour in human-machine interfaces, described as "virtual environments" once accepted by the user as indistinguishable from "real" experiences [1]. Has the time come to place the phenomenon of presence as a unique state of consciousness in the context of current neuroscientific understanding? As multidisciplinary research of presence continues to evolve, we propose that valuable lessons about the elusive nature of defining this phenomenon can be learned from the field of somnology.

Some would argue that dreams are in fact both the most vestigial yet also the most sophisticated virtual environments that our perceptions allow for. Sleep research has greatly advanced our evidence-based scientific understanding of conscious states, allowing for a unified model of the phenomenology and neuroscience of dreaming. Particularly within the past decade, a movement has emerged to reunite the more descriptive/psychoanalytic with the neuroanatomic/psychophysiologic approaches to consciousness [2-5], recognizing that rather than representing competing theories of Mind/Brain, an integrated approach is able to incorporate complementary elements of both to form a more unified picture. Central to this advanced understanding has been the study of the phenomenology and neurobiology of dreams. Following this approach, we review here the premise of presence as a dimension of consciousness, whether experienced via self-generated simulation during the process of dreaming, or through an externally generated media simulation. A speculative therapeutic approach, "dream simulation therapy", is proposed as a future possible area of study of this field. Our intent is bridge what is currently known about consciousness vis-à-vis dreaming and media technology, particularly when used in a therapeutic context.

5.2 Dreaming Consciousness as Semiotic Experience

Marshall McLuhan boldly predicted a state where "We have extended our central nervous system itself in a global embrace, abolishing both space and time"[6]. More recently, Frank Biocca proclaimed:

"Virtual Environments have less to do with simulating physical reality per se, rather it simulates how the mind "perceives" physical reality. A cyclotron of the mind can only be created by perfectly simulating the medium of the mind." (p. 2, [7]).

If a true state of "virtual reality" presence, indistinguishable from "physical" reality can be considered the ultimate communication experience, then from an evolutionary perspective, dreaming can be understood as the most archetypal form of virtual reality. Let us consider how we define what qualifies as media communication. Before virtual environments, there was the less well-defined concept of "multimedia". Before multimedia, there were media stimulating individual senses, in particular, the visual or auditory senses. Before we were able to create these through technologies such as cameras, audio recording devices or even the printing press, hand-produced facsimiles were used in attempts to communicate the sensory, emotional and cognitive/semantic aspects of experiences. The tradition of interpersonal communication in humans has always been about one individual's attempt to recreate, re-enact or describe their experiences to another individual. These experiences, encoded in infinitely interconnected "bits" of perceptual inputs constantly modify our pre-existing states of consciousness, consisting of memories, learned behaviours and expectations. As will be discussed later, there are some theories regarding evolutionary advantages of dreams used as an ancient biological defense and communication mechanism to make sense of and prepare for a variety of "real-world" experiences during the earliest human eras of communication [8,9].

Much of psychoanalytic theory and practice, with its historical emphasis on decoding complex messages embedded in our dreams, is in fact based on the deciphering of communication between self and the outside world, but this approach has fallen out of favour in the scientific community largely because of lack of provable hypotheses. However, the field has left as a residue a fascination amongst clinicians, philosophers and popular culture regarding hidden meanings of dreams   [10]. Conversely, within discussions of semiotic aspects of multimedia communication, representational systems, both in the aural and visual modalities are ultimately processed within the central nervous system (CNS) through complex decoding processes. For example, Jerome Bruner [11] classified semiotic systems into three types:

1.   enactive- based on physical movement and learning of the responses (e.g. actions required for riding a bicycle).
2.   iconic – depending on imagery and perception (e.g. photographs)
3.   symbolic- using symbols which do not have a perceptual relationship with concepts they signify (e.g. words, a traffic light)

Analogous to our later discussion of the phenomenology of dream mentation and phenomenology in normal and pathological states, communication through dreams, whether understood as a form of self-to-self or environment-to-self communication can also be understood to employ this type semiotic organization, all of which ultimately serve as an unconscious conduit towards learning and information processing.

Semantics aside, a neuroscientific understanding of presence remains in its infancy. In a recent review of the taxonomy of presence from a communications perspective [12], Lee comments:

"in addition to usual pencil-and-paper measures of presence, we need to develop novel and unobtrusive measures of presence based on physiological responses, behavioural reactions, brain waves, and so on." (p. 47).

That the scientific field of sleep research concerns itself intimately with the study of brainwaves in relation to conscious experiences is inarguable. There have also been exciting recent parallels to established models of consciousness research in terms of attempts to describe experiences in synthetic environments in neurophysiologic terms. While the field of somnology remains a relatively recent discipline, great advances have been made in terms of describing neural processes underlying the processes that allow for the unique perceptual experience of dreaming and other states of consciousness. By describing these in some detail, we aim to familiarize an audience truly interested in advancing the cognitive neuroscience of dreaming, or as per Antti Revonsuo's description, "inner presence" [9].

5.3 Dream Phenomenology

Wikipedia defines a dream as "the experience of images, sounds/voices, words, thoughts or sensations during sleep, with the dreamer usually not being able to influence the experience" [13]. The broadness of this definition is presumably meant to mitigate argument, although some may criticize its very all-inclusiveness and lack of specificity. Neilson for example distinguishes between non-specific "cognitive activity" in sleep, which may consist of "static visual images, thinking, reflecting, bodily feelings or vague fragmentary impressions"; from dreaming proper which is characterized by "sensory hallucinations, emotions, storylike or dramatic progression and bizarreness"[14]. Likewise, Hobson et al. argue against a broad definition for dreaming as "any mental activity occurring in sleep" [15] and for a narrower definition as follows:

"Mental activity occurring in sleep characterized by vivid sensorimotor imagery that is experienced as waking reality despite such distinctive cognitive features as impossibility or improbability of time, place, person and actions; emotions, especially fear, elation and anger predominate over sadness, shame and guilt and sometimes reach sufficient strength to cause awakening; memory for even very vivid dreams is evanescent and tends to fade quickly upon awakening unless special steps are taken to retain it." (p. 3).

In fact there is no generally accepted definition of dreaming, with definitions varying from study to study or no definition being provided at all. Even less consensus has been reached with regard to the phenomenology of dreaming. This may be a consequence of the universality of the phenomenon in question: it would hardly seem necessary to define something that each of us experiences on a more or less nightly basis (much as some researchers refer to "consciousness" without fully explicating it). Alternatively it may be a tacit acknowledgment that dreaming is in essence a subjective phenomenon and potentially indefinable outside of this boundary.

We will, as a preliminary step, describe some of the phenomenological characteristics of dreaming, occasionally stating the obvious, since it is sometimes only in stating the obvious that the remarkableness of this nightly phenomenon becomes evident.

5.3.1 Sensory Experience

All sensory modalities may be experienced in dreams with visual being the most common, followed by auditory, kinesthetic, touch and to a significantly less degree gustatory and olfactory [16, 17, 18]. Hobson also emphasises the sense of continuous movement in dreams [19]. Sensations and perceptions in dreams are often described as "vivid", meaning they are experienced in a manner similar to waking life, or as "hallucinatory" meaning they are taken by the dreamer to be real.

The actual qualities of sensory experiences in sleep have been sparsely studied. Rechtschaffen and Buchignani studied the visual qualities of dreams by awakening subjects from rapid eye movement (REM) sleep and asking them to compare the visual imagery in their dreams to a series of photographs representing varying amounts of colour saturation, brightness/illumination, figure clarity, background clarity and overall hue [20]. The authors found that the visual qualities of most dreams (40%) were categorized by subjects as "normal" i.e. similar to external reality. Mild deviations, however, were not uncommon, particularly with regard to decreased color saturation and a loss of background detail. The authors speculate that the latter finding may be a function of dream processes focusing on cognitively important images (figures etc.) rather than less cognitively relevant background details. In other words, "high fidelity" is not a requirement of dreams in their simulation of reality.

Researchers in the 1950's had commonly reported that dreams were predominantly experienced in black and white, in contrast to earlier writers, and a marked change of opinion in the 1960's onward that suggested we dream predominantly in colour [21]. This may be a consequence of methodological differences between studies [22, 23]. Schwitzgebel, however, has put forth the intriguing hypothesis that the frequent reports of black and white dreams in the 1950's may have been the result of the prominence of black and white film media in the first half of the twentieth century [21]. Schwitzgebel repeated the methodology of a 1942 study on colour in dreams and found a significantly greater proportion of students in 2001 reported dreaming in colour in comparison with their 1942 counterparts [23]. Furthermore he found that cultural groups with longer histories of exposure to colour media also report more dreaming in colour [24]. The perception of colour in dreams would thus seem to be an example of media technology influencing our experience of dreaming, if not conscious experience in general. Schwitzgebel even goes so far as to suggest that as future media incorporates more "haptic" elements, the perceived presence of such elements in dreams (now considered rare) will likewise change [25].

That dream reality is not solely dependent on visual imagery is illustrated by reports of blind individuals that indicate the presence of vivid dreams in this group in the absence of visual imagery [22, 26]. Solms reported two cases of "non-visual dreaming" owing to brain lesion in the medial-temporal region, after having reviewed a number of similar cases in the literature [27].

5.3.2 Narrative Structure

A detailed analysis of dream content is beyond the scope of this review, but it is evident that dreams contain a full range of settings, characters, objects, activities and social interaction; in fact all of the elements that might be said to encompass waking experience [18, 28]. Of more importance to the phenomenology of dreaming is that such elements do not take the form of isolated images and events, but rather within the context of a "narrative structure" i.e. a *sequence* of perceptions taking on a storylike quality [29]. Furthermore, Strauch and Meier in a dream series analysis found that the dreamer was present in all dreams (the "Dream Self"), with the dreamer usually taking on an active role [18]. The narrative structure of dreams is thus generally from a first-person perspective, with the dreamer experiencing him- or herself as moving through an environment and interacting with various characters and objects.

Of relevance to interpersonal and transpersonal aspects of presence, social interactions seem to be particularly common in dreams [18, 28]. Aggressive interactions have typically been felt to be more common than friendly ones, with sexual interactions placing a distant third [28]. Affective state during wakefulness has been reported as often correlating with themes and affective state experienced during dreams [25]. Strauch and Meier described that most social interactions in dreams were verbal rather than action oriented and usually centred on everyday "concrete themes" [18].

5.3.3 Bizarreness

Bizarreness in dreams, or the presence of the unusual or impossible (in comparison with waking life) may occur both with respect to their form and content [18]. Bizarreness of form may occur as disruption or rapid changes in the temporal sequence of dream images and themes. Bizarreness in content is represented by unusual or improbable combination of people, places and objects [15, 18, 29, 31-34]. While some authors have emphasized bizarreness as a distinctive feature of dreaming [29], other have not. Strauch and Meier felt that while all elements of dream experience could be subject to bizarre admixtures, this was neither general nor dominant [18]. Reinsel et al. found a greater level of bizarreness in waking fantasy than in rapid eye movement (REM) sleep [32].

5.3.4 Thought Processes

Rechtschaffen described the "single-mindedness" of dreams [35], a term which can be thought of as encompassing several elements of thinking within dreams. "Self-reflection" in dreams is generally absent or at best reduced. The dreamer is not only unaware that the reality he or she is experiencing is a dream (except in rare cases of lucid dreaming), but thought processes in general are simplistic and focused on the immediate dream content or theme [15, 18, 35, 36]. Dreamers lack "autonoetic awareness" or an appreciation of themselves as extending through time, with a sense of a continuous presence being maintained [14]. Reasoning, when present, is "ad hoc", arising after the fact to explain a particular incongruency [34]. Even if one does allow for the differences between cognition in dreaming and wakefulness to be more quantitative rather than qualitative [35, 36], metacognition is generally deficient [37, 38]. Such a narrowing of thought processes would account for the overall sense of coherence and narrative structure present in a dream despite the presence of otherwise bizarre elements. It would also account for the uncritical or "delusional acceptance" of the dream experience as real [34], much reminiscent of a state of immersion experienced in a virtual environment simulation [1].

5.3.5 Emotions

Emotions, while often underreported in dream reports and under-recognized by dream researchers [28], appear to be a prominent if not ubiquitous component of dream experience [39]. Emotions in dreams may take the form of specific emotions or generalized mood states [18, 40]. Intense emotions such as fear and anger may be experienced more frequently than more subtle ones such as guilt and disgust, and dreamers usually report only one emotion at a time [18]. Emotions in dreams likely exhibit the same single-mindedness as thought processes with a similar lack of self-reflection. While negative emotions are often reported as being more prominent than positive emotions [28, 30, 39], this may be the result of methodological issues, which once corrected result in an equal balance of reported emotions [39]. Specific emotions may be more negative in waking consciousness, and generalized mood states more positive [18], though this may relate to the increased ability to accurately label affective states while awake.

Although common experience suggests that emotions in dreams may be incongruous or disproportionate with dream content (either exaggerated or deficient), some authors have contended that emotions are almost always appropriate to the dream plot and may even determine/integrate dream images and plot features [39]. Kahn et al. have shown that characters in dreams are often identified by the emotions they evoke in the dreamer [41]. Given the potential ubiquity and primacy of emotions in dream experience and its potential relevance to analogous emotional experiences in other forms of presence, including synthetic, it is surprising how relatively unstudied this aspect of dreaming has been.

5.3.6 Memory

Born and colleagues have described sleep in general as crucial to the "off-line" consolidation of procedural memory [42], and have implicated REM sleep specifically in the formation and processing of emotional memories [43]. Memory deficits are a prominent feature of dreams [29], with dreams often not being remembered at all unless one is awakened in the middle of one, or quickly forgotten if not recorded. While this does not speak directly to the phenomenology of dreaming, it is noteworthy that while the dreamer perceives dreams as "real", this experience is not generally integrated into waking consciousness. This could, we hypothesize, be a protective mechanism to maintain a boundary between dreaming and waking experience (or simulated versus real world experience), without which a fragmentation of consciousness would result. One recent neuropsychoanalytic model has focused on the shared phenomenology of dream mentation and psychosis with aspects of virtual reality, in the sense that an individual's reality testing —and often, belief system— may be altered in such states [44].

5.3.7 Relationship to Waking Experience

Freud emphasised the effect of waking activity on dream mentation (the "day residue", [2]). Episodic memories however (accurate reproduction of specific events, characters and actions) seem to be rarely reflected in dreams, occurring in less than 2% of dream reports [14, 45]. Hartman noted that we rarely dream of the "3 R's": reading, writing and arithmetic, despite a large percentage of our waking lives engaged in such activities [46]. Schredl and Hofmann note that we rarely dream of using a computer (for either work or play activities) [47]. However, in a well-known experiment, Stickgold et al. found that subjects engaged in an extended Tetris playing paradigm reported experiencing stereotyped images at sleep onset consisting of falling and rotating Tetris pieces, but never images of a computer screen, keyboard, etc. [48]. The findings were similar in normals and in patients with amnesia secondary to bilateral medial temporal lobe damage (who could not even recall playing the game). Perhaps most convincingly, subjects developing blindness after the age of seven continue to experience visual dreaming over a lifetime [22].

Thus, overall, it seems that dreams are not a simple replaying of the day's events, but rather isolated fragments of waking experience, extracted and incorporated into conscious narrative in novel ways. Extracted elements may be those with emotional salience or those concerned with procedural learning [14, 43, 45].

5.4 Dreaming, Virtual Reality and Presence

Given the phenomenological characteristics of the dreams, it is not surprising that several authors have likened the dream experience to a form of virtual reality [14, 26, 44, 49, 50]. Foulkes has commented that while the dreamer creates dreams mentally, they are experienced as life rather than thought, and as perception rather than imagination [26]. Dreams, according to this perspective, take on the form of "credible world analogs", through which we move and interact with other individuals. In fact the simulation of reality is so complete, that for Foulkes the question is not why we accept it as real but "why we *shouldn't* believe it to be real." [27]. Neilson and Stenstrom describe dreaming as portraying "coherent virtual worlds" [14], noting:

"Dreams seem to take place in real, spatially coherent, environments with which the self interacts perceptually, for example, by orienting, seeking and assimilating sensory information, much as it does with the real world. The self also seems to engage realistic character in emotional and intellectual exchanges. Semantic information and a sense of knowing are often also present." (p. 1286).

Likewise Revonsuo describes dream consciousness as an "organized and selective simulation of the perceptual world" specifically referring to it as a form of virtual reality [49]. In an earlier paper Revonsuo even suggests that consciousness in general, be it in dreaming or waking, may be conceptualized as a virtual reality experience [50].

Lee defines presence as a "psychological state in which virtual (para-authentic or artificial) objects are experienced as actual objects in either sensory or nonsensory ways" [12]. Furthermore Lee delineates three types of presence – physical, social, and self; depending on the virtual objects being experienced as actual objects, be they physical objects, social actors or self/selves.

Dream experience, in the terminology proposed by Lee, may readily seen as exhibiting a high degree of presence in the physical, social and self domains. The dreaming mind, even in the absence of external perceptual inputs, is able to generate for itself an immersive environment that is taken by the dreamer to be completely real, perceptually and affectively. Furthermore the dreaming Mind/Brain accomplishes this without the need for either a high degree of fidelity ("vividness" as Lee puts it), or even elements corresponding directly to waking reality - dreams in their bizarreness are still taken to be real. This is a feat unmatched by any artificial immersive environment, akin to not only believing that a virtual environment is reasonably realistic, but is in fact a reality unto itself. Given that in the case of dreaming the brain is generating the very environment it perceives, such a standard may be unattainable by artificial - including digital/multimedia – means.

Lee [12] also distinguishes between three types of human experience: "real experience", the sensory experience of actual objects; "virtual experience", sensory or non-sensory experiences of para-authentic or artificial objects; and "hallucination", nonsensory experience of imaginary objects. Dream experience is most akin to "hallucination" in Lee's typology. Lee however proposes that hallucinatory experiences are neither real nor virtual, since the objects experienced are neither real nor mediated by man-made technology. As such, Lee argues, hallucination, along with real experience, is not pertinent to presence research. Certainly the sense of realness experienced during dreaming is complete enough that dreaming may be said to be not simply a simulation of reality, but an "experiential reality" in its own right [50]. Like Revonsuo [9, 49, 50], we would, however, argue with a proposition that claims nothing is to be gained in presence research by a study of the dreaming phenomenon.

Dreaming, firstly, may be regarded as a natural experiment in presence; in fact the "gold standard" by which other immersive environments may be compared. Secondly dreaming provides a unique window into the processes that determine how the brain organizes information (external and internal). Lee [12] himself has argued that one of the most important issues in the study of presence is the determination of the underlying, human-based mechanisms that make presence possible. In particular he expresses an interest in presence induced by low-tech, nonsensory media such as books, requiring significant self-generated cognitive "filling-in " processes to achieve presence.

Revonsuo has commented that dreaming represents a specific, and perhaps more basic form of consciousness as it is dissociated from the effects of external input (an "unaltered" state of consciousness as it were) [50]. He further adds that whatever neurophysiologic mechanisms of the brain are active while dreaming, they are sufficient for conscious experiences to exist. Thus dreaming may offer important insights into consciousness in its most basic form, and the manner in which it organizes external information, be it via the "real world" or through selectively chosen media interfaces. These insights may in turn be used to design even more immersive artificial environments. Similarly, as we begin to create more realistic artificially immersive environments, this may provide insights into the dreaming process, as well as consciousness in general.

5.5 The Function of Dreams

5.5.1 Psychoanalytic Theory

Despite the universality of the dream experience, there continues to be little consensus as to what function, if any, dreams serve. Freud postulated that sleep represents a regression by which infantile wishes buried in the unconscious threatened to surface to conscious awareness [2]. Dreams, or the "dream-work" functioned to disguise such wishes, converting the latent content of infantile wishes into the manifest content experienced by the individual (through the processes of condensation, displacement and symbolization). Dreams, according to Freud, first and foremost acted as the "guardians" of sleep, preventing the individual from waking up in response to otherwise threatening infantile wishes [2]. Subsequent analytic schools have broadened Freud's view of the function of dreaming to include a more active problem-solving capacity [51, 52]. Fosshage for example describes the function of dreams as the "development, maintenance (regulation) and, when necessary, restoration of psychic processes, structure and organization" [52].

5.5.2 Neuropsychoanalytic and Neural Network Theory

The view of dreams as a regulator of drives or emotions has persisted in sleep research, albeit from a neuropsychological rather than depth psychological perspective. Solms has speculated that brain activation during sleep stimulates centres in the brain responsible for "appetitive interest" (in the limbic frontal white matter) [27, 53]. Rather than such centres being allowed to activate motivational motor systems that would otherwise awaken the individual, their influence is instead shunted toward perceptual systems (in the occipito-temporo-parietal junction) that instead produce dreaming. Thus the system driving dream production serves as the guardian of sleep as proposed by Freud [2], although in this model dreaming in itself does not seem to have any particular function. Hartman, by contrast, has proposed that dreams function to contextualize the dominant emotional concern of an individual by cross-connecting or integrating new material into pre-existing neural networks (such as after a significant trauma) [54, 55].

5.5.3 Threat Simulation Theory

Revonsuo, perhaps more than any writer, has emphasized the concept of dreams as a simulation of reality, and has directly incorporated this perspective into a theory of their function. Dreaming, according to Revonsuo is a biological defence mechanism, evolutionarily selected for its ability to simulate threatening events - the "threat simulation theory" of dreaming [49, 56]. Such a simulation allows for the rehearsal of threat recognition and avoidance, which in turn leads to increased survival of the organism (this would account for the instinctive appeal of certain immersive, first-person perspective, action-based video games). Other authors have suggested a broadening of the simulation theory of dreaming to include other adaptive functions such as play [57, 58]. Revonsuo comments that the rehearsal of threat recognition and avoidance may still strengthen implicit or procedural learning without the need to remember such a rehearsal upon awakening [49]. We would add that such a loss of memory of dream mentation upon awakening may be necessary, serving to prevent dream mentation from being integrated into episodic memory and potentially being confused with waking experience. In fact the function of dreaming may be not only to rehearse behavioural responses in a "safe place" but to do so in a manner that will not interfere with waking episodic memory. For the simulation to function maximally it should be taken for real, but ultimately not confused with the reality of the waking world.

5.5.4 Dreams as Nonfunctional Epiphenomena

Finally, some investigators, while attributing a potential function of REM sleep in brain regulation, see dreaming as epiphenomena in nature, the result of non-specific cortical activation or arousal [15, 28, 49]. In other words, the perceptual experience of dreaming, while interesting and potentially meaningful, in and of itself serves no biologically useful function. As Domhoff comments [28]:

"On the basis of current evidence, it is more likely that dreams are an accidental by-product of two great evolutionary adaptations, sleep and consciousness." (p. 6).

5.6 REM, Non-REM and Wakefulness: Three States of Consciousness

We present here a broad and admittedly simplified overview of the neurobiology of dreaming in order to illustrate the potential value, if not the necessity of understanding dreaming in terms of fundamental neurobiological mechanisms underlying the experience of presence.

5.6.1 Historical Aspects

A breakthrough in understanding of the biological underpinning of dreaming occurred only as recently as 1953 with the discovery of REM sleep by Aserinsky and Kleitman [59], seen as a key landmark in heralding in the era of biological psychiatry that many would argue prevails to this present day, supplanting psychoanalytic approaches to understanding psychopathology. Shortly afterwards, Michel Jouvet's discovery of atonia (muscle paralysis) during REM sleep in cats [60] prompted him to describe REM sleep as *paradoxical sleep* [61, 62], in which an organism is neither asleep nor awake, but under the influence of a "new" third state of the brain. In this state, an individual would experience perceptual phenomena analogous to being awake, but with sensory and cognitive gating systems operational during wakefulness altered, and motor response systems including speech production "paradoxically" incapacitated. Furthermore early studies demonstrated that patients awakened during this phase of sleep reported dream mentation, while those awakened at other times did not [63]. Thus the association between REM sleep and dreaming became established.

5.6.2 Polysomnographic Measurement and Sleep Staging

These early developments also led to the refinement of polysomnography (PSG), or overnight sleep recording, which has become the essential diagnostic instrument of sleep medicine [63, 64]. PSG consists of continuous and simultaneous recording of the following core parameters:
1. electroencephalogram (EEG) recording of brain activity;
2. electro-oculogram (EOG) recording of eye movements;
3. electromyogram (EMG) recording of muscle activity.

Auxillary physiological parameters such as respiratory or cardiac functioning throughout a sleep period are also commonly monitored in PSG [64]. Through use of PSG recording techniques somnology researchers have been able to define three distinct and separate states of consciousness:
1. waking consciousness, characterized by a high frequency, low-amplitude EEG activity and normal muscle tone.
2. nonREM (NREM) sleep, divided into four stages and characterized by a progressive slowing of EEG frequencies and increase in amplitude, relaxed EMG muscle tone and slow rolling to absent eye movements.
3. REM or "paradoxical" sleep, characterized by a mixed-frequency low-amplitude EEG pattern akin to stage I sleep (which is often thought of as the transition between relaxed wakefulness and sleep proper), rapid eye movements and an absence of muscle activity (muscle atonia). REM sleep, it is worth noting, is distinguished from NREM sleep through its relatively active EEG pattern, despite a high arousal threshold characteristic of sleep (hence the term "paradoxical sleep") and from a wakeful state by the presence of muscle atonia which prevents the activation of motor response systems in the face of cortical activation (a useful evolutionary adaptation that prevents us from physically acting out our dreams).

PSG allows for the recording of a typical cycling between NREM (stages 1-4) and REM sleep, with REM sleep periods occurring every 90-100 minutes and taking up 20-25% of the night. A typical nocturnal sleep pattern hypnogram for a healthy adult is shown in Figure 1, demonstrating the fluctuating nature of consciousness during sleep.

It has traditionally been held that awaking from REM sleep results in reports of full-blown dream mentation while awakenings from NREM sleep produce reports of more "thoughtlike" processes. However, the view that REM sleep is synonymous with dreaming has recently come under challenge. It has been estimated that 5-30% of REM awakenings do not elicit dream reports, while 5-10% of NREM awakenings elicit dream reports indistinguishable from REM reports (particularly at sleep onset). Thus REM sleep can technically occur without dreaming and dreaming can occur without REM sleep [65, 66]. It is fair to say, however, that in general, dreaming is most likely to occur under the conditions of REM sleep.

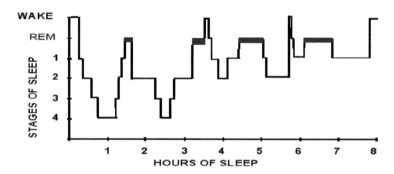

Figure 1: Hypnogram in a healthy individual, showing the dynamic nature of sleep stages, with dream-rich REM episodes (indicated by thick bars) recurring between non-REM sleep periods of varying depth at regular intervals. Note that longer periods of REM occur during the latter part of the sleep period.

5.7 The functional neuroanatomy of dreaming

Classic experiments by Jouvet in the 1960's isolated the centres that generate REM sleep to the pontine brainstem [67]. It is now known that cholinergic neurons located in specific nuclei (the laterodorsal tegmental nucleus and the pedunculopontine tegmental nucleus) are activated during REM sleep. These nuclei in turn send projections to nearby nuclei to produce rapid eye movements, downward into the medulla and spinal cord to paralyze muscle activity, and most importantly upward into the forebrain to produce diffuse cortical activation [15]. REM sleep, however, confined in its production to the brainstem is still only the generator of the process, leaving open the question of what areas of the forebrain are responsible for the generation of the complex conscious state known as dreaming. In a landmark study, Solms reviewed all reported cases of altered dreaming and neurological injury, prompting him to designate the following areas of the brain to be necessary for dreaming: the limbic system (the brain's core emotional centre), the medial occipito-temporal cortex (producing visual representations), the inferior parietal convexity (producing spatial cognition) and basal forebrain pathways (producing "appetitive interests") [27].

Neuroimaging studies have confirmed that during dreaming there is activation of the limbic and paralimbic regions and activation of specific cortical areas such as the associative visual and auditory areas [68].   Furthermore, dreaming seems to be associated with a *deactivation* of portions of the frontal cortex responsible for executive control, a finding which may account for the bizarreness of dreaming [15].

5.8 The Neurophysiology of Dreaming

5.8.1 The Activation-synthesis Hypothesis

Figure 2 illustrates the complexity of any attempt to anatomically delineate the dynamic process and experience of dreaming [15].

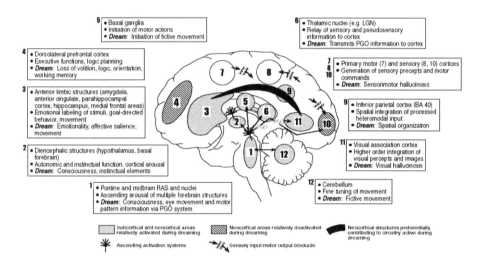

Figure 2 The Activation-Synthesis Functional Model of Dreaming
(reprinted with permission from Hobson et al, 2003)

One of the leading theories with respect to the neurophysiology of dreaming is the *activation-synthesis hypothesis*, a theory proposed by Hobson and McCarley in 1977 [69] and which has undergone substantial evolution over the years. This theory postulates that the process of dreaming is driven by REM sleep generators in the pontine brainstem which, as noted above, activate or send signals diffusely into the forebrain to a number of areas including the limbic system and selected cortical areas (in particular those subserving visual association and spatial cognition). Such internally driven signals are "chaotic" in nature, and in attempts to make sense of them, higher association areas in the brain synthesise or construct visual images and narrative plots around them. The end result is dreaming, with its unique phenomenology.

Further peculiarities of dreaming may be accounted for by decreased frontal lobe functioning and a shift to cholinergic (acetylcholine) neuromodulation during REM sleep from the aminergic (serotonin and norepinephrine) neuromodulation associated with wakefulness [15].

The activation-synthesis hypothesis has been a very influential model in understanding dream generation, but is of course not the only such model (for example, consider Solms' model as noted under the function of dreaming [27, 52]). One major controversy underlying competing models has been whether or not REM sleep is indeed the prime driver in the dreaming process.

5.8.2 The AIM Model of Conscious States

Dreams, similar to Biocca's conceptualization of media presence [7], obey not the laws of physics but the laws of the mind. The AIM (Activation-Input-Modulation) model was developed from the activation-synthesis model as an attempt to map conscious states onto an underlying physiological state space [15].   In this model, shown in Figure 3, conscious states in the Mind/Brain are determined by three interdependent processes which can be mapped along three dimensions . The three processes in the AIM model of conscious states include:

1.   the level of brain activation ("A");
2.   the origin of information input ("I") to the brain (external or internal); and
3.   the relative levels of aminergic and cholinergic neuromodulation ("M") which determines information processing.

These three Mind/Brain processes are hypothesized to exist at discrete points along the construed three-dimensional state space. A high level of activation, predominantly external information inputs and high levels of aminergic modulation characterize wakefulness. REM sleep (and dreaming), by contrast, is characterized by a high level of activation, predominantly internal information inputs and high levels of cholinergic modulation (hence the particular characteristics of dreaming in comparison with waking experience).

5.8.3 Applications to Presence in other States of Consciousness

A number of other partial or dissociated states may also be mapped in a similar manner such as quiet rest (or waking fantasy), lucid dreaming, hallucinosis etc. [15]. This relatively simple model has proven useful in the understanding of dissociated conscious states. It may also prove applicable in the understanding of immersive states of consciousness involving multimedia displays, which would presumably involve intermediate positions along any of these dimensions. The presence induced by reading a riveting novel, for example, is predominantly internally driven, as the reader individualizes the information imparted through perceiving text characters via a neurocognitive "filling-in process" process.   By contrast, the experiential state of an individual engaging in an immersive 3-dimensional software-generated environment via virtual reality goggles is predominantly externally driven. Thus, as fidelity and richness of perceptual information presented to an individual increases, the experience of presence is generated through different mechanisms using the AIM model. It remains clear, however, that a low fidelity simulation with a powerful affective impact imparts a strong feeling of presence.

It has been argued that in a virtual environment paradigm, there is a spectrum of immersion ranging from "presence" (completely engaged) to "absence" (completely disengaged) [70].   This can be applied to human-centred communication as well as engagement in media-related interactive tasks (see also the other chapters of this section). We have previously proposed that there may well be an electrophysiological correlate of absence, as defined by intrusion of EEG-defined sleep consciousness while engaged in a task [71].

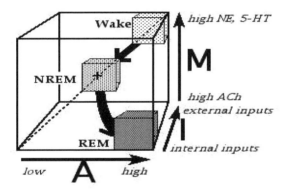

Figure 3: The AIM model.(NE=Norepinephrine, 5-HT=Serotonin, Ach=Acetylcholine.)
(reprinted with permission from Hobson et al, 2003).

Thus the term "absence", used by neurologists to define characteristic sleep-like EEG in certain types of seizures [72] could also be applied to the study of presence, even in the absence of epileptiform activity.   As an individual is decreasingly engaged in a perceptual experience, he or she will retreat into a state of absence that is both a psychological/perceptual experience and a neurophysiologic state. If this transition from wakefulness is towards a non-REM sleep state, this is experienced in the form of brief fragments of microsleep intruding into waking consciousness [73]. If it is towards a state of REM sleep (as in states such as sleep deprivation or narcolepsy) this may be experienced as pseudohallucinatory dream mentation [74]. Conversely, as an individual becomes increasingly perceptually immersed and experiences presence, a transition in consciousness occurs that can be described in qualitative/subjective as well as physiological/objective terms [1, 71].   Thus it must be noted that any fluctuations in consciousness relevant to experiencing presence involve far more complex neurophysiologic phenomena than a simple linear absence-presence spectrum.

5.9 Therapeutic Considerations

5.9.1 Applications to Presence in Virtual Environments

As discussed, REM, NREM and wakefulness are widely considered to be three separate states of consciousness, with occasionally overlapping features. We have established that dreaming (widely associated with REM) can be considered to be an auto-generated virtual reality simulation [49, 50], useful for rehearsal of dealing with threats [56], consolidation of memory [42, 43, 48] and expanding behavioural repertoire through play [57, 58]. Virtual environments may be thought of as simulations of real-world (i.e. waking) experiences, but it becomes clear that without an appreciation of dreaming consciousness, it will become difficult to approach an ultimate understanding of presence. A key difference between an individual's experience while dreaming and engaging in a multimedia-generated immersive environment is the degree of interactivity that it possible [1]. As discussed, the neurophysiology of REM/paradoxical sleep states involves muscle atonia. Thus even though an individual may perceive him- or herself interacting with the environment either verbally or behaviourally while in a dream state, the actual body of the dreamer remains paralyzed. By contrast, an individual in an interactive virtual environment can experience a high degree of immersion/presence, and retain the capacities of speech and motor movement. More intriguingly, the digital nature of most immersive multimedia simulations allows such behaviours to be encoded and executed through a variety of mechanisms. Thus, for example, a "real-world" mouse click or movement with a cyberglove can generate the movement of a "virtual" limb, an entire avatar or any group of virtual objects assigned to a keystroke or manipulation of a hardware device.

5.9.2 Psychopathological Aspects of Dreaming and Sleep Pathology

A survey of dream phenomenology and sleep abnormalities in psychiatric disorders involving disturbances of affect indicates that REM sleep regulation plays a prominent role in the brain's attempt to regulate such disturbances [75-78]. Recurrent disturbing dreams, along with flashbacks and intrusive re-experiencing of a traumatic event are typical symptoms experienced by sufferers of posttraumatic stress disorder (PTSD) [76, 77]. Mellman et al have summarized some of the polysomnographic characteristics of PTSD, including earlier onset REM, increased dream mentation during the initial REM period, increased REM density and fragmentation of REM [76]. Vividness of visual flashbacks to an experienced trauma may inappropriately occur during wakefulness through similar dysregulation of the REM-sleep memory consolidation circuits [76]. The general implication appears to be that the brain's internally generated threat simulation defence is on one hand powerfully activated by an attempt to process the trauma an individual has experienced, but on the other hand, is pathologically caught in a reverberating circuit of being unable to use its normally functioning 'software'.

A medical analogy to this might be a chronically overactive immune response to an environmental disturbance, which if working appropriately serves a useful role, but if overwhelmed or inappropriate, ultimately causes more pathology than it removes.

REM abnormalities are also found in a number of other anxiety disorders, as well as major depressive disorder, with shortened REM latency, increased total REM percentage and REM fragmentation commonly seen as sleep markers of a failure of affect regulation [76, 78, 79]. Dream content in depressive disorders has also been described by Nejad et al. as frequently disturbing and frightening, with themes such as death, separation, natural disasters, falling, aggression, frightening animals or situations, homicide and suicide [30]. Cartwright et al.'s "broken dream" study investigated dream content in a group of women undergoing divorce [80]. The dreams of those divorcing without major mood upset were longer and dealt with a wider time frame than those of control subjects and depressed divorcees. They also dealt with marital status issues, which were largely absent in the dreams of the depressed group. On follow-up those who had been depressed showed positive dream changes in mood, dreamlike quality, and identification of dream self with the marital role. This study implies a "problem solving" simulation role for dreaming sleep, which can correlate with an auto-therapeutic function for the dreamer.

5.9.3 Dream Simulation Therapy

Perhaps it is no coincidence that "sleep fragmentation" is a term commonly used by somnologists to describe the brittle EEG sleep characteristics of depressed and anxious patients [76, 78]. If one accepts the hypothesis that disturbed dreams are in essence errors of the brain's software used to defragment perceptual experiences and consolidate these appropriately into long-term memory, it is reasonable to consider the eventual possibility of "corrective" therapeutic digital simulations of disturbed dreams in psychiatric disorders, given the advances made in simulation paradigms.

A future goal to strive towards would be a collaborative simulation protocol paradigm developed by therapist and patient. Here, an eloquent patient is able to convey a recurring dream and the therapist is able to develop a simulation protocol, which need not necessarily be high-fidelity but confer a sufficient sense of presence to be emotionally salient and therefore potentially therapeutic. PSG recording techniques allow the therapist/researcher to readily recognize when a patient is engaged in REM sleep through characteristic extraocular muscle movements. Using standard PSG or an ambulatory nightcap unit, as described by Cantero et al. and shown in Figure 4, this could readily be performed in an ambulatory setting [81, 82].

Once awakened, a patient can then be encouraged to describe dream content to the clinician, who might select a scene from a digital library, and with the aid of appropriate modelling/rendering software tools and feedback from the patient could construct a simulation paradigm that would match the dream content, and attempt to personalize it to the patient's experience. This might be performed in a graded exposure paradigm, with the difference from traditional cognitive-behavioural technique being the advantage of a recreation of an immersive experience that is experienced during dreaming.

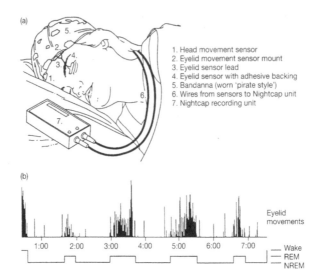

Figure 4: a) A nightcap unit is able to monitor sleep onset as well as REM sleep in an ambulatory setting, b) histogram plot of extraocular muscle movement detected using nightcap and computer-scored sleep stages. (Reprinted with permission from Hobson, 2002)

The key advantage of dream simulation therapy would be the high degree of control that patient and therapist would have on the manipulation of perceptual variables, a considerable advantage over more controversial dream-therapy techniques such a lucid dream therapy [83]. Furthermore, while recurrent auto-generated nightmares might frequently become derailed through the intrinsic pathology of the dream process in disturbed individuals, therapeutic use of immersive technologies allow the patient to persevere at different levels of affectively charged presence. In fact, verbally based dream rehearsal therapy has been used with some effect to treat recurrent nightmares in short-term psychotherapy [84]. Analogous to theories about use of virtual simulations in anxiety disorders, patients with alexithymia or restricted visual/imaginative capacities might benefit from such an approach that is able to provide a perceptual "filling in process" during therapy [85]. Successful outcome of dream simulation therapy would be increased level of mastery over dreams, with the dreamer becoming more of an active participant rather than passive observer, through practice gained in rehearsed therapeutic simulations. A reverse approach to this involves the delineation of specific neurocognitive processes occurring during high-presence immersive states induced by specific multimedia simulations (for example, salient immersive audiovisual imagery, whether aversive or hedonic) while awake, and to capture this data digitally through monitoring devices such as PSG/EEG or neuroimaging techniques. This requires gathering of multimodal subjective and performance-based response data from subjects in synthetic perceptual environments, and mapping these accurately to corresponding neurophysiologic data. We would stress that this is not currently feasible with any accuracy, although in recent years, attempts have been made to describe the elusive experience of presence in neuroscientific terms, including use of fMRI [86] and EEG monitoring [87, 88]. Once more reliable data regarding neurological commonalities underlying 'high presence' states contained in vivid or salient dreams and artificially generated immersive experiences becomes available, the next, and more ambitious step will become the introduction of externally generated virtual environments into unconscious sleep. This might occur through mirrored biofeedback mechanisms that would be able to store digitally recorded brain-state data (e.g. PSG/EEG patterns correlating with an immersive experience in a virtual environment), and to manipulate EEG amplitude, frequency and temporospatial patterns underlying dreaming consciousness to activate perceptual systems without waking up an individual.

Attempts have been made to affect sleep mentation through presentation of stimuli, intended to then subsequently affect dream processes. For example, Stickgold describes presenting auditory stimuli to sleeping subjects, with pure tones activating auditory processing regions, while subjects' names activated language centres as well as the left amygdala (thought crucial for processing emotionally salient perceptual information) as well as the prefrontal cortex [89]. The presentation of visual imagery to dreaming patients has not thus far been described during sleep, although during the process of parasomnia, there is a state dissociation-the brain is partially awake and partially asleep, with the possibility of both motor activity and intake of perceptual information without conscious awareness [90]. Outside of rigorous scientific scrutiny, there appears to be an emergence of industrial/commercial applications intimating this type of model that deserve mention [91]. In 2004, a Japanese toy manufacturer launched a product dubbed *Yumemi Kobo*- Japanese for "dream workshop", advertised to help individuals shape their dreams in specific predetermined directions. In this model, prospective dreamers are asked to look at a photo of what they would like to dream about and then record a story line using a combination of prerecorded video imagery, voice recording, along with lights, music and smells, which are activated for release during periods of rapid eye movement (REM) sleep. No data are available on this paradigm thus far.

5.9.4 Relationship to VR Therapy

Therapeutic virtual reality (VR) simulation for psychological indications historically stems from less complex anxiety disorders such as acrophobia and claustrophobia, with later established indications for fear of flying, driving and public speaking [92]. One of the most rapidly evolving therapeutic applications of VR simulation therapy involves the treatment of posttraumatic stress disorder (PTSD) [93, 94], which involves a more diffuse distribution of phobic responses paired with an experienced trauma, including dream abnormalities [76]. The content of PTSD dreams is often highly stereotyped, particularly if relating to a single traumatic event [76, 84, 95]. By contrast, the dream content of depressed individuals, while often profoundly immersive by VR simulation standards and frequently containing threat themes [30], tends to be more topically diffuse, and thus more difficult and time-consuming to artificially replicate. Use of personalized images, sounds or other media clips, semantically and affectively meaningful to the patient might be particularly useful to either incorporate into the simulation or to model the therapeutic environment, rather than using traditional imaginal-based cognitive techniques [77].

The challenge for a truly skilled "cybertherapist" using this methodology would thus be to unlock a remote and highly encrypted trauma that has triggered a depression using a combination of polysomnographic and simulation technologies. One might see irony in the apparent reliance on human-machine interfaces as a bridge to help the patient ultimately regain function and in domains of human-to-human function. If one, however, accepts the premise that everything we know and perceive about the "real" world is entirely subjective, and subject to our own creation of a simulated reality [50, 53], the precise mechanisms of activating or correcting these disturbances of consciousness matters less than their ability to generate a feeling of presence.

5.10 Connecting the Neuroscience of Dreaming and Media Presence

5.10.1 Theoretical Considerations

Some feel that the central place of face-to-face communication in the psychotherapeutic context will gradually erode in the multimedia era. We would argue that psychiatrists, psychologists and psychoanalysts with an interest in states of consciousness could find fertile ground for research and clinical interaction with their patients by being more aware of neurobiologic aspects of presence in multimedia displays. As display technologies continue to improve in fidelity, the ability to suspend perceptual disbelief in a prolonged state of immersion becomes increasingly relevant [96]. Is this more akin to waking consciousness, or REM sleep? To what degree does this depend on the amount of operator control in a human-computer interface? In therapeutic scenarios where the "virtual plot" is controlled by a separate agent such as a therapist controlling level of immersion, how analogous could this be construed to Jouvet's "paradoxical sleep" state [61, 62]? Conversely, designers of effective human-machine media communication interfaces need to appreciate the neurophysiologic complexities of presence. If currently there is an acceptance that there are three states of consciousness, i.e. wakefulness, non-REM sleep and REM sleep, where does artificially generated virtual reality experience, accepted as "real", fit into this spectrum? Is it appropriate to consider virtual reality as a "fourth state of consciousness", or is such taxonomy even necessary if one already accepts the notion of dreams as a unique self-generated simulation program?

5.10.2 Videohypertransference as Behavioural Outcome, Dreaming as Intermediary Process

When an individual begins to integrate simulated media experiences with a high degree of presence into his or her subsequent behaviour, whether through conscious or unconscious mechanisms, this could be described as videohypertransference [97], or perhaps more accurately multimedia-hypertransference. The example of Stickgold et al.'s experiment [48], in which Tetris images persisted into sleep consciousness, illustrates the role that dreams might play in such a transference process. Schutte et al. noted that young children who play video games tend to act similarly to how their video game character acted [98], and there is certainly abundant controversy surrounding immersive video games involving violence and antisocial behaviours [99]. On a less pessimistic level, the promise of VR or dream simulation therapy indicates a far more constructive and even transcendental role for using artificially generated media presence.

An intriguing question is whether increasingly immersive media experiences are likely to have an increasingly powerful influence on human behaviour, with sleep and dreaming being an unconscious conduit for this "learning" to occur [43]. It would be useful to gather more behavioural and neurophysiogic data about the bidirectional relationship between the types of consciousness an individual experiences in an immersive simulation paradigm and subsequent REM/dreaming episodes. This might be a more direct and controllable approach than attempts to examine effects on later waking behaviour, as dreams would appear to be one of, if not *the* key primary processes through which perceptual and emotional experiences are eventually integrated into behavioural changes.

5.10.3 Dreaming as Media Experience: Hot or Cool?

Ultimately, like any sort of simulation experience, dreams can be understood as a form of media affecting consciousness, both in current and evolutionary terms. McLuhan is credited with developing a "hot and cool" metaphor for defining media [100], based on the amount of information imparted on the consumer. In this taxonomy, orality is a "cool" or "low definition" medium because it presents very spare information. It therefore requires a lot of active participation on the part of the listener to decode the information for a strong experience of presence to occur. Writing, and particularly print, is "hot" because it presents a lot of information in high definition, although this does not necessarily imply an increased presence. McLuhan considered television "cool" because of the low resolution of its grainy picture, perhaps a controversial perspective in today's era of high-definition broadcast media. Improvements in computer simulation and digital communication technology will continue to strive towards approaching a "hot" high-fidelity model, with increasing involvement of integrated multisensory information including haptic, visual and auditory [25]. All of these experiences and more are already contained in the experience of dreams, which can be understood as both "cool" (requiring much active participation to extract the encoded information) and arguably, "hot" (with complex multisensory information presented in exquisitely "high definition") at varying times [20]. As with fluctuating states of REM density and intensity of dream state experience [20, 62, 63, 76], it is likely that there is some level of fluctuation even in highly immersive media experiences [86], as opposed to a continuous experience of presence. If dreams are to be understood as a form of media as well neurobiological events, this unique characteristic should be explored further.

5.11 Conclusions

If presence is a "psychological state", as proposed by Lee [12] and by the other authors of this Section, then what is the phenomenology and neurobiology underlying this state? The functional neuroanatomy and neurophysiology of dreaming has already been well established. We believe that a key step in advancing the field of presence-mediated communication will be for researchers to follow along a similar path, using multimodal assessment tools such as neuroimaging and psychophysiologic monitoring, as well as subjective user feedback (see also the chapter by Coelho and colleagues). From our perspective of clinician-researchers interested in both psychotherapeutic and fundamental neuroscientific aspects of media technology, we have discussed to what degree immersive media simulation will progress towards a productive convergence with advances in neuroscience.

The rapidly evolving and multidisciplinary understanding of presence shows promise in contributing significantly to an eventual solution to the problem of consciousness by future science. This chapter has explored the notion of dreams occupying a unique virtual space in our consciousness that underlies integration of all communication experiences, particularly from an evolutionary and perceptual perspective [10]. We have established that presence is the key phenomenology underlying immersive experiences in both dreaming and immersive media simulations. Furthermore we have presented evidence for a conceptual model of dreaming as an auto-generated virtual reality simulation from a number of divergent neuroscientific, philosophical and psychological models of consciousness (see also the chapter by Riva for a further discussion).

In our discussion of clinical aspects of dream pathology and virtual environments, we have specifically taken note of potential fertile ground for collaboration between researchers in both fields, attempting to understand the phenomenon of presence from either perspective. As outlined earlier, it is hoped that this discussion can bridge these areas of ongoing research of cognitive neuroscience. The tantalizing possibility of being able to manipulate consciousness through multimedia presence has been presented in a speculative model of dream simulation therapy, which remains a future goal to strive towards, depending on technological advances. Having argued for an inclusion of the dreaming process in immersive experiences synthesized by the Mind/Brain in response to our experiences, we predict that with the evolution of media presence, there will eventually be a far less distinct boundary between which of these experiences are organic/real and artificial/virtual.

We have reviewed here diverse theories explaining both the phenomenology and neurobiology of dreaming consciousness, in order to provide a neuroscientific benchmark for the study of presence-related conscious experiences in the future of media technology development. We emphasized the powerful role of presence in the context of dream mentation as both a neurophysiologic substrate and conceptual metaphor for understanding psychological aspects of virtual environments. Dreaming consciousness reminds us that the key factor in approaching an ultimate technology-mediated presence experience is the sum rather than its parts: a subjective/affective state of being.

5.12 References

[1]   M.K. Sanchez-Nunes, M. Slater, From presence to consciousness through virtual reality. *Nature Reviews Neuroscience.* 6(2005): 332-9.
[2]   S. Freud, *The Interpretation of Dreams (1900): Complete Psychological Works*, Standard ed, vols 4, 5. London, Hogarth Press, 1953.
[3]   M. Reiser, The Dream in Contemporary Psychiatry. *American Journal of Psychiatry* 158(2001): 351-9.
[4]   I. Whishlow, Locale and taxon systems: no place for neophrenology? *Hippocampus* 1(1991): 272-4.
[5]   M. Solms, *The Neuropsychology of Dreams: A Clinico-Anatomical Study.* Mahwah, NJ, Lawrence Erlbaum Associates, 1997.
[6]   M. McLuhan, L.H. Lapham, *Understanding Media: The Extensions of Man (1ˢᵗ MIT rev ed),* Cambridge MA: MIT Press, 1994.
[7]   F. Biocca, Media and Laws of the Mind. In G. Riva, F. Davide, F.A. Ijsselsteijn (Eds.), *Being There: Concepts, Effects and Measurements of User Presence in Synthetic Environments.* IOS Press Amsterdam, 2003.
[8]   M.J. Zyphur, M.S. Franklin, The Role of Dreams in the Evolution of the Human Mind. *Evolutionary Psychology,* 3(1978): 59-78.
[9]   A. Revonsuo, *Inner Presence: Consciousness as a Biological Phenomenon* Cambridge MA: MIT Press, 2006.
[10] M.I. Marozza, When does a dream begin to 'have meaning'? Linguistic constraints and significant moments in the construction of the meaning of a dream. *Journal of Analytic Psychology,* 50 (2005): 693-705.
[11] J.S. Bruner: "Culture and Cognitive Growth" In J.S. Bruner, R.R. Olver, P.M. Greenfield (Eds.), *Studies in Cognitive Growth.* New York: Wiley, 1966.
[12] K.M. Lee, Presence, Explicated. *Communication Theory* 14 (2004): 27-50.
[13] Wikipedia – Dream [Internet Webpage]. 2005. Online: http://en.wikipedia.org/wiki/Dreams
[14] T.A. Nielsen & P. Stenstrom, What are the memory sources of dreaming? *Nature.* 437 (2005): 1286-1289.
[15] J.A. Hobson, E.F. Pace-Schott and R. Stickgold, Dreaming and the brain: Toward a cognitive neuroscience of conscious states. In E.F. Pace-Schott, M. Solms, M. Blagrove, S. Harnard (Eds.), *Sleep and Dreaming: Scientific Advances and Reconsiderations.* Cambridge: Cambridge University Press; 2003: 1-50
[16] F. Snyder, The phenomenology of dreaming. In L. Madow, L.H. Snow (Eds.), *The psychodynamic implications of the physiological studies on dreams.* Springfield Ill: Thomas; 1970.
[17] A.L. Zadra, T.A. Nielsen, D.C. Donderi, Prevalence of auditory, olfactory and gustatory experiences in home dreams. *Perceptual and Motor Skills* 87(1998): 819-26.
[18] I. Strauch, B. Meier, *In search of dreams: Results of experimental dream research.* Albany: State University of New York Press; 1996.
[19] J.A. Hobson, *The Dreaming Brain.* New York: Basic Books; 1988.
[20] A. Rechtschaffen, C. Buchignani, The visual appearance of dreams. In: J.S. Antrobus, M. Bertini, (Eds.) *The Neuropsychology of Sleep and Dreaming.* Hillsdale, NJ: Lawrence Erlbaum associates; 1992: 143-155.
[21] E. Schwitzgebel, Why did we think we dreamed in black and white? *Studies in the History of Philosophy of Science* 33(2002):649-660.
[22] N.H. Kerr, Dreaming, imagery, and perception. In M.H. Kryger, T. Roth, W.C. Dement, (Eds.), *Principles and practice of sleep medicine.* 3ʳᵈ ed. Philadelphia: Saunders; 2000: 482-490.
[23] E. Schwitzgebel, Do people still report dreaming in black and white? An attempt to replicate a questionnaire from 1942. *Perceptual and Motor Skills* 96 (2003): 25-29.
[24] E. Schwitzgebel, C. Huang & Y. Zhou, Do we dream in color? Cultural variations and scepticism. *Dreaming* (2006)[In Press].
[25] E. Schwitzgebel, How well do we know our own conscious experience? The case of visual imagery. *Journal of Consciousness Studies* 9 (2002): 25-53
[26] D.Foulkes, *Dreaming: a Cognitive-Psychological Analysis.* Hillsdale, NJ: Lawrence Erlbaum Associates; 1985.
[27] M. Solms, *The Neuropsychology of Dreams.* Mahwah, NJ: Lawrence Erlbaum Associates; 1997.

[28] G.W. Domhoff, Finding meaning in dreams: a quantitative approach. New York: Plenum Press; 1996.
[29] J.A. Hobson & R. Stickgold. Dreaming: A neurocognitive approach. *Consciousness and Cognition,* 3 (1994): 1-15.
[30] A.G. Nejad, R.Z. Sanatinia & K. Yousofi, Dream contents in patients with major depressive disorder. *Canadian Journal of Psychiatry.* 49(2004): 864-5.
[31] J. Fookson, J. Antrobus, A connectionist model of bizarre thought and imagery. In: J.S. Antrobus, M. Bertini, (Eds.), *The Neuropsychology of Sleep and Dreaming.* Hillsdale, NJ: Lawrence Erlbaum Associates; 1992: 197-214.
[32] R. Reinsel, J. Antrobus & M. Wollman, Bizarreness in dreams and waking fantasy. In J.S. Antrobus, M. Bertini (Eds.) *The Neuropsychology of Sleep and Dreaming.* Hillsdale, NJ: Lawrence Erlbaum Associates; 1992. p.157-181.
[33] C.D. Rittenhouse, R. Stickgold & J.A. Hobson, Constraint on the transformation of characters, objects, and setting in dream reports. *Consciousness and Cognition,* 3(1994): 100-113.
[34] D. Kahn, E.F. Pace-Schott & J.A. Hobson, Consciousness in waking and dreaming: The roles of neuronal oscillation and neuromodulation in determining similarities and differences. *Neuroscience* 78(1997): 13-38.
[35] A. Rechtschaffen, The single-mindedness and isolation of dreams. *Sleep* 1(1978) : 97-109.
[36] T.L. Kahan, S. LaBerge, L. Levitan & P. Zimbardo, Similarities and differences between dreaming and waking cognition: An exploratory study. *Consciousness and Cognition,* 6(1997): 132-147.
[37] D. Kahn, J.A. Hobson, State-dependent thinking: A comparison of waking and dreaming thought. *Consciousness and Cognition,* 14 (2005): 429-438.
[38] P. Cicogna, M. Bosinelli, Consciousness during dreams. *Consciousness and Cognition,* 10 (2001):26-41.
[39] J.M. Merrit, R. Stickgold, E.F. Pace-Schott, J. Williams & J.A. Hobson, Emotion profiles in the dreams of men and women. *Consciousness and Cognition,* 3 (1994): 46-60.
[40] M. Schredl, E. Doll, Emotions in Diary Dreams. *Consciousness and Cognition* 7 (1998): 634-646.
[41] D. Kahn, E.F. Pace-Schott & J.A. Hobson, Emotion and cognition: Feeling and character identification in dreaming. *Consciousness and Cog*nition, 11 (2002): 34-50.
[42] J. Born, U. Wagner, Awareness in memory: being explicit about the role of sleep. *Trends in Cognitive Science* 8 (2004): 242-4.
[43] U. Wagner, S. Gais & J. Born, Emotional memory formation is enhanced across sleep intervals with high amounts of rapid eye movement sleep. *Learning and Memory,* 8(2001): 112-9.
[44] M. Leclaire, The 'mad scientists': psychoanalysis, dream and virtual reality. *International Journal of Psychoanalysis,* 84(2003): 331-346.
[45] R. Stickgold, Sleep-dependent memory consolidation. *Nature,* 437(2005): 1272-1278.
[46] E. Hartmann, We do not dream of the 3R's: implications for the nature of dream mentation. *Dreaming,* 10 (2000): 103-110.
[47] M. Schredl, F. Hofmann, Continuity between waking activities and dream activities. *Consciousness and Cognition,* 12 (2003): 298-308.
[48] R. Stickgold, A. Malia & D. Maguire, D. Roddenberry & M. O'Connor, Replaying the game: hypnagogic images in normals and amnesics. *Science* 290 (2000): 350-353.
[49] A. Revonsuo, The reinterpretation of dreams: An evolutionary hypothesis of the function of dreaming. In E.F. Pace-Schott, M. Solms, M. Blagrove & S. Harnard, (Eds.), *Sleep and dreaming: scientific advances and reconsiderations.* Cambridge: Cambridge University Press; 2003: 85-109.
[50] A. Revonsuo, Consciousness, dreams and virtual realties. *Philosophical Psychology,* 8 (1995): 35-58.
[51] M.R. Lansky, The legacy of the interpretation of dreams. In M.R. Lansky (Ed.), *Essential Papers on Dreams.* New York University Press; 1992: 3-31.
[52] J. L. Fosshage, The psychological function of dream: a revised psychoanalytic perspective. In: *Essential Papers on Dreams:* New York University Press; 1992: 249-271.
[53] M. Solms & O. Turnbull, *The Brain and the Inner World: An Introduction to the Neuroscience of Subjective Experience.* New York: Other Press; 2002.
[54] E. Hartmann, Outline for a theory on the nature and functions of dreaming. *Dreaming,* 6(1996): 147-170
[55] E. Hartman, Nightmare after trauma as paradigm for all dreams: a new approach to the nature and functions of dreaming. *Psychiatry,* 61(1998): 223-38.
[56] K. Valli, A. Revonsuo & O. Pälkäs, K.H. Ismail, K.J. Ali, R.L. Punamaki. The threat simulation theory of the evolutionary function of dreaming: Evidence from dreams of traumatized children. *Consciousness and Cognition,* 14(2005): 188-218.

[57] J.A. Cheyne, Play, dreams and simulation. In E.F. Pace-Schott, M. Solms, M. Blagrove & S. Harnard, (Eds.), *Sleep and dreaming: Scientific advances and Reconsiderations.* Cambridge: Cambridge University Press; 2003: 129-130.

[58] N. Humphrey, Dreaming and Play. In E.F. Pace-Schott, M. Solms, M. Blagrove & S. Harnard, (Eds.), *Sleep and dreaming: Scientific Advances and Reconsiderations.* Cambridge: Cambridge University Press; 2003: 164.

[59] E. Aserinsky, N. Kleitman: Regularly occurring periods of eye motility and concurrent phenomena during sleep. *Science*, 118(1953): 273-274.

[60] M. Jouvet, F. Michel, I. Courjon & H. Hermann, L'activite electrique du rhinencepale au cours du sommeil chez le chat. *Comptes Rendus de Societé Biologique, Paris*, 153 (1959): 101-105.

[61] M. Jouvet, F. Michel, Délenchements de la "phase paradoxale" du sommeil par stimulation du trone cerebral chez le chat intact et mesencephalique chronique. *Comptes Rendus de Societé Biologique, Paris*, 154 (1960): 634.

[62] M. Jouvet, (1993) *The Paradox of Sleep.* 2nd ed, MIT press, Cambridge, Mass, 1999.

[63] W. Dement, History of sleep physiology and medicine. In M.H. Kryger, T. Roth & W.C. Dement (Eds.) *Principles and Practice of Sleep Medicine.* 3rd Philadelphia: Saunders; 2000: 1-14.

[64] M.A. Carskaddon, A. Rechtschaffen, Monitoring and staging human sleep. In M.H. Kryger, T. Roth & W.C. Dement, (Eds.), Principles *and Practice of Sleep Medicine.* 3rd ed. Philadelphia: Saunders; 2000: 1197-1215.

[65] M. Solms, Dreaming and REM sleep are controlled by different brain mechanisms. In E.F. Pace-Schott, M. Solms, M. Blagrove & S. Harnard, (Eds.) *Sleep and dreaming: Scientific Advances and Reconsiderations.* Cambridge: Cambridge University Press; 2003: 51-58.

[66] M. Solms & O. Turnbull, *The brain and the inner world: an introduction to the neuroscience of subjective experience.* New York: Other Press; 2002.

[67] M. Jouvet & D. Jouvet, A study of the neurophysiological mechanisms of dreaming. *Electroencephalography and Clinical Neurophysiology* 24 (1963); Suppl.: 133

[68] E.A. Nofzinger, Functional neuroimaging of sleep. *Seminars in Neurology* 25(2005): 9-18.

[69] J.A. Hobson & R.W. McCarley, The brain as a dream state generator: an activation-synthesis hypothesis of the dream process. *American Journal of Psychiatry*, 134(1977): 1335-48.

[70] J.A. Waterworth & E.L. Waterworth, (2000) Presence and Absence in Educational VR: The Role of Perceptual Seduction in Conceptual Learning. *Themes in Education* 1(2000): 7-38.

[71] H.J. Moller, Assessment of Daytime Somnolence: More Complex Than You Might Think. *Advance for Managers of Respiratory Care,* 14 (2005): 12-15.

[72] H. Blumenfeld, Consciousness and epilepsy: why are patients with absence seizures absent? *Progress in Brain Research.* 150 (2005): 271-86.

[73] H.J. Moller, L. Kayumov, E.L. Bulmash & C.M. Shapiro, Assessing the effects of driver sleepiness on driving performance using combined electrophysiological monitoring and real-time computerized driving simulation: normative daytime circadian data. In D.A. Vincenzi, M. Mouloua & P.A. Hancock (Eds.), *Human Performance, Situation Awareness and Automation: Current Research Trends.* L. Erlbaum Associates, Mahwah, NJ, 2004: 296-301.

[74] M.M. Ohayon, R.G. Priest, M. Caulet & C. Guilleminault, Hypnagogic and hypnopompic hallucinations: pathological phenomena? *British Journal of Psychiatry.* 169 (1996): 459-67.

[75] C.R. Soldatos & T.J. Paparrigopoulos, Sleep physiology and pathology: pertinence to psychiatry. *International Review of Psychiatry.* 17(2005): 213-28.

[76] T.A. Mellman, V. Bustamente, A.I. Fins, W.R. Pigeon & B. Nolan, REM sleep and the early development of posttraumatic stress disorder. *American Journal of Psychiatry*, 159 (2002): 1696-1701.

[77] S.A. Rauch, E.B. Foa, J.M. Furr & J.C. Filip, Imagery vividness and perceived anxious arousal in prolonged exposure treatment for PTSD. *Journal of Traumatic Stress*, 17 (2004): 461-5.

[78] M.Y. Agargun & R. Cartwright, REM sleep, dream variables and suicidality in depressed patients. *Psychiatry Research*, 119 (2003): 33-9.

[79] N. Tsuno, A. Besset & K. Ritchie, Sleep and Depression. *Journal of Clinical Psychiatry,* 66(2005): 1254-69.

[80] R.D. Cartwright, S. Lloyd, S. Knight & I. Trenholme, Broken dreams: a study of the effects of divorce and depression on dream content. *Psychiatry,* 47(1984): 251-9.

[81] J.L. Cantero, M. Atienza, R. Stickgold & J.A. Hobson, Nightcap: a reliable system for determining sleep onset latency. *Sleep* 25(2002): 238-45.

[82]   J.A. Hobson, *Dreaming: An introduction to the science of sleep.* Oxford University Press: Oxford; 2002.
[83]   A.L. Zadra & R.O. Pihl, Lucid dreaming as a treatment for recurrent nightmares. *Psychotherapy and Psychosomatics,* 66 (1997): 50-5.
[84]   B. Krakow, M. Hollifield, R. Schrader, M. Koss, D. Tandberg, J. Lauriello, L. McBride, T. Warner, D. Cheng, T. Edmond & R. Kellner, A controlled study of imagery rehearsal for chronic nightmares in sexual assault survivors with PTSD: a preliminary report. *Journal of Traumatic Stress,* 13 (2000): 589-601
[85]   M.A. Lumley & R.A. Bazydlo, The relationship of alexithymia characteristics to dreaming. *Journal of Psychosomatic Research,* 48 (2000): 561-7.
[86]   H.G. Hoffman, T. Richards, B. Coda, A. Richards & S.R. Sharar, The illusion of presence in immersive virtual reality during an fMRI brain scan. *CyberPsychology and Behavior,* 6(2003): 127-31.
[87]   T. Baumgartner, L. Valko, M. Esslen & L. Jancke, Neural correlate of spatial presence in an arousing and noninteractive virtual reality: an EEG and psychophysiology study. *Cyberpsychology and Behavior,* 9(2006): 30-45
[88]   W.F. Bischoff & P. Boulanger, Spatial navigation in virtual reality environments: an EEG analysis. *CyberPsychology and Behavior,* 6(2003): 487-95.
[89]   R. Stickgold, Watching the sleeping brain watch us - sensory processing during sleep. *Trends in Neuroscience,* 24(2001): 307-9.
[90]   M.W. Mahowald, M.C. Bornemann & C.H. Schenck, Parasomnias. *Seminars in Neurology* 3(2004): 283-92.
[91]   Wikipedia- Yumemi Kobo [Internet Webpage]. 2006. Online: http://en.wikipedia.org/wiki/Yumemi_Kobo
[92]   G. Riva, Virtual reality in psychotherapy: review. *CyberPsychology and Behavior,* 8 (2005): 220-30
[93]   B.O. Rothbaum, L.F. Hodges, D. Ready, K. Graap, R.D. Alarcon, Virtual reality exposure therapy for Vietnam veterans with posttraumatic stress disorder. *Journal of Clinical Psychiatry,* 62 (2001): 617-22.
[94]   A. Rizzo, J. Pair, P. J. McNerney, E. Eastlund, B. Manson, J. Gratch, R. Hill & B. Swartout, Development of a VR therapy application for Iraq war military personnel with PTSD. *Studies in Health Technology and Informatics,* 111(2005): 407-413.
[95]   G. Pillar, A. Malhotra & P. Lavie, Post-traumatic stress disorder and sleep-what a nightmare! *Sleep Medicine Reviews,* 4 (2000): 183-200.
[96]   T. Marsh, P. Wright & S. Smith, Evaluation for the design of experience in virtual environments: modeling breakdown of interaction and illusion. *CyberPsychology and Behavior,* 4 (2001): 225-38.
[97]   Wikipedia- Videohypertransference [Internet Webpage]. 2006. Online: http://en.wikipedia.org/wiki/Videohypertransference
[98]   N.S. Schutte, J.M. Malouff, J.C. Post-Gorden & A.L. Rodasta, Effects of playing video games on children's aggressive and other behaviors. *Journal of Applied Social Psychology,* 18 (1988): 454-460.
[99]   C.A. Anderson & B.J. Bushman, Effects of violent video games on aggressive behavior, aggressive cognition, aggressive affect, physiological arousal, and prosocial behavior: A meta-analytic review of the scientific literature. *Psychological Science,* 12 (2001): 353-359.
[100] McLuhan, *Hot and Cool,* G.E. Stearn (Ed.), New York, Dial Press, Inc., 1967

SECTION III

FROM COMMUNICATION TO PRESENCE: EMOTION, COGNITION AND CULTURE

To understand communication, we should to bear in mind the continuous variation of meanings between stability and instability, as we said in previous section.

We should also take into account the range of signaling systems, and the plurality of expressive means available to the communicators in order to express their communicative intention.

We have to focus our attention on the semantic synchrony process, intended as the speaker's competence to organize, co-ordinate, and make the different communicative systems converge on each other in order to make explicit the meaning of one's own communicative intention in a unitary and coherent way.

Anolli, 2003

From Communication to Presence
G. Riva et al. (Eds.)
IOS Press, 2006

6   Structure and Communication in Interactions

Magnus S. MAGNUSSON

Abstract. The highly demanding study of meaning, intention, and communication including miscommunication, in human interaction seems to call for the development of powerful new approaches and in that context the astonishing raw power of modern computers may eventually be harnessed, given that adequate models, methods, algorithms and software be developed and made available. In this context, a proposed data structure, pattern definitions, algorithms, and a new statistical validation test are proposed. New additions are introduced to this theoretical/methodological system (called t-system) including special definitions of well known phenomena such as bursts and cyclical occurrence as well as of more novel concepts called "t-blocks", "t-metronomes" and "ghost cycles". A method is introduced to deal with the estimation of a priori probability (or statistical significance) of individual patterns without consideration of the arbitrary binary trees used for their detection and in this context "t-templates" and their matching are introduced. Statistical validation through shuffling of data is compared with a suggested method called (random series) rotation (t-rotation) and results obtained with each are compared for both human and neuronal interactions. It is pointed out that brain behavior as observed with brain scanners does not offer direct insight into meaning and intentions, but essentially means more behavior to observe and more patterns to be detected, while limitations in social neuroscience seem to repeat to those of earlier human interaction studies and also due to technical difficulties. Finally some thoughts and questions are put forward concerning possible relations between on one hand hidden patterns and symmetry in interactions and on the other hand meaning, intentions, communication and miscommunication in highly patterned human interactions as well as about the possible need for new and specialized mathematics for the study of these phenomena.

Contents

6.1 Introduction

Patterns in behavior are frequently hidden from the consciousness of those who perform them as well as to unaided observers. Considering this as a fact, the approach outlined here is about defining and discovering repeated temporal patterns in behavior with a special focus on interactive behavior. For this, algorithms have been developed as a kind of "seeing aids" somewhat like eye-glasses, microscopes, telescopes, sonar and various other instruments.

This approach has often led to the discovery of unexpected patterns some of which have been surprising and have often elicited the questions "But what does it mean?" referring to some particular detected pattern, or more generally, "What do they mean?" referring to many or all such patterns. Especially when no clear meaning is given to the term "meaning", answering such questions is no simple matter, but it seems that very strong demands in this direction are not always justified given the present level of understanding of human behavior and interactions. On the other hand, discovering previously unknown repeated patterns or symmetry is often considered a major goal and achievement in sciences such as physics (see below) and biology (for example, the discovery of the double helix) even before anything can be said about their "meaning" not to mention any kind of "intentions" behind their existence.

It has been said that in its rush to become a respectable science, psychology neglected its natural history phase, a part of which is to find out what phenomena exist and need explanation within the particular field of research. In astronomy such phenomena now include galaxies and galaxy clusters, which were at best only dots of light for the early unaided observers who frequently assigned all kinds of meaning and intentions to what little they could possibly see. Extensive regularities in the movements of various kinds of heavenly bodies were only discovered after thousands of years of systematic observation and record keeping, but neither meaning or intention have really been found even if many have bee assigned. No more than, for example, in the repeated interaction patterns or symmetries within the nuclei of atoms discovered through great efforts by a large number of highly trained specialists using extremely expensive instruments as in the case of, for example, leptons and quarks:

"So, it's simply not yet understood why, if there are three generations of leptons, there should necessarily be precisely three generations of quarks. It could just be an accident of nature, but past experience suggests that a symmetry pattern as simple and clear as this provides an essential, if yet undeciphered, clue about the workings of nature." ([1], p. 118).

Accounts of the concept of symmetry and its use as well as of the closely related Group Theory are easily available (for example, [2-4]).

6.2. Brain-patterns and Human Interaction

When the present repeated pattern discovery approach was adopted in the early seventies with a strong desire for objectivity, no real access was available to the inner events of the active human brain and intentions could only be inferred from observable verbal and nonverbal behavior including self-reports such as individuals' introspections about their own intentions and behavior. However, people often being unconscious about their intentions and how they communicate or bring about the corresponding wanted changes in others, self-report is known to be unreliable scientific evidence. Making inferences about others intentions on the basis of direct observations of their behavior, on the other hand, is usually colored by projections and general lack of context and situation awareness by the observer. These difficult matters related to conscience, intensions, miscommunications (see notably, [5]) will be briefly reconsidered at the end of this paper after considering some issues and results regarding patterning and its detection in interactive behavior.

As a mater of fact, there seems to be no easy track around these difficulties as context is so decisive for meaning and effect and frequently extends in such complex ways in time and space. Even now in times of brain scanners and imaging, although still mostly applicable to immobile individuals rather than to natural interactions, such information calls for non-obvious interpretations.

"Despite the impressive amount of research generated, social cognitive neuroscience is still in its infancy and has so far focused on the study of very basic social abilities… The simplicity of the studies to date may reflect the early stage of development of the field and the methodological limits imposed by neuroimaging and other neurophysiological techniques." ([6], p. xvii.)

So, in spite of the spectacular methodological progress offered by brain scanners they still do not provide direct access to conscious and/or unconscious meanings or intentions. Finding out with certainty what is "really" going on even in the simplest dyadic encounter is therefore still far beyond easy scientific reach. As brain scanner technology enters the realm of communication research, familiar concerns seem to resurface:

"Most of the neuroimaging studies that investigate social phenomena do so from a uni-directional perspective. The focus has been on understanding the effects of socially relevant stimuli on the mind of a single person. In contrast, the study of social interaction involves by definition a bi-directional perspective and is concerned with the question of how two minds shape each other mutually through reciprocal interactions." ([6], p. xvii.)

These concerns recall the evolution within psychology from "interaction studies" focusing on just one individual within an interaction to a focus on the interaction as an organized whole where both or all parties have to be considered together, that is, at the same time and as a single system. Before film or video it was difficult to fix the object of study for thorough analysis and when that problem was solved there came the difficulty of analyzing by hand the complex resulting data so that the analysis of painstakingly established real-time behavior records mostly concerned frequencies and durations of the behaviors. With computers such analysis was made extremely quickly, but no methods or software were available for relevant deeper analysis specially aimed at real-time behavioral data. Often methods and software were used that had been developed for very different purposes, even those intended for the analysis of questionnaire data rather than the real-time event-streams of interactive behavior. For those who wanted to delve deeper into the obscure structure they sensed before their eyes, no special purpose tools were available.

Technological and related methodological progress thus has long been a shaping factor in interaction and communication research. The future possibility of integrating behavioral data and data from ever more advanced brain-imaging technology that would amongst other allow scanning brain activity in freely moving individuals is certainly a stimulating perspective. But such technology also produces complex real-time streams of brain-events, which probably also form patterns that need to be discovered and interpreted in relation to other types of events and patterns and possibly at least some of the temporal patterning within the brain may be similar to that of the behavior it produces.

Unfortunately, observation of the active brain has not provided access to any kind of "little man" who can tell what is really going on and modern brain scanners only find more behavior and more, not less, behavioral patterns to discover. Application of t-pattern analysis to interactions within populations of neurons in living brains is in progress [7].

It has been the philosophy of the present pattern definition and detection approach to keep things as simple as possible for a number of reasons. One main reason is that mathematically/statistically complex methods tend to be misunderstood and/or misused if not simply (and often wisely) ignored. It also seems a reasonable pursuit to make available behavioral research models, methods and tools that can be fully understood and used without years of special mathematical/statistical preparation which is often impossible to include in either university studies or research carriers. Furthermore, approximation is here chosen when greater precision lies beyond available resources or represents uncertain scientific gain.

6.2.1 The Data Structure

The t-pattern model described below refers to a set of event-types $E = \{e_1, e_2, e_3...\}$ and their respective occurrence time point series $S = \{s_1, s_2, s_3...\}$ within a continuous observation period $(1, T)$ of T discrete time units; where e_i has occurrence time series s_i.

The event-types in E typically stand for the beginning or ending of some behavior by an actor (agent, system, etc.). For example, "Sue begins running" and "Bill ends laughing" are event-types and are here noted as "sue,b,run" and "bill,e,laugh". Similarly, the event-type "neuron 12 fires" may be noted simply as, for example, "n12", since a spike may be considered too short for coding its beginning and end separately and since firing may be all that is registered for a neuron. The coded behavior records thus consist of the occurrence time series of such types of events so a data set, D, therefore really consists of a set of labeled series: $D = \{(e, s)_1, (e, s)_2, (e, s)_3 ...\}$ and the observation time, T.

Such data is called t-data and is the basic reference for all definitions in the t-pattern system which integrates a growing number of structural types aimed at the analysis and description of behavior. Figure 1 shows a real example of such data, below referred to as *Data1*, including 82 event-type series resulting from the coding of approximately 13:30 min of dyadic toy-play and toy-exchange interaction between five-year-olds. A previously published [8] list of categories for ethological analysis of children's behavior with a few additions, was used for the coding that was carried out using a digitized 15 frames per second video recording and an interactive multimedia computer program.

As a matter of fact, the definitions only refer to S and [1, T] and the corresponding elements in E are only seen as series labels or names. However, once patterns have been detected they can be selected and analyzed on the basis of information contained in the labels.

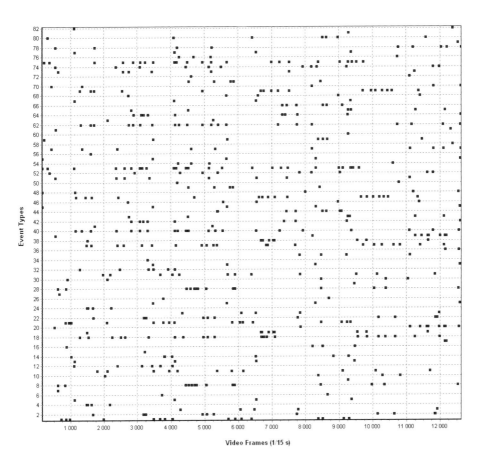

Figure 1. This figure shows all the occurrence time points of each of the 82 event-types coded in a 13.5 min toy-play & toy-exchange interaction between two five-year-olds. The occurrence times for each of the 1 to 82 event-types can thus be read from left to right across the chart. The event-types are listed in the order indicated in the Appendix. This data set is referred to as *Data1*. The event-types with their meanings are listed in the Appendix.

Analysis of data of this kind has often focused exclusively on the number of occurrences (frequency) of the event-types or of the durations of the periods from their beginnings to their ends (i.e., from sue,**b**,run to sue,**e**,run). This could be a demanding task when it had to be done by hand, but usually is now done in less than a second on a PC. Figure 2 shows the result of such analysis of *Data1* (shown in Figure 1) and indicates the limited information it provides about the real-time patterning of the interaction.

The number of other kinds of relationships that may exist between the points in S is infinite and exploring but the simplest is impossible by hand. As a matter of fact, such tasks can be very hard or even impossible using high speed computers. For example, given data with 100 series, considering all possible temporal patterns each involving up to all 100 of is such a task. Blind and unlimited search for any and all kinds of patterns even in the most ordinary kind of real-time behavior records is therefore doomed even if it made sense.

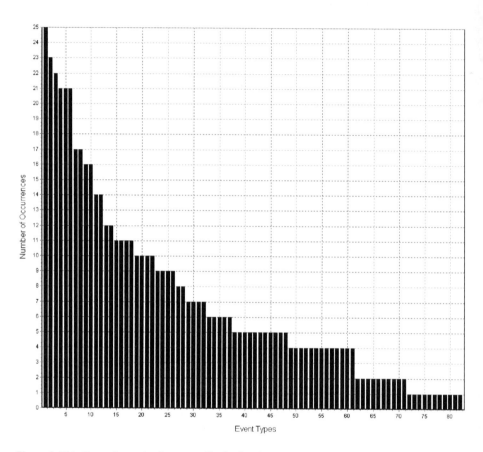

Figure 2. This figure shows the frequency distribution for the 82 event-types in *Data1*. The event-types are listed in the appendix.

To instead harness the amazing power of the modern PC now everywhere present and frequently idle, formalized ideas regarding things to look for are necessary.

A particular kind of structure, called a t-pattern and some derived aspects that together are called the t-system, have been proposed in this context and are described in detail elsewhere and various applications cited [9-12] but short descriptions will be presented below. Some new additions to the system will also be described and illustrative results of their application in the analysis of interactions presented.

6.2.2 The T-pattern

A t-pattern is basically a set of event-types occurring concurrently and/or sequentially with **significantly invariant** time distances between each consecutive pair within the pattern, which can be noted in the following way:

I) $X_1 \approx dt_1 \ X_2 \approx dt_2 \ X_3 \ ... \ X_i \approx dt_i \ X_{i+1} ... \ X_{m-1} \approx dt_{m-1} \ X_m$

Where each X term stands for some element of E (some event-type) and the general term $X_i \approx dt_i \ X_{i+1}$ means that during occurrences of the pattern, consecutive terms X_i and X_{i+1} are separated by the characteristic approximate time distance $\approx dt_i$.

The meaning of the term "significantly invariant" above must, of course, be defined formally amongst other for detection purposes using automatic computational algorithms.

For this purpose I) above is replaced by a consideration of the variation limits of each $\approx dt$ term, that is, the intervals between the lowest and the highest value of each $\approx dt_i$ within a given observation period (data set):

II) $X_1 \ [d_1, d_2]_1 \ X_2 \ [d_1, d_2]_2 \ X_3 \ ... \ X_i \ [d_1, d_2]_i \ X_{i+1} ... \ X_{m-1} \ [d_1, d_2]_{m-1} \ X_m$

Where the general term $X_i \ [d_1, d_2]_i \ X_{i+1}$ now means that within occurrences of the pattern, after an occurrence of X_i at t there is a time window $[t+d_1, t+d_2]_i$ within which X_{i+1} will occur. (Here, m is called the <u>length</u> of the pattern.)

To be truly useful for the detection of complex hierarchical patterns, the d_1 and d_2 parameters of each interval must be detected and the pattern detection process must be done bottom-up to be computationally feasible. For this purpose a binary tree structure is imposed such that a particular pattern of type II) above, for example,

A $[d_1, d_2]_1$ B $[d_1, d_2]_2$ C $[d_1, d_2]_3$ D

can be seen as the terminal string of one or more such a trees, for example,

((A $[d_1, d_2]_1$ B) $[d_1, d_2]_2$ (C $[d_1, d_2]_3$ D)) or
((A $[d_1, d_2]_1$ (B $[d_1, d_2]_2$ C)) $[d_1, d_2]_3$ D)) or (A $[d_1, d_2]_1$ (B $[d_1, d_2]_2$ (C $[d_1, d_2]_3$ D)))

In this way the $[d_1, d_2]$ can be seen as a binary relation between the two branches at each non-terminal node of the pattern. Significant invariance in the distance between any two branches is here defined on this basis and only trees with such a relation at each non-terminal node are t-patterns by definition. Between any two point series (as those in S), s_a and s_b, a particular relation is thus defined called a critical interval relation, $R(s_a, s_b, c, d_1, d_2)$, where c is the pre-specified level of significance and $[d_1, d_2]$ is the critical interval that needs to be detected. For the series s_a and s_b (respectively, noted as t_{ai} ; $i=1..N_a$ and t_{bj} ; $j = 1..N_b$) this relation exists, per definition, if for significantly more of the intervals $[t_{ai} + d_1, t_{ai} + d_2]$ than expected by chance, there is at least one point t in s_b such that $t_{ai} + d_1 \leq t \leq t_{ai} + d_2$; where $0 \leq d_1 \leq d_2$, and $[d_1, d_2]$ is the largest interval for which this is true, and N_a and N_b are, respectively, the number of occurrences of event-types e_a and e_b.

In other words, after occurrences of e_a at t there is a time window $[t + d_1, t + d_2]$ within which significantly more often than chance expectation there is at least one occurrence of e_b. The zero-hypothesis is that s_a and s_b are independently distributed and that s_b has constant probability $= N_b/T$ of occurrence per unit time throughout $[1, T]$. (Note that event-types are considered as a patterns of length m=1.) For examples of t-patterns, respectively, $X_1...X_{27}$ and $X_1...X_9$, with their imposed binary trees see the left sides of figures 3 and 4.

6.2.3 The detection algorithm

The detection algorithm searches for all possible critical interval relationships between all the initial series in the data as well as those created for the patterns found during the detection process and added to the data.

Each time a critical interval is found between A and B (whether event-types or patterns) all those instances of A and B where B begins within the critical interval measured from the last element of A are connected to form an instance of pattern (A B). If A and B are of lengths m_1 and m_2, respectively, the resulting pattern (A B) will be of length $m_1 + m_2$ and its instances will start the first element of A and end at the last element of B. (An event-type can be see as a pattern of length m = 1 and therefore as its own first and last element.) As many different significant binary trees may correspond to the same underlying t-pattern, this algorithm alone frequently makes many equivalent as well as partial (i.e., with missing elements) detections of the same underlying pattern which often leads to combinatorial explosions and results impossible to digest.

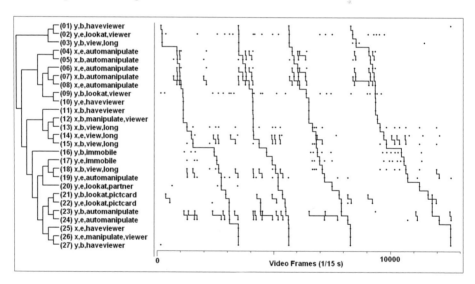

Figure 3. This figure shows the longest pattern m=27 detected in *Data1*. On the left is the terminal string of event-types: $X_1...X_{27}$ as well as the binary tree of critical interval relationships. On the right of each event-type its occurrence time series is shown. Connecting lines show how points from each series are connected to form the pattern that occurs four times and in this case begins and ends with the same series which therefore appears twice (that is, $X_1 = X_{27}$). The four occurrences of this single pattern cover 100% of the observation period of approximately 13.5 min. P(template) $< 10^{-25}$, P(4 template occurrences) $< 10^{-102}$. Longest pattern length after 1000 rotations was m=12 while the number of occurrences of patterns of that length was 107.16 standard deviations greater than random mean. See text.

By assuming the underlying t-patterns and comparing all patterns that are detected, a kind of completeness competition is thus set up between detected patterns such that only and most complete survives.

6.3 Searching for more structure

Looking at figures such as those above and just thinking about every-day behavior and interactions, it is obvious that multiple (countless) aspects of the temporal structure of behavior are not treated by the t-pattern type. In trying to discover further structure, some new terms, definitions and algorithms have recently been added to the t-system and are described here in essence.

The following sections deal with issues concerning aspects hitherto ignored in the t-system. Amongst these are familiar phenomena such as bursts and cycles including related phenomena referred to as "t-blocks", "t-metronomes" and "ghost cycles" ("t-gcycles"). To keep the t-system as simple as possible and to facilitate the development of corresponding algorithms, all definitions of these phenomena are based on the critical interval relationship.

A newly developed approach will also be described for assigning a priori probabilities to whole patterns without consideration of the arbitrary binary tree structure used for their detection. To deal with the critical issue of statistical validation a new randomization method, called (random) rotation, is also described.

6.3.1 Bursts

One of the terms that now have been given definitions specially adapted to the t-system is the burst, referring to a number of points (events of the same type) occurring in succession with distances between them that are much shorter than the average. Until very recently, the t-pattern detection algorithms have not dealt directly with such phenomena which have consequently been invisible to the corresponding software. But now a "t-burst" is defined and detected as a special kind of t-pattern and can therefore also occur as a component of more complex t-patterns (including higher-order bursts). Any t-pattern can also form t-bursts, which in turn may occur as components of more complex t-patterns.

The t-burst is defined and integrated into t-pattern detection on the basis of the critical interval relationship requiring minimal changes to the existing algorithms. The t-burst thus exists in a single series of n points, t_i ; i=1,2,..n, within [1, T] if a fast critical interval, [1, d] exists between the two sub-series t_i ; i = 1, 2, n-1 and t_i where i = 2, 3,..n and these bursts occur where consecutive points in t_i are separated by distances within the critical interval range; that is, where $t_i + 1 <= t_{i+1} <= t_i + d$. Since the series t_i may represent either an event-type (A) or a pattern (Q), patterns such as (A A) and (Q Q) may be formed and become components of higher order t-patterns. See, for example, the burst X_4 and X_5 in event-type "n,b,fou,tac" (novice begins providing information) in figure 4. A more unusual example can be seen in figure 5, the pattern $X_1...X_{12}$ which is a single burst of three occurrences of the pattern $X_1...X_6$ or $X_7...X_{12}$. This also shows that the detection of a burst that only occurs once is possible). Both figures are based on data from a previously published study of children's problem solving interactions [13].

6.3.2 Blocks

Some t-patterns have a strikingly similar duration each time they occur. This is most apparent when the patterns are long, including many critical intervals allowing for considerable variation in the total duration of different instances, that is, the time from X_1 to X_m.

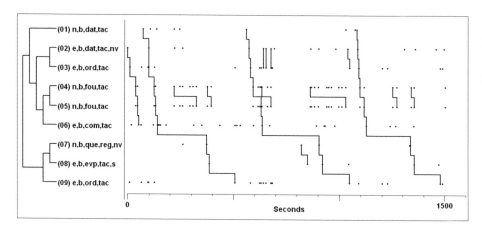

Figure 4. This figure shows a highly significant pattern detected in children's approximately 25-min puzzle-solving dyadic interaction. P(template) < 10^{-6} and P(3 template occurrences) < 10^{-18}. Maximum length after 1000 random rotations was m=7 with occurrence in the real data >26 standard deviations over random mean. It contains a burst in n,b,fou,tac, which is therefore shown twice; as X_4 and X_5 forming the first level pattern (X_4 X_5) sometimes occurring as parts of the larger pattern $X_1..X_9$. Actors are e and n. Only the beginnings of behaviors, "b", were coded. Temporal resolution = one second. Dat = directs the other's attention. Tac = task (solving a puzzle). "nv" = nonverbally; "ord" = gives and order; "que" = asks a question; "reg" = rule for the solution of the puzzle; "evp" = positive evaluation of progress (in solving puzzle); "com" = makes a comment; "s" = soliloquy (talking to oneself); "fou" = provides information. N,b,fou,tac thus means: n begins providing information regarding the task. Data from an earlier study [13].

To allow automatic detection and selection of such patterns they have been given a simple formal definition and named "t-blocks". A t-block is thus defined as a t-pattern where there is a critical interval relationship between its beginning and end elements, X_1 and X_m. For example, a repeated pattern ABCD is a t-block if there is a critical interval relation between the occurrences series of, respectively, A and D, when these occur as parts of ABCD. All first level patterns, having only two event-types related by a critical interval, are thus t-blocks by definition. The pattern $X_1...X_9$ in Figure 4 is an example of a t-block.

6.3.3 Cycles

A cyclical occurrence of event-types and t-patterns is frequently observed in interactions (see for example, Figures 3 and 4), but cyclical aspects are not involved in the definition of t-patterns, and the corresponding detection algorithms do not deal with them. The following definition of cyclical occurrence based on the critical interval relationship now allows consideration of this aspect for event-types as well as t-patterns. The definition is partly inspired by literature regarding (approximate translation) symmetry cited above. For a single series, the definition of cyclical occurrence is identical to that of bursts, except that the fast critical interval [1, d] is

replaced by a *free* critical interval [d_1, d_2] (where both the lower and the upper limit may vary). A pattern, Q, is by definition cyclical if at least one of its terms, $X_1...X_m$ (when occurring as such) is cyclical (and is therefore called a cyclical term in Q).
A pattern is said to be x% cyclical if x% of its terminals are cyclical in this way. Differing from bursts, no connection operation is at the moment used for this relationship. Patterns are thus classified as cyclical or not, but no new entities and occurrence series are formed.

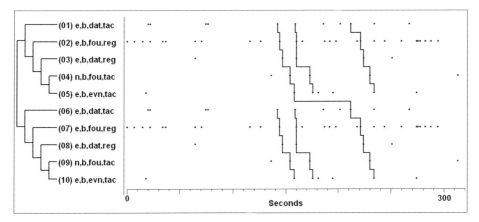

Figure 5. This figure shows a pattern of length m=10 that is a single burst of three occurrences of a t-pattern of length m=5: $X_1...X_5$ (or $X_6...X_{10}$). P(template) = P(1 template occurrence) < 10^{-6}; as the burst only occurs once. Occurrence deviation from random mean after 1000 rotations = 3.8 standard deviations. The binary detection tree is on the left side and the occurrence series of each event-type appears immediately to its right. Connection lines show how the three occurrences of pattern are constructed. For burst patterns, the pattern is shown twice as, respectively, $X_1...X_5$ and $X_6...X_{10}$. A horizontal line connects the ending (X_5) of the first instance and the beginning (X_6) of the last instance of in the burst; here of the first and third instances of pattern $X_1...X_5$ (or $X_6...X_{10}$). Evn = negative evaluation (of progress in solving the puzzle). See text and figure 4 regarding the meaning of the other codes. Data from an earlier study [13].

6.3.4 Metronomes

When looking at a t-pattern diagram, for example, Figures 3 and 4, not only might the cyclical occurrence of a pattern be striking, but also some of its terms considered *per se* (as independent event-types) may also seem cyclical with a similar periodicity and to act as a kind of metronome for the pattern. This is most striking when such event-types occur as the first element of a pattern and seem to direct or guide the cyclical rhythm of the full pattern (as, for example, in Figure 3). But as defined here, such "t-metronomes" may also happen at any position other than the first within $X_1...X_m$. Moreover, some such t-metronomes may occur in a cyclical fashion while the pattern, within which it is a cyclical term occurs more rarely, i.e. using a musical reference, the pattern may happen only on some of the metronome's beats. Per definition, a t-metronome is a cyclical terminal of a pattern with critical interval [d_1, d_2] which, when considered as an event-type independently of the pattern, it is also cyclical with a critical interval [xd_1, xd_2] such that there is an overlap between [k * xd_1, k * xd_2] and [d_1, d_2]; where k is a positive integer. A number of such metronome event-types have just been detected and will be reported later.

6.3.5 Cyclical patterns without a metronome

Cyclical patterns that do not have any metronome components are here called (for want of a better name) "ghost cycles" (t-gcycles) as they behave cyclically without any visible guidance. Such patterns are now routinely found and illustrate as earlier suggested that prior detection of patterns can be necessary for the discovery of cyclical organization, that is, when such organization is not present in any of the initial data series (14).

6.4 Templates and a priori probabilities

It is mainly for practical reasons that t-patterns are defined and detected as binary tree structures as the testing of all possible fairly long t-patterns would otherwise not be feasible even for the fastest computers. However, when a t-pattern has been detected, it is possible to ignore the tree structure and simply look at the pattern as under II) above and try to assign an a priori probability irrespective to any tree structure:

$$X_1 [d_1, d_2]_1 X_2 [d_1, d_2]_2 X_3 \ldots X_i [d_1, d_2]_i X_{i+1} \ldots X_{m-1} [d_1, d_2]_{m-1} X_m$$

And in the fully specified case of a detected pattern, for example, as:

$$A [3, 15]_1 B [17, 39]_2 C [5, 12]_3 D$$

Where A, B, C, and D are particular event-types.

   This kind of structure derived from a t-pattern is here referred to as a t-template, W.

It can also be expressed exclusively in terms of the lengths of the intervals:

$$A [13]_1 B [23]_2 C [8]_3 D$$

As simple estimate of the probability of finding a single match for such a structure in a shuffled version of data will here be used as an estimate of the a priori probability of the template. For the above template this a priori probability $P(W)$ is defined as the product P(of finding a B within a randomly placed interval of length 13) * P(of finding a C within a randomly placed interval of length 23) * P(of finding a D within a randomly placed interval of length 8). Any detected t-pattern can thus be assigned a probability equal to that of its implicit t-template, which also may be of other important use (see below).

   Thus if a pattern Q with t-template W is detected, for example, n times in real data, D, the a priori probability assigned to this is thus $P(W)^n$, which is also called the a priori probability of Q's occurrence in D. These probabilities are often extremely small so they are best expressed as logarithms (here, base 10, i.e., log10) and values between 10 and 200 are often seen. This is actually in good accordance with the extreme significance of differences between the numbers of detected patterns of each length in, respectively, real and randomized data, where frequently $p < 10^{-7}$ (approximately) for all but the shortest patterns (see below).

The computation of the p values for such deviation was done with Theme 6 beta version. At the time of this writing it uses the "NormDist" function in TurboPower's Systools for Delphi, which returns zero for values lower than approximately 10^{-7}, which happens not far from five or six standard deviations. For this reason p values are not presented for real versus randomized data comparisons below, but in terms of standard deviations that typically far exceed that number. (The NormDist routine is to be replaced in Theme by a more powerful routine.)

6.4.1 Statistical significance, shuffling and random rotation

The detection of critical intervals and therefore t-patterns is based a zero hypothesis that is tested possibly millions of times when exploring for patterns in a single data set. Obviously, many would thus be significant even if the data were random. A crucial issue here is thus whether findings are statistically significant, that is, whether much fewer patterns are detected after randomization of the data.

Already in the first version of THEME™ ([15, 16]; (copyright and development by PatternVision, www.patternvision.com; distributed by Noldus Information Technology, www.noldus.com), this issue was tackled quite directly as each search in real data was followed by a search in a shuffled version of the same data, that is, after the time points in each series in the real data have been randomly redistributed over the observation period. In this way the size of the data remains the same as the number of series, and the number of points in each, remain unchanged. By repeatedly shuffling and then searching for patterns in the same data set, an occurrence distribution with a mean and a standard deviation is obtained for each pattern length. This allows comparison with the findings in the original (un-shuffled) data and differences can be expressed in terms of standard deviations and p values.

For most data, these differences have been considerable, for example, between 5 and 20 standard deviations with corresponding (extremely) low p values, and as expected the differences are generally much greater for the longer patterns. For the longest patterns detected in real data, typically none at all are found after shuffling the data and even after repeating the randomization and search process more than a thousand times, which is, for example, the case for the patterns in figures 3 and 4. It is interesting that for the shortest patterns there may actually be no difference at all or it may even occasionally be negative, that is, slightly more very short patterns may be found in the randomized data. This could easily be the case if, for example, many of the coded event-types are of a kind that do not occur in t-patterns, except in randomized (non-sense) data.

6.4.1.1 Deciding significance for "synfire" patterns and t-patterns

With regard to the detection of so called "synfire" patterns in neuronal activity (see, for example, 17, and references therein) the possibility has been raised that shuffling data may give misleading results, exaggerating the difference between random and real data. Synfire patterns have some similarity with t-patterns and may in essence be described as t-patterns where all critical intervals are the same and very narrow, for example, [0, 1] or [1, 1]. The detection algorithm therefore does not detect critical intervals relationships, but tries to find matches for the prefixed one (which remains unchanged throughout). No completeness competition between patterns is involved either.

The number of synfire patterns detected in real data compared to shuffled data is small and may not be significant and the possibility exists that the differences do not reflect dependencies between series in the real data, but rather the particular structure of each of the series. Different from the synfire patterns, the differences between the number of t-patterns detected in real and shuffled data is typically great or somewhere between 5 and 200 standard deviations. However, a new randomization method has been developed that maintains practically unchanged the structure of each series while randomizing the relationship between them. This can be visualized as figure 1 being wrapped around a cylinder whereby each series forms, around the cylinder, a circle that can be rotated by a random number of degrees independently of the others. Thus, instead of shuffling every series, all series are left unchanged, but each one is rotated by a new random number of degrees (between 1 and 359).

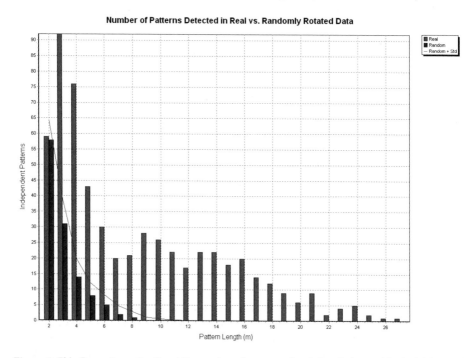

Number of Patterns Detected in Real vs. Randomly Rotated Data

Figure 6. This figure shows for *Data1* the number of patterns of each length detected in the initial (real) dataset as well as the mean number for each length detected in one thousand searches in the same number of randomly rotated (see text) versions of the same data. The line shows mean + 1 standard deviation for the 1000 random cases. Note that no patterns of length greater than 12 are detected in any of the randomized data, while patterns of length up to 27 are detected in the real data. (See also corresponding Figures 7 and 8.)

Since much more of the initial structure of the data is thus maintained than in the shuffle case, differences between randomized and real data are also smaller for rotated than for shuffled data. However, since the differences are generally much greater than usually required in significance testing, the differences between the two methods have not yet been important enough to change conclusions.

Both kinds of test have now been implemented in the Theme software (version 6) allowing easy comparison of the results. Using *Data1* (Figure 1), Figures 7 and 8, show results for, respectively, the shuffling and rotation test obtained through one thousand repetitions of randomization followed by detection for each type of test. Note that patterns longer than m=12 are not found in either kind of randomized data, while in the real data patterns up to length 27 are detected. For both types of randomization the differences obtained are extreme so finding the associated p value is usually impossible due to the above mentioned limitation in the currently used subroutine which returns $p < 10^{-7}$ as zero. Figure 8 only concerns cyclical patterns. For cyclical patterns in neuronal data, Figure 9 shows differences between real and random data using the rotation test (with one thousand repetitions). In this case due to over abundance of patterns, the analysis was limited to only two hierarchical patterns levels (i.e. in the binary pattern tree) so the longest patterns are of length m=4. The difference between random and real in this case began at 81 standard deviation for m=2 and went up to 240 standard deviations for m=4.

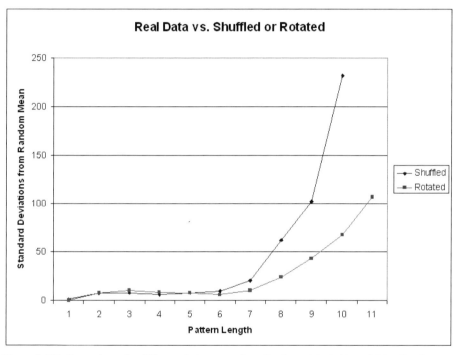

Figure 7. This figure shows the difference between number of patterns detected in real data, *Data1*, versus the average found over 1000 repetitions of, respectively, rotation and shuffling of that data. It can be seen that from about length 7 the deviation increases much faster with increasing pattern length in the shuffling case. No patterns of greater length were found in the randomized data, while patterns up to length 27 were detected in the initial *Data1*.

In general, the more inherent structural characteristics of behavior are considered, the greater the difference should be between results obtained from, respectively, real and randomized data (whether shuffled or rotated). In this respect the importance of the cyclical aspect is clearly indicated regarding the Data1 (Figure 1) since considering cyclical t-patterns only, the difference between real and randomized data increases considerably as may be seen by comparing figures 7 and 8. This has also been found in all other data hitherto analyzed including interactions in a population of neurons as exemplified in Figure 9. Figure 6 shows differences in pattern detection between real and rotated versions of *Data1* (shown in Figure 1).

6.5 Conclusions

Considering the above results of randomization, both shuffling and rotation, it seems that assignment of a priori probabilities to t-patterns (t-templates) in the way suggested above may be reasonable and that the arbitrary tree structure may be safely disregarded after detection. However, a new algorithm has been developed that successfully matches t-templates, without consideration of the tree structure, in the data set where they were detected while respecting the order and mutual exclusiveness of pattern occurrences and generating the same series of terminal occurrence times.

In terms of t-patterns, interactions between humans as well as neurons appear to be highly structured.

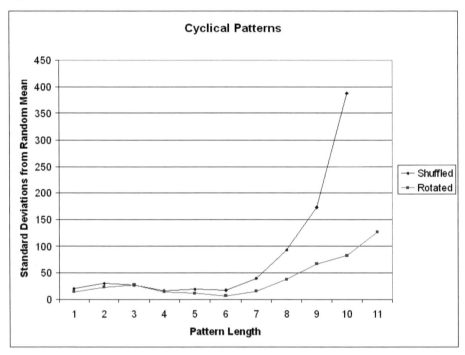

Figure 8. This figure only concerns cyclical patterns. It compares results obtained with the two different methods of randomization, shuffling and rotation, using *Data1*. It can be seen that from about length 7 the deviation increases much faster with increasing pattern length in the shuffling case. It also shows that the deviation is quite extreme in both cases. No patterns of greater length were found in the randomized data, while patterns up to length 27 were detected in the initial *Data1*.

But some questions arise. Are t-patterns equally relevant in the temporal organization of neuronal and human interactions? Are both organized according to a common principle somehow related to the t-pattern structure? What is that principle? Are the t-patterns seen in human interactions higher-level reflections of such underlying structure and, if so, how deep down in nature's organizational ladders might such structure be found?

"Human biology is anchored in concrete anatomy and genetics, providing fundamental elements from which to draw interconnections and with which to construct theory. The social world, in contrast, is a complex set of abstractions representing the actions and influences of the relationships among individuals, groups, societies, and cultures. The differences in levels of analysis have resulted in distinct histories, research traditions, and technical demands, leaving what some regard as an impassable abyss between social and biological approaches. The assumptions in social neuroscience, in contrast, are that the abyss can and must be bridged, that the mechanisms underlying mind and behavior will not be fully explicable by a biological or a social approach alone, that a multi-level integrative analysis may be required, and that a common scientific language – grounded in the structure and function of the brain and biology – can contribute to this goal." ([18], p. 5).

Such unity of language, however, is currently hardly favored by the often confusing use of the term "biological". For example, probably every biologist would consider social insect hives with all their social organization and interactions as biological, while hundreds of thousands of human hives (villages, towns and cities) with their however varied social structures, some ancient and others new, are typically not considered biological. Some biologists even appear to have a kind of dualistic view of human social phenomena including what often is referred to with limited clarity of definition as "culture". Moreover, the molecular view of life [19] is clearly dominant in modern biology and some biologists, at least in informal discussions hardly seem to view Darwin himself as a biologist. Rather amazing analogies in terms of structure and function of repeateded patterns actually seem to exist between information molecules and human cultural phenomena and even in terms of t-patterns [12].

All of science deals with the discovery of nature's recurrent patterns across time and/or space and much of the complex set of social abstractions mentioned above mostly seems to refer to (classes) of repeated interaction patterns of such general importance that they have been given names by systems of interacting humans. Clearly, the behavioral phenomena they refer to are no less observable or objective than those of, for example, physics and chemistry.

Like the behavioral and social sciences, molecular biology and genetics are about patterns and also depend on the truly common and ever expanding language of science, from chemistry to astronomy, "the science of patterns", mathematics, which has experienced such explosive growth and specialization in the 20th century. This special language, however, focuses less on the size and kind of elements, whether they be quarks, phonemes, molecules, texts, cells, or humans, but more on the joy of discovering unity of structure across different phenomena and scales. And possibly the study of interaction and communication still needs its own new mathematics to be developed.

The above results suggest that even toddlers playing freely with a toy for a few minutes quickly organize their time, the temporal structure of their interaction, in a surprisingly rigid and repetitive way, that is, showing striking translation symmetry. Other aspects of symmetry regarding t-pattern detection have been considered elsewhere [20]. Also surprising is that an adult watching the interaction is not aware of or is unable to detect but a minimum of the regularity that is developing in front of his/her eyes. All this calls to mind classical questions of nature versus nurture as, for example, in this paragraph from [21, p. 4]:

"A cross-specific comparison of courtship rituals highlights the fundamental distinction between naturally based and socially based sequential rigidity, and serves to demonstrate where nature ends and social convention begins. The courtship ceremonies of water salamanders or sticklebacks, for example, generally consist of biologically determined "reaction chains" wherein each link in the chain functions as a necessary "releaser" of the mate's next move. Ritualized fanning by the male, for instance, is indispensable for "releasing" the female's entrance to the nest and must, therefore, precede it." {Emphasis added.}

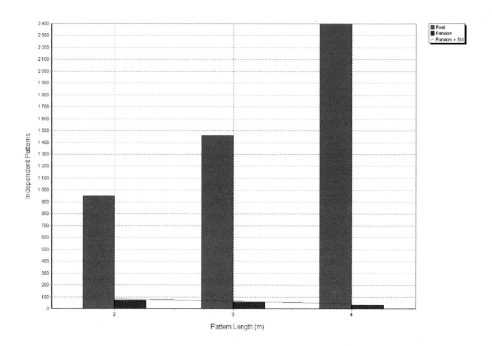

Figure 9. This figure shows the number of cyclical t-patterns detected in neuronal interaction data and the mean number detected in one thousand random rotations of the same data. The data used are form an ongoing study [7].

But at another level it may truly be in the *nature* of interacting humans, even quite unconsciously, to improvise patterns and then repeat them approximately unchanged as in so many other cases of nature's approximate translation symmetries. The meaning of it all may also be more or less unconsciously perceived. And while some such patterns may be short-lived others survive, that is, become more common for some time, much as in other evolutionary processes, which humans also used to be unaware of. The conventional structure of rituals, ceremonies and other more or less rigid routines of social existence, may thus in each case be more or less arbitrary, but the fact that they are there, that they are created and repeated by interacting humans, may still be a reflection of deep human tendencies and possibly with roots in nature's most general spatio-temporal symmetries.

It is hoped that t-pattern detection may be of help in dealing with issues of intention, meaning, and mistakes in communication and steps have already been taken in that direction [22]. In the context of communication, questions also clearly arise regarding how much of the patterning is semi-conscious, conscious, intentional and/or communicative? Furthermore, what communicative effects can be expected when such symmetries are broken?

6.6 Appendix

The following is a short list of the meanings of some of the terms that appear in Figures 1 to 3. The children are using a special viewer to look at picture-cards (pictcard). There is only one viewer. X and Y are the two actors; b and e indicate whether the behavior described is beginning or ending; Automanipulate = the actor touches any part of own body; immobile = the actor does not move any body part and is like frozen; order = verbally orders the other to give up the viewer; long = more than 3 seconds; short = less than 3 seconds. For example, x,e,walk means x ends walking.

The following list shows the the label of each event-type with its number as on the Y-axis in figure 1: **1** x,b,automanipulate; **2** x,b,glanceat,partner; **3** x,b,glanceat,pictcard; **4** x,b,glanceat,viewer; **5** x,b,haveviewer; **6** x,b,immobile; **7** x,b,kneel; **8** x,b,laugh; **9** x,b,lie; **10** x,b,lookat,partner; **11** x,b,lookat,pictcard; **12** x,b,lookat,viewer; **13** x,b,manipulate,viewer; **14** x,b,order,viewer; **15** x,b,pull; **16** x,b,sit; **17** x,b,stand; **18** x,b,view,long; **19** x,b,view,short; **20** x,b,walk; **21** x,e,automanipulate; **22** x,e,glanceat,partner; **23** x,e,glanceat,pictcard; **24** x,e,glanceat,viewer; **25** x,e,haveviewer; **26** x,e,immobile; **27** x,e,kneel; **28** x,e,laugh; **29** x,e,lie; **30** x,e,lookat,partner; **31** x,e,lookat,pictcard; **32** x,e,lookat,viewer; **33** x,e,manipulate,viewer; **34** x,e,pull; **35** x,e,sit; **36** x,e,stand; **37** x,e,view,long; **38** x,e,view,short; **39** x,e,walk; **40** y,b,automanipulate; **41** y,b,crawl; **42** y,b,glanceat,partner; **43** y,b,glanceat,pictcard; **44** y,b,glanceat,viewer; **45** y,b,haveviewer; **46** y,b,headtilt; **47** y,b,immobile; **48** y,b,kneel; **49** y,b,laugh; **50** y,b,lie; **51** y,b,lookat,partner; **52** y,b,lookat,pictcard; **53** y,b,lookat,viewer; **54** y,b,manipulate,nose; **55** y,b,manipulate,viewer; **56** y,b,order,viewer; **57** y,b,sit; **58** y,b,stand; **59** y,b,view,long; **60** y,b,view,short; **61** y,b,walk; **62** y,e,automanipulate; **63** y,e,crawl; **64** y,e,glanceat,partner; **65** y,e,glanceat,pictcard; **66** y,e,glanceat,viewer; **67** y,e,haveviewer; **68** y,e,headtilt; **69** y,e,immobile; **70** y,e,kneel; **71** y,e,laugh; **72** y,e,lie; **73** y,e,lookat,partner; **74** y,e,lookat,pictcard; **75** y,e,lookat,viewer; **76** y,e,manipulate,nose; **77** y,e,manipulate,viewer; **78** y,e,sit; **79** y,e,stand; **80** y,e,view,long; **81** y,e,view,short; **82** y,e,walk.

6.7 References

[1]   B. A. Schumm, Deep Down Things: The Breathtaking Beauty of Particule Physics. London: The John Hopkins University Press, 2004
[2]   R. McWeeny, Symmetry: An Introduction to Group Theory and ints Applications. NY: Dover Publications, Inc, 2002
[3]   J. Rosen, Symmetry Discovered: Concepts and Applications in Nature and Science. NY: Dover Publications, Inc, 1998

[4]   H. Weyl, Symmetry. New Jersey: Princeton University Press, 1989.
[5]   L. Anolli, MaCHT - Miscommunication as CHance Theory: Towards a Unitary Theory of Communication and Miscommunication. In Anolli, L., Ciceri, R., Riva, G. (Ed.) Say Not To Say. Amsterdam: IOS Press, 2001.
[6]   C. Frith. & D. Wolpert, The Neuroscience of Social Interaction: Decoding, Imitating, and Influencing the Actions of Others. NY: Oxford University Press, 2003.
[7]   A. U. Nicol, K. M. Kendrick & M. S. Magnusson, Communication within a neural network. In L Anolli, S Duncan Jr, MS Magnusson & G Riva, The hidden structure of interaction: from neurons to culture patterns, IOS Press, Amsterdam, NL, pp. 74-78, 2005.
[8]   W. C. McGrew, W. C. An Ethological Study of Children's Behavior. London: Academic Press, 1972.
[9]   M. S. Magnusson, "Hidden Real-Time Patterns in Intra- and Inter-Individual Behavior: Description and Detection." European Journal of Psychological Assessment, Vol. 12, Issue 2, p. 112-123, 1996.
[10] M. S. Magnusson, Discovering Hidden Time Patterns in Behavior: T-Patterns and their Detection. Behavior Research Methods, Instruments and Computers, 32(1): pp. 93-110, 2000.
[11] M. S. Magnusson, Repeated Patterns in Behavior and Other Biological Phenomena. In Evolution of Communication Systems : A Comparative Approach (Vienna Series in Theoretical Biology). D. Kimbrough Oller (Editor), Ulrike Griebel (Editor). London: The MIT Press, 2004.
[12] M. S. Magnusson, Understanding Social Interaction: Discovering Hidden Structure with Model and Algorithms. In Anolli, L., Duncan, S. , Giuseppe, R. & Magnussson, M.S. (Eds). The Hidden Structure of Interaction: From Neurons to Culture Patterns. Amsterdam: IOS Press, 2005.
[13] M. S. Magnusson, J. Beaudichon, "Détection de "marqueurs" dans la communication référentielle entre enfants." In J. Bernicot, Caron-Pargue, J. , Trognon, A. (Ed.), Conversation, Interaction et Fonctionnement Cognitif (pp. 315-335). Nancy: Presse Universitaire de Nancy, 1997.
[14] M. S. Magnusson, "Structures syntaxiques et rythmes comportementaux: sur la détection de rythmes cachés." Siences et Techniques de l'Animal du Laboratoire 14, 143-147, 1989.
[15] M. S. Magnusson, "Temporal Configuration Analysis: detection of an underlying meaningful structure through artificial categorization of a real-time behavioral stream." Paper presented at Workshop on Artificial Intelligence, University of Uppsala, in April 1982. Part of a Ph.D. thesis at the Psychological Laboratory, Copenhagen University 1983.
[16] M. S. Magnusson, "Theme and Syndrome: Two Programs for Behavior Research." In Edwards, D. & Hoeskuldsson, A. (Eds.), Symposium in Applied Statistics, pp. 17-42. Copenhagen: NEUCC, RECKU & RECAU, 1983.
[17] G. L. Gerstein, Searching for significance in spatio-temporal firing patterns. Acta Neurobiol Exp, 2004, 64: 203-207, 2004.
[18] T.J. Cacioppo, G. G. Berntson, R. Adolphs, et al (Ed) Foundations in Social Neuroscience. London: MIT Press, 2002.
[19] S. Sarkar, Molecular Models of Life. London: MIT Press. 2002.
[20] T. Anguera, Microanalysis of T-patterns: Analysis of Symmetry/Asymmetry in Social Interaction. In Anolli, L., Duncan, S. , Magnussson, M.S. & Giuseppe, R. (Ed.). The Hidden Structure of Interaction: From Neurons to Culture Patterns. Amsterdam: IOS Press, 2005.
[21] E. Zerubavel, Hidden Rhythms: Schedules and Calendars in Social Life. Berkley: University of California Press.
[22] L. Anolli, The Detection of the Hidden Design of Meaning. In Anolli, L., Duncan, S. , Magnussson, M.S. & Giuseppe, R. (Eds). The Hidden Structure of Interaction: From Neurons to Culture Patterns. Amsterdam: IOS Press, 2005.

From Communication to Presence
G. Riva et al. (Eds.)
IOS Press, 2006

7 Zooming on Multimodality and Attuning: A Multilayer Model for the Analysis of the Vocal Act in Conversational Interactions

Rita CICERI, Federica BIASSONI

Abstract. The most recent research about both human-human conversational interaction and human-computer agents conversational interaction is marked by a multimodal perspective. On the one hand this approach underlines the co-occurrence and synergy between different languages and channels, on the other hand it highlights the need for joined and coordinated action between various subjects (attuning and mutual tuning in). In a similar way recent research on human computer interaction points out the need to consider the vocal interaction in a multicomponential perspective, both as a multilayer phenomenon in itself and as one component in wider interactive patterns. As the communicative action is seen with its features of comprehensiveness and multicomponentiality, so the vocal act needs to be seen as a complex event. Research on models aimed at new interfaces analysis, outline the way beyond the distinction traceable in the majority of studies, where conversational action is split up into its factors and analysis focuses on the factors one by one: conversation analysis or content analysis or suprasegmental analysis. The purpose of this chapter is to offer a contribution to the creation of an analysis model that allows for the complexity of the vocal act and for its *being-in-context* in the interactive flow, so applying the Embodied Conversational Agents (ECAs) qualifying multicomponential focus to the vocal act. Two levels of analysis so emerge: a vertical, morphological analysis, and a horizontal, sequential analysis.

Two kinds of vocal interaction are here examined according to the proposed model, a human face-to-face and an interaction between an ECA and its user.

Contents

7.1 Introduction

Think of the way we converse nowadays, imagine the way we will talk tomorrow: a progressive modification in communication media, languages, modalities and actors is occurring [1]. On one side, the attempt to define conversational experience arouses the same sensation as when from a height you can see and suddenly realize a dizzy outlook enlargement. On the other side, conversation needs joined and coordinated action between various subjects (attuning and mutual tuning in; [3, 4, 5]). Finally, both the advent of technology and the collateral development of theoretical and analysis models about communication show the scarce utility of rigid categorization, calling the attention to the need of new explanation models [6]. What role for conversation and specifically for vocal communication within this new scenery? Let us peruse two paradigmatic examples.

a. An ordinary face-to-face conversation between two human agents.

C: You could have answered, at least!!
F: Don't you check SMS on your cell?
C: (Takes out the cell phone and looks at the screen).
Carlo → SMS content: ☺:)) "Bought rings"
C: But this news must be told by word of mouth! Really it's a bad idea to write it in a message!!
F: Damn! What are you saying? Don't be ridiculous ...

Who's right? F or C? Thanks to the use of communicative artifacts the conversation chronological dimensions are multiplied: the SMS has been couched formerly, but F learns these piece of information just in a certain moment; at that time, C thinks F has already learned it some time before, more or less when he typed and sent it. The possible choice between a multiplicity of communicative modalities and media expands the freedom and the chance to overcome physical constraints, such as space and time bonds. But at the same time misunderstanding possibilities increase, altering the standard sequential model and arising disagreement about pertinence and appropriateness in the use of various modalities.

b. The described conversation occurs between a user and an avatar (actually, simulated through the Wizard of Oz procedure; [7]):

Oz: What did you eat at breakfast?
S: Only two 'espressioni' today. How about you?
Oz: Maybe you forget I'm only an artificial agent.
S: So you don't eat? How do you feed yourself?

This piece of conversation introduces a further, interesting application area: research about conversational rules and protocols aims at modeling believable interactive interfaces. In this case conversation is the requisite for the system effectiveness.

Knowledge got from studies in human face-to-face communication and models describing natural occurring interactions need to be imported in the field of computer science, as to implement interactive Agents modeling. On the other hand interactions between virtual and human Agents are "a new form of relationship", different from the previously examined ones, so that "what form such mediated interactions take and what implications they might have for the human Agents are a matter of speculation" [8]. This means that research on human-computer interactions may provide insights into manners and conditions of human interaction.

From Austin's Speech Act Theory to the most recent observations produced by the Embodied Conversational Agents' (ECAs) theory, we are experiencing a progressive focusing from the message-word to the concept of action. The common element is the attention directed to the communicative joint-action of Agents and to agency, that is awareness of one's own and others' capability to act and inter-act [9]. The communication development from *homo loquens* to Agent (*subject-in-action*) matches different analysis modalities: from the utterance analysis, where the speech act is split into its components analyzed one by one: conversation analysis [10] or content analysis [11] or suprasegmental analysis [12] to a global approach. The purpose of this chapter is to offer a contribution to the study of an analysis model that allows for the complexity of the vocal act and for its *being-in-context* in the interactive flow, so applying the ECAs qualifying multicomponential focus.

7.2. From Multimodality to Semantic Modal and Intermodal Architecture

Communication in face-to-face interactions occurs through a variety of modalities and different semantic systems need to be integrated into a unique communicative act. Recent studies about the multimodality of the communicative act [13, 14] have stressed the role of both verbal and non verbal codes in the meaning process. The meaning of each sign depends on its use in the whole communicative act, and its semantic value takes place in the relation with other signs [15]. Research on multimodal presentations has taken into account the different affordances of the verbal and pictures language, so reminding that in writing as in speaking communicative goals may be differently mapped into different modalities [16]. The semantic and pragmatic compatibility seen in the gesture-speech relationship recalls the interaction of words and graphics in multimodal presentations [17]. In fact, gesture and speech arise together from an underlying representation that has both visual and linguistic aspects and so the relationship between gesture and speech is essential to the production of meaning and its comprehension [18]. Sense multimodality is a feature of the embodied interaction between an Agent and the environment. The exploration of reality occurs through different senses. In the communicative action, then, a transition from perceptive multimodality to semantic intermodality takes place, both in *face-to-face* and in artifact mediated communication, as shown in Figure 1. In perceptive multimodality different information channels are processed, whereas in communicative intermodality different semiotic systems are integrated to empower semantic effectiveness [5].

Moreover, it is possible to create modal communicative artifacts: in these messages different languages, all belonging to the same modality (all made up of visual or auditory stimuli, for example) are synergically integrated to convey the message meaning. Intermodal artifacts, instead, are featured by the combination of different languages belonging to different codes and by the simultaneous managing of signals from different perceptive modalities. Within a communicative act anyway constituted by a multiplicity of signs, we can so distinguish, a modal architecture and an intermodal one.

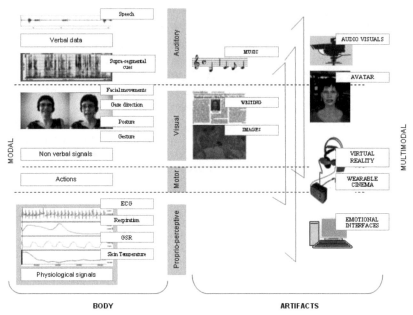

Figure 1. Modal and multimodal signals.

An example of modal architecture is the speech act, which includes and integrates signs from different codes although all of them belonging to the auditory modality (e.g. verbal dimension, prosodic dimension and cry); an example of intermodal architecture, instead, is an audio-visual artifact or a conversational act, where gesture, posture and mimicry are used together, as shown in Figure 2. The link between language and thought can be described by two events: a referential and a communicative one. Through the referential event the information we experience (perceptual, psychological, cultural) is organized into different format of knowledge (propositional, procedural, narrative knowledge and mental imagery); the communicative event requires the declension into languages (verbal and non verbal) through a medium, generating a modal or intermodal message. It is possible to highlight three integrated modules concerned with the shift from multimodal exploration to intermodal expression: sense exploration (perceptual experience); concept construction (concepts and creation of mental relationships); meaning expression and communication (achieved through languages and media).

These are the three phases of reality exploration and knowledge processes, joint into a bidirectional and non-sequential flow [19]. They make possible – as said by Jackendoff [20] - "the giant leap from senses to concepts" and, to fulfil the definition, the leap from the concept to the sharable and co-constructed (through communicative artefacts) meaning. Human beings, therefore, own a set of skills to integrate signs belonging to different semiotic systems both in language comprehension and production processes; these skills -in the form of sets of rules to link meaning to signals that work in different modalities- need to be owned also by synthetic Agents, in order to manage the combination of signals taken from different communicative codes and the distribution of meaning across them. This means that virtual Agents, too, need to plan conversation exchanges so that multiple and different communicative goals may be realized by a composite communicative action (molar entity) including different elements (molecular entities) -not only speech but also coverbal signs- fitting with the context and the conversational grounding in ways similar to human communicative exchanges [18]. All the more if we consider that people are more likely to consider computers lifelike and to rate their language skills more highly if those computers display not only speech but also non verbal communicative behavior. The ability to use signs from different semiotic system in a synergic way, with a communicative aim, influences both the pleasantness and the usability of computer interfaces.

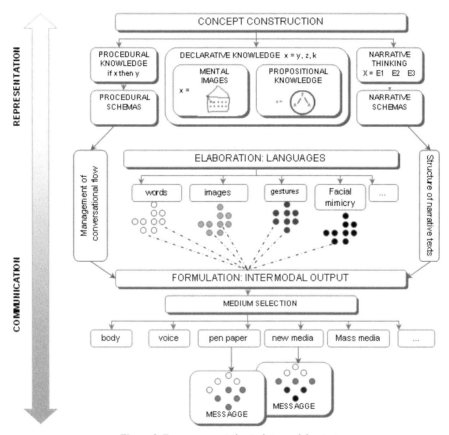

Figure 2. From representation to intermodal output

In their works aimed at modeling ECAs architectures, some authors [21] assigned a different, specific role for verbal and non verbal language: semantic functions to speech and conversational functions, such as conversation and interaction management, to non verbal language.

However, as previously said, in each communicative action the meaning emerges from the relationships occurring between different signs belonging to different codes; a message featured by inconsistency between the meaning expressed by verbal and non verbal language is a good example in this sense. Imagine to ask someone if she/he has understood some content you expressed; you can listen to her/his saying "Yes" and you can see her/his nodding and, at the same time, frowning. Of course your decoding of the meaning expressed by your interlocutor won't be a simple sum of meanings expressed through speech and mimicry, as a linear process of addition of single elements. To likely decode the real meaning expressed by your communication partner behaviors a process of integration of different signs is needed: the signifying process overlaps the process of building a whole, combined meaning, that is something different from the simple summation of different components, exactly because the meaning arises from the *being-in-relation* of different signs, combined in function of the conversational context and temporal flow.

Modal architectures, including verbal and suprasegmental dimensions, are often employed to empower communication and make it more flexible (MaCHT, [14]). An example of modal architecture in a communicative act is ironic communication. Irony has been defined as "a *complex communicative act*. It involves a plurality of the semantic and intentional levels of an utterance pronounced by the speaker"[22]. Four experiments [23] showed that the ironist's intention is expressed through an antiphrastic process and syncoding aimed at "hitting" the victim of the irony. So the ironic intention can be re-enacted and interpreted just through an integrated perusal of signals from different codes. Within the "fencing game" perspective, the ironic utterance is a global communication act and it is the unitary outcome of different signaling systems. In it linguistic (segmental) inputs are combined with paralinguistic (supra-segmental) patterns, face expressions, and gestures. Each of these aspects contributes effectively, each for its part, to produce the ironic meaning of an utterance said by a given speaker in a certain situation. They converge to produce an ironic comment that is coherent in itself, even if complex and articulated, since it displays a determinate communicative intention. Differently said, irony is a "multi-modular" communicative act.

Therefore, as Anolli has pointed out [24], irony is the result of a semantic synchrony process. As previously said, for irony we have a specific "*contrastive semantic synchrony*", since the paralinguistic pattern appears to be in contrast to the linguistic input. With the linguistic unit speakers convey a certain meaning obtained by a pure linguistic encoding; with the paralinguistic pattern they convey an alternative (in most cases, opposite) meaning. The synchronic combination of these signaling systems generates the ironic meaning, which is not to be grasped as an addition of "linguistic meaning plus paralinguistic (and nonverbal) meaning", but it is to be intended as the unitary outcome of the simultaneous convergence of these communicative signs.

To endow a synthetic Agent with non-verbal communication abilities means to provide it with a range of multimodal behavior, all aimed at communicative functions when executed in temporal synchronization with verbal language. As Cassel et al. put into evidence [25], the contributions to a conversation can be propositional or interactional; propositional information correspond to the content of the communicative exchange, and is conveyed by speech as by non verbal signs: I can express my preference between two options by saying "I prefer the red one", by indicating by finger pointing, by a movement of the head, by stressing a word increasing the pitch and intensity in my speech or acting all these behavioral units in a unique and complex molar communicative act . And, most likely, the truthfulness and the degree of my choice will not emerge but from the integration and coordination of different molecular acts. Interactional information consist of the cues that regulate conversational process and includes a wide range of non verbal behavior such as speech. For example, results from Kelly et al. [26] show that information from both speech and gesture is used to provide context for the ongoing talk and that the speakers' common ground can be updated by both speech and gesture.

On the way to the implementation of the ECA Rea, Cassel et al. [18] collected a sample of real-estate conversation; the conversations were transcribed and utterances were distinguished from referential gestures. Analysis of the data revealed that for 50% of gesture-accompanied utterances, gesture was redundant with speech hence expressing the same meaning, while for the other 50%, gesture provided different and complementary content to that expressed by speech. In addition, we hypothesize that a significant amount of meaning arises from the relationship between speech and gestures, in respect of their duration, synchronization and timing. The rules to search for in the investigation on conversational protocols transferable to human-machine interaction are not simply rules of co-occurrence and coordination between verbal and non verbal behavior, but rules of integration and mutual meaning attribution within the relationship between signs.

In a recent work [27] Ciceri et al. examined adult crying as global act. Aim of the study was to trace the acoustic profile of adult cry, through the analysis of vocal patterns, pinpointing a possible methodological approach.

The examined sample consisted of 238 cry episodes, extracted from 40 movies. Three level analysis included: frame analysis, perceptive analysis and acoustic digitalized analysis. On the one hand, frame analysis put into evidence the polisemic function of adult cry, emerging as a complex phenomenon between confidentiality and self-expression, and characterized by a rich emotional frame, different from the dyadic-care pattern typical of the caregiver-infant relation. On the other hand, acoustic analysis highlighted the semantic pattern of adult cry, rich in paralinguistic elements conveying discontinuity, intermittence and lower intensity.

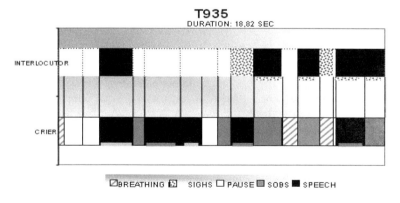

Figure 3. Modal architecture of a cry production

What's more interesting is that adult crying emerges as a composite phenomenon, composed by signals belonging to different systems (verbal and suprasegmental code), organized in a complex architecture. It's not possible to isolate the different elements without losing the communicative effectiveness of a cry production both in expressing the crier intentions and emotions and in influencing the listener behavior. Figure 3 puts into evidence the modal architecture of a cry fragment.

Multimodal organization seems to play a functional role when one communicative channel is impaired. In deaf children, for example, the vocal-auditory channel becomes unavailable involving as a consequence the need to rely on a visual-gesture modality to communicate. In contrast to the single vocal channel for spoken languages, where multiple functions (linguistic and emotional information) are simultaneously transmitted through this single channel, in sign languages there is a distribution of linguistic and emotional information across channels and languages that results in the integration of emotion and language across multiple channels and behavioral systems simultaneously [28]. This kind of integration was proved by T-pattern analysis [29] as shown in Figure 4: while communicating an emotion deaf children rely upon different systems of expression (vocal behavior, facial expressions, signs) and behavioral units belonging to those systems are organized in complex multimodal patterns.

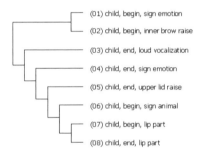

(01) child, begin, sign emotion
(02) child, begin, inner brow raise
(03) child, end, loud vocalization
(04) child, end, sign emotion
(05) child, end, upper lid raise
(06) child, begin, sign animal
(07) child, begin, lip part
(08) child, end, lip part

Figure 4. Intermodal architecture

7.3 Intentional Attuning and Attuning as Behavioral Accommodation and Synchronization

Preconditions for any communicative interaction are cooperation and mutual accreditation between the partners, who show through cooperative behavior their willingness to be involved in the exchange. In such a perspective, the other is deemed as an "intentional Agent", that is an Agent endowed with her/his own communicative intentionality and the ability to act as to achieve her/his goals [30]. More recently, within the neuroscience approach, starting from his empirical studies on mirror-neurons, Gallese [31, 4, 32] defined the concept of "*Intentional Attuning*": according to this author, at the basis of our social competence there is the capacity to co-construct a directly shared inter-subjective space enabling us to establish links and relations with others. We are not alienated from the actions, emotions and sensations of others, because "we are attuned to the intentional relations of others".

By means of the intentional attunement, "the others" are much more than being different representational systems: they become persons, like us. The attunement so conceived constitutes the prerequisite of other competences such as imitation, the recognition of other people behavior as intentional and similar to ours, the representation of the others as intentional beings, the ability to recognize and feel emotions and, in a broader sense, empathy, all phenomena that are precondition of our ability to interact.

In a second meaning, indeed, attuning constitutes a co-management of the other's presence, first in the sense of reciprocal coordination in the action planning and realization and, secondly, in the sense of empathy. The acknowledgment of the partner in the communicative exchange entails the sense of the need to regulate one's behavior in regard to the other's action, in an uninterrupted management of the co-presence. Sensing the other as Agent and not as a tool, thereby endowed with intentionality and acting faculty, represents the basis for recognizing and identifying her/his internal states. Secondly, the reciprocal influence of conversation partners is based upon such an awareness. Attuned people tend to modulate some characteristics of their non verbal behavior in relation to the actions of their interlocutor; the shifts produced in this way can be used in a convergent or divergent direction to signal the need of a change in the behavior and hence direct the joint action [33, 3]. Since we are considering the communication process not simply as a semiotic process, but also as "structuring relation" [14, 34], accommodation means not only the adjusting of portions of a language, but rather the inner assent to the local way of being of the conversational partner and the adoption of behavioral units consonant not only with those displayed by her/him but also with her/his internal world [35].

Verbal communication in the seduction context provides an example of the attunement attitude just described as reciprocal influence. Research by Singh [36] shows that fondness increases when two people observe a likeness or similarities in their attitudes and behavior. Grammer's studies [37] show that fondness is born out of the ability to coordinate one's attitudes with those of the other person.

This overview was confirmed by recent research [38] focused on the analysis of suprasegmental transitory characteristics (variations in rhythm, duration, pitch and intensity of speech) in seductive interactions. In particular, the aim was to describe any variations undergone by the persons involved in the seductive interaction and finally to highlight the differences between successful and unsuccessful seductive language as far as vocal communication is regarded. Data were collected from the analysis of male subjects' vocal behavior during interactions aimed at succeeding in obtaining a subsequent meeting from the partner and showed that, in general, successful seducers differ from those who failed as they were able to modulate the prosodic aspects of their voice in a more flexible way during seductive interaction with their female partner. The authors interpret the result of the successful seducers according to the theory of the local management of communication [39]. In fact, successful seducers show they possess in all situations a stronger ability to regulate the features of their voice while interacting with the partner. It is not only a matter of planning and programming the communication of a message. It is also necessary to know how to choose the most effective move at that moment in consideration of the hints offered by the partner, hence putting to use an unrehearsed modulation of one's own behavior.

An emerging issue is thereby that human communicative partners show a natural and continuous disposition to attuning. In a similar way, affective interaction in human-computer interchanges cannot be reduced to sequences of recognitions and expressions: the defining, fundamental feature of human interaction is contingent responsiveness and such a feature needs to be achieved in human-computer interactions [8]. Responsive interactions are the regularized patterns of messages from one person that influences the messages sent in turn by the other over and above what they would otherwise be [40]. Davis has defined responsive social interactions in term of two kinds of contingency [41]. The first refers to the probability of a person's response to the actions of a partner in an interaction. The second one concerns the proportion of responses related to content of the previous message. In this sense, responsiveness can be defined by an equation expressing that B's behavior must influence the probability of A's behavior at some significant level and, more importantly, that the size of the probability must be greater than the probability that A will emit the behavior in the absence of B's behavior [8]. Much of the research in modeling human interaction has focused on the coordination between different components of a single person's behavior, but the attuning theme suggests the central importance of identifying rules useful to describe the mutual coordination between the partners of a communicative dyad. Cassell et al. [25], too, put into evidence that the conversational ability does not just imply the recognition of the partner's behavior and the coordinated utilization of signs belonging to different semiotic systems, but is a *truly responsive or co-constructed activity*.

A third perspective looks at *attuning* as it is generally defined in communication psychology: a set of interpersonal behavioral units aimed at the achievement of the joined intention (see also the "*we-intention*", [42]) through which the speakers arrange, maintain and coordinate their communicative interaction. In this sense, attuning can be defined as a sequence of interactions mutually coordinated between the speakers [43, 5]; it includes a temporal dimension (synchronization) and a qualitative aspect (mutual tuning in). As far as the temporal dimension is regarded, the role of interactive coordination along the communicative flow emerges as a central element; concerning the qualitative aspect, many studies have revealed the disposition to shift, modulate and accommodate some behavior properties, such as the frequency and intensity of behavioral patterns [44].

In a work in progress, Ciceri et al. have examined communicative interactions aimed at gossiping.

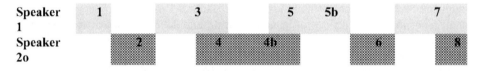

Periodicity of speech turns.

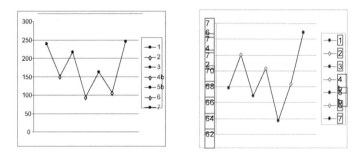

Figure 5. Interaction of the speakers' pitches (Hz) and intensity profiles

The vocal production of each speaker was collected and analyzed through the acoustic parameters extraction. A second step analysis focused on the relationship between different speakers' vocal flow. Data put into evidence an interesting feature of the examined gossip conversation: an attunement trend. Each speaker joined the conversational exchange independently, displaying his/her own vocal characteristics (measured during the first speech turn). As shown in Figure 5, throughout the conversation advance, then, a gradual adjustment to the partner modalities emerged, in the shape of reproducing the acoustic trend of her/his speech, as observable in the example below. When speaker 1's speech decreases in frequency and intensity, the same happened to speaker 2's speech.

A further central aspect in attuning is the strategic dimension of the coordination of different codes in the chronological going through of the communicative flow. Verbal and non verbal signals are synchronized within the speaker action, with the conversational context and with the partner Agent's activity. Some authors underline the need for a believable (and comfortable, we would add) synthetic Agent to display behavior in a way that is "appropriate and well-timed". Any Agent needs to be able to get a representation of the state of the conversational context and of the partner state, as well as of her/his own, in each moment of the exchange, as to display the appropriate behavior with regard of real-time interactional frame. Finding rules that describe changes in the individuals' state and consequent behavior *over time* and that correspond to the empirical realities is the essence of the enterprise of modeling [8].

To describe the interaction synchronological workflow, two types of rules are needed: one set concerns sequence, or when to change a state; the other one concerns distributional rules or how long to remain in a state before leaving. Evidently, the description of a dyad of communicating Agents workflow is expressed by two crossing algorithms or a composite algorithm. Chronological dimension and context sensitivity converge in the synchronization of each behavior but also as far as the communicative plan is concerned. Besides synchronization, intended as punctual event, a timing strategic dimension can be pinpointed. Context sensitivity and the ability to be suitably responsive implies the skill to keep a monitoring activity on the context changes and micro-changes and to store the interaction history as the point of departure for subsequent communicative actions. Moreover, timing ability represents the sensitivity to contextual and conversational cues and the competent, intentional use of those cues to plan the chronological structure of the conversational exchange. The placement of some multimodal pattern of behavioral units along the time *continuum* is endowed with intentionality and is a part of the strategy worked out by the communicative Agent. In this perspective the chronological dimension of the Agents' behavior within the interaction undertake a semantic function.

In a recent work [45] some interviews were analyzed, from both a verbal and suprasegmental point of view. In particular, an interviewing strategy was pinpointed: the repetition of a question. An interesting issue emerged: the repeated questions pattern shows the importance of the timing aspect. Both the verbal and suprasegmental dimensions are used along the chronological continuum in a strategic manner, as to achieve the speaker communicative goal. For instance, we can examine the following questions repetition.

Q1: Were you alone?
A1: (Silence, no answer).
Q2: Were you alone or was there anyone with you?

A2: (Silence, no answer).
Q3: Was there anyone with you or were you alone?
A3: (Silence, no answer).
Q4: Were you alone?
A4: No, I was not alone.

The complex structure of the pattern (see Figure 6) puts into evidence firstly the coordination between the interviewer and the interviewed speaking turn; secondly, the synergic action of verbal and suprasegmental in both semantic and relational function. The coordinated use of different codes turns out to be functional on one hand to the conversation management, on the other hand to the effectiveness in achieving the speaker's communicative intention.

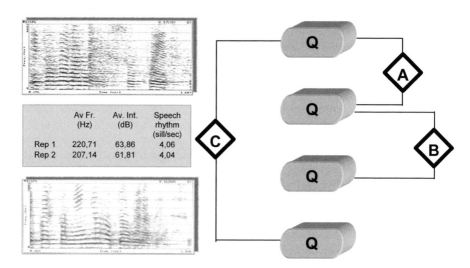

Figure 6. Repeated questions pattern

We can observe three different repetition strategies: strategy A ("repetition with focusing question"): the repetition uses the "funnel technique", and so the second question provides a narrower focus; strategy B ("repetition with focus reverse"): the same words are used in the repetition, but with a different order in the sentence; the result is the change of position of the emphatic stress; and strategy C ("identical repetition"): the question is repeated just alike in the verbal streak, but there are significant changes in the suprasegmental profile, as shown by the sonographic outlines and the acoustic parameters values. The speaker's choice to repeat the question in a different way, as far as both the verbal streak and the suprasegmental profile is concerned, is related to the intention to get an answer and finally turns out to be effective. What's more interesting in this example is the speaker's ability to get into contact with the interlocutor's state and to hit her intention (not to answer) and the behavior displayed to get such an intention; account of these signals, the interviewer modulates her speech behavior in an unrehearsed and on-going way.

Of course the possible strategic use of the chronological placing demands on one hand for the management of multimodality, that is the possibility to operate, combine and integrate various channels into a single semantic representation aimed at a communicative goal; on the other hand it requires to be able to notice, decode and integrate the partner's internal states signals. This is in fact the essence of responsiveness, defined by Cappella [40, 8] "not simply the generation and recognition of social signals, nor it is just receiving and sending such signals. Neither (responsive interaction) can be reduced to the interleaving of two monologues (…)". Responsive interactions are the regularized patterns of messages from one person that influence the messages sent in turn by the other over and above that they would otherwise be".

According to the first illustrated meaning, intentional attuning is the prerequisite for human communication, but it's more difficult to ascribe this characteristic to H-M interaction. An interesting work has been carried out, aimed at assessing the presence of attuning within a human-machine interaction [46, 47]. Participants were asked to use the computer where an avatar (Baldi, CSLU Toolkit) guided them across the three different kinds of computer games. They were divided into two different groups, according to the kind of information received by the avatar. In particular, this experimental research made use of the Wizard of Oz approach [48]. In the experimental condition, the subjects were exposed to a simulated emotional-intelligent computer, where the avatar provided a simulated intelligent feedback to the user to decode his emotional state and to adapt the tasks accordingly. In the control condition the avatar guided the subjects in the same activities but did not simulate to decode emotion. All subjects were alone in the room with the computer.

Results showed that during the interaction with the computer, the subject exhibits communicative verbal and non verbal behavior. In particular, user's communicative responses changed with respect to the interactivity level of the tasks and their emotional events (high interactive tasks elicit more communicative signals, e.g. the quiz game and avatar interaction).

Subjects in the experimental condition assigned higher scores to the computer's ability to understand emotion, to adapt the task according to them and to answer to his reactions, while in the control condition subjects assigned high scores to the ability to give information. Evidently, the described data questions about the possibility of attuning between human user and machine. The shift in the machine definition from *tool to use* to *Agent tool to interact with* seems to be acquired, and yet it is troublesome and somewhat risky to define an ECA as an intentional Agent tool.

Actually, although in a multimodal interaction the imitation of a real conversation can be so great to increase significantly both pleasantness and involvement in the interaction itself, it can't be said so plainly that the user attributes intentionality to the artificial Agent. As pinpointed by Hook [33], human-machine interaction seems distinguished by specific rules, since though interacting with the machine the user goes on regarding it as a tool. For this reason, we more suitably ascribe to human-machine interaction the second meaning of the concept "attuning". In this acceptation, the enhancement of effectiveness and pleasantness is explained predominantly by means of mutual coordination.

7.4. The role of Embodiment and a Wider Outlook on Agency

The human body enables the use of certain communication protocols in face-to-face conversation, providing a otherwise unconceivable richness and variety of signs.

Moreover, the affordances of embodiment represent the channels through which each speaker get plenty of information about the conversational context, her/his own state and the partner's internal states, such as thinking processes and emotional situation. It can be said that the role of embodiment is to perceive and collect pieces of information from the outer interactional environment, be communicative and conversational or affective and relational, and to convey and express signals telling the individual internal processes. In this sense, the role of embodiment is in integrated manner both propositional and interactional [25]. Not by chance user studies showed that users rated the smoothness of the interaction and the Agent's *language skills* significantly higher when the ECA Gandalf [49] utilized conversational behavior than when he didn't. So, by now, the studies showed that the mere presence of an embodied character improves the pleasantness and the efficacy of a conversational exchange; the future challenge of research is to understand the role of embodiment in fully functional conversational interfaces [25]. Our proposal is to regard embodiment as the place of the dynamic monitoring , through the sensitivity to and the expression of signs belonging to various languages, to the conversational and contextual field, to the partner state and to the speaker's own condition. In other words: embodiment as *being-in-context*.

Cappella & Pelachaud [8] focus on the importance of finding rules predicting sequences of behavior in dyads, underlining that people committed in a conversational transaction must be *sensitive to the behavior of the partner and not just the behavior of the person*. A way to achieve that goal is to define states of persons as in the following example:

State definition for 2 persons, On-Off behavior (Example behavior: Smiles)

A's Behavior	B's Behavior	Dyad's Behavior
Smile is off (=0)	Smile is off (=0)	NEITHER smiling (00)
Smile is on (=1)	Smile is off (=0)	A ONLY smiling (10)
Smile is off (=0)	Smile is on (=1)	B ONLY smiling (01)
Smile is on (=1)	Smile is on (=1)	BOTH smiling (11)

In a diachronic perspective, the dyad matrix shows that in any moment of the time continuum the dyad state depends on both partners behavior; in fact, changes in A's state entails a change in the state of the whole dyad, therefore affecting B's state and so on. The simultaneity of the partners' behavior is a kind of mutual responsiveness required by the social nature of human beings and an indication for synthetic conversational Agents modeling. The core of embodiment is represented by the possibility to sense the partner behavior as related to her/his communicative intention, to one's own state and the signals uttered regarding that state, as well as to the conversational contest and the conversation history till the present moment.

Moreover, embodiment affordances are instrument and bond of our *being-in-relation*, since just by means of embodiment it is possible to make oneself accessible to a communication partner. An interesting example of the affordances of embodiment is CUEX (Cue Extraction), a system for extracting acoustic cues from an expressive music performance [50]. The cues can be mapped into a 2-dimensional space that represent the expressivity of the performance, for example the 2-dimensional space originated by the pleasure-displeasure continuum and arousal degree continuum [51]. The acoustic cues extracted by CUEX are then turned into a visual feedback, expressed by a virtual Agent system: Greta. Greta is the embodied representation of a virtual human able to communicate using verbal and non verbal behavior. A set of acoustic cues is mapped into the behavior of an expressive animated human like character, simulating the process of perception, integration and decoding of signals uttered by the communication partner and simultaneously displaying one's own set of signals, aimed at providing a feedback and at the same time at conveying further meanings.

The acoustic cues that can be extracted by CUEX are: articulation (legato or staccato), local tempo (number of events in a given time window), sound level, spectrum energy and attack time. Research on music performance has shown that musicians use acoustic cues in a particular way and combination in order to communicate emotions [50, 52]; moreover, studies on vocal expression and music performance reveal strong similarities between voice and music in the use of acoustic cues to communicate emotions. The Agent system linked to CUEX and intended at providing the user with continuous feedback through an animation in real time uses a variety of signals such as: head movements, blink and facial expression. Each category of signals is parameterized by a set of dimensions of expressivity, which modify the Agents animation qualitatively. The six dimensions are: overall activation (amount of activity, number of movements per time), spatial extent (amplitude of movements), temporal extent (duration of movements), fluidity (smoothness and continuity of movement), power (dynamic properties of movement) and repetitivity (number of repetition of the same expression).

Keeping in mind the observation that the musicians' body movements are correlated with their emotional intention [53], the extracted acoustic cues are mapped into the corresponding expressivity parameters:

- *volume*: the current sound level of the music performance is linearly mapped into the *spatial* and *power* expressivity parameters;
- *tempo*: the speed of the musical performance influences the *temporal* and *overall activation* expressivity parameters;
- *articulation*: it reflects the style and the quantity of the articulation in the music performance, i.e. the amount of staccato and legato; it influences the *fluidity* dimension.

This system, aimed at providing feedback to expressivity in music performances, is able to perceive signals of the partner's affective state and to utter correlated behavior, modulating them along different parameters in relation to a feedback intention. Not only it works in a multimodal perspective, but it shows that the communicative process wholly makes use of the embodiment affordances to place into an interactional context.

A noticeable consequence of embodiment is the influences affecting and modifying the behavior an Agent will display to communicate a certain meaning within a specific context [54]. The taxonomy of influences includes intrinsic factors, such as personality, age, sex, nationality, culture, education and experiences; contextual factors, such as environment settings and the relationship with the interlocutor; dynamic factors, due to the Agent's internal states. According to literature, two meanings of the term "embodiment" can be depicted.

On one hand, an Agent is embodied in so far as physically, socially and culturally defined by her/his body and her/his history. With regard to this first meaning, speech embodied features are permanent factors: vocal timber, pronunciation, accent, discourse style. They have been labelled "voice quality" because they designate the speaker's permanent vocal setting. Voice quality is semantically very rich: it provides information about speaker's age, sex, origin, social status, ...; not by chance a listener can recognize a familiar voice even in unique situations, such as from behind a door or when the speaker has a cold, or she/he can get acquainted with a new voice in a short time [55]. The accent, too, becomes a customary discourse style and is perceived by a listener as different from her/his own style. For this reason, not only it has an informative function about geographic origin and social placement, but it is also at the origin of social labeling. Many works, have tested accent influence on judgment about the speaker's *status* and personality.

With regard to the previously expressed remarks, agency or the self-awareness to be an Agent [5], the awareness to be apart from the object of one's own action and the recognition of the others' intentional action assumes an eminently intersubjective nature. The attribution of the acting faculty to oneself as to other persons and the simultaneous coding of the other as possible object of one's action [56] find their appropriate context within interaction. In brief, the meaning of agency is empowered by the perspective of *agency-in-interaction*.

7.5 Conclusions: Towards a Multilayer Model for the Analysis of the Vocal Act in Conversational Interactions

Two considerations arise from the facts and observations told insofar.

The communication development from *homo loquens* to Agent (*subject-in-action*) is a central issue for research on communication since it associates the analysis of human communication, mediated communication and human-artificial Agents communication. Some recent works here presented show that people judge interactions with synthetic Agents as more pleasant and effective if they are not only emotionally responsive [9] but, more important, if they are able to engage in social interactions, applying conversational skills and protocols typical of human communicative exchanges. In a similar way, human communicative exchanges analysis needs to take into account and to focus on the interactive flow, so as to detect both the communicative action features and their chronological and co-ordination links. The multidimensional focus about modal and intermodal architecture, attuning process and embodied skills allows to outline a multilayer system, where all the three factors are taken into account. Figure 7 provides an overview of the features traceable in the analysis of a vocal act. In the light of this model, we can go back to the adult cry fragment previously examined (Figure 3). To draw the showed visual display a multilayer analysis has been required. Firstly we analyzed the vocal act "morphological" factors and their modal architecture: pitch, loudness and articulation rhythm, integration of the extralinguistic and linguistic elements and of their relationships into pattern of recurring configurations. These patterns allows to describe the phenomenon: it is a piercing cry, drawn out and composed by sobs and verbal elements. Nevertheless this analysis, although thorough and refined, can't tell very much about the vocal flow and the vocal interaction in which the communicative action takes place. For this reason, we need a further analysis level, able to describe how the different communicative actions come one after the other along the chronological continuum. We focus therefore on the two speakers, on their mutual vocal actions and on the coordination and accommodation patterns between them. We will see their vocal production occurring simultaneously and synchronically and we will notice the way speaker A's action affects speaker B's action. And yet we don't really know a lot about that cry event. Information about the two interacting Agents and about the action space and time placement, allows us to re-enact the intentional hierarchy and the Agents cultural transitory and permanent characteristics. As in a Chinese box game, this multilayer focus on vocal action represents one component in a complex intermodal act. Within this complexity it must be placed and analyzed, in his very interaction with different languages (vocal and motor, and visual, and so on). The overview on some elements is of course just a beginning in the direction of getting out from purely associative analysis models. To find out and describe the links and relationships between the three levels is a big amount of a complex work, to be done in the future.

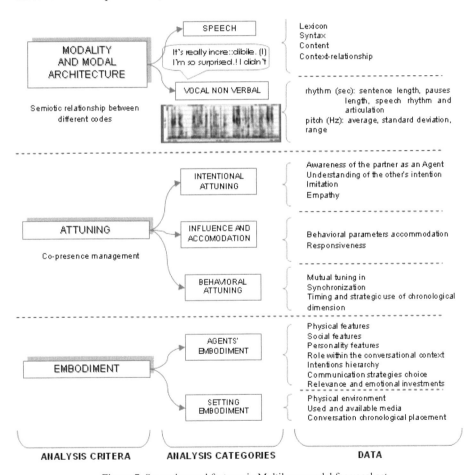

Figure 7. Synoptic vocal features in Multilayer model for vocal act

In the present work the dialog and comparison between experimental analysis on human-human and on human-ECA conversation have been continuous, fecund and challenging. Virtual environment simulation and implementation allows to evaluate bonds, effects and characteristics of the conversational architectures between two

Agents, as well as to indicate and study new interaction modalities. In other respects, data about human conversational interaction in different contexts provides an extraordinary complex model; at the same time, such a model provides the ergonomic effectiveness to which AI aims although being yet far from it. About this, it's fundamental to assess if, according to the famous Media Equation [57, 58], the rules of human-human interaction can be applied and extended to human-machine interaction. Several studies have suggested that users speak more to humanoid or "anthropomorphic" interfaces [59] and these are evaluated as more intelligent and pleasant [60, 61]. More recently, however, several authors have started to arise doubts on the applicability of such hypothesis, suggesting the need to investigate more deeply the nature of the interaction between human user and technology [33], rather than simply try to model artificial agents on the bases of human characteristics. Research on Embodied Conversational Agents has shown how these two kinds of interactions are not so similar and that human users actually adapt their dialog style when aware of interacting with a tool [62].

According to the multilayer model here presented, this means that HM interaction is governed by its own specific features and principles of attuning and embodiment [33]. That makes the equation between emotion, natural forms of interaction, usability and efficiency more problematic: it's not only through the use of believable avatars able to use facial or vocal emotional expression very similarly to the human ones that a system will be capable to involve the user in a true affective and effective interaction [63]. An intriguing challenge seemingly without limits, as we can see in the human-machine conversation imagined by Norman, Ortony & Russell, in an article published on IBM System Journal [64]. The authors describe a grid computer, assembling a number of machines prior to doing a computation and suppose that each machine were queried about its state of readiness, asking:

User: How are you feeling?
Machine1: I had a disk failure in my RAID, so if this is an important calculation, you had better not count on me.
Machine 2: I am feeling a bit anxious because I have had some errors, so I will be slowed by the need to do continual checks.
Machine 3: I am feeling anxious because of recent virus or hacker attacks.
User: Ok, let's wait, then, we can try later on.

The authors suggest to endow the machines not only with the ability to detect errors through algorithms, but also with the ability to engage in a conversation with the user during the processes, so as to signal an unforeseen and therefore beyond control situation, representing a source of surprise and anxiety. This competence would increase robustness and error tolerance, as proved by those animals which have developed sophisticated mechanisms, as emotional appraisal and expression, for surviving in an unpredictable, dynamic world.

7.6 References

[1]   L. Anolli, *Fondamenti di psicologia della comunicazione*, Il Mulino, Bologna, 2006.
[2]   J. Cassell, H. Vilhjálmsson, K. Chang, T. Bickmore, L. Campbell, and H. Yan, Requirements for an architecture for Embodied Conversational Characters, in: *Computer animation and simulation '99*

(Eurographics Series), D. Thalmann and N. Thalmann, Eds., Vienna, Austria: Springer Verlag, 109-120, 1999.

[3]   H. Giles, C.A. Shepard and B.A. Le Poire, Communication Accommodation Theory, in: *The new handbook of language & social psychology,* P. Robinson and H. Giles, Eds., Chichester, UK: Wiley, 33-56, 1991.

[4]   V. Gallese, *The manifold nature of interpersonal relations: The quest for a common mechanism.* Phil. Trans. Royal Soc. London, 358, 517-528, 2003.

[5]   R. Ciceri, Ed., *Mente Inter-Attiva. Media, Linguaggi, Competenze,* Omega Edizioni, Torino, 2005.

[6]   T. Bickmore and J. Cassell, Social dialogue with Embodied Conversational Agents, In: *Advances in Natural, Multimodal Dialogue Systems,* J. van Kuppevelt, L. Dybkjaer, and N. Bernsen, Eds.,. New York: Kluwer Academic, 2005.

[7]   F. De Rosis, A. Cavalluzzi, I. Mazzotta and N. Novelli, Can embodied conversational agents induce empathy in users? AISB Virtual Social Characters Symposium, 2005.

[8]   J.N. Cappella and C. Pelachaud, Rules for responsive robots: Using human interactions to build virtual interactions, in: *Stability and Change in Relationships*, A.L. Vangelisti, H. T. Reis and M. A. Fitzpatric, Eds., New York: Cambridge University Press, 2001.

[9]   R.W. Picard, *Affective Computing,* Cambridge, MA: MIT Press, 1997.

[10] K. Fitch and R. Sanders, R., Eds., *Handbook of language and social interaction,* Lawrence Erlbaum, 2005.

[11] A. Trognon, Sur l'analyse du contenu des interlocutions, *Psychologie et éducation, X, 1,* 21-48, 1986.

[12] J.M., Jakobi, A. Blanchet and M. Bromberg, Effects of prosodic focus in referential reiterations during interviews/Les effets du focus intonatif dans les réitérations référentielles en situation d'entretien de recherche., *Revue Internationale de Psychologie Sociale*, 1, 345-363, 1988.

[13] R. Ciceri, L'intenzione comunicativa, in: *Comunicare il pensiero,* M.R. Ciceri, Ed.,Omega Edizioni, Torino, 2001.

[14] L. Anolli, MaCHT- Miscommunication as chance THeory: Towards a unitary theory of communication and miscommunication, in:, *Say not to say. New perspectives on Miscommunication,* L. Anolli, R. Ciceri, G. Riva, Eds., IOS Press, Amsterdam, 3-42, 2002.

[15] L. Anolli and R. Ciceri, *Elementi di psicologia della comunicazione. Aspetti semantici e tattici,* LED, Milano, 1995.

[16] R. Ciceri, P. Colombo and C. Antoniotti, Pictures and Words: Analogies and Specificity in Knowledge Organization, in *Neural Nets, WIRN* Vietri - 03, Springer-Verlag, Londra, 358-366, 2003.

[17] N. Green, G. Carenini, S. Kerpedjiev, S. Roth and J. Moore, A mediaindependent content language for integrated text and graphics generation, in: *CVIR '98 – Workshop on Content Visualization and Intermedia Representations,* 1998.

[18] J. Cassell, M. Stone and H. Yan, Coordination and context-dependence in the generation of embodied conversation, *INLG 2000,* Mitzpe Ramon, Israel, 2000.

[19] M. Cole, *Cultural Psychology: A once and future discipline,* Cambridge: Harvard University Press, 1996.

[20] R. Jackendoff, *The architecture of the language faculty,* Cambridge, Mass., MIT Press, 1997.

[21] C. Pelachaud, V. Maya and M. Lamolle, Representation of Expressivity for Embodied Conversational Agents, Workshop Balanced Perception and Action, Third International Joint Conference on Autonomous Agents & Multi-Agent Systems, New-York, 2004.

[22] R. Ciceri, L. Anolli and M. Infantino, You' re a Real Genius!: Irony as miscommunication design, in: *Say not to say. New perspectives on miscommunication,* L. Anolli, R. Ciceri, G. Riva, Eds., IOS Press, Amsterdam, 135-159, 2002.

[23] L. Anolli, R. Ciceri and M.G. Infantino, Irony as game of implicitness: Acoustic profiles of ironic communication, in: *Journal of Psycholinguistic Research*, 29, 275-311, 2000.

[24] L. Anolli, R. Ciceri and G. Infantino, Behind the dark glasses. Irony as strategy for implicit communication, In: *Genetic, Social and General Psychology Monograph's*, 128,76-95, 2002.

[25] J. Cassell, T. Bickmore, H. Vilhjalmsson and H. Yan, More than just a pretty face: Conversational protocols and the affordances of embodiment, *Knowledge-Based Systems,* 14, 55-64, 2001.

[26] Kelly, S. D. J. D.Barr, R. B. Church, and K. Lynch, Offering a hand to pragmatic understanding: The role of speech and gesture in comprehension and memory. *Journal of Memory and Language*, 40:577–592, 1999.

[27] R. Ciceri, F. Biassoni and V. Valloggia, Frame emotivo e componenti acustiche del pianto adulto nella cinematografia degli anni '50/'90, paper presented to the International Society for Research on Emotion General Meeting, Bari, 2005.

[28] J. Reilly, M.L. McIntyre and U. Bellugi, BABYFACE: A new perspective on universals in language acquisition, in: *Theoretical issues in sign language research: psycholinguistics,* P. Siple, Ed., Chicago, IL, University of Chicago Press, 1991.

[29] R. Ciceri and S. Balzarotti, Recognition and narration of emotional scenes in deaf children: Analysis of the strategies used to organize and coordinate communicational behavior, *XVIII Biennial Conference of the International Society for the Study of Behavioural Development* ISSBD, Ghent, pp. 248, 2004.

[30] R. Ciceri and M. Marini, The attunement in mother-infant communication from 2 to 7 months: Synchronicity of interactive behavior, *XI European Conference on Developmental Psychology,* Milano, 201-202, 2003.

[31] V. Gallese, The "Shared Manifold" Hypothesis: From mirror neurons to empathy, *Journal of Consciousness Studies,* 8, 33-50, 2001.

[32] V. Gallese, "Being like me": Self-other identity, mirror neurons and empathy, in: *Perspectives on Imitation: From Cognitive Neuroscience to Social Sciences,* S. Hurley, N. Chater, Eds., MIT Press, Boston, MA, 2005.

[33] K. Höök, Steps to take before IUIs become real, *Journal of Interaction with Computers,* 12, 2000.

[34] L. Anolli and P. Legrenzi, *Psicologia generale,* Il Mulino, Bologna, 2003.

[35] P. Boylan, Accommodation through a transformation of consciousness, in: *Globalisation, foreign languages and intercultural learning,* K. Koch and T. Muggin, *SIETAR-UK Conference,* South Bank University, London, 9-12, 2001.

[36] D. Singh, Adaptive significance of female physical attractiveness: Role of waist-tohip ratio, *Journal of Personality and Social Psychology,* 65, 293-307, 1973.

[37] K. Grammer, Human courtship behavior: Biological basis and cognitive processing, in: *The sociobiology of sexsual and reproductive strategies,* C. Vogel and E. Voland, Eds., London: Chapman & Hall, 1989.

[38] L. Anolli and R. Ciceri, Analysis of the vocal profiles of male seduction: From exhibition to self-disclosure, *The Journal of General Psychology,* 129,149-169, 2002.

[39] J. O'Keefe and B.L. Lambert, Managing the flow of ideas: A local management approach to message design, in *Communication Yearbook 18,* B.R. Burleson, Ed., Thousand Oaks, CA: Sage, 1995.

[40] J.N. Cappella, The management of conversational interaction in adults and infants, in: The handbook of interpersonal communication, M.L. Knapp and G.R. Miller, Eds., Thousand Oaks, CA: Sage, 2nd ed., pp. 380-419, 1994.

[41] D. Davis and W.T. Perkowitz, Consequences of responsiveness in dyadic interaction: Effects of probability of response and proportion of content-related responses on interpersonal attraction, *Journal of Personality and Social Psychology,* 37, 534-550,1979.

[42] M.E. Bratman, What is intention? In: *Intention in Communication,* P.R. Cohen, J. Morgan and M.E. Pollack, Eds., Cambridge, MIT Press, 1990.

[43] A. Schutz, Making music together, in: *Collected Papers II: Studies in social theory,* A. Schutz, Ed., The Hague: Martinus Nijhoff, 1971.

[44] A.W. Siegman and S. Feldstein, *Of Speech and Time,* Erlbaum, Hillsdale, 1979.

[45] R. Ciceri and F.Biassoni, Sulla funzione semantica dei tratti soprasegmentali e sul loro ruolo nel significare e comprendere domande reiterate nella self-disclosure di eventi traumatici, in: *Significare e comprendere. La semantica del linguaggio verbale,* F.Lo Piparo , Ed., Aracne, Milano, 389-406, 2005.

[46] R. Ciceri, P. Colombo and S. Balzarotti, Analysis of the human physiological responses and multimodal emotional signals to an interactive computer, in: *Proceedings of AISB 2005 Agents that want and like: motivational and emotional roots of cognition and action,* published by The University of Hertfordshire, Hatfield, AL10 9AB UK, 25-33, 2005.

[47] G. Andreoni, B. Apolloni, S. Balzarotti, F. Beverina, R. Ciceri, G. Palmas, L. Piccini, Emotional interfaces with ambient intelligence, in: *Ambient intelligence, wireless networking, and ubiquitous computing,* A. Vasilakos, W. Pedrycz, Eds, Artech House, USA, 125-156, 2006.

[48] C. L. Lisetti, Personality, affect and emotion taxonomy for socially intelligent agents, in: *Proceedings of the 15th International Florida Artificial Intelligence Research Society Conference* (FLAIRS'02), Menlo Park, CA, AAAI Press, Pensacola, FL, 2002.

[49] J. Cassell and K.R. Thorisson, The power of a nod and a glance: Envelope vs. emotional feedback in animated conversational agents, *Applied Artificial Intelligence,* 13, 519-538,1999.

[50] M. Mancini, B. Hartmann, C. Pelachaud, A. Raouzaiou and K. Karpouzis, Ex-pressive avatars in MPEG-4, in: *IEEE International Conference on Multimedia &Expo,* Amsterdam, 2005.

[51] J.A. Russell, A circumplex model of affect, *Journal of Personality and Social Psychology,* 39, 1161-1178, 1980.

[52] A. Gabrielsson and P.N. Juslin, Emotional expression in music, in: Music and emotion: Theory and research, H.H. Goldsmith, R.J. Davidson and K.R. Scherer, Eds., Oxford University Press, New York, 503-534, 2003.

[53] S. Dahl and A. Friberg, Expressiveness of musician's body movements in performances on marimba, in: *Gesture-Based Communication in Human-Computer Interaction, 5th International Gesture Workshop*, A. Camurri, G. Volpe, Eds., GW 2003, Genoa, Italy, April 2003, Selected Revised Papers. Volume LNAI 2915., Berlin Heidelberg, Springer-Verlag, 479-486, 2004.

[54] V. Maya, M. Lamolle and C. Pelachaud, Influences and Embodied Conversational Agents: Tools for automatic processing of effects, *Third International Joint Conference on Autonomous Agents & Multi-Agent Systems*, AAMAS'04, New-York, USA, 2004.

[55] W.A. van Dommelen, The contribution of Speech Rhythm and Pitch to Speaker Recognition, *Language and Speech*, 30, 313-318, 1989.

[56] M.S.A. Graziano and C.G. Gross, Spatial maps for the control of movement, *Curr. Op. Neurobiol.*, 8, 195-201, 1998.

[57] B. Reeves and C. Nass, *The media equation*, New York, Cambridge University Press, 1996.

[58] C. Nass and K.L. Lee, Does computer-generated speech manifest personality? An experimental test of similarity-attraction, in: *Proceedings of the Conference on Human Factors in Computing Systems*, ACM Press, NY, 329-336, 2000.

[59] S. Brennan and J. Ohaeri, Effects of message style on users' attributions toward agents, *Conference Companion on Human Factors in Computing Systems*, Boston, Massachusetts, 281-282, 1994.

[60] T. Koda and P. Maes, Agents with faces: The effect of personification, paper presented at the *Proceedings of the Fifth IEEE International Workshop on Robot and Human Communication (ROMAN'96)*, 1996.

[61] F. De Rosis, C. Pelachaud, I. Poggi, V. Carofiglio, and B. D. Carolis, From Greta's mind to her face: Modelling the dynamics of affective states in a conversational embodied agent, *International Journal of Human-Computer Studies. Special Issue on Applications of Affective Computing in HCI*, in press.

[62] S. Oviatt and B. Adams, Designing and evaluating conversational interfaces with animated characters, in: Embodied Conversational Agents, J. Cassell,, J. Sullivan, S. Prevost and E. Churchill, Eds., MIT Press, Cambridge, MA, 319-343, 2000.

[63] P. Rizzo, Emotional agents for user entertainment: Discussing the underlying assumptions, in: *International Workshop on Affect in Interactions: Towards a New Generation of Interfaces*, Siena, Italy, AC'99, Annual Conference of the EC I3 Programme, 1999, 21-22.

[64] D.A. Norman, A. Ortony, D.M. Russell, Affect and machine design: lessons for the development of autonomous machine, *IBM Systems Journal*, 42 (2003), 38-43.

From Communication to Presence
G. Riva et al. (Eds.)
IOS Press, 2006

8   Strategic Emotion in Negotiation: Cognition, Emotion, and Culture

Shu LI, Michael E. ROLOFF

Abstract. This chapter is an overview of research on emotion in negotiation that integrates cognitive, affective, and cultural aspects of the field. We address the following issues: (1) the effects of mood and emotion on negotiator cognition and performance and the potential of emotion as a negotiation strategy; (2) individual differences in emotional expression and individual traits, such as self-monitoring and emotional intelligence, that impact on the use of strategic emotion; and (3) cultural influences on negotiation and on emotional experience and expression.

Contents

8.1 Emotion in Negotiation

Much emotion research has been devoted to the study of its relationship with cognition. According to psychologist Klaus Scherer [1], the dichotomous approach that views cognition as "an antagonist to emotion" and that sees emotion "as an impediment to the proper functioning" of cognition and rational thought has its roots in Plato and Aristotle's philosophical musings (p. 563). In modern psychology, the debate over the primacy of cognition over emotion has and continues to draw a great deal of attention. On one side, cognition is championed as a necessary condition of emotion [2]. In this tradition, appraisal theories trace the elicitation of emotions to "subjective evaluations of the significance of events to the well-being of the person concerned" (p. 564) [1]. On the other side of the debate, Robert Zajonc, a major proponent of the independence of emotion, argues that emotion and cognition are distinct and separate processes and that experience of emotion is possible without cognitive input (i.e., cognitive evaluations) [3, 4]. These disparate perspectives, while promoting and deepening our understanding of the mechanism of the cognition-emotion interactions, unnecessarily cast cognition and emotion in opposition and preclude one in the smooth functioning of the other. In recent years, however, more efforts have been made to "integrate rather than oppose the two"—to incorporate affect in rational decision-making and cognitive appraisal in emotional reactions [1, 5].

This bit of history in the study of emotion provides a good context for an overview of research on emotion in negotiation, which began as a branch of psychological studies. For a long time, emotion was ignored while cognition (rational thinking) was treasured in negotiation. In the 1980s and 1990s, most negotiation research was conducted under a cognitive decision-making framework, which viewed the negotiator as a decision maker faced with an opponent and a situation [6]. The negotiator's perception and interpretation of the opponent and situation greatly influence the judgments and decisions that he/she makes. Max Bazerman and Margaret Neale (see [7]) argue that "much of the suboptimality that can be observed in negotiation is the result of deviations from rationality in the judgmental processes of negotiators" (p. 247). For example, negotiators systematically make judgment errors about their opponent's priority (the relative importance or weight of negotiation issues) and the compatibility of interest between the two (whether the two parties' preferences for alternatives within a given issue are compatible). They often assume that the opponent assigns the same value to issues as they do and therefore there can be only a win-lose outcome on any issue; they also assume that the other party's preferences must be completely incompatible with their own. In a distributive-integrative bargaining paradigm, in which the negotiator is guided with a win-lose or a win-win perspective, such perceptive errors can lead bargainers to work within a distributive frame and to focus on their individual interest only, thus reduce the potential for integrative gains and result in suboptimal outcomes [8].

Significant advances in negotiation research were achieved during this phase. However, it was also characterized by a disregard for emotion that deemed emotion as a hindrance to rational decision-making. Is negotiation all about the mind and rationality of the negotiator? What influence does emotion have on negotiator behavior and outcomes? And how do emotion and cognition interact in negotiation processes? In this chapter, our goal is to review recent developments in emotion and negotiation research that provide evidence for the importance of emotion in negotiation and that address the effective use of emotion by negotiators. We begin with a delineation of current literature on the influences of mood and emotion on negotiator cognition and behavior. We then turn our focus to a specific type of emotional display that can be highly cognitive and influential, i.e., strategic emotion, or the "on-demand emotional expression" [9]. Next we move on to a discussion of individual traits of the negotiator that affect the use of strategic emotion. Because strategic emotion involves the use of emotional expression as influence tactics, it requires cognitive evaluation on the part of the negotiator who uses these tactics (the *strategist*). We will explore individual characteristics that impact on the strategist's assessment of the situation and the partner, his/her planning capacity for the appropriate and effective emotional expression needed for the situation, and the strategist's behavioral control in communicating the tactical emotions. Before conclusion, we will also touch on the influence of culture on emotional expression and its implications for the emotional strategist who is faced with cultural variations. With this chapter we hope to integrate rather than contrast emotion and cognition. Negotiation, as a simultaneously cognitive (decision-making) and emotional (conflict-ridden) interaction, offers us an ideal venue for this endeavor.

8.1.1 Affect in Negotiation: Mood and Emotion

By the late 1990s, emotion was rediscovered by negotiation scholars; research interest in emotion has since been on the rise [10-12]. The conflict nature embedded in negotiations makes the activity frequently contentious and emotional. Thus, in Barry's [9] words, "as an impetus for and byproduct of social conflict, emotion is potentially central to understanding how individuals think about, behave within, and respond to bargaining situations"(p. 94). Cognitive decision-making is not the only determinant of negotiation behavior; negotiators are human beings under the influence of their own emotions.

A delineation of research on emotion in negotiation calls for a conceptual distinction between mood and emotion, both of which are encompassed under the umbrella of the broader concept of affect. Mood and emotion are distinguished from each other by their relative pervasiveness and specificity. Moods are undifferentiated affective states that are relatively more pervasive, more enduring and less intense than emotions, and may not have an identifiable antecedent cause or a target [9]. We often identify our mood in broad, unspecific terms, such as good or bad. In contrast, emotions are discrete, of relatively short duration, and intentionally directed at a target [13-16]. The emotions we experience also come in a much wider variety than do moods—happiness, sadness, anger, fear, etc. Yet moods and emotions are also interdependent [17]. A person in a bad mood may be more likely to experience negative emotions like distress, anger, or sadness in response to certain stimuli, whereas a person given a pleasant surprise in the morning may bathe in a good mood for the rest of the day.

The majority of affect and negotiation research focuses on the intrapersonal effects of mood on negotiator behavior, i.e., the effects of mood on the negotiator's own behavior [e.g., 11, 18-20]. Despite the heavier interpersonal nature of emotion and its potential as an influence strategy, it has been neglected and played second fiddle to the more pervasive but less differentiated mood as a predictor of negotiator cognition, behavior, and outcome. In a series of seminal studies, Alice Isen and her colleagues induced positive mood in experimental subjects prior to an experimental task by giving them cookies or leaving them a dime in the coin return of public phones, by asking them to sort funny cartoons and giving them a gift, and by making them watch a comedy film or giving them candy [19-21]. Results verified the effects of positive mood on cognition: negotiators' good mood carried over into the negotiation task and made the negotiators' cognitive processing more flexible and creative. In the words of the researchers [20], "good feelings increase the tendency to combine material in new ways and to see relatedness between divergent stimuli," thus facilitate creative thinking and problem solving (p. 1130).

Other researchers used similar positive mood manipulations, such as pleasant artificial scents, humorous videos, and false positive feedback on task performance [12, 18]. These studies consistently demonstrate ways in which positive affect influences social information processing. According to Forgas [22], people in a good mood are more likely than those in a neutral or bad mood to "adopt more creative, open, constructive, and inclusive thinking styles" (p. 18). This cognitive processing style in turn promotes a cooperative and integrative orientation in negotiators, making them more altruistic and helpful, confident and optimistic, and less contentious and more concessionary than their non-emotional counterparts [18, 19, 21, 23]. Thus, good mood appears to increase the use of cooperative and integrative strategies and lead to higher joint outcomes [11, 19, 24].

In a similar vein, negative mood affects negotiator behavior through a cognitive processing. Where positive mood leads to heuristic and flexible thinking, negative mood leads to more systematic and rational decision-making in negotiators [25]. Negative mood tends to create a focus on self-interest and increase the use of such distributive and competitive strategies as decreasing initial offers and using threat and aggression in the development of profitable agreements [26, 27]. Hertel, Neuhof, Theuer, and Kerr found that sad and insecure subjects (in a bad mood) displayed more rational behavior, such that they tended to defect when the other was cooperative and to cooperate when the other was uncooperative [28]. In terms of its effect on negotiation outcome, this cognitive and behavioral orientation easily contributes to conflict spirals, lower joint gains, and less satisfactory relationships [25, 29, 30].

The above findings suggest that while positive mood leads to cooperation and greater joint gain, negative mood leads to competition and greater individual gain because of the different cognitive processing styles associated with each. Mood is believed to influence negotiators' cognitive processing, thus their behavior, and thus affect negotiation outcomes. However, emotion, especially its tactical expression, works not only on self but on other cognition and consequently influence other behavior. In other words, emotion has a stronger interpersonal effect. We devote the rest of the section to an examination of the interpersonal effects of emotion, i.e., the effects of one negotiator's emotion on the other negotiator, to contribute to the small but growing body of research in this area [31-34].

The study of emotion and negotiation is characterized by a social functionalist approach that posits that emotion is informative, evocative, and serves as an incentive in social interactions and causes social consequences [35]. For example, positive emotion can signal cooperativeness and trustworthiness, elicit cooperation, trust, and concession from others, and promise rewards for others. Negative emotion, on the other hand, impresses the other party as aggressive, competitive, and reckless, elicits compliance from the other party, and signals punishment or negative consequences for the non-complying opponent [36]. Perhaps because positive emotion shares an undertone of cooperativeness with principled, integrative bargaining, it has received relatively more scholarly attention. On the other hand, negative emotions such as anger, frustration, and depression seem to violate the rational principle of integrative bargaining, which might be the reason that negative affect has not been studied as much. Then, in what is now a classic study of ultimatum games, Madan Pillutla and Keith Murnighan brought negative emotion back to the study of negotiator behavior [37]. Bargainers would reject economically beneficial offers, the authors found, out of anger and spite caused by their perception of unfairness in their opponents' offers, rather than on the basis of rational economic consideration. This study is a wonderful antidote to the purely rational and emotion-free approach to negotiation: negotiator behavior is not always guided or determined by rational analyses of utility. However imperfect and irrational negative emotions might be, they actually led bargainers to "revolt," despite knowledge of potential economic damage associated with such outbursts of feelings.

Since then we have seen fast growth in the amount of research on negative emotion (as compared to positive emotion), both because of a realization of its intricacies and complexities and of our insufficient understanding of its nature and impact on negotiation (e.g., see [36-39]). Despite their risk of relational damage, negative emotions do serve important social functions, because the stance negative negotiators take is likely to impress the other side as extreme, risky, reckless, and seemingly out of control [34, 36].

For this reason, they may be highly effective when used tactically to achieve an agreement. If negotiators do fall under the influence of negative emotions, e.g., anger, how exactly will it impact on negotiation outcomes? Arif Butt and colleagues report that anger expression of a negotiator lowers his/her opponent's outcome, possibly because displays of anger are signals of strong positions or threats, which in turn increase a negotiator's power [40]. Keith Allred, however, cautions that the use of anger may also bring retaliation. When negative emotions are used intentionally throughout the negotiation, targets will most likely feel unfair, offended, and angry. Once they are provoked to retaliate and to match their opponents' behavior with equal or greater anger, the strategy becomes counterproductive [38].

The lesson, then, seems to be that negotiators should be aware of messages of power hidden in emotions, which may be highly effective sources of social influence. If negotiators intend to influence their partners through affective displays, they first need to know which emotions are more powerful. Larissa Tiedens juxtaposes power messages behind expressions of anger and sadness. The expression of anger implies confidence and capability, whereas the expression of sadness (e.g., over disappointment) implies incompetence and subjugation. People confer more power and status on those who express anger than those who express sadness [41]. Although the study was not carried out in the negotiation context, Tiedens's findings fittingly apply to negotiation interactions. The normative integrative bargainer is taught not to get emotional and to maintain a positive, cooperative affect state during negotiations. However, when negotiators find it necessary to express their dissatisfaction, frustration, or hurt feelings, it might help establish their power status if they coat it in a high-power emotion like anger rather than in a low-power emotion like sadness or disappointment.

Anger has also been studied with other "powerful" negative emotions. Michael Morris and Dacher Keltner [34] argue that anger and contempt are major emotions displayed in the positioning phase of negotiation. Contempt works to convey information about status and is likely to evoke complementary emotions. Either the counterpart "internalizes the message of low regard, loses self-control and becomes easier to persuade, or he may become motivated to make concessions to win back the contemptuous one's approval" (p. 30). In either case, contempt displays help establish relational dominance. Anger, on the other hand, signals one's commitment to a position and warns the opponent that one may be prone to rash action, such as abandoning the negotiation and taking alternative measures. Thus anger-expressing people are seen as dominant and they evoke such complementary, low-power emotions as fear and guilt in the counterpart [42, 43]. Fear can lead a negotiator to yield and avoid behaviors that could offend or upset the other. Guilt may bring about restitution in the form of concessions. Both emotions steer the negotiator toward behaviors that benefit the angry opponent.

This limited body of research on emotion in negotiation suggests that emotions do not only affect negotiators' cognitive processing, but also their social perception and relationships. Hence the social functional framework of emotional expression in negotiation [34]. Under this framework, negotiator emotion should be studied with regard to its functions in social interactions, i.e., "emotions that arise in response to one's counterpart" and interaction dynamics (p. 5). As we mentioned earlier, a functionalist view posits that emotions serve informative (signaling information about feelings and intentions to one's opponent), evocative (eliciting emotional or behavioral responses from others), and incentive (signaling rewards or punishments on the behavior of the other side) functions [35].

If emotion serves such important social functions, we may profit in both theory and practice by consciously managing and utilizing it as an influence strategy in social interactions such as negotiations. Such potential of emotion perfectly illustrates its complex relationship to cognition: there is rationality in the seemingly irrational use of emotions.

8.1.2 The Management of Emotion

A few lines of research in the area of emotion management (e.g., emotional control, emotional regulation, and emotion work) bear on our discussion of strategic emotion in negotiation. Emotional control refers to an individual's ability to exhibit (or avoid exhibiting) an emotional response as a matter of personal desire rather than as an involuntary consequence of environmental conditions [44]. It varies along four major dimensions: direction—it may lead to either the amplification or inhibition of emotional expression; target of control—whether it is directed at the management of one's own emotions, or at the emotional expression of another party; onset of control—whether it is the effort at initiating control prior to experiencing an actual emotion, or the effort to redirect an emotional response following the onset of that response; and finally, nature of transformation—some control efforts are intended to alter the intensity levels of existing emotions; others entail the substitution of one emotion for another; still others attempt to mask emotions [9, 45].

Similarly, emotional regulation is a "heterogeneous set of processes by which emotions are themselves regulated" [46]. Basic processes are reappraisal and suppression. Reappraisal modifies how we evaluate situations that induce emotions.

For example, we may tell ourselves that a sad scene in a movie is cheap cliché without genuine feelings so that we do not find it moving and cry about it. Robert Sutton observed that when bill collectors followed the professional norm of conveying urgency and irritation to debtors that they did not genuinely feel and thus encountered emotive dissonance, they used reappraisals to help them become emotionally detached [47]. Suppression is about inhibiting emotion-expressive behavior, which decreases self-reported experiences of such emotions as pain, pride, and amusement (but not disgust or sadness). In other words, by suppressing the expression of certain emotions, we may reduce the intensity with which we feel them.

Emotion work is defined as "the management of feelings to create a publicly observable facial and bodily display" [48]. Social contexts provide cues to display rules—expectations and obligations regarding appropriate emotional expression in a given situation or a given role—which in turn guide emotion work by individuals. For example, humility and modesty are behavioral norms in some East Asian societies, and individuals are expected to behave accordingly. When someone wins a valued prize for extraordinary work, no matter how happy and excited he/she is about the honor, the particular display rule in that society stipulates that this individual work on his/her emotions so that he/she displays not exaltation but only mild satisfaction and even a touch of self-deprecation. Emotion work takes the forms of surface acting, when an individual expresses or displays emotions that are not personally felt, and deep acting, when the individual seeks to internalize the emotion that is to be displayed [48]. In the context of negotiation, to the extent that negotiators follow display rules to express "appropriate" and desired emotions, they are doing emotion work, very likely surface acting. But who would choose, under what circumstances, to adopt emotion work?

8.2 Strategic Emotion and the Negotiator

As a negotiator displays sadness or frustration that he does not genuinely feel in order to evoke the opponent's compassion, as he tries to mask the happiness of achieving a desired outcome so that the opponent does not become alarmed and discontent, or when he makes an effort to stay calm while truly infuriated by his opponent just because that is the appropriate thing to do, the negotiator engages in emotion management. Therefore, the question raised above resonates in all three lines of conceptually related, complementary research—emotional control, emotional regulation, and emotion work. The emotion management literature indicates that emotional expression as negotiation strategy is closely linked with one's goals, tendencies, and competencies regarding expressive display. Imagine a negotiator who plans for a display of fury to extract a concession from his opponent but who, having a generally happy and agreeable disposition, is incapable of executing such negative behavior and, contrary to his intention, exhibits a much milder affect state that is not compelling to his opponent at all. Put another way, successful strategic emotion requires accurate assessment of the emotional needs in specific situations, integration of such needs with one's affective tendencies (e.g., some are more prone to positive or negative emotional display than others), and efficacy in deploying the strategy.

This brings us to the second segment of the paper—what individual differences influence emotion management in negotiation? Surely we do not all share the same emotional management styles and competencies. Next we discuss some individual characteristics that we believe to be most proximately related to the strategic expression of emotions, drawn from literature in personality, emotion, communication, and impression management. We consider each of the following in terms of its bearing on the strategic use of emotions in a negotiation setting: affectivity, emotional expressivity, emotional intelligence, and self-monitoring.

8.2.1 Individual Differences in Emotional Expression

8.2.1.1 Affectivity

Dispositional affectivity—which captures individual tendencies in emotional experience—includes positive affectivity and negative affectivity, the latter of which has received more scholarly attention [49]. Individuals who score high on this dimension are susceptible to tension, anxiety, and nervousness and are much more likely to experience these emotions than those who score low on this dimension [50]. Jack Haney suggests that high negative-affectivity individuals tend to judge ambiguous stimuli in a much more negative light than low negative-affectivity individuals [51]. As negotiators, high negative-affectivity individuals are not only more likely to experience negative emotions during typical conflict-ridden moments of contention, but also when they are faced with ambiguity in the situation and the opponent. Therefore, they may prefer negative to positive emotions as well.

8.2.1.2 Emotional Expressivity

Emotional expressivity depicts a stable individual trait associated with emotion-expressive behavior, i.e., how much emotion is displayed [52]. Early expressivity measures treated this trait as a unidimensional construct varying from low to high on a single continuum [53]. James Gross and Oliver John noted the inadequacy of this conceptualization and developed a multifaceted scale that incorporated multiple dimensions such as positive expressivity, negative expressivity, impulse strength, the confidence with which individuals express emotion, and the ability to mask emotion [52]. The first two aspects are most relevant to our purpose here: Individuals high in positive expressivity, for example, laugh more when they find something funny, and individuals high in negative expressivity cry more when they are sad. According to the rational (emotionally neutral) negotiation approach, high expressivity, either positive or negative, could be detrimental for a negotiator, because the overflowing emotions may reveal too much about a negotiator's positions, preferences, and strategies. An unsuppressed smile or frown at an offer obviously signals to the opponent that the negotiator is satisfied or dissatisfied with the offer and therefore implies his/her position and goal. An emotionally expressive bargainer may also be considered lacking in his/her ability to regulate or control emotions. However, emotional expressivity also has implications for the conscious and tactical use of emotions. For example, if I am an expressive individual with high expressive confidence and masking abilities, I might be more willing to choose to use emotional strategies than a low-expressivity individual.

Therefore, affectivity and emotional expressivity both center around natural individual tendencies toward emotion, with affectivity focusing on emotional experience and expressivity capturing emotional expression. These traits would presumably impact on affective   behaviors in negotiation, but since they do not capture the cognitive and strategic-motivational processes (e.g., evaluating the situation to determine specific needs for emotional display, goal-setting guided by such evaluation, and behavioral planning for the enactment of strategy), we believe strategic emotional display would be influenced more heavily by the following traits that do embody individual differences in the conscientious management of emotions.

8.2.1.3 Emotional Intelligence

Emotional intelligence (EI) refers to four branches of core emotional regulation competencies—perceiving emotions, using emotions to facilitate thinking, understanding emotions, and managing emotions [54, 55]. The first two branches constitute Experiential EI; the last two branches make up Strategic EI. As part of Strategic EI, understanding involves knowledge of "emotional information, how emotions combine and progress, and how to reason about emotional meanings." Managing emotions, on the other hand, "specifically pertains to a person's ability to manage and regulate feelings in oneself and others" (p. 178) [56]. Thus strategic EI may be directly related to strategic emotional displays in negotiations—it depicts both cognitive and behavioral capacity needed for the task. Individuals high in EI, especially strategic EI, are more likely to be able to maintain control over their affective state than those low in EI. They may be able to use emotions strategically, "knowing when to and when not to express emotion, and knowing how much and in what form to express emotion when its use is necessary" [57].

8.2.1.4 Self-Monitoring

Self-monitoring might well be the most important dispositional trait considered in this chapter in relation to emotion in negotiation. Self-monitoring is concerned with the processes by which individuals actively plan, enact, and guide their behavior in social situations. Mark Snyder prescribes two sources of information that guide these activities—cues to situational or interpersonal specifications of behavioral appropriateness and cues to inner states, dispositions, and attitudes [58]. Individuals differ in the extent to which they rely on either information source to guide their actions in social contexts. High self-monitoring individuals ask the question: "What does the situation demand of me and what image should I project?" They demonstrate exquisite situation-to-situation discriminativeness and variation in their social behavior, and the correspondence between behavior and attitude is often low [59-61]. In contrast, low self-monitoring individuals ask: "Who am I and how should I be me?" They are characterized by a heavier reliance on relevant inner states to guide their behavior and by a lower level of responsiveness to situational and interpersonal specifications of appropriateness. With these individuals, correspondence between behavior and attitude is typically substantial.

Research suggests that emotional self-regulation is essential to understanding the link between emotional expression and self-monitoring, because how well expressive behavior—at center stage in our social interactions—is interpreted and received depends on effective regulation of such behavior [62]. High self-monitors are good at controlling and concealing their emotional displays, because they are not only sensitive to, but also willing to adapt their behavior in a manner consistent with, situational requirements [58, 63-64]. For example, high self-monitors may be more sensitive to the power differential implied in various emotions discussed earlier (e.g., anger and contempt vs. fear and guilt), and thus more adept at choosing to display the appropriate emotion to their advantage. Emotion-expressive behavior, falling in their repertoire of behavioral control, is their strength in comparison to low self-monitors. This control, as well as the ability to signal a wide range of emotional states, could potentially make high self-monitoring negotiators effective emotional strategists [65].

If self-regulation of emotional expression proves an issue of centrality to emotional intelligence and self-monitoring, it gives us reason to consider conceptual similarities between the two characteristics. Both require cognitive and perceptive processing of the situation and "on-demand" emotions; and both presume behavioral competency to display emotions befitting a particular context. The major difference between the two is that emotional intelligence focuses on emotional expression, while self-monitoring guides a wider range of self-presentation behaviors. Both traits might predict the effective use of strategic emotions.

Closely related to emotional intelligence and self-monitoring is the idea of impression management, which is involved with the behaviors people direct toward others to create and maintain desired perceptions of themselves [66]. Impression management is rooted in Erving Goffman's dramaturgical theory. According to Goffman, people are "actors" engaging in "performances" in various "settings" before "audiences" [67]. Actor and audience interactions define the situation and provide stimuli or motivation for the actor's behavior. Because the act of managing impressions requires a certain degree of comprehension of the specific demands of situations and audiences, self-monitoring ability may play a moderating role in the process as it reflects one's sensitivity to such demands.

When the presentation of an intended image requires affective behavior, a connection is established between impression management and emotional expression. For example, a bill collector's professional image in front of a debtor is intentionally emotional—urgency represented by "high arousal with a hint of irritation"—so as to increase the likelihood that debtors would pay off their debt [47]. A negotiator who wants to gain an edge might decide to present him/herself in an arrogant manner to signal status, contempt, and, ultimately, dominance, thus eliciting complementary emotional reactions in the opponent, which may indeed lead the latter to lose the edge. In this sense, emotion management (emotional control, regulation and emotion work, etc.) is other-directed, affective impression management—both comprise a cognitive mechanism and impact not only presentation of the self but also experience of the other person (or, through interpersonal influence, eventually own experience). Impression management research has not paid adequate attention to emotion in the past, but it will certainly benefit from the inclusion of emotion [68].

The four individual differences reviewed in this section can be grouped into two categories. Dispositional expressivity and affectivity are stable personality traits that predict the emotions individuals habitually, genuinely, or "unconsciously" experience and express. Emotional intelligence and self-monitoring, on the other hand, guide expressive behavior that individuals plan and manage to display or withhold from displaying and that does not necessarily correspond to their genuine emotional experience. The latter group has an individual efficacy component and involves one's ability to plan and execute strategies. It is this quality that links these traits to the strategic use of emotion in negotiation and provides insights into the mechanism of strategic emotion. We address the planning and enacting aspects of self-monitoring and its significance in negotiation strategies next.

8.2.2 Strategic Use of Emotion and Self-Monitoring in Negotiation

The strategic use of emotion in negotiation, according to Barry [9], is "the willful use of emotional display or expression as a tactical gambit by an individual negotiator" (p. 94). Also called on-demand emotional expression, it could reflect dissociation from one's genuine emotional experience, in that a negotiator displays emotions that are sometimes altered in intensity or nature, and at other times not driven by real emotional experience at all. Our review of emotional management suggests that the strategic use of emotion is a type of management work and overlaps with some of the management concepts discussed earlier. In order to use emotions strategically, individuals need to be able to exercise emotional control and engage in emotion work if they intend to project a desired self image. The strategy also calls to attention individual differences considered previously. A strategic negotiator assesses the need for specific emotions, plans for the display of such emotions, and executes the plan with appropriate expressive behavior. The components of this task render certain individual traits considerably influential in emotional strategies, especially those affecting the negotiator's management efficacy of expressive behavior, e.g., emotional intelligence and self-monitoring.

We want point out that although the strategic use of emotion may be initiated by one party in a negotiation, it is not merely an other-directed tactic that either succeeds or fails in its attempt at interpersonal influence. Negotiators interact with each other and their emotions evolve in the process. One party's planned emotional expressions may arouse genuine changes in the other party's emotions, attitudes, and behaviors. In turn, the interdependency between two negotiators makes it likely that genuine, rather than planned, emotional encounters and interactions proceed after the initial acting. As strategic and genuine emotions entangle, it might become difficult for even the strategist to distinguish the two. Emotional responses from the target, whether or not anticipated by the initial strategist, might affect the emotional experience of the strategist, whose emotional display may detract from the original path he/she designs. Because of this interpersonal effect of emotion, it is imperative that we study both the strategist and the target, rather than considering the general negotiator indiscriminately. Next we turn to a discussion of individual differences that influence the performance of the strategist and the target.

8.2.2.1 The Strategist

The specific goals of the negotiator determine which emotions are in demand and how they should be displayed. Are emotions used to maintain good relationships, to assert oneself, to seek agreements and/or concessions, to manage ambiguities and uncertainties, as when a negotiator has very little knowledge of the opponent's interests and alternatives, or to inform an opponent of one's power, commitment, or position? What emotional strategies are called for in each of these circumstances? Because of the unlimited range of contexts that require emotional strategies, self-monitoring seems to be an individual characteristic most well suited for our investigation of the predictors of strategic emotional expression—possibly more so than emotional intelligence, if only because of the broader scope of strategic, "managed" behaviors that are guided by self-monitoring. After all, high self-monitors, by definition, are more sensitive to situational cues. They may be better at recognizing circumstances that demand the use of emotional (as well as substantive) strategies and they may plan and act accordingly. Therefore, even though self-monitoring is not as directly related to emotion as it is to self-presentation in general, it represents an important mechanism of evaluation, planning, and enactment, which is key to strategic emotions.

Before negotiators initiate an emotional strategy, they must be sufficiently aware of the negotiation situation and of their opponent and accordingly choose the specific emotions needed. Evidence clearly points to high self-monitors' heightened awareness of what the situation and the opponent demand and their superior ability to modify behavior in accordance. In a study by Roloff and Campion, self-monitoring was examined in the context of negotiator accountability to a constituency. When held accountable, high self-monitors were more likely than low self-monitors to conform closely to their constituency's objectives when making initial offers but then to stray away in their final offers [69]. This finding indicates that high self-monitors' self-presentation is indeed adjusted on the basis of perceived situational or relational demand. Early in the negotiation, when initial offers were an indication of responsibility to one's constituency, accountable negotiators, both high and low in self-monitoring, complied with the goals of the constituency. Later in the negotiation, however, high self-monitors' sensitivity to situational and relational cues took over and made them more cooperative with their opponents in order to reach an agreement, whereas low self-monitors continued to adhere to the objectives of their constituents.

Applying this feature of high self-monitors to the strategic use of emotions, we surmise that they are more likely to be better emotional strategists because of their greater awareness and more accurate assessment of what emotions the situation demands. After evaluating the situation, emotional strategists begin to plan for emotional expression. Jordan and Roloff demonstrated that high self-monitoring negotiators were better at interaction planning of impression management strategies and integrative tactics. They concluded that high self-monitors were better able to accomplish negotiation goals as a result of their superior planning skills [70].

Additionally, we may speculate that self-monitoring is related to communication skills required to express intended emotions through verbal or nonverbal channels. In general, high self-monitors, guided by their behavioral sensitivity and adaptability, may be more effective communicators than are their low self-monitoring counterparts.

Thus it is very likely that self-monitoring is positively related to the planning and enactment of emotional strategies. Future research is needed to empirically test the link between self-monitoring and the variability and complexity of strategic emotion planning and the behavioral repertoire representing strategic emotional behaviors.

Although an exhaustive contemplation of all the individual differences is well beyond the scope of this review, factors discussed previously—emotional expressivity, affectivity, and emotional intelligence—do seem to bear significantly and positively on the strategic use of emotions. They also appear to be positively related to or overlap with self-monitoring ability, the primary individual quality examined in this chapter.

8.2.2.2 The Target

The strategist alone does not determine the success of tactical emotions. As we offered earlier, the target, so called because he/she is the intended destination of the strategist's emotional influence, is not a mere receiver of emotional strategies. Since the strategist's ultimate goal is to exert influence on the perception, attitude and emotion of the target, it is important that we explore how the target perceives and reacts to emotional expressions of the strategist, and when strategic emotions are most likely to be successful with targets.

8.2.2.2.1 Emotional Congruence

Impression management sheds light on the target's interpretation of and reaction to strategic emotion, in which process both actor and audience contribute to the definition of a situation and stipulate behavioral requirements. The audience's definition of and response to the situation are significant components in impression management processes [68]. Schneider asserts that just as important as the actor's situational definition, the audience's definition of the situation includes expectations regarding appropriate roles and actor behavior. Together, "the perceived congruence between the actor's actual behavior and the audience's expectations is a key determinant of audience attributions and affective reactions" [66]. Since impression management is all about presenting a desired image, it is crucial that the impression manager gauge the attitudes and emotions of the audience so as to make the impression compelling.

Drawing on this stream of research, we may regard strategic emotional expression as actual actor behavior, and consider the possibility that the success of this strategy largely depends on the emotional expectations of the target/audience. The greater the emotional congruence the target perceives between the strategist's actual and target's anticipated emotional expression, the more likely the emotional strategy will succeed. A grim negotiator who sees the negotiation at hand as a critical last encounter in a series of talks and who is ready to be combative to achieve preset goals may not appreciate the positive emotions displayed by his counterpart in an effort to dissipate past grievances and lead the interaction onto a cooperative track. Or, if one party still holds grudges about unfair prior transactions with the other party and expects the latter to show remorse and solemnity, emotional incongruence will again dampen the actor's attempts at jovial smiles and hearty jokes. In other words, strategic emotion might be more influential if it is consistent with what the target anticipates as appropriate behavior.

We do acknowledge that emotional congruence is not a necessary condition for emotional tactics to be effective. A strategically angry negotiator might take the opponent by surprise and even compel a concession from the latter, even though the opponent has not anticipated or identified with the affective display. However, observations of real or simulated negotiations suggest that there may be just as many instances where emotional congruence does matter, which again puts a demand on the emotional intelligence and self-monitoring abilities of the negotiator. The specificity of emotional congruence, therefore, is ripe for empirical inquiry. In particular, under what conditions is emotional congruence vital to the success of the strategist? Would emotional congruence be particularly important to relational negotiations as compared to transactional negotiations? Also, are there emotions whose efficaciousness relies more heavily on perceived emotional congruence than other emotions? An example of a successful strategy that defies the principle of emotional congruence could be that when I expect my opponent to be angry with me but instead he deliberately adopts a happy and forgiving style, I might actually be more willing to comply with his requests. On the contrary, if I expect my opponent to be guilty and apologetic but he decides to be cheerful and to remind me to "look to future opportunities," I might feel utterly disgusted and refuse to cooperate. These are realistic concerns about the target that the strategist needs to consider in advance.

8.2.2.2.2 Self-Monitoring

Research on self-monitoring consistently depicts high self-monitors as experts with people. For instance, they are more likely than low self-monitors to notice and accurately remember information about someone they expect to interact with [71]. High self-monitoring individuals are not only keenly attentive to the actions of other individuals, but also particularly skilled at interpreting the nonverbal expressive behavior of other individuals to correctly infer their affective experience and emotional states, which is emphasized in Lennox and Wolfe's revision of the Self-monitoring Scale (sensitivity to expressive behavior of others and ability to modify self-presentation subscales) [72, 73]. In summary, high self-monitors seem to be more perceptive than low self-monitors of the emotions, motivations, and behaviors of others [74]. How does this play out for the target? A logical development from the description above is that high self-monitoring individuals may be better detectors of implicit strategic emotion and less approving of such manipulative tactics. Research on self-monitoring and reaction to emotional tactics is nonexistent, but we may infer from empirical work on ingratiation, another self-presentation and influence tactic. Mark Snyder shows that high self-monitors are less receptive to ingratiation than low self-monitors [58]. Edward Jones and Roy Baumeister report that high self-monitors reacted positively when the actor was moderately agreeable but reacted negatively when the actor was overly ingratiatory. Low self-monitors, on the other hand, just liked the actor more as he tried to be more agreeable [75]. Different evaluations of ingratiatory behavior emerged possibly because high self-monitors were not only more sensitive to the actor's behavior, but also to his incentives; and their evaluation changes under the actor's different incentive frames. Would the strategic use of emotions be similarly detected and interpreted by high self-monitors? People do not like to be manipulated, and high self-monitoring individuals know it when they are!

Ironically, however, the scenario could also play out in the opposite direction. High self-monitors are characterized by sensitivity to other behavior and adaptability of self-presentation. They might be so attuned to others' needs that they would fall easier preys to the strategist's manipulations than low self-monitors would. Therefore, we believe that these two competing hypotheses would be a worthy topic for future research on the relations between target self-monitoring and the effectiveness of emotional strategies. The same trait that enhances emotional strategies when possessed by the strategist may turn into its own nemesis when possessed by the target; conversely, it might also help the strategist in achieving his/her goals.

8.3 Cultural Influences on Negotiation

The growth of a global economy necessitated intercultural communication and exchange, much of which involves negotiation, be it the starting up of a joint venture, the purchase of a foreign player by a professional athletic club, or the arrangement for a musician to give a concert in another country. As negotiators repeatedly report miscommunication and misunderstandings on the bargaining table, it becomes increasingly important that we study cultural influences on negotiation [76-77]. Cultural psychologists have long promoted a "culture-inclusive" psychology that affords wonderful insights into the study of negotiation [79]. So far, most of negotiation research was done within Western cultures, which makes the generalizability of findings across cultures problematic as emotional processes and negotiation behaviors are not universal but rather predicated on specific cultural norms. Negotiation research can benefit greatly from cross-cultural perspectives.

Culture differences, such as those between vertical and horizontal cultures, are found in how people process social information [80]. Vertical cultures are characterized by social hierarchy and deference to status; horizontal cultures, on the other hand, are characterized by social equality and a low power distance. Negotiators from these two types of cultures are likely to interpret and use power differently. Power distance is expected to be highest in vertical collectivist cultures and lowest in horizontal individualist cultures. People from vertical, high power distance countries such as China, Japan, or Turkey are more likely to resort to their superiors rather than their own experiences and peers to resolve conflicts within their work groups; they are less likely to argue against or negotiate with their bosses; and they are more likely to use their position power when negotiating with those lower in the hierarchy [81]. A professor from an American business school who taught negotiation in a Chinese executive MBA program observed that managers in her class were hesitant to contend with their superiors from work who were in the same negotiation training program. As a result, they did not realize the level of individual gain achieved by managers who negotiated with their peers.

The influence of culture is also seen in the experience and expression of emotions. Hazel Markus and Shinobu Kitayama introduced the categorization of independent and interdependent cultures and drew comparisons between the two in the areas of self concept, socialization, and everyday emotional experience [82-84]. Through development of the self and socialization processes, culture determines the origin, content, and intensity of one's emotional experience. In independent cultures like the US, the ideal self is positively unique from others, independent and self-reliant, and associated with positive self feelings and high self-esteem. Feelings and expressions of happiness are central in social interactions [85]. In an interdependent culture like Japan, however, happiness relies more on "an awareness and assurance of connection and interdependence" (p. 129) than on a positive self-concept [84]. In terms of the intensity of emotions, Japanese respondents reported lower intensity levels of both positive and negative affect than American ones. An explanation for the difference might be found in the socialization process of the Japanese respondents, which typically does not pay as much attention to the registration and recall of self-feelings [86].

Culture also provides an important explanation for different patterns of emotional expression. Taking the individualism vs. collectivism conceptualization [80], we may assume that, compared to Americans (in an individualist, independent culture), Chinese negotiators (in a collectivist, interdependent culture) are more likely to remain calm and less likely to reveal the true emotions they feel during an negotiation so as to keep conflicts minimal and maintain good relations with their opponents. Given the independent/interdependent culture categorization, we may predict that negotiation behaviors are influenced by the already existing social relationships between negotiators, such that more competitiveness and aggressiveness are expected in independent relationships whereas more cooperation and compromises are expected in interdependent relationships. Further, we can speculate on how Chinese negotiate with Americans—how do they display their emotions, whether positive or negative, and how do they interpret the other's display? Are there inaccuracies or errors in understanding and interpreting one's opponent? If so, what are the consequences?

To answer all these questions and to be able to apply this knowledge in cross-cultural negotiations requires a general understanding of cultural psychology. Moreover, negotiators also need a capacity for cognitive processing and emotional control so that individuals can accurately perceive, interpret, and create meanings in specific cultural environments, especially when strategic behavior and emotion are concerned. In the current global environment, this will be an area of negotiation research that proves especially fruitful and rewarding.

8.4 Conclusions

In this chapter we have discussed several aspects of research on emotion and negotiation. The effects of mood and emotion on negotiator cognition and performance led us to ponder the strategic potential of emotional expression. Incorporating research on individual differences in emotional expression, we turned to the use of strategic emotions in negotiations. Individual factors, self-monitoring in particular, in both the strategist and the target, were considered, as well as the dynamics between negotiators that affect the effectiveness of strategic emotion. Finally, we discussed the issue of cultural influences in negotiation and briefly reviewed research on cultural differences in emotional experience and expression.

Negotiation is indeed a fascinating site where we can observe the intertwining of cognition, emotion, and culture in shaping social behaviors. Strategic emotion, in particular, is the tactical display of emotions that calls for the negotiator's cognitive evaluation and planning, emotional regulation and presentation, and cultural sensitivity. Even the individual traits we addressed have both cognitive and emotional elements in them. Empirical work on strategic emotion and the emotional strategist is needed to advance our knowledge of negotiation and strategy. We conclude this chapter with a look at one of our recent efforts in this direction.

In a study on how negotiators enact positive and negative emotional strategies, we found that strategic negative negotiators (i.e., those instructed to adopt a negative emotional strategy) not only increased their negative display during the negotiation, as instructed, but also significantly increased their positive display [87]. Eventually, these strategists outperformed their targets and their strategic positive counterparts (i.e., negotiators instructed to employ a positive emotional strategy). A plausible interpretation is that, in order to maximize the effect of strategic negative emotions, these strategists decided to also maintain a seemingly contradictory positive display, either in an effort to counteract the negative relational impact of negative emotions or to induce more cooperative behaviors by means of a contrast strategy of positive display. Past research on negotiation has touched on this "dual display" phenomenon. In a study of role-differentiation as a negotiation team tactic, Brodt and Tuchinsky reported that the bad-cop/good-cop routine was more successful than just the good-cop/good-cop or the bad-cop/bad-cop arrangement. In the latter case, pressuring by two "bad cops" actually backfired [88]. Hilty and Carnevale addressed a similar tactic—what they called the "black-hat/white-hat" strategy—in an earlier study and found that strategy shifts played an important role in negotiation, such that when a new strategy was presented, participants made more and bigger concessions [89].

Interestingly enough, two people were not necessary for executing this dual strategy. In fact, one person playing both the good and the bad cop, so long as the transformation is coherent and stable, is sufficient in producing the intended influence on the opponent [64, 89]. That participants in our study adopted this dual contrast strategy strongly suggests that strategic emotion is a highly complex behavior that is simultaneously cognitive and affective.

Existing research on the highly nuanced interpersonal effects of dual play strategy invites direct empirical exploration of whether the combination of negative and positive emotional strategies is more effective than either strategy alone in its influence on individual outcomes. If emotional strategies, especially dual strategies, are complex and subtle processes that require much evaluation, planning, and execution, individual traits like self-monitoring could have a vital part in this process, because it represents negotiators' capacity for such cognitive and behavioral tasks. It is possible that high self-monitoring negotiators can accurately judge how much positive versus negative emotional display is needed and how to maintain the balance between the two; they may also be superior than low self-monitors at administering the right "dose" of the needed emotions. If this explanation can be tested in future research, it will offer valuable information on the dynamics of strategic emotion in negotiation and communication in general.

8.5 References

[1]   K. R. Scherer, Introduction: Cognitive components of emotion. In R. J. Davidson (Ed), *Handbook of affective sciences* (pp. 563-571). Cary, NC: Oxford University Press, 2003.
[2]   R. S. Lazarus, On the primacy of cognition. *American Psychologist,* (1984), *39*, 124-129.
[3]   R. B. Zajonc, Thinking and feeling: Preferences need no inferences. *American Psychologist,* (1980), *35*, 151-175.
[4]   R. B. Zajonc, Feeling and thinking: Closing the debate over the independence of affect. In J. P. Forgas (Ed), *Feeling and thinking: The role of affect in social cognition* (pp. 31-58). New York: Cambridge University Press, 2000.
[5]   For a review, see G. Loewenstein and J. S. Lerner, The role of affect in decision making. In R. J. Davidson (Ed), *Handbook of affective sciences* (pp. 619-642). Cary, NC: Oxford University Press, 2003.
[6]   M. A. Neale and M. H. Bazerman, Negotiator cognition and rationality: A behavioral decision theory perspective. *Organizational Behavior and Human Decision Processes,* (1992), *51*, 157-175.
[7]   M. H. Bazerman and J. S. Caroll, Negotiator cognition. In L. L. Cummings and B. Staw (Eds.), *Research in Organizational Behavior,* (1987), *9*, 247-288.
[8]   L. L. Thompson and R. Hastie, Social perception in negotiation. *Organizational Behavior and Human Decision Processes,* (1990), *47*, 98-123.
[9]   B. Barry, The tactical use of emotion in negotiation. *Research on Negotiation in Organizations,* (1999), *7*, 93-121.
[10] B., Barry and R. L. Oliver, Affect in dyadic negotiation: A model and propositions. *Organizational Behavior and Human Decision Processes,* (1996), *67*, 127-143.
[11] J. P. Forgas, On feeling good and getting your way: Mood effects on negotiator cognition and bargaining strategies. *Journal of Personality and Social Psychology,* (1998), *74*, 565-577.
[12] R. M. Kramer, E. Newton and P. L. Pommerenke, Self-enhancement biases and negotiator judgment: Effects of self-esteem and mood. *Organizational Behavior and Human Decision Processes,* (1993), *56*, 110-133.
[13] J. A. Russell and L. F. Barrett, Core affect, prototypical emotional episodes, and other things called emotion: Dissecting the elephant. *Journal of Personality and Social Psychology,* (1999), *76*, 805-819.
[14] K. Oatley and J. M. Jenkins, *Understanding emotions.* Cambridge, MA: Blackwell, 1996.
[15] N. H. Frijda, Moods, emotion episodes, and emotions. In M. Lewis & J. M. Haviland (Eds.), *Handbook of emotions* (pp. 381-403). New York: Guilford Press, 1993.

[16] G. A. Van Kleef, C. K. W. De Dreu and A. S. R. Manstead, The interpersonal effects of anger and happiness in negotiations. *Journal of Personality & Social Psychology,* (2004), *86*, 57-76.

[17] R. J. Davidson, On emotion, mood, and related affective constructs. In P. Ekman & R. J. Davidson (Eds.), *The nature of emotion: Fundamental questions* (pp. 51-55). New York: Oxford University Press, 1994.

[18] R. A. Baron, Environmentally induced positive affect: Its impact on self-efficacy, task performance, negotiation, and conflict. *Journal of Applied Social Psychology,* (1990), *20*, 368-384.

[19] P. J. Carnevale and A. M. Isen, The influence of positive affect and visual access on the discovery of integrative solutions in bilateral negotiation. *Organizational Behavior and Human Decision Processes,* (1986), *37*, 1-13.

[20] A. M. Isen, K. A. Daubman and G. P. Nowicki, Positive affect facilitates creative problem solving. *Journal of Personality and Social Psychology,* (1987), *52*, 1122-1131.

[21] A. M. Isen and P. F. Levin, Effect of feeling good on helping: Cookies and kindness. *Journal of Personality & Social Psychology,* (1972), *21*, 384-388.

[22] J. P. Forgas, Introduction: Affect and social cognition. In J. P. Forgas (Ed.), *Handbook of affect and social cognition* (pp. 1-24). Mahwah, NJ: Lawrence Erlbaum Associates. 2000.

[23] A. M. Isen, Positive affect, cognitive processes, and social behavior. In L. Berkowitz (Ed.), *Advances in experimental social psychology* (Vol. 20, pp. 203-253). San Diego, CA: Academic Press, 1987.

[24] G. Hertel, & K. Fiedler, Affective and cognitive influences in a social dilemma game. *European Journal of Social Psychology,* (1994), *24*, 131–146.

[25] J. P. Forgas, Mood and judgment: The Affect Infusion Model (AIM). *Psychological Bulletin,* (1995), *117*, 39-66.

[26] R. A. Baron, S. P. Fortin, R. L. Frei, L. A. Hauver, and M. L. Shack, Reducing organizational conflict: The role of socially-induced positive affect. *International Journal of Conflict Management,* (1990), *1*, 133–152.

[27] M. Deutsch, *The resolution of conflict: Constructive and destructive processes.* New Haven, CT: Yale University Press. 1973.

[28] G. Hertel, J. Neuhof, T. Theuer, and N. L. Kerr, Mood effects on cooperation in small groups: Does positive mood simply lead to more cooperation? *Cognition & Emotion,* (2000), *14*, 441-472.

[29] K. G. Allred, J. S. Mallozzi, F. Matsui and C. P. Raia, The influence of anger and compassion on negotiation performance. *Organizational Behavior and Human Decision Processes,* (1997), *70*, 175-187.

[30] W. Ury, J. M. Brett and S. B. Goldberg, *Getting disputes resolved.* San Francisco: Jossey-Bass, 1988.

[31] See R. S. Adler, B. Rosen, and E. M. Silverstein, Emotions in negotiation: How to manage fear and anger. *Negotiation Journal,* (1998), *14*, 161-179.

[32] M. N. Davidson and L. Greenhalgh, The role of emotion in negotiation: The impact of anger and race. In R. J. Lewicki, R. J. Bies, & B. H. Sheppard (Eds.), *Research on negotiation in organizations* (Vol. 7). Greenwich, CT: JAI Press, 1999.

[33] S. Kopelman, A. S. Rosette and L. L. Thompson, The three faces of Eve: An examination of strategic positive, negative, and neutral emotion in negotiations, *Organizational Behavior and Human Decision Processes* (2006), 99, 81–101

[34] M. W. Morris and D. Keltner, How emotions work: The social functions of emotional expression in negotiations. In B. M. Staw (Ed.), *Research in Organizational Behavior, 22,* 1-50, 2000.

[35] D. Keltner and A. M. Kring, Emotion, social function, and psychopathology. *Review of General Psychology,* (1998), *2*, 320-342.

[36] L. Thompson, V. H. Medvec, V. Seiden and S. Kopelman, Poker face, smiley face, and rant'n'rave: Myths and realities about emotion in negotiation. In M. A. Hogg, & R. S. Tindale (Eds.), *Blackwell handbook of social psychology: Group processes* (pp. 139-163). Malden, MA: Blackwell Publishers, 2001.

[37] M. M. Pillutla and J. K. Murnighan, Unfairness, anger, and spite: Emotional rejections of ultimatum offers. *Organizational Behavior and Human Decision Processes,* (1996), *68*, 208-224.

[38] For example, K. G. Allred, Anger and retaliation: Toward an understanding of impassioned conflict in organizations. In R. J. Bies & R. J. Lewicki (Eds.), *Research on negotiation in organizations* (Vol. 7, pp. 27-58). Stamford, CT: JAI Press, 1999.

[39] C. Anderson and L. L. Thompson, Affect from the top down: How powerful individuals' positive affect shapes negotiations. *Organizational Behavior and Human Decision Processes,* (2004), *95*, 125-139.

[40] A. N. Butt, J. N. Choi and A. M. Jaeger, The effects of self-emotion, counterpart emotion, and counterpart behavior on negotiator behavior: a comparison of individual-level and dyad-level dynamics. *Journal of Organizational Behavior,* (2005), *26*, 681-704.

[41]   L. Z. Tiedens, Anger and advancement versus sadness and subjugation: The effect of negative emotion expressions on social status conferral. *Journal of Personality & Social Psychology, (*2001), *80*, 86-94.

[42]   M. S. Clark, Reactions to and strategic self-presentation of happiness, sadness, and anger. Paper presented at an invited symposium at the meeting of the American Psychological Society, Chicago, IL, 1993.

[43]   U., Dimberg and A. Ohman, Behold the wrath: Psychophysiological responses to facial stimuli. *Motivation and Emotion,* (1996), *20*, 149-182.

[44]   J. R. Averill, Emotions unbecoming and becoming. In P. Ekman & R. J. Davidson (Eds), *The nature of emotion: Fundamental questions* (pp. 265-269). New York: Oxford University Press, 1994.

[45]   R. W. Levenson, Emotional control: Variation and consequences. In P. Ekman & R. J. Davidson (Eds.), *The nature of emotion: Fundamental questions* (pp. 273-279). New York: Oxford University Press. 1994.

[46]   J. J. Gross, Emotion regulation: Past, present, future. *Cognition and Emotion,* (1999), *13*, 551-573.

[47]   R. I. Sutton, Maintaining norms about expressed emotions: The case of bill collectors. *Administrative Science Quarterly,* (1991), *36*, 245-248.

[48]   A. R. Hochschild, *The managed heart: The commercialization of human feeling.* Berkeley: University of California Press, 1983.

[49]   D. Watson and L. A. Clark, Negative affectivity: The disposition to experience aversive emotional states. *Psychological Bulletin,* (1984), *96*, 465-490.

[50]   J. M. George and A. P. Brief, Feeling good-doing good: A conceptual analysis of the mood at work-organizational spontaneity relationship. *Psychological Bulletin,* (1992), *112*, 310-329.

[51]   J. N. Haney, Approach avoidance reactions by repressors and sensitizers to ambiguity in a structured free association task. *Psychological Reports,* (1973), *33*, 97-98.

[52]   J. J.,Gross and O. P. John, Revealing feelings: Facets of emotional expressivity in self-reports, peer ratings, and behavior. *Journal of Personality and Social Psychology,* (1997), *72*, 435-448.

[53]   A. M. Kring, D. A. Smith and J. M. Neale, Individual differences in dispositional expressiveness: Development and validation of the Emotional Expressivity Scale. *Journal of Personality and Social Psychology,* (1994), *66*, 934-949.

[54]   P. N. Lopes, M. A. Brackett, J. B. Nezlek, A. Schütz, I. Sellin and P. Salovey, Emotional intelligence and social interactions. *Personality and Social Psychology Bulletin,* (2004), *30*, 1018-1034.

[55]   J. D. Mayer and P. Salovey, What is emotional intelligence? In P. Salovey & D. Sluyter (Eds.), *Emotional development and emotional intelligence: Implications for educators* (pp. 3-31). New York: Basic Books, 1997.

[56]   M. A. Brackett, P. N. Lopes, Z. Ivcevic, J. D. Mayer and P. Salovey, Integrating emotion and cognition: The role of emotional intelligence. In D. Y. Dai and R. J. Sternberg (Eds.), *Motivation, emotion, and cognition: Integrative perspectives on intellectual development and functioning* (pp. 175-194). Mahwah, NJ: Lawrence Erlbaum, 2004.

[57]   R. Salovey, C. K. Hsee and J. D. Mayer, Emotional intelligence and the self regulation of affect. In D. M. Wegner & J. W. Pennebaker (Eds.), *Handbook of mental control* (pp. 258-277). Englewood Cliffs, NJ: Prentice Hall, 1994.

[58]   M. Snyder, Self-monitoring processes. In L. Berkowitz (Ed.), *Advances in experimental social psychology* (Vol. 12). New York: Academic Press, 1979.

[59]   M. Snyder and T. C. Monson, Persons, situations, and the control of social behavior. *Journal of Personality and Social Psychology,* (1975), *32*, 637-644.

[60]   M. Snyder and W. B. Swann, Jr. When actions reflect attitudes: The politics of impression management. *Journal of Personality and Social Psychology,* (1976), *34*, 1034-1042.

[61]   M. Snyder and E. D. Tanke, Behavior and attitude: Some people are more consistent than others. *Journal of Personality,* (1976), *44*, 501-517.

[62]   W. G. Graziano and W. H. M. Bryant, Self-monitoring and the self-attribution of positive emotions. *Journal of Personality and Social Psychology,* (1998), *74*, 250-261.

[63]   H. S. Friedman and T. Miller-Herringer, Nonverbal display of emotion in public and in private: Self-monitoring, personality, and expressive cues. *Journal of Personality and Social Psychology, 61*, 766-775, 1991.

[64]   A., Rafaeli and R. I. Sutton, Emotional contrast strategies as means of social influence: Lessons from criminal interrogators and bill collectors. *Academy of Management Journal,* (1991), *34*, 749-775.

[65]   R. Kumar, The role of affect in negotiations: An integrative overview. *Journal of Applied Behavioral Science,* (1997), *33*, 84-100.

[66]   D. J. Schneider, Tactical self-presentations: Toward a broader conception. In J. T. Tedeschi (Ed.), *Impression management theory and social psychological research* (pp. 23-40). New York: Academic Press, 1981.

[67] E. Goffman, *The presentation of self in everyday life*. Woodstock, NY: Overlook Press, 1959.
[68] W. L. Gardner and M. J. Martinko, Impression management in organizations. *Journal of Management,* (1988), *14*, 321-338.
[69] M. E. Roloff and D. E. Campion, On alleviating the debilitating effects of accountability on bargaining: Authority and self-monitoring. *Communication Monographs,* (1987), *54*, 145-164.
[70] J. M. Jordan and M. E. Roloff, Planning skills and negotiator goal accomplishment: The relationship between self-monitoring and plan generation, plan enactment, and plan consequences. *Communication Research,* (1997), *24*, 31-63.
[71] E. Berscheid, W. Graziano, T. Monson, and M. Dermer, Outcome dependency: Attention, attribution, and attraction. *Journal of Personality and Social Psychology,* (1976), *34*, 978-989.
[72] R. S. Geizer, D. L. Rarick and G. F. Soldow, Deception and judgment accuracy: A study in person perception. *Personality and Social Psychology Bulletin,* (1977), *3*, 446-449.
[73] R. D. Lennox and R. N. Wolfe, Revision of the self-monitoring scale. *Journal of Personality and Social Psychology,* (1984), *46*, 1349-1364.
[74] M. Snyder, & N. Cantor, Thinking about ourselves and others: Self-monitoring and social knowledge. *Journal of Personality and Social Psychology,* (1980), *39*, 222-234.
[75] E. E. Jones and R. Baumeister, The self-monitor looks at the ingratiator. *Journal of Personality,* (1976), *44*, 654-674.
[76] R. Cohen, *Negotiating across cultures*. Washington, DC: United States Institute of Peace, 1991.
[77] E. Glenn, *Man and mankind: Conflicts and communication between cultures*. Norwood, NJ: Ablex, 1981.
[78] H. C Triandis, *Culture and social behavior*. New York: McGraw-Hill, 1994.
[79] M. Cole, *Cultural psychology: A once and future discipline*. Cambridge, MA: Harvard University Press, 1996.
[80] H. C. Triandis, (1995). *Individualism & collectivism*. Boulder, CO: Westview Press.
[81] See G. Hofstede, *Culture's consequences: International differences in work-related values*. Beverly Hills, CA: Sage, 1980.
[82] H. R. Markus and S. Kitayama, Culture and the self: Implications for cognition, emotion, and motivation. *Psychological Bulletin,* (1991), *98*, 221-253.
[83] H. R. Markus and S. Kitayama, The cultural construction of self and emotion: Implications for social behavior. In S. Kitayama & H. R. Markus (Eds.), *Emotion and culture: Empirical studies of mutual influence* (pp. 89-130). Washington, DC: American Psychological Association, 1994.
[84] H. R. Markus and S. Kitayama, The cultural construction of self and emotion: Implications for social behavior. In W. G. Parrott (Ed.), *Emotions in social psychology: Essential readings*. Philadelphia, PA: Psychology Press, 2001.
[85] A. Wierzbicka, Emotion, language, and cultural scripts. In S. Kitayama & H. F. Markus (Eds.), *Emotion and culture: Empirical studies of mutual influence* (pp. 133-196). Washington, DC: American Psychological Association, 1994.
[86] H. Akiyama, Measurement of depressive symptoms in cross-cultural research. Paper presented at the International Conference on Emotion and Culture, University of Oregon, Eugene, 1992.
[87] S. Li, & M. E. Roloff, Strategic negative emotion in negotiation. Paper presented at the International Association for Conflict Management Conference in Pittsburgh, PA, 2004.
[88] S. E., Brodt and M. Tuchinsky, Working together but in opposition: An examination of the "good-cop/bad-cop" negotiating team tactic. *Organizational Behavior and Human Decision Processes,* (2000), *81*, 155-177.
[89] J., Hilty, and P. Carnevale, "Black-hat/White-hat" strategy in bilateral negotiation. *Organizational Behavior and Human Decision Processes,* (1993), *55*, 444-469.

From Communication to Presence
G. Riva et al. (Eds.)
IOS Press, 2006

9 Personality and Self-Esteem in Social Interaction

Gudberg K. JONSSON

Abstract. There is a long-standing interest in hidden temporal patterns in behavior. The current chapter discusses the idea that face-to-face interaction can be construed as having a definite organization or structure, just as language is understood in terms of its grammar. The participant has, within that organization, options he can exercise, including the option of violating aspects of the organization. Numerous studies, using the T-pattern detection algorithm, have demonstrated that the organization of behavior is influenced by situation, personality and culture. Strong relationships have been found between the structure of verbal and non-verbal communication and cognition and social adaptation. Little research exists though on the relation between real-time behavior organization and self-esteem and personality. An earlier study suggests a strong relationship between level of subject's self-esteem and number of real-time behavioral patterns produced in dyadic interaction situations. Significant differences have also been found in real-time behavioral patterns produced in dyadic interactions between subjects who considered themselves to be friends versus those who were strangers. It is unknown whether such behavioral analysis would reveal a difference in real-time patterns produced by persons with different scores on the Eysenck Personality Questionnaire. These ideas have been tested by analyzing twenty-four dyadic interactions between male students. A special software, THEME, was used to detect real-time patterns in real-time behavior records. Results indicate that these interactions are highly synchronized and structured. Strong correlation was found between subjects' self-esteem and complexity and frequency of behavioral patterns detected. Positive correlation was also found between subject's personality and complexity and frequency of patterns. Certain pattern types were found exclusively to be produced by extraverts and other by introverts. High and low self-esteem subjects' were also found to produce different types of behavioral patterns.

Contents

9.1. Introduction

9.1.1 Behavior and Patterns

Our universe is full of patterns. Every night the stars move in circles across the sky and the season's cycle at yearly intervals. Our hearts and lungs follow rhythmical cycles whose timing is adapted to our body's needs. Many of nature's patterns are like the heartbeat: they take care of themselves, running "in the background." Once we have learned how to identify the patterns, exceptions start to stand out. Using mathematics to organize and systematize our ideas about patterns, we have already discovered that nature's patterns are not just there to be admired; they are vital clues to the rules that govern natural processes [1].

Considering the everyday world of face-to-face encounters, the commonplace activities in these encounters - greeting, discussing, joking, bargaining, directing, and the like - make up the fabric of an individual's social world. Individuals of all societies move through life in terms of a continuous series of social interaction. It is in the context of such social encounters that the individual expresses the significant elements of his culture, whether they are matters of economics, social status, personal values, self-image, or religious belief.

It can be argued that goal of psychology is to discover the scientific viable constructs or categories that will characterize what is variant and invariant in the working of the human mind. Psychologists, like all scientists, model variance. By observing people's thoughts, feelings, or behavior in some sort of controlled or measured environment, psychologists turn those observations into numbers by some recording method, and then examine the numbers to provide a description of what was occurring in the minds of the people who were studied [2].

Much has been written for professional and popular audiences about interpersonal interaction and about specific actions that occur in these encounters. These have included both insightful commentaries based upon general observation and investigations of single behaviors [3]. But what is communication? There are numerous definitions and the differences between them clearly demonstrate the difficulty of describing the communication structure. A theory able to address all the features of the communication process is still lacking. The earliest communication frameworks were based on the process of signal transmission in telecommunication systems. Shannon and Weaver's model, still the best known and most widely used, fails to take account either of the specifically linguistic features of verbal language or of the sense-making of the communicative processes [4]. Given the difficulties of these models, some theorists have taken another approach by differentiating between standard communication and miscommunication. According to Anolli [5], miscommunication does not only include its standard meaning such as a lacking, defect and violation of communication rules, but also mismatching interpretation as well as misrepresentation of information. And studying miscommunication, as a part of the communication process, should not only consider the negative aspects but also the positive ones.

There is a long-standing interest in hidden or non-obvious temporal patterns in behavior in various areas of behavioral research [6-8] and it is now a common believe that human interaction is much more regular than has yet been reported. In the opening words of his book *Ethology: The biology of behavior*, Eibl-Eibesfeldt [9] argues that behavior is composed of patterns in time and that investigation of behavior deal with sequences that are, unlike bodily characteristics, not always visible. An integrated study of the structure of verbal and nonverbal behavior has also been repeatedly proposed [e.g. 10, 11]. But regardless of this believe and growing interest in studying the organization or structure of behavior it might come as a surprise to many that only about 8% of all psychological research is based on any kind of observation. Only a fraction of that research is programmatic research, and a fraction of that sequential in its thinking [12].

Numerous studies, using the T-pattern detection algorithm [6-8], have demonstrated that the organization or structure of behavior, both verbal and non-verbal, is influenced by variables such as situation, personality and culture. And a strong relationship has been found between the structure of verbal and non-verbal communication and cognition and social adaptation [e.g. 13-29].

Little research exists on the relation between real-time behavior organization and self-esteem and personality. An earlier study suggests a strong relationship between level of subject's self-esteem and number of real-time behavioral patterns produced in dyadic interaction situations [17, 18]. Jonsson also reported finding significant differences in real-time behavioral patterns produced in dyadic interactions between subjects who considered themselves to be friends versus those who were strangers, the level of patterning being much higher between friends. It is unknown whether such behavioral analysis would reveal a difference in real-time patterns produced by persons with different scores on the Eysenck Personality Questionnaire.

9.1.2 The Person Situation Debate

The fundamental issues of the variant vs. invariant in personality have recurred in different forms and under various labels for the past several decades. The most common of which is the "*person situation debate*" [30]. This translates into a concern over whether the behavior of a person is consistent (invariant) enough across time and situations to be usefully attributed to individual characteristics [29]. The other possibility is that behavior is so inconsistent (variable) that only the situation matters.

The person-situation debate has generated no shortage of arguments, but directly relevant data remain scarce. To yield relevant data, the behavior of a sample of subjects must be directly measured in more than one situation, so that their consistency can be assessed. Direct behavioral measurement is difficult and expensive and for that reason has been rare in personality research [31]. Repeated behavioral measurement has been even rarer. And apart from those reported in this chapter no research seems to exist on the temporal structure of behavior and how it transforms between situations. The recent literature includes signs that this may be starting to change [e.g. 32, 33], which is good, because when behavior is directly measured on more than one occasion, illuminating analyses become possible.

Funder and Colvin [34] observed hundred and forty undergraduate subjects in two experimental situations. In the first, two undergraduates of the opposite sex who had never met before were shown into a small room containing little except a couch and a video camera. They where told that they could "talk about whatever you like," and that someone would be back in a few minutes. The second situation occurred a few weeks later, and was exactly like the first, except that each subject was paired with a different opposite-sex partner, both of whom were there for the second time. Even though results demonstrated that the situation amounted to a kind of getting-acquainted conversation, within that limit there were great variations across individuals. At the first session trained independent raters, using the Riverside Behavioral Q-sort [35] rated the subject's behavior as relatively awkward, tense, disinterested, distant, insecure, and fearful. In the second session, behavior was observed to have become more relaxed, socially skilled, interesting, expressive, fluent, and all-around enjoyable. It should not be hard to explain these results. In the second session subjects are at much more ease, already familiar with the situation, the environment had transformed itself from one that was strange/unpredictable to on that felt more comfortable. Overall, 20 of the 62 behavioral items observed changed between the two sessions, all of which are consistent with the interpretation [29]. The evidence offered here demonstrates how seemingly small changes in situation can have major psychological importance.

These results might imply that the influence of personality on behavior is low. However, the influence of personality is reflected in individual differences in behavior and thus requires a separate analysis. Calculating correlations between individuals' behavior at *Time 1* and *Time 2*, Funder [29] reported consistencies were numerous. Subjects were consistent in the relative degree to which they spoke loudly, acted timidly, laughed, smiled, and were expressive, awkward and enthusiastic. So these seemingly similar situations turned out to be psychologically very different. People felt differently between them and changed their behavior accordingly. Funder's results also suggest that the more similar a person rated the two situations, the more consistently the subject behaved across them. This suggests that the "same" two situations can differ in how similar they seem to different participants.

It can be argued that situations are under-studied but the matter is even worse when it come to behaviors. Only a few attempts have begun to address the question of how to think about differences between different kinds of behavior. Skinner [36] and McClelland [37] argued that is was important to differentiate between "operant" and "respondent" behaviors. Operant behaviors should be more consistent across situations than are their respondent behaviors. This was confirmed by Furr and Funder [38] gathering ratings of behaviors as to the degree to which they were "automatic", e.g. laughing, as opposed to "controlled", e.g. offering advice. Over all the behaviors assessed, ratings of the degree to which a behavior was automatic as opposed to controlled correlated with cross-situational consistency with an $r = .50$.

9.1.3 Self-Esteem

Looking at the research history on self-concepts, it seems there is no topic that has been more studied than self-esteem. Most probably this is the case because low self-esteem is a vulnerability that has been linked to susceptibility to mental illness, relationship dissatisfaction, and even physical illness [e.g. 39-41].

There is no shortage of ways to define self-esteem. Perhaps the simplest one is found in the New Webster's Dictionary [42], which says that self-esteem is "satisfaction with oneself." In psychology, self-esteem or self-worth includes a person's subjective appraisal of himself or herself as intrinsically positive or negative to some degree [43]. Generally, self-esteem is described as a personal evaluation that an individual makes of her or himself, their sense of their own worth, value, importance, or capabilities [44, 45]. Though the descriptions of different levels of self-esteem might sound a little general most would probably agree on that self-esteem could be regarded as a filter mechanism. As such, it plays a significant part in how we generally perceive the world and hence how we behave.

It can be assumed that self-esteem could be construed as a permanent characteristic (trait self-esteem) or as a temporary psychological condition (state self-esteem). Traits are often conceptualized as dispositional forces that create consistency in individuals' experiences and actions; as such they carry the past into the present and across the diverse circumstances. According to Robinson and Cervone [46] this perspective has two limitations. First, the predictive value of global trait constructs can sometimes be surprisingly low. Second, the explanatory value of the trait construct is potentially limited.

There are at least two types of consistency are to the trait construct: consistency across situations and over time [46]. Efforts to explain cross-situational consistency have been to some extent successful. We would for example expect people to be more consistent across situations to the extent that they appraise or categorize diverse situations in a similar manner [47].

People's self-evaluation, whether explicit or implicit, are presumably formed through interaction with significant others. According to theories in the tradition of symbolic interactionism, people develop a sense of self on the basis of how other people treat them, and according to the sociometer theory of self-esteem, people's self-esteem is formed through their interactions with others [48]. Individuals with low self-esteem have been reported to have repeatedly experienced perceived interpersonal rejection. Conversely, people with high self-esteem have experienced many subjectively successful or non-rejecting interpersonal relationships [48].

Self-esteem has been studied in relation to many different variables, e.g. violence, drug abuse, bullying, relationships and academic achievement. From the late 1960s to the early 1990s it was assumed that a student's self-esteem was a critical factor in the grades that they earn in school, in their relationships with their peers, and in their later success in life. That being the case, many American groups created programs to increase the self-esteem of students, assuming that grades would increase, conflicts would decrease, and that this would lead to a happier and more successful life [49]. Recent studies indicate that inflating students' self-esteem in and of itself has no positive effect on any objective aspect of their lives. One study has shown that inflating self-esteem by itself can actually decrease grades [50]. Global self-esteem has also be positively correlated with extraversion and negatively with neuroticism [51] and therefore has particular relevance to experiences of subjective well-being.

9.1.4 Personality

It is evident that there are individual differences in social behavior. People have traditionally been distinguished in terms of such personality traits as extroversion or dominance. According to the Columbia Encyclopedia [52] personality refers to the patterns of behavior, thought, and emotion unique to an individual, and the ways they interact to help or hinder the adjustment of a person to other people and situations.

Numerous theories have attempted to explain human personality. In recent years, trait theories have arisen with the object of determining aspects of personality that compel an individual to respond in a certain way to a given situation. Objections to trait theories point out that behavior is largely situation dependent, and that such traits as "honesty" are not especially helpful in characterizing personality and behavior. Despite such objections, trait theories have been popular models for quantifying personality [52]. Eysenck [53] has proposed three fundamental dimensions of personality: extroversion-introversion, neuroticism, and psychoticism. Extroversion-introversion includes the trait of sociability, which can also be related to emotion (e.g., interest, as expressed toward people, versus shyness). Neuroticism includes emotionality defined, as in temperament theory, as nonspecific negative emotional responsiveness.

According to Eysenck's Personality Inventory test, an introvert is associated with controlled behaviors, seriousness, pessimistic and reliability. He does not act on impulse nor does he like excitement. An extrovert, on the other hand, is associated with sociable tendencies, optimistic, aggressiveness and impulsive behaviors. He does not keep his feelings under control nor does he like to do things by himself [54, p.180]. Extroverts appear to be more open to change their judgments under the influence of prestige suggestions. However, when an introvert encounters an extrovert with different views on a controversial issue, the introvert is more likely to be persuaded to modify his position [54, p.205].

Studies on differences in communication style between extraverts and introverts, suggest that people who are extraverts speak more rapidly, using higher pitch, and give more feedback than introverts [55, 56]. Introverts have also been found to be more likely to take the role of the "interviewer" in dyadic situations [56]. According to Argyle [57] several studies have confirmed that extraverts gaze more frequently, with longer glances, especially while talking, than introverts.

9.1.5 Objectives and hypotheses

The object of the current pilot research is to search for a particular type of repeated behavior patterns, both intra- and inter- individual, and relate the patterns to self-esteem and personality types. The search was based on a method developed by Magnusson [e.g. 6-8] to detect real-time behavior patterns using a system of computer software, called THEME. The research combines two different approaches "structural" and "external" [3]. While the structural approach attempts to discover the sequential structure of social systems, the external variable approach is concerned with individual and group differences in behavior as a function of external variables, here self-esteem and personality.

9.2 Method

9.2.1 Participants

Twenty-four pairs of male students at the University of Iceland, aged 20-26 (mean 22,5 years), participated in the study.

9.2.2 Procedure

The students were informed that they would participate in a filmed interview about the major qualities and faults of the Icelandic Educational System. They were given 10 min to prepare for the interview. The 10 min long preparation time was recorded with a video camera.

9.2.3 Measures

The Rosenberg [44] Self-Esteem Scale (RSE) and the Eysenck Personality Questionnaire [52] were demonstrated to all subjects prior to the video-recorded sessions. A self-esteem score between 10-20 indicates low self-esteem, 21-30 indicates moderate self-esteem, and a score between 31-40 indicates high self-esteem. EPQ scores on the extraversion dimension can range from 0-12 where high scores indicate extraversion and low scores introversion.

ThemeCoder, a multi-media module of the THEME computer software, was used to code behavior events frame by frame, using digitized video recordings. Following the coding, THEME was used to detect and analyze behavior patterns.

Verbal behavior was coded according to a system designed by Bromberg and Landré [58] (see Appendix A), and non-verbal behavior was coded using McGrew's category system [59], further developed by Jonsson [18], studying the relation between self-esteem, friendship and the temporal structure of verbal and non-verbal interaction (see Appendix B).

9.2.4 Inter-observer reliability

Estimates of inter-observer reliability were calculated using the formula (McGrew 1972, p. 24):

$$\frac{No. \ of \ agreements \ (A + B)}{No. \ Of \ agreements \ (A + B) + No. \ seen \ by \ B \ only + No. \ seen \ by \ A \ only}$$

Standards for inter-observer reliability are not uniform, but agreement below .70 was regarded as unacceptable. Two observers were randomly assigned one minute clips from each dyad. The inter-observer reliability scores was 0.74 for all classes of behavior, but over .85 for "looking behavior" and "verbal behavior".

9.2.5 Independent observers

Two independent observers were asked to estimate the level of subject's self-esteem and personality dimensions of extraversion, using a 5 point Likert Scale, by watching selected video recordings. The scores were compared to the actual scores of participants and their level of patterning in the interaction process.

9.2.6 Temporal Pattern Analysis

Underlying the THEME method [e.g. 6-8] is a structural model that is concerned with the temporal organization of verbal- and non-verbal behavior. THEME detects regular, hierarchical real-time behavior patterns, where large patterns are composed of smaller ones, somewhat like phrases in language are made out of words that again are patterns of phonemes, etc.

A Temporal pattern (T-Pattern) is essentially a combination of events where the events occur in the same order with the consecutive time distances between consecutive pattern components remaining relatively invariant with respect to an expectation assuming, as a null hypothesis, that each component is independently and randomly distributed over time. As stated by Magnusson 'that is, if A is an earlier and B a later component of the same recurring T-pattern then after an occurrence of A at *t*, there is an interval [*t*+d1, *t*+d2](d2≥d1≥d0) that tends to contain at least one occurrence of B more often than would be expected by chance'. The temporal relationship between A and B is defined as a critical interval and this concept lies at the centre of the pattern detection algorithms.

Through use of the Theme 5.0 software package, pattern detection algorithms can analyze both ordinal and temporal data however, for the algorithms to generate the most meaningful analyses the raw data must be time coded i.e. an event must be coded according to time of occurrence as well as event type. The method of time-motion computerized video analysis therefore lends itself to the use of T-Pattern detection and through use of the Bloomfield Movement Classification detailed and highly complex patterns that are specific to the performance of competition can be identified.

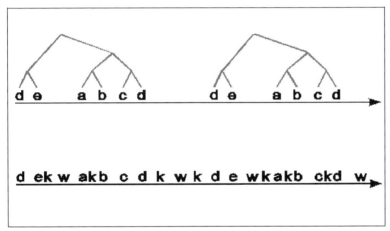

Figure 1. The lower part of this figure shows a simple real-time behavior record containing a few occurrences of several event types, a, b, c, d, & e, indicating their respective instances within the observation period. The upper line is identical to the lower one, except that occurrences of k and w have been removed. A simple t-pattern (abcd) then appears, wich was difficult to see when the other events were present.

9.3 Results

The proportion of different behavior patterns subjects participated in, relative to all patterns, correlated positively with self-esteem (r = .66; p < .05). The proportion of pattern occurrences subjects participated in, relative to all patterns, also correlated positively with self-esteem (r = .67; p < .05) (see Figure 2).

This indicates that behavior emitted by subjects with high self-esteem was more patterned than the behavior of those with moderate self-esteem (none of the participants scored low on the self-esteem scale).

The type, frequency and duration of behavioral events emitted differed between the high and moderate self-esteem subjects. High self-esteem subjects emitted more verbal events and feedback and hesitated less during their speech. They looked more frequently at their partner, with longer glances, and talked for a greater percentage of the time than subjects with moderate self-esteem.

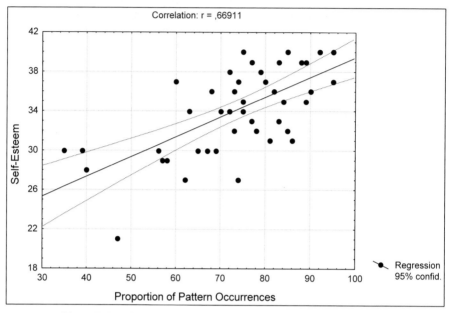

Figure 2. Correlation between Self-Esteem and Proportion of Pattern Occurrences

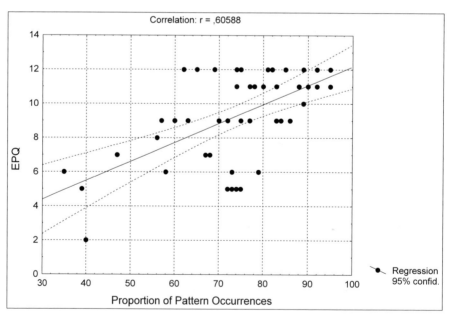

Figure 3. Correlation between EPQ scores and Proportion of Pattern Occurrences

No difference was detected in number of different types of behavior emitted by high and moderate self-esteem subjects, but the frequency of events emitted was higher for high self-esteem subjects.

Scores on the EPQ were positively correlated with proportion of pattern occurrences that each individual participated in (r = .60; p < .05) (see Figure 3). These findings indicate that individuals who scored high on EPQ (extraverts) participated more frequently in detected patterns than those who scored low on the EPQ (introverts). Introverts on the other hand seemed to participate in a larger variety of pattern types.

Extraverts produced longer patterns and more patterns including gesticulation than introverts, even though extraverts did not gesture more in general. Introverts, on the other hand, produced more patterns including adaptations (adjusting cloths, hair, etc.) and certain types of verbal patterns (ask & answer) than extraverts.

Introverts, on average, looked less at their partner than extraverts and with shorter glances, and also talked for a lesser percentage of the time. Extraverts hesitated less and provided more verbal feedback. Overall there was no difference detected in number of different types of behavior emitted by intro- and extraverts, but the frequency of events emitted was higher for extraverts.

Introverts with high self-esteem (EPQ scores ≤ 6, RSE scores 31-40) participated in a higher proportion of detected patterns than introverts with moderate self-esteem (EPQ scores ≤ 6, RSE scores 21-30) (t = -9.8; df = 9; p < .001) (see Figure 4).

Extraverts with high self-esteem (EPQ scores ≥ 7, RSE scores 31-40) participated in a higher proportion of detected patterns than extraverts with moderate self-esteem (EPQ scores ≥ 7, RSE scores 21-30) (t = -4.9; df = 35; p < .001) (see Figure 5.).

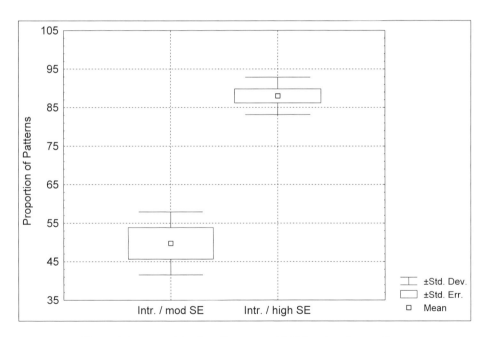

Figure 4. Pattern participation of introverts with high and moderate self-esteem

On average 418 (min=46, max=1139, S.d.=309) different pattern types were detected in the 24 dyads (mean occurrence=2208, min=262, max=5356, S.d.=1535). The maximum length of patterns was on average 14,5 (min=4, max=34, S.d.=6.3) (mean maximum level=6.6, min=3, max=9, S.d.=1.6).

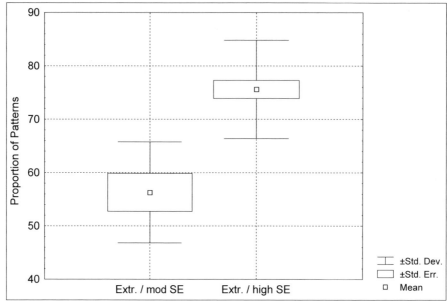

Figure 5. Pattern participation of extraverts with high and moderate self-esteem

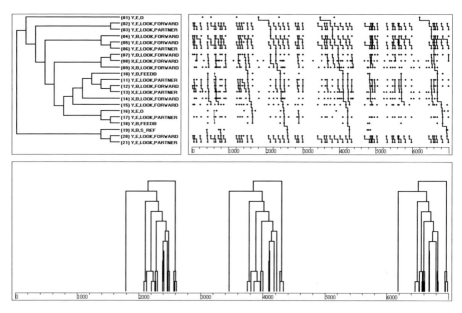

Figure 6. Two *introverts* (*X & Y*) with *high* self-esteem [The pattern figure has three main parts, each involving the same observation period. The upper-left box shows the hierarchical construction of the pattern, whereas the upper-right box shows the occurrence time points of each of its event types and the connection of points to form pattern occurrences. The bottom-box is like the upper-right box but with only complete patten instances showing]. <u>Events</u> - (**01**) Y, end (e), expressing opinion; (**02**) Y,e, look forward; (**03**) Y,e, look partner; (**04**) Y, begin (b), look forw; (**05**) Y,e, look forw; (**06**) Y,e, look partn; (**07**) Y,b, look forw; (**08**) X,e, look forw; (**09**) X,b, look forw; (**10**) Y,b, oral feedback; (**11**) Y,e, look partn; (**12**) Y,b, look forw; (**13**) X,e, look partn; (**14**) X,b, look forw; (**15**) Y,e, look forw; (**16**) X,e, expressing opinion; (**17**) Y,e, look partn; (**18**) Y,b, oral feedback; (**19**) X,b, referring to himself; (**20**) Y,e, look forw; (**21**) Y,e, look partn - (p<.001).

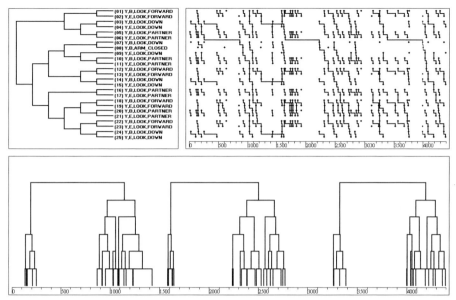

Figure 7. Extrovert (Y) with high self-esteem. Events - (01) Y, begin (b), look forward; (02) Y, end (e), look forw; (03) Y,b, look down; (04) Y,e, look down; (05) Y,b, look partner; (06) Y,e, look partn; (07) Y,b look down; (08) Y,b, arm open; (09) Y,e, look down; (10) Y,b, look partn; (11) Y,e, look partn; (12) Y,b, look forw; (13) Y,e, look forw; (14) Y,b, look down; (15) Y,e, look down; (16) Y,b, look partn; (17) Y,e, look partn; (18) Y,b, look forw; (19) Y,b, look forw; (20) Y,b, look partn; (21) Y,e, look partn; (22) Y,b, look forw; (23) Y,e, look forw; (24) Y,b, look down; (25) Y,e, look down - (p<.001).

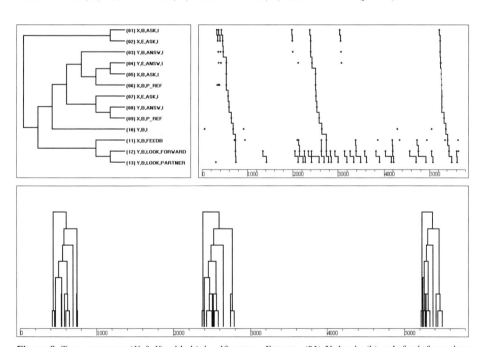

Figure 8. Two *extroverts* (*X & Y*) with *high* self-esteem. Events - (**01**) X, begin (b), ask for information; (**02**) X, ends (e), ask for information; (**03**) Y,b, answer; (**04**) Y,e, answer; (**05**) X,b, ask for information; (**06**) X,b, referring to partn; (**07**) X,e, ask for information; (**08**) Y,b, answer; (**09**) X,b, referring to partn; (**10**) Y,b, give information; (**11**) X,b, oral feedback; (**12**) X,b, look forw; (**13**) Y,b, look partn - (p<.001).

Subjects participated, on average, in 72.4% of detected pattern types (min=40, max=94, S.d.=14) and in 74.1% of pattern occurrences (min=35, max=95, S.d.=14.4).

Pattern occurrences were higher in dyads were both individuals scored high on the self-esteem scale than in mixed dyads (high vs. mod. self-esteem). Both "high self-esteem" and "extravert" dyads produced on average longer patterns than mixed dyads. Certain pattern types were found exclusively to be produced by extraverts and others by introverts. High and moderate self-esteem subjects were also found to produce different types of behavioral patterns (see examples in Figures 6, 7 and 8). Significant differences were found between scores from independent observers and actual scores from subjects; $F(4,98)=2,967$ $p<0,05$ for self-esteem, and $F(4,99)$ $=5,896$ $p<0,05$ for personality dimension of extraversion. The observers were more successful identifying extroverts with high self-esteem and introverts with average self-esteem than extroverts with average self-esteem and introverts with high self-esteem. None of the observers correctly identified all subjects observed according to their scores on the inventories.

9.4 Discussion and conclusion

The number, frequency and complexity of detected patterns, indicates that behavior is even more synchronized than the human eye can detect. This synchrony was found to exist on different levels, with highly complex time structures that extended over considerable time spans where many of the patterns occurred in a cyclical fashion. The results indicate a strong relation between self-esteem, personality and complexity and frequency of behavioral patterns. Certain patterns were found exclusively to be produced by extraverts and introverts, and others by high and moderate self-esteem subjects.

How can the difference between introverts and extraverts, and high and moderate self-esteem subjects, described in the results, be explained? Self-esteem is a concept that describes a general feeling of own worth. As such it might affect both social skills and the desire to communicate. The type and amount of behavior emitted by extraverts and subjects with high self-esteem differed from behavior emitted by introverts and subjects with a moderate self-esteem. This could explain different types of patterns produced, as well as differences in pattern frequency.

Extraverts and high self-esteem individuals might also be the "time giver", that is, the external stimulus the other person has to synchronize his behavior with. Extraverts and high self-esteem individuals could then, to some extent, control pattern production. Possible functions of synchronization might be found in mutual understanding; the higher the degree of synchronization, the higher the degree of mutual understanding. Synchronization might also serve as an indicator of compatibility in interactions. The amount of synchronization that can be achieved would thus be the indicator of compatibility by interactants [20].

Haynal-Reymond, Jonsson, & Magnusson [22], analyzing behavioral patterns in patient-doctor interaction, reported that the Theme pattern analysis was more successful in predicting future suicide attempts, by patients who had already tried taking their own life, than evaluations from their trained therapists. The current results suggest that the Theme pattern analysis might also be more successful in identifying the level of subject's self-esteem and scores on extraversion/introversion than independent observers.

Identifying and explaining trait-related consistencies remains a scientific challenge. While two situations may at first seem only slightly different, on a psychological level the difference can be powerfully important, with observable effects on behavior. But it is difficult to identify just how situations are important. This is partly because of the common practice of assigning "the situation" responsibility for all the behavioral variance not accounted for by a particular personality trait.

The results of the current study suggest that when behavior is analyzed using advanced methods like the T-pattern detection algorithm, illuminating analyses become possible.

Numerous studies have demonstrated that the organization of behavior is influenced by situation, personality and culture. Significant differences have been found between the structure of verbal and non-verbal communication in dyadic interaction of different culture groups [21] and different levels of attraction between subjects in mixed-sex dyadic interaction [23].

Strong relationship has been reported between level of subject's self-esteem and number of real-time behavioral patterns produced in dyadic interaction situations [17, 18]. Using repeated measures, analyzing therapeutic interviews, Jonsson [17] reported that as self-esteem of subjects increased the amount and type of behavior emitted changed. The increasing self-esteem also resulted in different types and an increasing number of patterns being detected. But what is perhaps most interesting is the increase of the complexity of patterns detected; seemingly augmented linear with increased self-esteem.

Jonsson [18] also reported finding significant differences in real-time behavioral patterns produced in dyadic interactions between subjects who considered themselves to be friends versus those who were strangers, the level of patterning being much higher between friends. The current study reveals a clear difference in real-time patterns produced by persons with different scores on the Eysenck Personality Questionnaire; certain patterns were exclusively produced by extraverts and others by introverts. Positive correlation was also found between subject's personality and complexity and frequency of patterns.

People's self-evaluation, whether explicit or implicit, are presumably formed through interaction with significant others. Parenting style should then be regarded as an important aspect in this formation [39]. Same might apply to caregivers and teachers. The failure of external observers, in correctly identifying the level of extraversion and self-esteem of subjects, raises some questions concerning miscommunication and misinterpretations between interactants. According to Anolli [5], miscommunication does not only include its standard meaning such as a lacking, defect and violation of communication rules, but also mismatching interpretation, as well as misrepresentation of information.

The concept of self-fulfilling prophecy might also be of some importance within the framework of the current study and the formation of self-esteem/personality. It certainly seems a valid question to ask, whether a belief or expectation, correct or not, affects the outcome of a situation or the way a person will behave. Thus, for example, labeling someone a "high self-esteem individual" or an "extravert", and treating that person as such, may foster high self-esteem or extravert behavior in the person who is subjected to the expectation. Studying mismatching interpretation and miscommunication should thus not only consider the negative aspects but also the positive ones.

9.5 Appendix

Table 1. Verbal categories [58]

Actes à visée collaborative	Actes à visée agonale
Actes de demande	*Actes de refus d'accéder à des demandes*
- d'information	- d'information
- de confirmation	- de confirmation
- de validation	- de validation
- de prise de position	- de prise de position
Actes d'acceptation de satisfaire à des demandes	Actes d'acceptation de satisfaire à des demandes (actes anti-orientés)
- de confirmation	- de confirmation
- de validation	- de validation
- de prise de position	- de prise de position
Actes auto-initiés et co-orientés	Actes auto-initiés et anti-orientés
- d'information	- de confirmation
- de confirmation	- de validation
- de validation	- de prise de position
- de prise de position	- d'attaque de face

Table 2. A category system for non-verbal behavior was adopted from McGrew [59] and further developed for this study. Note that many events can be combined and like that make up a different behavior (for example look can be combined with up, down, partner or right).

Metaphors	Objects, Person, Attitude, Opinion, Intention
Punctuators	Punctuators
Adaptations	Face, Hands, Object, Cloths
Face & head	Look, Smile, Nod head, Shake head, Nod head (punctuator), Bite lips, Frown, Eye brown up, Eye closed, Eye open
Direction	Partner, Forward, Backward, Up, Down, Left, Right
Postures	Sit, Stand, Lean, Change, Lift shoulders
Paralinguistic	Silence, Hesitation, Cough, Laugh, "Uhum" (feedback), Interrupt
Hands & fingers	Hands crossed, Hands stretch, Hands rest, Hands "drum"
Legs	Legs crossed, Legs floor, Legs shake, Legs "tab"

9.6 References

[1]   I. Stewart, *Nature's Numbers: Discovering Order and Pattern in the Universe*. London, Weidenfeld & Nicolson, 1995.
[2]   L. F. Barret, Valence is a basic building block of emotional life. *Journal of Research in Personality, 40*, 35-55, 2006.

[3]   S. D. Jr. Duncan & D. W. Fiske, *Face-to-Face Interaction: Research, Methods and Theory.* Hillsdale: Lawrence Erblaum Associates, 1977.

[4]   L. Anolli, R. Ciceri, & G. Riva, Introduction. In L. Anolli, Ciceri, R., & G. Riva (Ed.), *Say No to Say*, 2002.

[5]   L. Anolli, MaCHT – Miscommunication as Change Theory: Toward a unitary theory of communication and miscommunication. In L. Anolli, Ciceri, R., & G. Riva (Ed.), *Say No to Say*. IOS Press, 2002.

[6]   M. S. Magnusson, Hidden Real-Time Patterns in Intra- and Inter-Individual Behavior: Description and Detection. *European Journal of Psychological Assessment, 12*, (2), 112-123, 1996.

[7]   M. S. Magnusson, Discovering Hidden Time Patterns in Behavior: T-Patterns and Their Detection. *Behavior Research Methods, Instruments & Computers, 32* (1), 93-110, 2000.

[8]   M. S. Magnusson, Understanding Social Interaction: Discovering Hidden Structure with Model and Algorithms. In L. Anolli, S. Duncan, M.S. Magnusson, & G. Riva (Ed.), *The Hidden Structure of Interaction: From Neurons to Culture Patterns*. IOS Press, 2005.

[9]   I. Eibl-Eibesfeldt, *Ethology: The biology of behavior*. New York: Holt, Rinehart & Winston, 1970.

[10]   K. L. Pike, *Language: In relation to a unified theory of the structure of human behavior*. Glendale, CA: Summer Institute of Linguistics, 1960.

[11]   B. F. Skinner, *Verbal behavior*. New York: Appleton-Century-Crofts, 1957.

[12]   R. Bakeman & J. M. Gottman, *Observing interaction: An introduction to sequential analysis*. Cambridge: Cambridge University Press, 1997.

[13]   R. Ghiglione, *L'Homme Communiquant*. Armand Colin, 1986.

[14]   A. Blanchet & M. S. Magnusson, Processus cognitifs et programmation discursive dans l'entretien de recherche. *Psychologie Francaise, 33*, 91-98, 1988.

[15]   J. Beaudichon, S. Legros, & M. S. Magnusson, Organization des regulations inter et intrapersonnelles dans la transmission d'informations complexes organisees. *Bulletin de Psychologie, 44*, (Whole No. 399), 110-120, 1991.

[16]   L. Bensalah, *Effets de la relation amicale sur les comportements interactive : En situation dyadique de résolution de probléme*. Unpublished doctoral thesis. Université Rene Descartes - Paris V, 1992.

[17]   G. K. Jonsson, Self-esteem, friendship and verbal and non-verbal interaction. In K. Grammer (Chair), *Communication, Cognition and Evolution*. Symposium conducted at the 13th Conference of the International Society for Human Ethology. Vienna, Austria, 1996.

[18]   G. K. Jonsson, Self-esteem, friendship and verbal and non-verbal interaction [Abstract]. In A. Schmitt, K. Atzwanger, and K. Grammer (Eds.), *New Aspects of Human Ethology*. Plenum Pub Corp, 1997.

[19]   G. K. Jonsson, Relation between self-esteem, personality dimensions of extraversion and emotionality and real-time patterning of social interaction. In L.P.J.J Noldus (Ed.), *Measuring Behavior 2000, 3rd International Conference on Methods and Techniques in Behavioral Research*. Nijmegen (pp. 167-168), Netherlands, 2000.

[20]   K. Grammer, K. Kruck & M. S. Magnusson, The Courtship Dance. *Journal of Non-Verbal Behavior, 22* (1), 3-29, 1998.

[21]   A. Agliati, A. Vescovo & L. Anolli, Conversation Patterns in Iceladic and Italian People: Similarities and Difference in Rhythm and Accommodation. In L. Anolli, S. Duncan, M.S. Magnusson, & G. Riva (Ed.), *The Hidden Structure of Interaction: From Neurons to Culture Patterns*. IOS Press, 2005.

[22]   V. Haynal-Reymond, G. K. Jonsson & M. S. Magnusson, Nonverbal Communication in Doctor-Suicidal Patient Interview. In L. Anolli, S. Duncan, M.S. Magnusson, & G. Riva (Ed.), *The Hidden Structure of Interaction: From Neurons to Culture Patterns*. IOS Press, 2005.

[23]   K. Sakaguchi, G. K. Jonsson & T. Hasegawa, Initial interpersonal attraction between mixed-sex dyad and movement synchrony. In L. Anolli, S. Duncan, M.S. Magnusson, & G. Riva (Ed.), *The Hidden Structure of Interaction: From Neurons to Culture Patterns*. IOS Press, 2005.

[24]   L. Anolli, A. Agliati, G. K. Jonsson, M. S. Magnusson & R. Ciceri, Dynamic Typicality in the Communication of Emotions by Preschool Children. *Cognition & Emotion* (submitted), 2005.

[25]   A. Blanchet, M. Batt, A. Trognon, & L. Masse, Language and Behavior Patterns in a Therapeutic Interaction Sequence. In L. Anolli, S. Duncan, M.S. Magnusson, & G. Riva (Ed.), *The Hidden Structure of Interaction: From Neurons to Culture Patterns*. IOS Press, 2005.

[26]   M. H. Plumet & C. Tardif, Understanding the Functioning of Social Interaction with Autistic Children. In L. Anolli, S. Duncan, M.S. Magnusson, & G. Riva (Ed.), *The Hidden Structure of Interaction: From Neurons to Culture Patterns*. IOS Press, 2005.

[27]   S. Sastre-Riba, Tutoring Adjustment and Infants' Cognitive Gain. In L. Anolli, S. Duncan, M.S. Magnusson, & G. Riva (Ed.), *The Hidden Structure of Interaction: From Neurons to Culture Patterns*. IOS Press, 2005.

[28] C. Hardway, & S. Jr. Duncan, "Me first!" Structure and Dynamics of a Four-Way Family Conflict. In L. Anolli, S. Duncan, M.S. Magnusson, & G. Riva (Ed.), *The Hidden Structure of Interaction: From Neurons to Culture Patterns*. IOS Press, 2005.
[29] D. C. Funder, Towards a resolution of the personality triad: Persons, situations, and behaviors. *Journal of Research in Personality 40*, 21-34, 2006.
[30] D. T, Kenrcik & D. C. Funder, Profiting from controversy: Lessons from the person-situation debate. *American Psycholist, 43*, 23-34, 1988.
[31] D. C. Funder, Personality. *Annual Review of Psychology, 52*, 197-221, 2001.
[32] M. R. Mehl & J. W. Pennebaker, The sounds of social life: A psychometric analysis of students' daily social environments and natural conversations. *Journal of Personality and Social Psychology, 84*, 857–870, 2003.
[33] H. Wolf, P. Borkenau, A. Angleitner, R. Riemann & F. M. Spinath, Multi-method assessment of personality: An observational study of adult twins. *Behavior Genetics, 34*, 665, 2004.
[34] D. C. Funder & C. R. Colvin, Explorations in behavioral consistency: Properties of persons, situation and behavior. *Journal of Personality and Social Psychology, 52*, 197-221, 1991.
[35] D. C. Funder, R. M. Furr & C. R. Colvin, The Riverside behavioral Q-sort: A tool for the description of social behavior. *Journal of Personality, 68*, 450–489, 2000.
[36] B. F. Skinner, *The behavior of organisms: An experimental analysis*. New York: Macmillan, 1938.
[37] D. C. McClelland, Is personality consistent. In D. McClelland (Ed.), *Motives personality and society* (pp. 185–211). New York: Praeger, 1984.
[38] R. M. Furr & D. C. Funder, Situational similarity and behavioral consistency: Subjective, objective, variable-centered and person-centered approaches. *Journal of Research in Personality, 38*, 421-447, 2004.
[39] A. M. Bardone, K. D. Vohs, L. Y. Abramson, T. F. Heatherton & T. E. Jr. Joiner, The confluence of perfectionism, body dissatisfaction, and low self-esteem predicts bulimic symptoms: Clinical implications. *Behavior-Therapy, 31*, 265–280, 2000.
[40] T. DeHart, S. L. Murray, B. W. Pelham, & P. Rose, The regulation of dependency in parent-child relationships. *Journal of Experimental Social Psychology, 39*, 59–67, 2003.
[41] J. D. Brown & K. L. McGill, The cost of good fortune: When positive life events produce negative health consequences. *Journal of Personality and Social Psychology, 57*, 1103–1110, 1989.
[42] *New Webster's Dictionary*, New York: Delair, 1984.
[43] C. Sedikides & A. P. Gregg, Portraits of the self. In M. A. Hogg & J. Cooper (Eds.), *Sage handbook of social psychology* (pp.110-138). London: Sage Publications, 2003.
[44] G. E. Myers & M. T. Myers, *The dynamics of human communication: A laboratory approach*. New York: McGraw-Hill. 1992.
[45] F. R. Rosenberg & M. Rosenberg, Self-Esteem and Delinquency. *Journal of Youth and Adolescence, 7*, 279-291, 1978.
[46] M. D. Robinson & D. Cervone, Riding a wave of self-esteem: Perseverative tendencies as dispositional forces. *Journal of Experimental Social Psychology, 42,* 103–111, 2006.
[47] W. Mischel, *Personality and assessment*. New York: Wiley, 1968.
[48] T. DeHart, B. W. Pelham & H. Tennen, What lies beneath: Parenting style and implicit self-esteem. *Journal of Experimental Social Psychology, 42,* 1–17, 2006.
[49] B. Lerner, Self-esteem and excellence: The choice and the paradox. *American Educator*, 1985.
[50] R. F. Baumeister, J. D. Campbell, J. I. Krueger & K. D. Vohs, Exploding the self-esteem myth. *Scientific American, 292* (1), 84-91, 2005.
[51] D. Watson, J. Suls & J. Haig, Global self-esteem in relation to structural models of personality and affectivity. *Journal of Personality and Social Psychology, 83*, 185–197, 2002.
[52] *Columbia Encyclopedia*, Sixth Edition. Columbia University Press, 2005.
[53] H. J. Eysenck & S. B. G. Eysenck, *Manual of the Eysenck Personality Scales (EPS Adult)*. London: Hodder & Stoughton, 1991.
[54] G. Wilson, Extroversion/Introversion. In T. Blass (Ed.) *Personality Variables in Social Behavior*. New Yourk: Lawrence Erlbaum Associates, 1977.
[55] M. Argyle, *The Social Psychology of Everyday Life*. London: Routledge, 1992.
[56] A. Thorne, The Press of Personality: A Study of Conversations Between Introverts and Extraverts. *Journal of Personality and Social Psychology, 53*, 718-726, 1987.
[57] M. Argyle & M. Cook, *Gaze and Mutual Gaze*. Cambridge: Cambridge University Press, 1976.
[58] M. Bromberg & A. Landré, Analyse de la Structure Interactionnelle et des Stratégies discursive dans un talk-show. *Psychologie Francaise, 38* (2), 99-109, 1993.
[59] W. C. McGrew, *An Ethological Study of Children's Behaviour*. New York: Lawrence Erlbaum Associates, 1972.

From Communication to Presence
G. Riva et al. (Eds.)
IOS Press, 2006

10   Methodological Approaches in Human Communication: From Complexity of Perceived Situation to Data Analysis

M. Teresa ANGUERA, Conrad IZQUIERDO

Abstract. Human communication is a highly complex phenomenon that can be approached from numerous theoretical perspectives of varying nature. It is a good example of how traditional metatheoretical, epistemological and methodological controversies can be channeled through a body of knowledge whose aim is the rational and systematic search for different approaches, interconnections and complementary features.

The extraordinarily wide range of aspects to be considered and the experiential richness that goes hand in hand with every communicative episode make it necessary to choose observational methodology, capable of being both flexible and objective.

In the first stage of the process involving observational methodology, qualitative methodology is preferred for the study of communication given the wide range of options it provides in terms of data collection, but it's high relevant the characterization and application of a quantitative approach in the second stage of an observation of communicative behaviour. Current advances involving the use of sophisticated methodological resources, which enable much greater rigor through the process.

Contents

10.1 The field of Interpersonal Communication and Non-verbal Behavior

Human communication is a highly complex phenomenon that can be approached from numerous theoretical perspectives of varying nature. In this regard, psychology offers a rich and extensive range of approaches which reflect the many different aspects addressed within this field: interpersonal communication, non-verbal behavior and communication, language and social interaction, group communication, organizational communication, intercultural communication, mass media, new communication technologies, cultural studies, the study of performance, communication and health, and communication applied to problem solving.

Indeed, the field of interpersonal communication — a well-established research area within the social sciences [1] — is a good example of how traditional metatheoretical, epistemological and methodological controversies can be channeled through a body of knowledge whose aim is the rational and systematic search for different approaches, interconnections and complementary features.

During the 20th century the themes addressed within the field of interpersonal communication developed as a result of contributions from various scientific disciplines: anthropology, linguistics, psychology and sociology. Thus, the field today is characterized by plurality in terms of the choice of fundamental units, the identification of basic processes, and the theoretical and methodological attention which must be paid to the communicative contexts of everyday life [2].

The consideration of non-verbal signals as fundamental units of human communication [3, 4] and the greater number of studies conducted with improved technical resources for observing, coding and measuring non-verbal behavior [5] have resulted in this topic becoming a research area in its own right, one that is mainly geared toward the study of interpersonal behavior [6, 7, 4].

From the methodological point of view, the research activity arising out of interpersonal communication (verbal and non-verbal) is based on two key features: 1. A pragmatic approach with respect to understanding the objectives of scientific knowledge: *Thus, none of the "paradigms" of inquiry occupies a privileged position in the court of truth; all share the burden of justification* [8]; 2. Awareness of the need to link the choice of methodology with the theoretical approach taken by researchers: *Significant progress depends both on substance and on method, and neither can be slighted without harming the whole* [9].

It appears, therefore, that the confrontation between positivist strategies and naturalistic research methods in the area of interpersonal communication has lessened:

[Interpersonal Communication] *As a traditional bastion of quantitative and positivist and post-positivist research, this subfield has been relatively slow and cautious in accommodating interpretative epistemology (Leeds-Hurwitz, 1992). Groundbreaking qualitative studies have treated personal relationships (e.g., family and friendships) and episodes of interaction (e.g., conflict) as situated accomplishments of speech and nonverbal (Ray, 1987) communication (e.g., Jorgenson, 1989; Rawlins, 1983, 1989). In their premises and practices, most of these studies reflect the influence of social-constructionism, "conventional" explanation and "grounded theory"* (Lindlof & Taylor, 2002, p. 20).

As Poole & McPhee [9] point out, conventional explanation is regarded as a goal associated with qualitative studies. By means of conventional explanation the perspective adopted by subjects with respect to their own world is taken as the starting point of the relationship between behavior and social norms. However, this goal can also be detected in the hypothetico-deductive approach to research and in the generation of models. Moreover, the goal of causal explanation, traditionally associated with hypothetico-deductive research and considered, more recently, in theoretical models [10], has also been adapted to qualitative research (ethnography, symbolic interactionism and grounded theory) in the field of interpersonal communication (e. g., [11]).

In what follows we offer a contemporary and stepwise discussion of how the methodological options available within scientific observation, both qualitative and quantitative, can be used to approach a number of — succinctly described — problems in the field of human communication research.

10.2 From Opposing Paradigms to Methodological Decision-making

The communicative process is an event or activity characterized by the different levels, which can be considered: interpersonal distance, gaze exchange, gestural behavior, vocal emissions, verbal behavior, etc. It is deeply imbued with cultural norms, is capable of being contextualized and re-contextualized at any given moment, and can be considered as comprising various episodes, each one of which is formed by a sequence of communicative acts produced by the transmitter.

This conceptual and experiential complexity raises many questions, uncertainties and doubts on the methodological level. However, the discipline that can be imposed through use of a given procedure should not prevent us from maintaining spontaneity, or at least the sense of everydayness with which we consider the production of communicative acts, that is, in terms of molecules — each one formed by atoms — that interact with one another in various ways and form groups of greater or lesser magnitude.

Undoubtedly, the conceptual perspective adopted — which is always both feasible and open to debate — will constitute the reference point that in each case provides the backbone of the approach taken.

The extraordinarily wide range of aspects to be considered and the experiential richness that goes hand in hand with every communicative episode make it necessary to choose methodological approaches that are, above all, capable of being both flexible and objective.

The former, flexibility, must take into account the constant search for fit between transmitter(s) and receiver(s) with respect to diverse elements such as existing prior knowledge, the thematic nature of the situation, the physical location, social norms and uses, and the expressive capacity of the communicating parties, to name but a few of the key aspects. The second attribute, objectivity, is non-negotiable due to it being an inherent feature of all scientific research, and, therefore, it should characterize the methodological procedure followed, in this case, *observational methodology*. Undoubtedly, combining the various elements of this process poses a great challenge.

10.2.1 Adequacy and Possibilities of a Qualitative Approach in the First Stage of an Observation of Communicative Behavior

Once the specific object has been defined (initiative in communication, single or multi-channel forms of communication, communicative symmetry/asymmetry, communicative networks, etc.) the scientific observation of human communicative behavior begins with the recording.

Recording simply implies the representation of reality in a given format, and will involve the use of a coding system. In procedural terms this capturing of reality can only be carried out qualitatively.

Until recently such a methodological approach was widely considered to be marginal and attracted the attention of few researchers. Nowadays a shift appears to be underway, although the dominant paradigm (in Kuhnian terms, but without the exclusive meaning he attributed to the term) continues to be the positivist-empiricist one.

Qualitative research may be described as a form of systematic inquiry aimed at understanding human beings and the nature of their interactions with one another and with their environment. Indeed, qualitative research is often described as holistic, as being concerned with the complexity of human beings and their surroundings, and fits neatly into the recording stage of an observational study of behavior, performance and situations involving individuals, groups or a given organization; in this regard, it is possible to classify the different types of recording. All this is illustrated by the way in which it can readily be adapted to what is implied by the study of communication in everyday life [12-15].

Qualitative methodology is based on a number of assumptions and there are certain key characteristics which define it. Method or methodology means "way to", and in the context of communication this will be defined by the content and, therefore, the substantive questions to which it *can* and *should be* applied. At times a choice is available as regards the initial reductionism implied by data collection (for example, in the case of someone going on a trip organized by a group of friends, this would be the transcription of a series of episodes, which may include a detailed description of the specific actions that constitute the aim of the trip or merely a list of distances covered, times, angles, etc.); in other cases, however, the approach is restricted by the nature of the situation and the basis of the theoretical framework (for example, communication with an acquaintance who is going through a personal crisis). Although both form part of everyday life it is only in the first example that we can *strictly* refer to the occurrence of perceivable behavior.

The root problem here is one of operationalization, or what amounts to the same, of the "correctness" of the reductionism which will enable *the information considered to be relevant to be selected from the communicative process, and thus collect the data in one form or another*. This is both the heart of the problem and the crucial question around which attitudes in favor or against will emerge, thus giving rise to the development of a qualitative or quantitative methodology. *In the first stage of the process involving observational methodology, qualitative methodology is preferred for the study of communication given the wide range of options it provides in terms of data collection* [16].

10.2.2 Characterization and Application of a Quantitative Approach in the Second Stage of an Observation of Communicative Behavior

In the first stage of an observational study in communicative research, particular care must be taken in justifying the adequacy of qualitative methodology, and the greatest difficulty lies in obtaining data. Once the latter have been obtained, and quality control procedures have been applied to detect and rectify possible errors, the process enters *a second* stage involving *adequate analyses based on the adequate observational design* [17], which will be discussed below. Traditionally, it has been stated that followers of quantitative methodology tend to translate their observations into figures, and these numerical values are produced through the counting, measurement or verification of the order or sequence, or from interval or ratio data, thus enabling researchers to discover, verify or identify the relationships between concepts derived from a theoretical framework developed in accordance with the criteria governing each one of the communicative situations to be studied. In terms of the *assumptions of quantitative methodology*, hypothesis testing requires that the criteria of representativeness and randomization are fulfilled, which implies the use of adequate sampling techniques, as well as the possible use of sophisticated univariate and multivariate analytic procedures. A general review of the scientific journals in the field of communication reveals that a great many communicative studies in natural contexts (that is, excluding laboratory studies) merit the criticism of *endemic methodological weakness*. However, what is also observable, and on an increasingly widespread scale, are *important advances involving the use of sophisticated methodological resources* which enable much greater rigor [18]; although not all of them come from studies conducted in natural contexts they would nonetheless constitute adequate analyses in many of them provided that adequate data were available.

10.2.3 Complementary Use of Methodological Options

In the above sections we have considered the appropriateness of qualitative and quantitative perspectives in the first and second stage, respectively, of the observation of communicative behavior. The logical succession of stages in an organized way should enable this change of perspective (from qualitative to quantitative) to occur smoothly, and avoid creating tension within the procedure to be followed.

The two methodological perspectives can mutually benefit one another, and indeed they are often used together, thus assuring their complementarity. Although it is true that this option may pose serious problems in terms of time and money, or due to the lack of trained personnel, the aim is to overcome the idea of opposing perspectives.

The nature of most — if not all — communicative situations in which the adequacy, complexity and multifaceted character of observational methodology are justified implies methodological diversity in terms of how such situations are approached. For even those authors most strongly associated with the quantitative perspective recognize that no method holds the patent on scientific correctness. This situation is helped by the fact that research is increasingly being carried out by multidisciplinary teams which, using a variety of techniques, seek to join forces in order to achieve greater research rigor [16]. Thus, the way ahead is increasingly clear, although considerable effort will still be required to consolidate new possibilities for collaboration.

10.2.4 Privileged Position of Observational Methodology for the Study of Communication in Terms of the Complementarity between Qualitative and Quantitative Approaches

Our starting point here is that the very nature of observational methodology enables it to be used for studying communicative behavior in contexts that are natural or usual for the individual or group.

We can then ask to what extent observational methodology is consistent with the above description of qualitative methodology in an initial stage and the application of quantitative methods in a second stage. Although we have always argued in favor of this compatibility, support for such a view can also be found in the work of two prestigious authors. Bakeman and Gottman [19] specifically define systematic observation as a particular way of quantifying behavior and, indeed, they code and analyze it rigorously; furthermore, they dedicate several chapters of their book to explaining and exemplifying recording methods, as well as their subsequent coding, the point where qualitative and quantitative approaches meet. *We can thus categorically state that observational methodology is the one which best reflects the complementarity between qualitative and quantitative approaches* [16] as, in highly simplified terms, it will always require the development of an *ad hoc* instrument on the basis of which a recording (qualitative methodology) can be made, this then being subjected to quality control and an adequate analysis (quantitative methodology).

Obviously, empirical studies of communication conducted according to such a perspective produce data by translating reality into systems of written notation. However, there will be an initial and provisional dichotomization (not a real dichotomy) depending on how this is done, which in turn will depend to a great extent on the nature of the problem at hand. To give an example of an unusual case, in a study of gaze exchange times between a mother and child, data collection will involve a certain type of data which will no doubt be expressed in conventional time units (seconds, tenths of a second, milliseconds, etc.). However, there are many fields of study in which "data" are produced but where it is not possible to operationalize them, or where this is not feasible without resorting to excessive reductionism. For instance, if we consider programs that provide health and/or social services to multi-problem families, in which there is a clear communicative relationship, the question is whether it would be feasible to conduct a quantitative count of a given phenomenon. The answer is no, due to the multiplicity of existing problems, the poorly defined nature of some of them, the need for contextualization, and the various factors involved, among many other aspects.

10.2.5 Is Integration Possible?

Finally, having established the complementarity of qualitative and quantitative methodological options in studies of communication [16] brief consideration should be given to their possible integration. Bericat [20] considers that such integration is both possible and useful within the framework of a pluralistic attitude toward methodology, and regards it as a step beyond "legitimate and recognized plurality" (p. 31).

This shift toward integration is already being undertaken by mathematicians and social data analysts on the basis of two premises [20]: The first of these recognizes that a great amount of the information dealt with by many researchers in the field of communication, and within the social and behavioral sciences, is qualitative in nature; thus, attempts are being made to develop suitable analytic mathematical models. According to Alvira [21], this work is being carried out on three fronts: Firstly, by finding ways of transforming something qualitative into a quantitative form by means of advances in measurement theory; secondly, by developing new statistical techniques that use qualitative data; and thirdly by creating formal languages, which are not necessarily numerical, that enable data treatment, for example, the analysis of correspondences, *logit* and *probit* analyses, and graph theory.

The second — and more radical — integration premise is based on the idea that what can be postulated is not a quantity but rather a predetermined quality, and vice-versa, i.e., that what can be postulated is not a quality but rather a predetermined quantity [20, 22]. In other words, quality and quantity lose their meaning unless viewed in light of one another.

Although the road may be long and tortuous it would seem that we are now closer to a point where this reciprocity between quantity and quality will materialize in empirical studies of communication; although Bericat [20] argues that their complementarity already implies an initial degree of integration we believe that sustained developments will occur on other levels.

10.3 From the Complexity of the Perceived Situation to the Descriptive Recording

10.3.1 The Importance of Perceivability

Communicative reality can be regarded as largely perceivable since, although there is undoubtedly a cognitive factor, we are concerned here with its behavioral aspect, regardless of the specific setting to be studied. Initially, recording a perceived situation involves a *transduction* of reality, that is, its representation within another format.

The recording process involves a number of common characteristics, whose purpose is to obtain information about communicative behavior in the situation studied, as well as about its context. The step from perceived reality to the descriptive recording forms part of the research strategies on which scientific method is based in the behavioral sciences, as well as in others such as the social sciences.

Although all the various forms of recording will be characterized by the kind of data collected, they should be classified according to their nature; this gives rise to the taxonomic system proposed in Table 1, in which direct and indirect observation complement one another (the latter being focused here on verbal behavior capable of being transformed into documental material), and where there is the possibility of gathering documental and graphic material [23], of great importance in studies of communication. This ranking covers the range of possibilities between data obtained from the recording of perceivable behavior — which are the easiest to code and subsequently quantify — and those gathered from documental sources (reports or dossiers), in which such data treatment is practically impossible.

Anyone wishing to study the reality of perceivable communicative situations must pay special attention to objectivity when collecting data, and this will mean respecting a number of prior methodological safeguards which will, in turn, lead to a series of actions. Obviously, the decisions made in this regard will be determined by the purpose of the research, the nature of the setting, the people involved in the study, and any practical limitations or issues of feasibility.

Table 1. Taxonomic criteria regarding ways of accessing reality according to perceivability.

DIRECT OBSERVATION	Total perceivability	Narrative recording Descriptive recording Coded recording
INDIRECT OBSERVATION	Partial perceivability	Documental material obtained in its original form Verbal behavior able to be transformed into documental material

The problem and question arising out of all this is how to begin the process of obtaining information about communicative behavior in the home, classroom, hospital, therapist's room, department store, office, street, etc., about which nothing is yet known.

10.3.2 Defining the Boundaries of the Observational Sesign

The observational design acts as a criterion or guide throughout the empirical process, but especially when collecting, managing and analyzing data. Various criteria can be established in drawing up a map of possible designs.

The model of Anguera, Blanco & Losada [17] comprises eight zones divided into four quadrants, corresponding to the eight different observational designs (Figure 1).

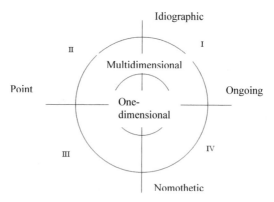

Figure 1. Observational designs (Anguera, Blanco & Losada, 2001)

The vertical axis refers to the units of study (interactive dyad, small group of participants carrying out a shared task, etc.), the horizontal axis to the temporal dimension of the evaluation (from one session to a series of sessions over a period of time), and the concentric circles to the dimensionality.

The upper pole of the vertical axis refers to an *idiographic study* (of units), for example, that of communication in a mother/child dyad or a small group of communicating people considered as a single unit. In contrast, the lower pole refers to a *nomothetic study* (group of units), such as that of a group of elderly married couples taking part in leisure activities.

The left-hand pole of the horizontal axis refers to a *point recording* (normally, a single session), while the right-hand pole is for *ongoing* recordings, such as the total number of group psychotherapy sessions included in a program for people who wish to stop drinking.

The inner concentric circle refers to a *one-dimensional design*, when what is of interest is just one type of observed element, for example, a single communicative channel. The outer circle refers to a *multidimensional design*, used in situations where the aim is to study a multi-channel communication (or a single channel one that can be broken down into different parts, for example, in gestural behavior, where different examples of such behavior can be derived topographically from different parts of the body).

10.3.3 Segmentation of the Communicative "Continuum"

Anyone wishing to collect data about communicative data must address a number of issues that have proved controversial since the beginnings of the discipline, for example, the pyramidal structure of the molecularization-molarization *continuum* and the definition of units according to the communicative aim, among many others.

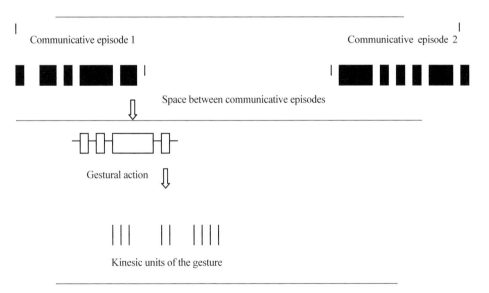

Figure 2. Hierarchical structure of behavioral units, where it can be seen that a unit of given molarity is broken down into further molecular units across a continuous dimension.

The continuous dimension to which we have referred stretches between two poles, the molar and the molecular, and this dichotomy is characterized by a number of advantages and disadvantages [24, 25], as shown in Table 2.

Table 2. Advantages and disadvantages of the molar/molecular dichotomy.

	Advantages	Disadvantages
Molecular	Greater objectivity	Disconnectedness
Molar	Greater interconnectedness	Risk of subjectivity

The flow of communicative behavior appears as a continuous succession of episodes, events and actions, etc., which develop into a session-based structure governed by established temporal rules (such as professional activities that involve a given duration), although these may also be absent (as in the spontaneity of interpersonal communicative relationships). Given that a session is usually understood as an uninterrupted recording time, adequate criteria must be established in order to break up the session conceptually into elements containing the minimum amount of information, which will then be taken as the units of recording, coding or analysis.

The nature of these units may vary widely. Although there is a *continuum* between the molar and the molecular levels [19], it should be remembered that these terms are somewhat relative, since, for example, a conversation between man and wife may be considered as a molecular unit in accordance with certain study objectives. However, it could also be regarded as a molar unit in another study whose aim was to analyze the multi-channel integration of dimensions involving, for example, speech, gestures and gaze exchange which appear during the succession of various episodes, each one of which will have a (relatively) molecular nature; however, each one — for example, a communicative action in the form of a gesture — could also be considered as a molar unit if it forms part of a kinesic or movement study, in which they have all been broken down into units of displacement and of gesture (Figure 2).

The decision regarding which criteria to use in segmenting the flow of communicative behavior is far from easy, and the specific aim of the study must always be the main criterion upon which this decision is based. The various possibilities must be considered and evaluated in each case, the investigator being aware that this will influence the results obtained. However, these differences appear not to be relevant if we adopt the position taken by Dickman [26], according to which groups of untrained observers confirm the tendency to detect certain "cut-off points" along the behavioral continuum which, although they do not always coincide, are generally consistent with what are termed the *modal division*, or most relevant cut-off points.

There is no inevitable equivalence or assimilation between event and molecularity, on the one hand, and states and molarity, on the other. One could imagine the study of a communicative episode consisting of a conversation (Figure 2), something which, on a highly ordered hierarchical scale, would constitute the highest level of molar behavior and be a point from which we would descend successively through various communicative actions along the molecular scale. However, there may be great mobility and variability in the channel corresponding to the gestural behavior of upper extremities, while the seated body posture remains constant. In this case, we would need to consider events for gestural behavior and states for body posture, although this does not mean that this body posture cannot readily be molecularized by means of approaches such as that of Birdwhistell [27].

Also worth noting in this context is the work of Barker & Wright [28], who established *segmentation indicators* by means of which untrained observers marked the boundaries of behavioral segments. These could be applicable to certain communicative episodes, and thus we have adapted them to communicative behavior:

a) Change in the type of communicative episode.
b) Change in the communicative action.
c) Change in the implied communicative channel.
d) Change in the identity of the transmitter and/or receiver.
e) Change in the behavior setting.
f) Change in the action modulators.

In our view, how the boundaries of the behavioral unit are defined will inevitably depend on the specific objectives which are set, and must also be consistent with the following modulatory criteria [24, 25]:

a) It must be possible to define the boundaries of each behavioral unit; in other words, to define and distinguish it from the previous and subsequent unit.
b) It must be possible to name each behavioral unit. Assigning a specific name is enormously helpful in terms of the unit acquiring its own identity, and in differentiating it from other similar behavioral units.
c) For a behavioral unit to be considered as such, it must be able to be defined in a way that captures its particular features.

Having fulfilled these three requirements, and in accordance with the stated aim, each study will then proceed to establish the size and characteristics of the behavioral units.

10.4 From the Descriptive Record to Analyzable Data

10.4.1 From the Descriptive to the Systematized Recording

Although the raw information is always obtained at the point of recording, the nature of this recording may take any one of an enormous variety of forms. The taxonomic criteria also cover a wide range of possibilities.

When it comes to recording communicative behavior we believe a relevant approach is that adopted by Martin & Bateson [29], who propose three types of description:

a) Description of the structure, appearance, physical form or temporal patterns of the behavior. Behavior is described in terms of the subjects' posture and movements, which may involve a great amount of detail, and a skilled observer is thus required in order to perceive subtle differences.

b) Description in terms of consequences, or effects of the behavior on the context (in the widest sense, and including both other subjects and material objects and their particular arrangement) in which it takes place, or on the subject producing it, but without reference to how these effects are produced. This is easy to distinguish from the previous category, and as such it is obvious that "hanging up during a telephone conversation" is a description in terms of consequences, whereas "using a finger to press the appropriate key on a mobile phone" or "putting a traditional telephone back on the hook" is a structural description.

c) A third form of description can be made in terms of the *spatial relationship* between subjects in a given setting, the emphasis here being on where and with whom subjects do something rather than what they do. For example, "moving closer" can be defined in terms of changes in the spatial relationship between subjects.

If a flexible approach is adopted to the question of which descriptive levels are the most suitable, such that there is a continuum which includes a range of intermediate levels between its two extremes, then there will be a better fit and interconnectedness between the perception of the communicative behavior and its interpretation, or the capturing of its meaning, and this will improve the quality of the observational recording. In most cases, the inclusion of several descriptive levels within the same recording will produce an overlap of various units and enable the behavioral "continuum" to be covered; thus, different types of analysis will also converge.

When studying communicative behavior we are interested in studying the process rather than the result, and therefore the *transduction* of the behavioral flow into the recording is of particular importance. In this regard it is necessary to consider whether we can always guarantee that a description of a behavioral episode captures its essential aspects and all the required nuances, let alone provide a perfect correspondence between data collected by means of descriptions located on different levels, between the use of strictly empirical terms and others which are far more conceptual in nature. Moreover, one can ask whether there will be reciprocity between the 'communicative event' and its corresponding description.

The empirical stage of the observation starts at the point when the observer begins to gather and classify information about events or behavior. These first data, the result of a transduction of reality, must be progressively systematized and this process may involve many intermediate steps (from passive to active observation) which usually follow on from one another, at least partially, as the observer develops increasing knowledge about the behavior studied and the specific approach adopted unfolds.

Firstly, as in quantitative studies, it is important to confirm that the data are complete, of good quality and in a format that facilitates their organization. Furthermore, any transcriptions that are meant to be *word for word* must be checked to ensure that this is indeed the case.

The main task in organizing qualitative data involves developing a way of indexing the material; for example, lists that match the identification numbers of material with other types of information such as dates and places of data collection.

Given the aim described earlier, any recording involves selecting those behaviors considered to be important and then, on the basis of their characteristics, the chosen recording technique and the resources available, it is necessary to choose a system (which nowadays will be almost entirely computerized) which facilitates their simplification and storage. Programs such as *The Observer* [30], SDIS-GSEQ [31], *State Space Grids* [32], *ThèmeCoder* [33] and *Match Vision Studio* [34] are easy to use in the study of various communicative settings.

However, this level of recording will be insufficient if what we are seeking is, as stated above, the subsequent elaboration — and quantification — of spontaneous behavior represented through systematic observation. Hence the need, by means of *coding*, to develop and use a system of symbols (which may be of various kinds) that enables the measurements required in each case to be obtained.

The complete systematization of communicative behavior is achieved through a system of codes (iconic, literal, numerical, mixed, chromatic, etc.) which may adopt the form of a string, module or cascade, etc. Naturally, the coding used may be binary (presence/absence, which could be coded, respectively, as 1/0) or focus on a single type of element, for example, verbal interactive behavior. Alternatively, it may be useful to *simultaneously code several concurrent aspects*, for which the researcher may develop a *complete syntax for any observation situation*, which reaches a maximum degree of systematization without the need for any descriptive term. In this case, it would be necessary to draw up a *coding manual*. Obviously, this transformation would have to be validated in terms of how feasible decoding was, that is, the process through which the corresponding descriptive recording would be obtained in its original non-systematized form; indeed, it is precisely in those cases where this operation does not work (the descriptive record obtained having been distorted or deformed by the decoding) that we can diagnose the nature of the errors committed during coding.

The coding manual comprises two different parts. The first will include all the terms (behaviors) used in the systematized recording, along with the corresponding code which represents them, and without any limitations being placed on the type of code used. The second part of the coding manual must contain the syntactic rules which govern the use of the codes, and specifically set out the syntax of the code combinations and the sequences of these combinations.

10.4.2 Notational system

A notational system transforms the behavioral flow into a certain kind of unit [35]. The need for the recording of units to be as objective as possible, at the same time as being efficient, is the key issue in the debate about the role played by a notational system in obtaining data. The literature on this issue illustrates the disappointment felt by scholars in the field as a result of the proliferation of individual systems and the disagreement this generates. This pessimism is clearly set out by Badler & Smoliar [36], who refer to:

[...] *an almost total lack of agreement on how movement should be described. It is almost as if each research project started from scratch with an arbitrary set of movement characteristics to be observed* (1979, p. 19).

Donaghy [37], following on from the work of Frey & Pool [38] and Hirsbrunner, Frey & Crawford [39], locates the notation system problem in terms of the attempt to develop a vocabulary of symbols for representing the positions and/or patterns of body movement which the human eye can discriminate. Given that there is an unlimited number of discernible movements in non-verbal communication, a notational system must inevitably function as a low-resolution instrument if the aim is to develop a useful and efficient system. According to Bernese Time-Series Notation [38], the methodological basis for using a limited vocabulary of codes is the recording of "moment-to-moment" movement. In each time interval unit, regardless of its size, a localized movement is identified by its location along the cardinal plane in which it takes place, and a gesture (e.g., of the hand) by the form (e.g., closed). Its space-time or figurative definition is a scale value assigned in accordance with its perceived position along the cardinal plane, or the presence of an attribute in the case of a gesture.

Through this procedure, almost every body movement can be notated by using a limited alphabet of codes which distinguish one type of visible behavior from another according to the spatial dimensions (e. g., sagittal dimension: *Up/down tilt head*) or characteristics of the specified form (e. g., closure dimension: *Opening/closing of fist*). It should be noted, however, that the most important aspect of the Bernese Time-Series Notation is not the codes it proposes but the structuring principles of the system: "moment-to-moment" notation and the selective assignation of characteristics and reference points that may be considered pertinent. Thus, for each notation problem it is necessary to define the relevant codes [37]:

The system is designed to code nonverbal behavior obtained from individuals sitting in a chair and conversing. If an investigator is interested in coding persons standing or walking and talking, many of the coding dimensions and reference points would have to be changed (1989, p. 301).

Izquierdo & Anguera [40] have continued the debate about notational systems within the theoretical and technical framework of observational methodology in psychology [41]. Unfortunately, for many investigators of non-verbal communication, systematic observation continues to be no more than a technique for obtaining and recording direct or recorded data, and moreover the study of the kinesics present in everyday written texts and literary works is overlooked [42]. Given such a limited approach, it is unlikely that Donaghy's proposed solution to the problem faced by the notational system for movement will go beyond the practice described, that is, an agreement regarding the two criteria which structure the coding process, namely, temporalization and restrictive coding. When direct observation is considered as a methodology [17], the perceptual/linguistic framework of the observer/analyst and the way in which this is represented through the chosen observational design become central issues when it comes to addressing the structural criteria and rules of use which may be shared by investigators when developing and adopting a notational system for non-verbal behavior. Although we accept that the criterion of "moment-to-moment" coding must be preserved, we believe that the notational system could be more readily normalized through the addition of new theoretical and methodological rules regarding how to achieve a restrictive coding which truly represents the morphokinetic characteristics of human action, whether observed live or through photographs, films or videos, and not forgetting the reading of written texts.

The progress made towards a new approach that normalizes the structure and use of notational systems for body movement [43, 40, 25, 44] has crystallized in the proposed *Common Morphokinetic Alphabet* (CMA) (in press). The basis of this theoretical and methodological conception of notation is that it combines the perceptual/linguistic process of the observer/analyst with the choreographic approach [45, 46]; it also adopts field formats as the observation instrument [41].

With respect to the choreographic approach there are three systems with a sound scientific basis: those of Laban [47], Benesh [48] and Eshkol-Wachman [49]. Apart from the differences between them their writing sequence provides information about the following basic questions: What moves?; What has changed?; and How has it changed? The search for answers to these questions structures the perceptual/linguistic behavior of the observer/analyst and means that the description of demonstrable movement (What has changed?) is rooted in the recognition of the communicative functions related to the expressive capacity of body zones and the use of the body through space [50-53].

One way to ensure that the linking of codes (or morphokinetic phrase) which transcribes the motor event (what is seen and the order in which it is seen, in accordance with the search for answers to the above three questions) remains cohesive (rather than aggregated) is by assigning a phrase marker grammatical structure [54, 55] to the string of concurrent morphokinetic codes in one time unit of the recording. The formal grammatical model of morphokinetic syntactic categories (Figure 3) provides a rule-based morphokinetic phrase as a reference point, although this does not, of course, imply the need to translate the dynamic body movement observed into natural language:

$$ {}_K[{}_{NG}[{}_F{}^{[codes]}{}_F \; {}_S[{}_P{}^{[codes]}{}_P \; {}_O{}^{[codes]}{}_O \; {}_T{}^{[codes]}{}_T]_S]_{NG} \; {}_{DG}[{}_{Det}{}^{[codes]}{}_{Det} \; {}_M{}^{[codes]}{}_M]_{DG}]_K $$

Figure 3. Phrase marker structure [K] of the string of morphokinetic codes. The block NG comprises the codes "what moves?" [F] and "what has changed?" [S]. The block DG refers to contextual characteristics: how has it changed?

Thus, two further criteria can be added to the previously mentioned criteria of agreeing "moment-to-moment" notation and restrictive coding: these are the structured perceptual/linguistic search for movement and the syntactic comparison of the string of codes which go to make up the morphokinetic description.

The second aspect of the CMA's theoretical and methodological framework, and one which also provides criteria for agreeing on how to use notational systems, is the adoption of field formats as the observation instrument.

10.4.3 Breaking down dimensions and field formats

All authors in the field agree that communication is multidimensional in nature, dimensions being understood as the levels of response or channels that are activated in every communicative process, and which correspond to those considered in the four multidimensional observational designs. Furthermore, each of these dimensions may be broken down into others of lesser depth. In other words, the hierarchical structure of communication should correspond to the various dimensions or channels or levels of response, each one of which would have its corresponding codes for use in the recording.

Obviously, given the enormous range of behaviors, which are generated in a communicative episode, the development of an *ad hoc* observation instrument is perfectly justified. As it is almost impossible to categorize the perceivable behaviors corresponding to each one of the channels (since this would imply meeting the requirements of exhaustiveness and mutual exclusivity) the only instrument which can be used in the study of communicative behavior is that of field formats; this approach does not necessarily require a theoretical framework and is open (and therefore deliberately non-exhaustive), multidimensional, based on multiple codes and self-regulatable [41, 24, 43, 40, 25].

The following figure (4) illustrates the role of a field format (comprising six criteria or dimensions) and provides an example of a recording made by means of a series of configurations (rows of the recording matrix); these show concurrence between all the codes recorded (in each row of the matrix) and the succession of configurations (rows) is ordered sequentially over time.

In terms of its characteristics the recording obtained from the field format is no different from the notational structures — also in the form of matrices — proposed by Frey, Jorns & Daw [56], Frey *et al.* [57] and Hirsbrunner, Frey & Crawford [39], and which are known as *time-series notation.*

In both cases the content of the matrix reveals, through a simple example, the enormous complexity of information contained within the communicative flow, and constitutes a meeting point between the qualitative and quantitative perspectives on research into communicative behavior. Once data are available in the form of codes, with whatever transformations may be necessary, they can be subjected to quality control procedures and subsequently analyzed. This analysis may adopt various perspectives: relationship between dimensions, cross-section with respect to time, sequential patterns of codes for one or several dimensions, etc.

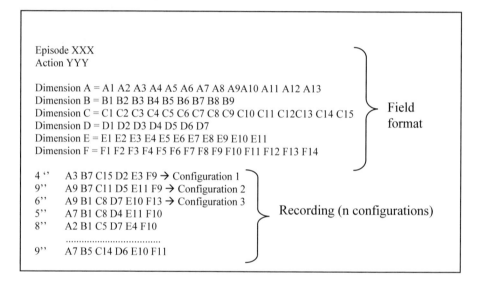

Figure 4. A field format example

10.4.4 The code as Datum and its Transformations

Although we have referred to various recording options, in all of them it is necessary to decide how to obtain the clean data, which will be extracted from the recording. Technological progress has enabled the development of various computer applications capable of recording generically every perceivable behavior, and they can also be used to record sports behavior in real time [58]. A rough estimate suggests that there are currently around two hundred computer programs, which can be used to conduct observational recordings, and some of these were mentioned above. Obviously, the codes themselves are interchangeable as they are merely labels which enable data to be collected by means of a given appearance, the aim being to gather information about reality in a way that is manageable and suitable in terms of the transformation which will be carried out, where necessary, and which allows the data obtained to be subsequently subjected to quality control and analysis.

Thus, the same recorded session could be recorded using many different types of codes. Although both primary and secondary parameters may be considered we believe the former to be essential for the study of communicative behavior. Here we present them as levels that progressively acquire greater power in terms of data and their progressive order of inclusion [24].

The primary parameters are: frequency, order and duration.

- *Frequency* consists merely in counting behavioral episodes. It is without doubt the weakest parameter, although it has probably been the most widely used.

- *Order* involves describing the sequence of the different behavioral episodes. In addition to information about frequency it also provides information that enables sessions to be distinguished from one another, whereas they may appear to be identical when considering the *frequency* parameter alone.

- *Duration* is the most consistent recording parameter and that which contains the richest information, as it encompasses the *order* parameter and also indicates the number of conventional time units (minutes, seconds, etc.) corresponding to each behavioral episode; this additional information enables sessions which may appear identical when only contemplating the *order* parameter to be distinguished from one another.

Most computerized recording programs take account of these three parameters. If a recording is based on the order parameter, there are various programs, which can be used, for example, the SDIS-GSEQ [31], using the options sequential event data, sequential interval data or sequential multi-event data. In terms of the duration parameter it is useful to distinguish between programs such as SDIS-GSEQ (SDIS module), which records in seconds (for the options sequential state data and sequential event data with time), and *Codex* [59], with respect to the program *ThèmeCoder* [33], which records in frames. Similarly, the program *Match Vision Studio* [34] is able to record in both seconds and frames.

10.4.5 Quantitative analysis on the basis of basic parameters

Traditionally, observational methodology suffered from being used in research lines in which the many different ways of analyzing its data were put to the test. The main reason for this was probably the superficial approach used in obtaining the data or, consequently, their inconsistent nature. However, observational methodology is a particular strategy within the scientific method, which aims to quantify the spontaneous behavior occurring in unprepared situations, and this requires that an ordered series of stages be followed. Its aim is quantification precisely because the mere recording of behavior as a form of data collection in direct observation is, by nature, qualitative. The purpose of the behavioral record in direct observation is to be found in the verification of problems (of description, covariation, causation, sequentiality, etc.) that arise in relation to the behavior of subjects in their habitual context. Clearly, therefore, there are a number of minimum requirements, which must be fulfilled, for example, setting an objective, planning the study in stages, optimizing the data collected and matching the analytic strategy to the objective.

The data analysis used will depend on the proposed observational design [17] and the nature of the data recorded, that is, on the recording parameter chosen. Once the coded recording is available and the data quality is shown to be satisfactory, then the data can be analyzed. Obviously, it is necessary to conduct a qualitative analysis of the recording made. Indeed, the staunchest supporters of qualitative methodology accept no other way of treating information, which they then triangulate and reduce in size before drawing conclusions.

However, this radical approach, under the pretext of capturing the wealth of information, suffers from a serious drawback, namely, the high risk of subjectivity [60]. In an earlier section of this chapter we argued that observational methodology occupies a privileged and unique position that bridges qualitative and quantitative procedures. Indeed, it is possible to capture the wealth of information by means of adequate recording, coding and the development of an *ad hoc* instrument, while at the same time using analytic techniques to ensure maximum rigor is applied in obtaining objective results.

According to their defining characteristics each one of the eight observational designs suggests certain kinds of data analysis, without these being imposed in any restrictive sense [17]. Once again, observational methodology can be seen to be characterized by the duality of flexibility, on the one hand, and precision, on the other. The various ways of analyzing data now available within observational methodology provide a fertile ground within the field of evaluation, and offer a range of alternatives which must be properly chosen and used. However, it should be remembered that almost all data are categorical in nature (with the exception of time, which is continuous), and this constitutes an important limitation. On a purely anecdotal level it is worth noting the somewhat "deceptive" nature of the abovementioned time-series notation, since the technique of analyzing time series is not actually possible due to the categorical nature of such data.

10.5 Epilogue

In this chapter we have sought to offer a dynamic overview of a methodological process whose aim is the objective observation of perceivable communicative behavior. This process will depend on the extent to which it is possible to represent this communicative reality in a recording before systematizing it, coding it and obtaining data, which can be subjected to quality control, thus converting raw into clean data. It is in this sense that observational methodology can be regarded as an attempt to quantify behavior.

10.6 Acknowledgements

The preparation of this chapter has been possible thanks to the funding received through the research project *Analysis of interactive behavior in team sports: Methodological and technological innovations in the process of communication and play action*, being carried out by a team comprising M.T. Anguera Argilaga, A. Blanco Villaseñor, J.L. Losada López, P. Sánchez Algarra, A. Hernández Mendo, A. Ardá Suárez, O. Camerino Foguet, J. Castellano Paulis and G. Jonsson, and awarded by Spain's *Dirección General de Investigación* (DGES) [SEJ2005-01961/PSIC] for the period 2005-2008.

10.7 References

[1]   M. Knapp & G. Miller, *Handbook of Interpersonal Communication*, Beverly Hills, CA, Sage, 1985.
[2]   M. Knapp & J. Daly, *Handbook of Interpersonal Communication* (3rd. ed.), Thousand Oaks, CA, Sage 2002.
[3]   W. Crouch, The nonverbal communication literature: A book review. *Australian Scandinavian, 7-8*, 1-11, 1980.
[4]   J.K. Burgoon & G.D. Hoobler, Nonverbal Signals. In *Handbook of Interpersonal Communication*, Ed. M. Knapp & J. Daly, 3rd. ed., Thousand Oaks, CA, Sage, p. 240-299, 2002.
[5]   J.M. Wiemann & R.P. Harrison, *Nonverbal interaction,* Vol. 11, Sage Annual Reviews of Communication Research, Beverly Hills, Sage, 1983.
[6]   A. Wolfgang, *Nonverbal Behavior. Perspectives, Applications, Intercultural Insights*, 2nd. ed., Göttingen, Hogrefe & Huber, 1997.
[7]   L.K. Guerrero, J.A. DeVito & M.L. Hecht , *The Nonverbal Communication Reader. Classic and Contemporary Readings* (2nd. ed.), Long Grove, Ill., Waveland, 1999.
[8]   A. Bochner, Perspectives on Inquiry: Representation, Conversation, and Reflection. In *Handbook of Interpersonal Communication*, Ed. M. Knapp & G. Miller, Beverly Hills, CA, Sage, p. 27-57, 1985.
[9]   M. Poole & R. McPhee, Methodology in Interpersonal Communication Research, In *Handbook of Interpersonal Communication*, Ed. M. Knapp & G. Miller, Beverly Hills, CA, Sage, p. 100-169, 1985.
[10] J. Gómez Benito, *Los modelos causales como metodología de validez de constructo,* Barcelona, Alamex, 1986.
[11] E. Bott, *Family and social network,* New York, Free Press, 1971.
[12] M.S. Valles, *Técnicas cualitativas de investigación social. Reflexión metodológica y práctica profesional,* Madrid, Síntesis, 1997.
[13] M.T. Anguera, *Hacia una evaluación de la actividad cotidiana y su contexto: ¿Presente o futuro para la metodología?* Lecture of admission to the Reial Acadèmia de Doctors, Barcelona, 1999.
[14] G. Pérez Serrano, *Modelos de Investigación Cualitativa en Educación Social y Animación Sociocultural. Aplicaciones prácticas,* Madrid, Narcea, 2000.
[15] C.A. Denman y J.A. Haro (Comps.), *Por los rincones. Antología de métodos cualitativos en la investigación social*, Sonora, México, El Colegio de Sonora, 2002.
[16] M.T. Anguera, Posición de la metodología observacional en el debate entre las opciones metodológicas cualitativa y cuantitativa. Enfrentamiento, complementariedad, integración. *Psicologia em Revista* (Belo Horizonte, Brasil), *10* (15), 13-27, 2004.
[17] M.T. Anguera, A. Blanco, y J.L. Losada, Diseños observacionales, cuestión clave en el proceso de la metodología observacional. *Metodología de las Ciencias del Comportamiento, 3* (2), 135-160, 2001.
[18] M.T. Anguera, Recogida de datos cualitativos. En *Métodos de investigación en Psicología*, Ed. M.T. Anguera, J. Arnau, M. Ato, M.R. Martínez, J. Pascual y G. Vallejo, Madrid, Síntesis, p. 523-547, 1995a.
[19] R. Bakeman & J.M. Gottman, *Observing interaction. An introduction to sequential analysis,* Cambridge: Cambridge University Press, 1986.
[20] E. Bericat, *La integración de los métodos cuantitativo y cualitativo en la investigación social. Significado y medida,* Barcelona, Ariel, 1998.
[21] F. Alvira, Perspectiva cualitativa - Perspectiva cuantitativa en la metodología sociológica. *Revista Española de Investigaciones Sociológicas*, *22*, 53-75, 1983.
[22] E. Bericat, *Sociología de la movilidad espacial. El sedentarismo nómada*, Madrid, Centro de Investigaciones Sociológicas, 1994.
[23] M.T. Anguera, Del registro narrativo al análisis cuantitativo: Radiografía de la realidad perceptible. *En Ciencia i cultura en el segle XXI. Estudis en homenatge a Josep Casajuana,* Barcelona, Reial Academia de Doctors, p. 41-71, 2000.
[24]   M.T. Anguera y A. Blanco, Registro y codificación en el comportamiento deportivo. En *Psicología del Deporte (Vol. 2). Metodología*, Ed. A. Hernández Mendo, Buenos Aires, Efdeportes (www.efdeportes.com), p. 6-34, 2003.
[25] C. Izquierdo y M.T. Anguera, Propuesta preliminar de un alfabeto morfo-cinésico común en el marco de la metodología observacional: Cuestiones clave y componentes básicos. *Metodología de las Ciencias del Comportamiento, vol. especial,* 305-309, 2002.
[26] H.R. Dickman, The perception of behavioral units. In *The stream of behavior*, Ed.: R. Barker, New York, Appleton-Century-Crofts, p. 23-41, 1963.
[27] R. L. Birdwhistell, *Kinesics and context: Essays and body motion communication,* Philadelphia, University of Pennsylvania Press, 1970.
[28] R.G. Barker & H.F. Wright, *One boy's day,* New York, Harper, 1951.
[29] P. Martin & P. Bateson, *La medición del comportamiento,* Madrid, Alianza Universidad, 1991.

[30] *The Observer [Software]*, Sterling, VA, Noldus Information Technology [*www.noldus.nl*], 1993.
[31] R. Bakeman y V. Quera, *Análisis de la interacción. Análisis secuencial con SDIS-GSEQ*, Madrid, Ra-Ma [*http://www.ub.es/comporta/sg/sg_e_programs.htm*], 1996.
[32] M.D. Lewis, A.V. Lamey & L. Douglas, A new dynamic systems method for the analysis of early socioemotional development. *Developmental Science, 2*, 458-476 [*www.statespacegrids.org*], 1999.
[33] PatternVision, *ThèmeCoder [software]*, Retrieved January 15, 2002 [*http://www.patternvision.com*], 2001.
[34] A. Perea Rodríguez, L. Alday Ezpeleta y J. Castellano Paulis, Software para la observación deportiva Match Vision Studio. *III Congreso Vasco del Deporte. Socialización y Deporte / Kirolaren III Euskal Biltzarra. Sozializazioa era Virola*. Vitoria, 2004.
[35] N. Freedman, Toward a Mathematization of Kinetic Behavior: A Review of Paul Bouissac's "La Mesure de Gestes". In *Nonverbal Communication, Interaction, and Gesture* (Ed.: A. Kendon), The Hague, Mouton, 1981.
[36] N.I. Badler & S.W. Smoliar, Digital representations of human movement. *Computing Survey, 11*, 19-38, 1979.
[37] W. Donaghy, Nonverbal Communication Measurement. In *Measurement of Communication Behavior*, Ed. Ph. Emmert & L. Barker, New York, Longman, p. 296-332, 1989.
[38] S. Frey & J.A. Pool, *A new approach to the analysis of visible behaviour*, Research Reports from the Department Psychology of the University of Berne, 1976.
[39] H.P. Hirsbrunner, S. Frey & R. Crawford, Movement in human interaction: Description, parameter formation, and analysis. In *Nonverbal behavior and communication*, Ed. A.W. Siegman & S. Feldstein, Hillsdale, N.J., Lawrence Erlbaum Associates, p. 99-140, 1987.
[40] C. Izquierdo & M.T. Anguera, The role of the morphokinetic notational system in the observation of movement. En *Oralité et Gestualité. Interactions et comportements multimodaux dans la communication*, Ed. Ch. Cavé, I. Guaïtella et S. Santi, Paris, L'Harmattan, p. 385-389, 2001.
[41] M.T. Anguera, Observational Methods (General). In *Encyclopedia of Psychological Assessment*, Vol. 2, Ed. R. Fernández-Ballesteros, London, Sage, p. 632-637, 2003.
[42] F. Poyatos, New Perspectives in Nonverbal Communication: Studies in Cultural Anthropology, Social Psychology, Linguistics and Literature and Semiotics, Oxford, Pergamon, 1986.
[43] C. Izquierdo y M.T. Anguera, Hacia un alfabeto compartido en la codificación del movimiento corporal en estudios observacionales. *Psicothema, 12* (Supl. N°2), 311-314, 2000.
[44] C. Izquierdo & M.T. Anguera, Reglas sintácticas de articulación de un alfabeto morfocinésico común para la observación y análisis del movimiento. *VII Congreso de Metodología de las Ciencias Sociales y de la Salud*, Valencia, 2003.
[45] A. Hutchinson-Guest, *Dance Notation. The Process of Recording Movement on Paper*, New York, Dance Horizons, 1984.
[46] B. Farnell, Moving Bodies, Acting Selves. *Annual Review Anthropology, 28*, 341-373, 1999.
[47] I. Bartenieff & D. Lewis, *Body Movement: Coping with the Environment*, Amsterdam, Gordon and Breach, 1980.
[48] R. Benesh & J. Benesh, *An Introduction in Benesh Notation*, London, A&C Black, 1956.
[49] N. Eshkol & A. Wachman, *Movement Notation*. Israel: Tel Aviv University, 1958.
[50] P. Ekman & W.V. Friesen, The repertoire of nonverbal behavior: Categories, origins, usage, and coding. *Semiotica, 1*, 124-129, 1969.
[51] E.T. Hall, *The silent language*, Garden City, NY, Anchor Press/Doubleday, 1973.
[52] A. Mehrabian, *Public places and private spaces*, New York, Basic Books, 1976.
[53] M.L. Knapp, *Social intercourse: From greeting to goodbye*, Boston: Allyn & Bacon, 1978.
[54] N. Chomsky, *Syntactic Structures*, The Hague, Mouton, 1956.
[55] N. Chomsky, *Aspects of the Theory of Syntax*, Cambridge, The MIT, 1965.
[56] S. Frey, U. Jorns & W. Daw, A systematic description and analysis of nonverbal interaction between doctors and patients in a psychiatric interview. In *Ethology & nonverbal communication in mental health. An interdisciplinary biopsychosocial exploration*, Ed. S.A. Corson & E.O. Corson, p. 231-258, 1980.
[57] S. Frey, H.P. Hirsbrunner, A. Florin, W. Daw & R. Crawford, A unified approach to the investigation of nonverbal and verbal behaviour in communication research. In *Current Issues in European Social Psychology*, Ed. W. Doise & S. Moscovici, Cambridge, England, Cambridge University Press, 1983.
[58] T. Thompson, D. Felce & F.J. Symons, *Behavioral Observation. Technology and applications in developmental disabilities*, Baltimore, Paul H. Brookes Publishing, 2000.
[59] A. Hernández-Mendo, M.T. Anguera & M.A. Bermúdez, Software for recording observational files. *Behavior Research Methods, Instruments & Computers, 32* (3), 436-445, 2000.
[60] M.T. Anguera, Metodología cualitativa. En *Métodos de investigación en Psicología* Ed. M.T. Anguera, J. Arnau, M. Ato, M.R. Martínez, J. Pascual y G. Vallejo), Madrid, Síntesis, p. 513-522, 1995b.

From Communication to Presence
G. Riva et al. (Eds.)
IOS Press, 2006

11 Multimodal Temporal Patterns for the Analysis of User's Involvement in Affective Interaction with Virtual Agents

Alessia AGLIATI, Fabrizia MANTOVANI, Olivia REALDON,
Linda CONFALONIERI, Antonietta VESCOVO

Abstract. Given the growing interest in developing embodied virtual agents
with multimodal communication and emotional expression abilities, the issue of
user's involvement is a relevant topic to take into account in determining how
to assess and interpret the quality of user-agent affective interaction. Main goal
of this paper is the definition of a methodology for the analysis of user-agent
interaction synchrony considered as an index of user's involvement. The
proposed approach is based on recent advances in communication psychology,
which on the one hand show the importance of considering the hidden temporal
organization underlying communicative interaction and on the other hand
provide a specific methodology for the structural analysis of the interactive flow
(analysis of intra- and inter-individual multimodal behavioral patterns through
Theme software). From a theoretical point of view, the crucial assumption is
that the more synchronic interactions are, the more pleasant and fulfilling they
are experienced, and consequently more related to positively valenced
emotional states. Our main objective is to tune and to test this methodology
(typically used in analyzing human-human communication exchanges) within
user-agent interaction, in order to detect interactive temporal patterns of actions
in affective interactions with virtual agents. This approach has been developed
within the European project MYSELF, where we are a preliminary evaluation
study of an interactive pedagogical agent by combining self-report measures,
physiological measures and multimodal behavioral patterns approach is being
carried out.

Contents

11.1 Introduction

The challenge of developing virtual agents meant to be engaged as social interactive conversational partners within communicative exchanges with humans is currently being addressed with considerable empirical and theoretical efforts in the HCI field [1, 2, 3].

Communicative exchanges are the framework within which interpersonal relationships are generated and fostered, hence granting interaction sequences with predictability and regularity [4]. At the same time, the shaping of interpersonal relationships is due to emotions that, as situated practices occurring through repeated interactions [5], give sense, direct and modify the relationship patterns. As such, emotions grow up, are redefined and modified within relationships, while relationships provide the context for the generation of emotions and their management. Within this perspective, emotions, being eventually rooted in interactions, should not be seen as involuntary intra-personal events, but, rather, as resulting from personal choices and options, that become manifest within the communication flow. Within the spatial and temporal boundaries of interactive communicative exchanges, emotions, more often than thoughts and intentions, tend to be expressed, mainly by non verbal extra-linguistic systems (like facial expressions, gestures, posture, etc.). As widely agreed in literature, emotion expression and management is mainly performed via non verbal signaling systems, that, in the relationship-building process tend to be synchronically shaped and tuned in order to attain the desired goal [6, 7].

Within this theoretical framework, the evaluation of affective interactions with virtual agents begs the relevant issue regarding how and at which degree multimodal agent's and user's expressions reciprocally match in a synchronic way.

Basically, the crucial assumption is that, the more synchronic interactions are, the more pleasant and fulfilling they are experienced, and consequently more related to positively valenced emotional states. Therefore it is reasonable to suppose that, on the one hand, positively valenced emotions contribute in shaping and maintaining functionally adaptive relationships, and on the other hand, complex synchronic interactions, featured by coordinated interpersonal timing, are related to more adaptive relationships, at least in terms of attachment security [8, 9].

Given these premises, this contribution mainly aims at introducing a pioneering evaluation method of human-agent interaction quality, by detecting interactive multimodal temporal patterns of actions occurring within user-agent affective interactions. To reach this goal, recent contributions in developing multimodal embodied conversational agents will be introduced. Then, starting from the premise about multimodality expression abilities as an essential requisite for both interactants in order to eventually converge in their communication styles, theoretical perspectives connecting interaction synchrony with positively valenced interpersonal relationships will be discussed, presenting tentative researches conducted on this theme within user-agents interactions.

After that, a methodology for detecting the degree in quality (as resulting from different signaling systems) and quantity (i.e., frequencies) of co-occurring patterns of action, considered as valid indexes of interaction synchrony, will be proposed. Finally, a preliminary study aimed at evaluating user-agent affective interactions by employing this methodology will be briefly presented.

11.2 Embodied Virtual Agents Devised to Participate in Communicative Interactions with Users

When conceived as communicative partners, embodied virtual agents need to be equipped with multimodal expressive abilities. As, among others, Anolli [4] pointed out, besides language, there are several other communicational devices to show interactants' own communicative design, like the paralinguistic (or supra-segmental), the face and gestures system, the gaze, the proxemic and the haptic, as well as the chronemic. Each of these communicative systems bears its contribution and participates in defining the meaning of a communicative act in an autonomous way. Therefore, meaning is not connected with a unique and exclusive signaling system, but comes out of the network of semantic and pragmatic connections between different signaling systems (multimodal configurations). Such semantic and pragmatic connections are organized, coordinated and made convergent, in communicative exchanges, according to the principle of semantic synchrony, which enables interlocutors to make explicit the meaning of their own communicative intentions in a unitary and coherent way [10].

Along this theoretical line, research trends on Embodied Conversational Agents (ECAs) [11], focusing specifically on communicative and conversational agents, concern the development of humanoid software agents that use speech, gaze, gesture, intonation and other signalling systems in the way humans use them in the communication process [12, 13].

The assumption of this perspective can be considered as one of the most relevant turning points in the development of embodied virtual agents. Indeed, in the early nineties, the challenge in this domain of study was focused basically on agents' appearance. More specifically, establishing and defining the agents' visual physical appearance in terms of anthropomorphism and human-likeness basically represented the main rationale in agents' design and development [14-16].

From the late nineties, studies on agents' embodiment and animation have started taking into account the agent being featured and acting as an interlocutor and a conversational partner, engaged and participating in a communicative interaction [12], animated in order to use different signalling systems [1, 17, 18].

Considerable efforts are being spent on this issue, with interesting and convergent findings from the several research groups addressing it. De Rosis and colleagues proposed a research project aimed at implementing Greta, a 3D Embodied agent that can be animated in real-time, able to coherently communicate complex information through the combination and the tight synchronization of verbal and nonverbal signals [19]. Consistent with the issue of multimodal animation, Cosi and colleagues proposed Lucia, an Italian talking head based on a modified Cohen-Massaro's Model [20]. Likewise, within the MIT group [13, 21], virtual agents named LAURA (a physical trainer) and REA (a salesperson) were developed, with the aim of supplying them with a wide range of conversational affordances, including the synchronic use of hand gestures, body posture, eye gaze, and facial expressions, to act as believable partners in communicative interactions.

11.3 Bridging Multimodality and Interaction Synchrony within Affective Interactions

11.3.1 Theoretical Perspectives

Although agents' multimodal expression abilities are recognized as a basic requisite in developing virtual agents, the issue connected with their synchronizing ability and the role such ability plays in affective interactions and in establishing and maintaining positively valenced relationships still need to be addressed in order to provide the development of agents' architecture with a robust theoretical backbone and to gather a valid frame for their evaluation.

Within human face-to-face interactions, people naturally tend to synchronize their rhythms of speech and body movements: many biological processes are known to be cyclical or rhythmical in nature and to be driven by the central nervous system, and there is evidence to suggest that human interactions have rhythms as well [22]. Such a rhythm has to do, and develops over time, within communicators' reciprocal matching and convergence in the way they shape their verbal and non verbal communication. In other words, people tend to converge their communication style (encompassing vocal features and non verbal behavior) towards the style used by the listener, even exhibiting exactly the same behaviors (*mirroring phenomenon*). From this perspective, rhythm and synchrony in the communicative interaction can be seen as powerful indexes of participation, agreement and closeness between interactants, showing that one is "with" his/her interlocutor in his/her attention and expectancies [23]. Moreover, according to the Accommodation Theory [24, 25], synchrony reflects *reciprocity,* since it meets the underlying psychological need to evoke listeners' social approval, to attain communication efficacy and to maintain positive social identities. Consistent with this point of view, results in recent researches exploring the relationship between interaction synchrony and initial attraction in first-met couples, showed that a higher degree in interaction synchrony was more strongly connected with participants' interest in their partner in the first minute than in last minute of their interaction [26].

These findings support the idea that interaction synchrony as resulting in complex co-occurring multimodal patterns of action (thus showing a more robust convergence in communication styles) can be viewed as valid and accurate indexes of perceived closeness, reciprocity and more positively valenced relationships. As such, interaction synchrony can be considered as a way of shaping interactions, which varies along the communicative flow as a function of reciprocal participation and involvement, hence placing a suitable frame for sharing positive affect.

Indeed, in turn, emotions are viewed as a communicatively structured, convention-based and rule-governed process [6, 7, 27], that are originated in, and give sense to one's patterns of relationships. As such, they can be thought of as embodied practises through which people build and organize interactions in their life worlds. According to Goodwin [5], emotions are situated practices within specific sequential positions in interaction, whose relevant unit for analysis is not the individual, but the sequential organization of action in interaction.

11.3.2 Tentative applications to human-artificial agents interactions

Starting from these theoretical perspectives, it is likely to assume that fulfilling and satisfying user-agent relationships are related to high degree in interaction synchrony between user and agent.

A tentative application of these concepts to human-computer interaction has recently been proposed by Bailenson and Nick [28]. In their study, assuming the theoretical paradigm of the *chameleon effect* [29], participants interacted with a virtual agent in an immersive virtual reality environment. The agent either mimicked the participant's head movements at 4-s delay or utilized pre-recorded movements of another participant as it verbally presented an argument. Mimicking agents were perceived as more persuasive and received more positive trait ratings that nonmimickers, despite participant's inability to explicitly detect the mimicry.

Moreover, research trends on *humanoid robots* [30, 31, 32] seem to follow the same pathway, highlighting how (as well as in human-human interactions) mutual coordination between human's and robot's body movements is a valuable key aspect to warrant compelling smoothness and naturalness in the communication exchange. Empirical results by Sakamoto and colleagues [31, 33] showed that such cooperative body movements as eye-contact and synchronized arm movements mutually related to a more positive user's subjective evaluation of the robot.

In sum, the effectiveness in synthonically and synchronically using bodily expressions and movements, as well as other communicative signalling systems, represents the added value in producing compelling human-like bonding between humans and artificial agents, be they Embodied Conversational Agents or robots.

11.4 A Methodology for Evaluating the Quality of User-agent Interaction

This methodology roots in the same theoretical premises but is aimed to demonstrate that user's tendency to synchronize and in case even mimic the agent is per se a signal of involvement in the interaction with him/her.

Consequently, the proposed method to assess the user's involvement in interaction with a virtual agent, may provide fruitful advances in this field by measuring interaction synchrony. In particular, a structural analysis of interaction aimed at hidden temporal organization detection should be integrated with a detailed qualitative analysis of visible behaviors. The methodology below describe meets this requirement, since it is observational in nature and aims at interactive multimodal patterns detecting, using Theme software [34, 35].

11.4.1 The Theme Method

11.4.1.1 General Description

Theme software is a tool for the detection and analysis of patterns in time-based data. It detects relationships that human observers typically overlook, and that are not commonly found by means of traditional statistical methods. Theme uses a unique pattern detection algorithm that has especially been designed for behavioral research. It gives insight into the structure of behavior in time, and gives measures for its complexity and organization.

The main assumption of this method is that behaviors are made of multimodal temporal patterns (*T-patterns*), which are sequences of behaviors regularly recurring within a certain temporal period [36]. Given the link between synchrony and positive affect in interactions, it is likely to expect that detected temporal patterns indicate the user involvement in the ongoing interaction with the agent.

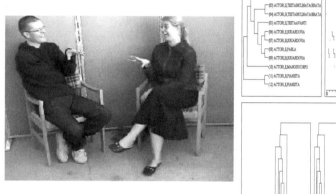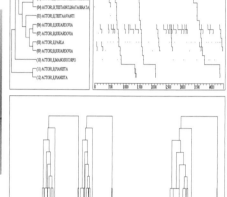

Figure 1. *This* figure includes a picture and a T-pattern of a dyadic interaction between two Icelandic participants. The picture on the left presents the "pianist" gesture displayed only by Icelandic subjects. The T-patterns show the different use of turnover displayed by Italians and Icelanders. The T-pattern on the right refers to an Icelandic interaction between friends, it includes twelve events ((1) *subjectB, e, turn*; (2) *subjectA, b, turn*; (3) subjectA, b, tilt head; (4) subjectA, e, tilt head; (5) subjectA, b, head forward; (6) subjectA, e, look away; (7) subjectB, b, look away; (8) subjectA, e, turn; (9) subjectB, b, look away; (10) subjectA, e, hand on body; (11) subjectA, b, pianist; (12) subjectA, e, pianist), and it recurs three times in the same observation period.

Theme application to studies on emotion and communication is turning out to be heuristically useful and powerful. Applicative opportunities encompass several kinds of face-to-face interactions: from conversation in cross-cultural perspective [22, 34] to adult-children emotion communication [37], to friendship [38] and courtship interactions [39], to clinical married couples exchanges [40] and siblings. Results, in such studies, give evidence to the idea that a higher degree in interaction synchrony is related to the perception of closeness and bonding between interactants.

Examples of T-patterns are illustrated in Figure 1. T-pattern on the left was detected from a dyadic interaction between Italian friends, whilst T-pattern on the right was detected from a dyadic interaction between Icelandic friends. Results drawn from this study suggested a relationship between interaction synchrony and culture [41, 42].

11.4.1.2 The Theme Procedure

The Theme procedure entails two main steps: first, coding individual's behaviors following a grid; second, detecting multimodal temporal patterns.

11.4.1.2.1 Coding Behavior

So far, non verbal behavior only has been coded and analyzed using Theme. However, considerable efforts are being spent in analyzing behavioral patterns related to verbal productions by means of Theme, since the quality of interaction is closely linked also to speech production [40, 43].

To code participants' facial and body movements, a grid has to be developed. Behavior units, divided in categories, have to be mapped into the grid. Facial expressions, gaze and head orientation, trunk and shoulders, arms and hands, self-contact, turn-taking are usually included in the grid and coded. Behaviors included in the grid are identified by using specific action units (AU) defined by Facial Action Coding System [44] for upper face, lower face, gaze and head orientation. Other behavior units for hands, arms, trunk and shoulders movements and self-contact are usually taken from grids used in previous studies on nonverbal behavior [39, 41, 45].

Category	Behavior units
Hands	rotation, hand contact, crossed hands, hand on face, hand on body, hand on chair, hand on hair, palm inward, palm forward, palm down, palm upward, palm back, palm outside, fist, bag-hand, mirror-hands, rubbing hands, ax-hand, hitchhiking, ring, hands away, ball-hands
Fingers	pointing, counting, negation, pianist
Arms	arms upward, crossed arms, arm forward, open arms, dangling arms, arms back, bend arms
Head	head forward, head down, head back, tilt head l/r, tilt head up/down, negation by head
Trunk	trunk forward, tilt trunk l/r, trunk back, swinging
Face	AU 6 + AU 12 + AU 26; AU 6 + AU 12 + AU 27
Gaze	avert gaze
Shoulders	shoulders shrug
Turn	Speak

Table 1. Example of grid. Fifty behavior in nine categories.

11.4.1.2.2 Detecting Multimodal Temporal Patterns

The occurrences of all event-types within the observation period herein taken into account constitute the so-called *T-data* (or T-dataset) which is the input to the T-pattern detection algorithm. T-pattern algorithm has been implemented in a specialized software package, called Theme, [34, 35] (http://www.patternvision.com and http://www.noldus.com). A T-pattern is essentially a combination of such event-types occurring in the same order with the time distances between consecutive pattern components remaining *relatively* invariant (that is, the time difference between A and B will be $x \pm y$). To be detected a T-pattern should recur at least three times (minimal occurrence) within the observation period.

A schematic representation of a T-pattern is shown in Figure 2. Especially, the letters in the upper line correspond to specific event-type appearing in proportion to the time of their occurrence. Thus, the line 1 is the visual representation of the temporal sequence of movements shown by a given subject during his/her interaction with the other interactant. Within the upper line, a sequence of four event-types – *A, B, C*, and *D* – recurs but it is masked by the occurrence of two other event-types, *W* and *K*. Even a highly expert human observer by visually inspecting the data string would most unlikely be able to detect any kind of pattern. On the contrary, a T-pattern analysis allows to identify the repeated pattern *A, B, C*, and *D* because of its consistent temporal structure. The T-pattern detection algorithm enables an analyst to discover repeated temporal patterns, even when various other event-types occur between the components of the pattern itself, masking its detection at a naked eye.

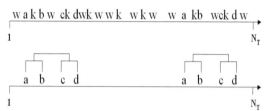

Figure 2. Example of repeated T-pattern

The pattern in Figure 2 illustrates how a larger pattern ((AB) (CD)) is detected as a combination of the two simpler patterns (AB) and (CD). Even in moderate data sets, the number of potential T-patterns is very high. For instance, when the potential number of event-types is 100, the number of potential patterns involving up to 10 event-types is many orders of magnitude greater than 100^{10} if all possible time windows are also considered. Even for supercomputers, it becomes an impossible task to search for each possible temporal pattern separately.

To deal with this issue, simple patterns are detected first – that is, identifying relationships between two event-types such as the (*AB*) or (*CD*) relationship in Figure 2 – while more complex patterns are detected as patterns of patterns (a so called "bottom-up" search strategy). The simpler patterns (*AB*) and (*CD*) are detected first and, then, the larger pattern (*(A B)(C D)*) as a combination of these. The new larger pattern may then become a part of even more complex patterns as it combines with other simple or complex patterns.

A further phase of the T-pattern detection deals with completeness competition between all the detected patterns. In this phase, those patterns that are less complete versions of one or more alternate patterns are deleted. As a matter of fact, during the detection process, a pattern $P_X = (ABCDE)$ may be partially detected as, for instance, (*ACDE*) or (*BDE*) or (*ABCE*). Since components of P_X are missing, these three patterns constitute less complete description of the underlying patterning, and consequently they are eliminated. This completeness competition ensures that only the most complete patterns survive and constitute the outcome of the detection process [47].

11.4.1.3 The Theme Output

Using Theme, three kinds of data should be obtained, indicating interaction synchrony. In particular, the first two kinds of data, *pattern number and complexity* outputs, reveal the hidden temporal organization of interaction. The third output (Event-Types in Raw Data) has to do with the type of behavior exhibited by each actor during their interaction.

Number of interactive patterns. In each observed interaction, it is possible to detect N. different interactive patterns including both actors' behaviors: interactive patterns imply that both the actors jointly contribute to their combination. Number of patterns is used as an indicator of interaction synchrony: higher number of patterns implies a higher number of co-occurring sequences of behaviors within the observational period. Thus, higher number of patterns means a higher interaction synchrony.

Pattern complexity. It refers to the number of event-types included in each pattern. Each observation period is defined by the average of patterns complexity usually exploited as a further indicator of interaction synchrony, since it indicates that synchrony occurs on different verbal and non-verbal systems of communication.

Event types in raw data. It refers to the proportional occurrences (%) of a given event-type recorded in the observation period. Each of these data are represented in Figure 3.

A further kind of data should be obtained using Theme, by means of a qualitative approach, allowing to measure *mirroring phenomenon* [24]. Within each interactive pattern it is possible to identify identical behaviors simultaneously exhibited by both the actors. For instance, Icelandic friends showed in the right picture of figure 1 simultaneously exhibit the hand-gesture called *"pianist"*. The number of these behaviors integrate quantitative data on interaction synchrony.

11.4.2 Using Theme in Human-computer Interaction Analysis

Given the methodological framework above advanced, and considering that a higher degree of interpersonal interaction's synchrony tightly links to the experienced quality of relationship in interacting with virtual agents as well as with humans, some advantages should be pointed in using Theme for evaluating the quality of human-agent interaction.

The first benefit is its quantitative and qualitative integrated approach to the analysis of interactions. Whilst the quantitative approach is aimed at detecting the hidden temporal structure of interaction, the qualitative one makes possible the analysis of visible behaviors and gives a measure of mirroring. In such way, user's involvement in interaction with an agent may be evaluated throughout a structural measure (interactive patterns) that reveals his tendency to synchronize to the agent's movements. A qualitative measure (mirroring) of user-agent interaction may be provided as well, indicating the user's tendency to mimicry agent's movements.

Quantitative and qualitative measures of emotional involvement may be fruitfully integrated with subjective measures (self-report questionnaires) and physiological measurement (changes in subject's heart rate, skin temperature, skin conductance, respiration rate, etc.) provided by other existing approaches in evaluating the quality of human-computer interaction, [48, 49, 50].

A further strength of this method is its lack of intrusion for users, avoiding risks of users' discomfort and inhibition related to survey-devices application. A video-camera and a webcam for virtual agent's and users' movements and facial expressions recording are only required.

Moreover, the collecting data session is simultaneous with the user-agent interaction: it makes possible the replication of the procedure on a significant number of subjects (forty at least), allowing proper statistical analysis. Obviously, observed behaviors are coded and analyzed post-session from videotapes.

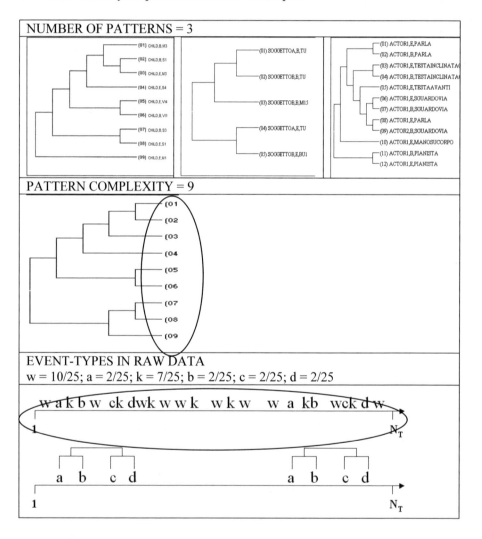

Figure 3. Pattern number, pattern complexity and event-types in raw data are shown with graphical example.(N Event-Types = 25)

11.5   User-Linda Agent Interaction Analysis Through Theme: a Preliminary Study

A first application of the Theme method in human-computer interaction analysis has been developed within the European project MYSELF - "*Multimodal e*-learning System based on *Simulations*, Role-Playing, Automatic Coaching and Voice Recognition interaction for Affective Profiling" (http://www.myself-proj.it) [51, 52], where a preliminary evaluation study of an interactive pedagogical agent is being carrying out, by combining self-report questionnaires, physiological measures and analysis of multimodal behavioral temporal patterns (synchrony and accommodation). The study basically aims at investigating user-agent interaction quality, within a learning environment involving an animated pedagogical agent called 'Linda'. Agent's multimodal expressivity and treatment of users' expectations' on the forthcoming interaction were considered as main factors.

Taking into account the agent's multimodal expressivity as independent variable, participants were randomly assigned to two different conditions, operationalized as follows: *(a₁)* agent with high multimodal expressive animation ('Linda' agent with voice, blink, lip movements, smile, eyebrow raise, head movements); *(a₂)* agent with limited multimodal expressive animation ('Linda' agent with voice, blink and lip movements). The main hypothesis under investigation is that the occurrence and the complexity of interactive patterns will be greater in the condition of 'Linda' agent with high multimodal expressive animation. Both virtual agent's and user's behavior was observed, coded and analysed using Theme software.

Even though further specific data analyses have to be carried out, first results show that participants tend to enact more synchronized behavioral patterns when interacting with 'Linda' agent with high multimodal expressive animation, compared to the condition of 'Linda' agent with limited multimodal expressive animation (see Figure 4). Thus, the occurrence of a higher degree of interaction synchrony between user and agent along the whole interactive flow, indicates that users seem to naturally experience greater participation and involvement within the interaction and higher relational closeness to agents with high multimodal expressive animation.

This trend of results is consistently corroborated by self-report measures indicating that participants clearly reported more fulfilling and positively valenced experience in condition of interaction with highly multimodal expressive agent.

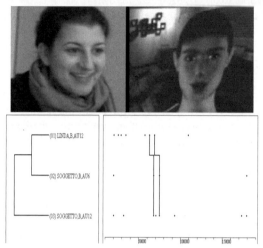

Figure 4. Example of synchronized behavioral patterns of a user interacting with 'Linda' agent with high multimodal expressive animation

11.6 Conclusions

Tuning and employing the Theme method to evaluate user-agent interaction does entail a substantial change in the perspective of the evaluation process itself: not only a rigorous device and a procedure for the detection of patterns of interaction is advanced, but also a radically different view on how to segment and define the phenomenon to be evaluated is proposed.

Indeed, the minimal unit of analysis is identified in interaction, hence entailing that the object to be observed and explored is not the outcome of contingent though frequent connections between two isolated individuals (user and agent), but is social in its nature, since the communicative process is intrinsically social in itself. Moreover, not only does communication require at least two interlocutors to be generated and performed, but also requires participation [53], as a necessary condition for both interactants to define the relationship between them.

Given that relationships-building processes via communication exchanges substantially affect emotions and the perceived valence of the quality of the interaction, the Theme method reveals itself as a fruitful option in evaluating human-agent interaction, by providing valid indexes of the affective quality of the interaction itself. Therefore, Theme represents the affordance for a valuable connection between cutting edge research trends in communication psychology and current technological advances.

11.7 References

[1]   J. Cassell, J. Sullivan, S. Prevost and E. Churchill, Embodied Conversational Agents. The MIT Press, Cambridge, MA, 2000.
[2]   J.N. Bailenson, J. Blascovich, A.C. Beall and J.M. Loomis, Interpersonal Distance in Immersive Virtual Environments. In Personality and Social Psychology Bulletin, 2003.
[3]   L. Schilbach, A.M. Wohlschlaeger, N.C. Kraemer, A. Newen, N.J. Shah, G.R. Fink, and K. Vogeley, Being with virtual others: Neural correlates of social interaction. Neuropsychologia, (2006), 44, 718-730.
[4]   L. Anolli, The Detection of the Hidden design of Meaning. In: L. Anolli, S. Duncan, M.S. Magnusson, G. Riva, Eds. The Hidden Structure of Interaction, 23-50. IOS Press, Amsterdam, 2005.

[5] M.H. Goodwin and C. Goodwin, Emotion within Situated Activity. In: Linguistic Anthropology: A Reader, Blackwell Press, Oxford. 239-253, 2000.
[6] L. Anolli, Psicologia della Cultura [Psychology of Culture]. Il Mulino, Bologna, 2004.
[7] A. Fridlund, Human Facial Expression. An Evolutionary View. Academic Press, San Diego, 1994.
[8] A.A. Hane, S. Feldstein and V.H. Dernetz, The Relation Between Coordinated Interpersonal Timing and Maternal Sensitivity in Four-Month-Old. Journal of Psycholinguistic Research, (2003), 32, 5.
[9] R.A. Isabella and J. Belsky, Interactional synchrony and the origins of infant-mother attachment: A replication study. Child Development, (1991), 62, 373-384.
[10] L. Anolli, Psicologia della Comunicazione [Communication Psychology]. Il Mulino, Bologna, 2006.
[11] C. Pelachaud and I. Poggi, Multimodal Embodied Agents. In: C. Pelachaud e I. Poggi, Eds. Multimodal Communication and Context in Embodied Agents. Proceedings of the Workshop W7 at the 5th International Conference on Autonomous Agents, Montreal, Canada 95-101, 2001.
[12] J. Cassell, More than just another pretty face: Embodied Conversational Agents. Communication of the ACM, (2000), 43, 4, 70-78.
[13] J. Cassell, T. Bickmore, L. Campbell, H. Viljailmsson and H. Yan, More than just a pretty face: Conversational protocols and the affordances of embodiment. Knowledge- Based System, (2001), 14, 55-64.
[14] J. Bates, The role of emotion in believable agents. Communications of the ACM, (1994), 37, 7, 122-125.
[15] T.J., Norman, Motivated Goal and Action Selection. In: Working Notes: AISB workshop, Models or Behaviors-Which Way Forward for Robotics?. University College London, Department of Computer Science research note 94/32, 1994.
[16] T.J. Norman, N.R. Jennings, P. Faratin and E.H. Mamdani, Designing and implementing a multi-agent architecture for business process management . In: J.P. Müller, M.J. Wooldridge, N.R. Jennings, Eds. Intelligent Agents III: Proceedings of the Third International Workshop on Agent Theories, Architectures, and Languages, Vol. 1193 of Lecture Notes in Artificial Intelligence, Springer Verlag, 261-275, 1997.
[17] D.N. Chorafas, Agent technology handbook. Mc Graw Hill, New York, 1997.
[18] S. Franklin, Autonomous Agents as Embodied AI. Cybernetics and Systems, special issue on Epistemological Issues in Embodied AI, (1997), 28, 499-520.
[19] F. De Rosis, C. Pelachaud, I. Poggi, V. Carofiglio and B. De Carolis, From Greta's mind to her face: modelling the dynamics of affective states in a conversational Embodied Agent. International Journal of Human-Computer Studies, (2003), 59, 81-118.
[20] P. Cosi, A. Fusaro and G. Tisato, Lucia: A new Italian talking head based on a modified Cohen-Massaro's Labial Coarticulation Model. Proceedings of EuropeSpeech 2003, Geneva, Switzerland, 3, 2269-2272, 2003.,
[21] T. Bickmore and R.W. Picard, Towards Caring Machines. Conference on Human Factors in Computing Systems, 2004.
[22] L. Anolli, S. Duncan, M.S. Magnusson and G. Riva, The Hidden Structure of Interaction. Amsterdam, IOS Press, 2005.
[23] A. Kendon, Movement coordination in social interaction: Some examples described. Acta Psychologica, (1970), 32, 1-25,
[24] H. Giles, N. Coupland and J. Coupland, Accommodation Theory: communication, context and consequence. In: H. Giles, N. Coupland & J. Coupland, Eds. Contexts of Accommodation, 1-68. Cambridge University Press, Cambridge, 1991.
[25] R.L. Street Jr. and D. Buller, Patients' characteristics affecting physician- patient nonverbal communication. Human Communication Research, (1988), 15, 60-90.
[26] K. Sakaguchi, G.K. Jonsson and T. Hasegawa, Initial interpersonal attraction and movement synchrony in mixed-sex dyads. In: L. Anolli, S. Duncan, M.S. Magnusson, G. Riva, Eds. The Hidden Structure of Interaction, IOS Press, Amsterdam, 107-122, 2005.
[27] J.M. Fernández-Dols, F. Sánchez, P. Carrera and M.A. Ruiz Belda, What are the spontaneous expressions of basic emotions? New views on old questions. Journal of Nonverbal Behavior, (1997), 21, 3, 163-177,
[28] J.N. Bailenson and Y. Nick, Automatic assimilation of nonverbal gestures in immersive virtual environment. Psychological Science, (2005), 16,10, 814-819.
[29] T.L. Chartrand and J.A. Bargh, The chameleon effect: The perception-behavior link and social interaction. Journal of Personality and Social Psychology, (1999), 76. 893-910.
[30] K. Hirai, M. Hirose, Y. Haikawa and T. Takenaka, The development of HONDA humanoid robot. Proceedings of the IEEE INt. Conf. on Robotics and Automation, 1321-1326, 1998.

[31] T. Kanda, H. Ishiguro, M. Imai and R. Nakatsu, Development and evaluation of an interactive humanoid robot "Robovie". IEEE International Conference on Robotics and Automation, 1848-1855, 2002.

[32] T. Ono, M. Imai and H. Ishiguro, A model of embodied communication with gestures between humans and robots. Proceedings of the Twenty-third Annual Meeting of the Cognitive Science Society, 8, 732-737, 2001.

[33] D. Sakamoto, T. Kanda, T. Ono, M. Kamashima, M. Imai and I. Hiroshii, Cooperative embodied communication emerged by interactive humanoid robots. Human-Computer Studies, 2005, 62, 247-265.

[34] M.S. Magnusson, Modelling complex real-time behavioral streams as optimised sub-sets of mutually exclusive and nested T-patterns. In: Measuring Behavior 2000. Proceedings of the 3rd International Conference on Methods and Techniques in Behavioral Research (15-18) August 2000. Nijmegen, The Netherlands, 2000.

[35] M.S. Magnusson, Understanding social interaction: Discovering hidden structure with model and algorithms. In: L. Anolli, S. Duncan, M.S. Magnusson & G. Riva, Eds. The Hidden Structure of Interaction, IOS Press, Amsterdam, 3-22, 2005.

[36] I. Eibl-Eibesfeldt, Ethology: The biology of behavior. Rinehart & Winston, New York, 1970.

[37] A. Agliati, L. Anolli and G.K. Jonsson, Time patterns of emotional Communication in children. Measuring Behavior 2002. Proceedings of the 4th International Conference on Methods and Tecniques in Behavioral research. Noldus Infomation Technology, Amsterdam, 2002.

[38] G.K. Jonsson, Self-Esteem, friendship and verbal and non verbal interaction, 1996. On-line: http://www.hi.is/~msm/poster1996gkj.htm .

[39] K. Grammer, K. B. Kruck and M.S. Magnusson, The courtship dance: patterns of nonverbal synchronization in opposite- sex encounters. Journal of Nonverbal Behavior, (1998), 22, 3-29.

[40] L. Pullini, Communication and discommunication in married couples: interactive nonverbal behavior and temporal structure analysis. Unpublished doctoral dissertation, Catholic University, Milan, 2006.

[41] A. Agliati, A. Vescovo and L. Anolli, Conversation patterns in Icelandic and Italian people: Similarities and differences in rhythm and accommodation. In: L. Anolli, S. Duncan, M.S. Magnusson & G. Riva, Eds. The Hidden Structure of Interaction, IOS Press, Amsterdam, 210-223, 2005.

[42] A. Agliati, A. Vescovo and L. Anolli, A new methodological approach to nonverbal behavior analysis in cultural perspective. Behavior Research Method, (in press).

[43] A. Blanchet, M. Batt, A. Trognon and L. Mass, Language and behavior patterns in a therapeutic interaction sequence. In L. Anolli, S. Duncan, M.S. Magnusson, G. Riva, Eds. The Hidden Structure of Interaction, IOS Press, Amsterdam, 210-223, 2005.

[44] P. Ekman and W.V. Friesen, Manual for Facial Action Coding System. Consulting Psychology Press, Palo Alto, CA, 1978.

[45] D. Morris, Human and his gestures (L'uomo e i suoi gesti). Arnoldo Mondatori, Milano, 1990.

[46] W.C. McGrew, An ethological study of children's behavior. Academic Press, New York, 1972.

[47] A. Borrie, G.K. Jonsson and M.S. Magnusson, Temporal pattern analysis and its applicability in sport: an explanation and preliminary data. Journal of Sport Science, (2002), 20, 845-852.

[48] K. Hook, K. Isbister and J. Laaksolhati, Sensual evaluation instrument. Proceedings of CHI 2005 Conference. Workshop on "Evaluating Affective Interfaces", 2005.

[49] R.W. Picard and S.B. Daily, Evaluating affective interactions: Alternative to asking what users feel. Proceedings of CHI 2005 Conference. Workshop on "Evaluating Affective Interfaces", 2005.

[50] R.L. Mandryk, Evaluating Affective Environments Using Physiological Measures. Proceedings of CHI 2005 Conference. Workshop on "Evaluating Affective Interfaces", 2005.

[51] L. Anolli, F. Mantovani, M. Balestra, A. Agliati, O. Realdon, V. Zurloni, M. Mortillaro, A. Vescovo and L. Confalonieri, The Potential of Affective Computing in E-Learning: MYSELF project experience. Proceedings of INTERACT 2005 Conference - Workshop on "eLearning and Human-Computer Interaction: Exploring Design Synergies for more Effective Learning Experiences". Rome, 12-15 september 2005.

[52] L. Anolli, F. Mantovani, M. Mortillaro, A. Vescovo, A. Agliati, L. Confalonieri, O. Realdon, V. Zurloni and A. Sacchi, A Multimodal Database as a Background for Emotional Synthesis, Recognition and Training in E-Learning Systems. In: J. Tao, T. Tan, R. Picard, Eds. Affective Computing and Intelligent Interaction, Lecture Notes in Computer Science, Springer Verlag, Berlin, 567-573, 2005.

[53] A. Duranti, Linguistic anthropology. Cambridge: University Press, Cambridge, 1997.

SECTION IV

COMMUNICATION AND PRESENCE IN PRACTICE: LEISURE, THERAPY AND LEARNING

When people communicate, they have to adapt their interaction styles to one another, matching and synchronizing their behavior.
The notion of interactive co-ordination and mutual adaptation in communication covers a broad range of processes, such as synchrony, mirroring, matching, reciprocity, compensation, convergence as well as divergence.
In our perspective we collect all these processes under the label of communicative synchrony as a global and basic property of communication, that has been developing since birth in newborn babies through the interaction system with their caregivers.

Anolli, 2003

From Communication to Presence
G. Riva et al. (Eds.)
IOS Press, 2006

12 Communication and Interaction in Multiplayer First-Person-Shooter Games

Jan-Noël THON

Abstract. Since their emergence in the 1960s, computer games have developed into a central part of popular culture. An ever-increasing number of players plays games using their computers. One of the most successful forms of computer games is the phenomenon of multiplayer games, i.e. computer games that more than one player can participate in. In these games, various interaction and communication processes take place between the players as well as between the players and the virtual game spaces that these games provide. This chapter attempts to describe multiplayer games as a form of computer-mediated communication (CMC). This mode of communication has often been described as lacking certain social cues that a face-to-face situation provides. However, to understand communication and interaction processes, one needs to understand the situation in which these processes take place. The situation in which multiplayer games take place makes a large amount of cooperation and task-oriented interaction between the players necessary. This chapter attempts to examine communication processes in multiplayer first-person-shooter (FPS) games as determined by the gaming situation in as well as the social context of these games, emphasizing that communication in these games is successful despite the constraints it has in common with other forms of CMC.

Contents

12.1 Introduction

Computer game studies are still a new academic field. Nevertheless, computer games have been studied from the perspective of various disciplines [1-3].

In the last few years, one could observe an increasing research interest in the phenomenon of multiplayer games, focussing on massive multiplayer online role playing games (MMORPGs) in particular.

The analysis of MMORPGs has been very fruitful with regard to questions of social interaction and communication [4-6].

There are, however, other multiplayer games that enable communication and create social spaces. But the number of academic studies concerned with the communicative and social structures of, e.g., multiplayer first-person-shooter (FPS) games seems rather modest compared to the research on MMORPGs. Contributions that treat multiplayer FPS games are scarce even at conferences exclusively concerned with multiplayer games [7].

Our aim is the development of a model for the description of the social structures and processes of communication and interaction in multiplayer games based on a general model of computer game structure as well as on recent communication research. For this purpose, it is necessary to focus on one computer game genre, since it is problematic to talk about "computer games in general" due to the differences between the various genres [8]. Instead of describing the highly complex social structures of MMORPGs, we will develop a model of communication and interaction processes in FPS games. This model may later be applied to the analysis of MMORPGs or other multiplayer games.

PC-based multiplayer FPS games such as *Doom* (1993), *Quake* (1996), *Unreal Tournament* (1999), *Halo* (2003), *Counter-Strike: Source* (2004) or *SWAT 4* (2005) are either played over Local Area Network (LAN) connections between computers that are located relatively near to each other or over the Internet, in which case the locations of the players may be practically anywhere [9]. The various games and game modes all revolve around some version of the mutual shoot-out, i.e. the players - or, more precisely, their avatars - fight against each other using a huge number of different weapons, vehicles and tactics.

This relatively "straight-forward nature" [10, p. 390] of multiplayer FPS games allows us to describe their social and communicative structure in some detail. These communication processes occur in a situation that is defined by highly cooperative and goal-oriented activity, but is also part of an "online community that is vocal, influential, highly social and considers itself self-regulating and, to a certain degree, self-determining" [11, n.p.].

Among the relatively few studies of computer games concerned with the communicative and social aspects of multiplayer FPS games, these of Morris [9, 11, 12] and Manninen [10, 13-15] are probably the most useful for our purpose.

In addition to these, we will consider some of the research that has been concerned with other forms of computer-mediated communication (CMC) in the last few years.

12.2 Previous Research on CMC

Among the most influential approaches in early research on CMC were *Social Presence Theory* [16] and *Media Richness Theory* [17]. *Social Presence Theory* is concerned with the effect that different communicative media have on the degree to which their mutual presence in the interaction is salient to the interlocutors. This social presence is seen as the quality of a given medium that is determined by the number of communication channels it supplies. Although most CMC is text-based, some forms make use of the audio channel that allows for intonation and other features of the voice to be perceived in communication. Furthermore, there are some applications that use the video channel, i.e. enable the participants to see each other and communicate non-verbally using physical appearance, gesticulation, facial expression etc. The more communication channels a user can use in a given medium, the higher will the social presence of this medium be. *Media Richness Theory* makes similar claims, in that it emphasizes the use of a large number of communication channels as a prerequisite for the processing of rich information, including a medium's ability "to interlink a variety of topics, render them less ambiguous, and enable users to learn about them in a given time-span" [18, p 10].

Many papers based on *Social Presence Theory* as well as *Media Richness Theory* describe CMC as lacking a number of cues that are necessary for the transmission of certain social, emotional and contextual types of information [19-21]. On the one hand, it is certainly true that CMC generally does not provide its users with a number of communication channels comparable to that of face-to-face conversation. Hence, part of the information that is transmitted in a face-to-face situation cannot be transmitted similarly in CMC. On the other hand, such a "cues-filtered-out" approach [22] has been criticized by many researchers. Claiming that CMC does not provide its users with as many communication channels as face-to-face-communication is not the same thing as claiming that CMC is "less friendly, emotional, or personal, and more businesslike and task-oriented" [19, p. 88]. Participants in CMC are no less part of a social context than are participants in face-to-face-communication, since "[a]ll interaction, including that which is task oriented, conveys social meaning and thus creates social context" [23, p.151].

Walther [24-26] has shown that users of CMC find ways to substitute the social (relational) and emotional cues CMC lacks with cues that can be realized in the signalling systems CMC provides. As far as text-based CMC is concerned, Walther notes that less social information is transmitted than is the case in a face-to-face situation due to the absence of nonverbal cues. The cues in CMC, however, are given more importance, since "whatever subtle social context cues or personality cues to appear in CMC take on a particularly great value" [26, p. 18]. Another point that is of relevance here is that CMC users develop new ways to convey social and emotional cues through (written) language, using emoticons and other substitutions for para- and nonverbal cues [27-29]. Building on Anolli's *Miscommunication as Chance Theory* [30], Riva [28] has characterized CMC as a form of miscommunication, emphasizing that "a strategic use of miscommunication may enhance the degrees of freedom available to the communicators during an interaction. If a user handles well the miscommunication processes typical of CMC, he/she may even achieve results difficult to obtain in face-to-face meetings" [28, p. 229].

Such general claims about the nature of CMC are, however, somewhat problematic. Even early research on CMC has emphasized that it "is not homogenous, but like any other communicative modality, manifests itself in different styles and genres" [31, p. 3], such as e-mails, discussion forums, Internet Relay Chat, instant messaging, MUDs or networked virtual environments such as computer games. While these various forms of CMC may share some basic characteristics, their differences make it seem difficult to speak of "CMC in general" much in the same way that it is difficult to speak of "computer games in general". Especially with regard to social presence and richness of communication, these differences matter. One can distinguish between chronologically synchronous and asynchronous CMC. Furthermore, one should distinguish between exclusively text-based, i.e. verbal CMC, these forms of CMC that use the audio channel, thereby allowing for paraverbal cues and CMC that also uses the video channel, thereby allowing for nonverbal communication. While the original Internet Relay Chat was text-based, contemporary Instant Messaging allows for the inclusion of audio or even video messages [28]. Similarly, traditional text-based MUDs have long evolved into networked virtual environments that allow their users to interact and communicate with each other using avatars, i.e. virtual representations of themselves. Multiplayer games can be understood as a form of these networked virtual environments. While they are a form of synchronous CMC, they also have certain unique structural properties that need to be taken into consideration to arrive at an understanding of the situation in which communication takes place in these games.

12.3 Towards a Model of Computer Game Structure

In order to understand the communication processes that take place in multiplayer FPS games, it is important to understand the situation in which this communication takes place. For this purpose, one can use as a basis the general model for the description of computer game structure developed by Thon [32-34]. This general model consists of four levels of computer game structure that represent different perspectives from which the structure of computer games can be described, i.e. the levels of spatial, narrative, ludic and social structure. These levels have a rather heuristic quality, and there are, of course, other perspectives from which computer games can and should be analysed. Furthermore, not every level will be of the same relevance in the analysis of every game. This is also the case with multiplayer FPS games. Hence, while such a general model is a good starting point, it has to be modified in order to arrive at an appropriate conceptualisation of the communicative situation of multiplayer FPS games.

The level of narrative structure plays an important role in singleplayer FPS games [9, 34, 35], but in multiplayer FPS games, the narrative aspects are reduced to the occasional reference to a narrative context. Instead of a narrative framework that guides the players' actions, there "is a social environment formed at the intersection of the text of the game, the specific rules of whichever game modification the server may be running and the presence of other human participants, who may communicate with each other during the game by typing" [9, p. 84]. Hence, the structure of multiplayer FPS games can be described referring to only three of the four levels, i.e. the level of spatial structure, the level of ludic structure and the level of social structure (cf. Figure 1).

The level of spatial structure refers to the game space and the objects therein. The level of ludic structure refers to the rules of the game that govern the interaction of players with the spatial structure (including the representations of other players). The level of social structure can further be distinguished into the parts of computer game structure that allow for social interaction between the players, i.e. the communicative devices, and the social space that is constituted by that social interaction (communication).

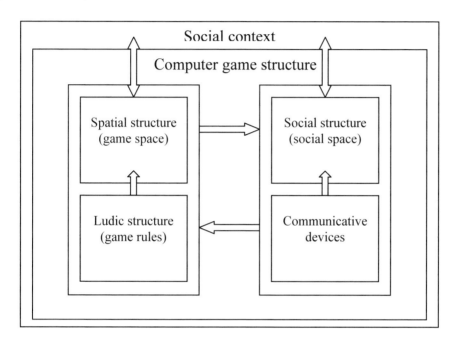

Figure 1. Model of computer game structure in multiplayer FPS games

Finally, the social context of the game influences the spatial and ludic structure (probably most drastically through mods, player-made modifications of the game spaces or game rules [11]) as well as the social structure of the game (and *vice versa*). Although our focus is on communication processes as a part of the level of social structure, the levels of spatial and ludic structure have to be discussed in some detail since they play an important role in these communication processes.

12.3.1 Spatial Structure and Ludic Structure

With regard to the level of spatial structure it is to be noted that many contemporary computer games are set in complex fictional worlds. Here, one has to distinguish between the space of the fictional world as a whole and the spaces that the player can interact with through the interface [34]. These are the spaces in which the game actually takes place. Juul draws a similar distinction between "world space" and "game space" [36, p.164-167]. Since most of the events in computer games take place in the game space, it is mainly this part of the space of the fictional world that is of interest with regard to the spatial structure of computer games, especially when it comes to multiplayer FPS games. Since singleplayer games generally use a certain number of narrative techniques to refer to the non-game space of the fictional world, this space is of greater importance in singleplayer games than it is in multiplayer games [34]. In contrast to singleplayer FPS games, multiplayer FPS games generally consist exclusively of different game locations that are not connected by any sort of narrative structure.

Such game spaces or *maps* are three-dimensional virtual environments, arenas in which the players let their avatars compete with each other in different variations of the game or game modes. Wolf notes that these spaces are often presented according to the conventions of space representations in classic Hollywood film. "Spaces and the objects in them can be viewed from multiple angles and viewpoints which are all linked together in such a way as to make the diegetic world appear to have at least enough spatial consistency so as to be navigable by the player" [37, p. 66]. Of course, the spaces in classic Hollywood film are not exactly navigable by the film viewer. In fact, even the players of multiplayer FPS games do not navigate the game space personally. Rather, they take control of an avatar, a representation of themselves in the virtual game space. In FPS games, this game space is presented using a subjective point-of-view, i.e. the spatial perspective used in the presentation of the game space is that of the player's avatar. This perspective is the most common in shooter games, and it may even be assumed that the subjective point-of-view increases the immersion of the player, i.e. his or her sense of presence in the virtual environment.

The inventory of the game spaces may vary considerably in different games, but opponents and weapons are generally a part of it. Furthermore, game spaces have certain borders that take the form of obstacles such as walls, chasms or locked doors. But the freedom of interaction that computer games suggest is restricted not only by the spatial borders but also by the rules of the game that determine the often quite narrow range of actions that are actually possible. It is equally true for single- as well as for multiplayer FPS games that the possible movement of the avatar can be seen as part of the ludic structure of the game. Running, jumping, and crouching as well as picking up and using a wide variety of weapons are essential abilities of the avatar in a FPS that are governed by the rules of the game. However, in multiplayer FPS games players play not only against the artificial intelligence of computer opponents, but also against other human players. This does, of course, have a certain impact on the ludic structure of the game.

Aarseth *et al.* [38] note that "it is common to distinguish between singleplayer and multiplayer games" [38, p. 51] but that this distinction is not differentiated enough to appropriately describe the various forms of multiplayer games in existence. It does indeed seem problematic to label games as different as chess with up to two players, multiplayer FPS games with usually around ten players, and MMORPGs with often more than hundred players all as multiplayer games. Aarseth et al. propose distinguishing between singleplayer, twoplayer, and multiplayer as well as between singleteam, twoteam, and multiteam game modes. This distinction seems useful for describing multiplayer FPS games as well, since there are significant differences between the ludic (as well as the social) structure of a multiplayer FPS game played in a multiplayer game mode, i.e. with a number of players each of whom is playing against every other player, and the same multiplayer FPS game played in a twoteam game mode, i.e. with two teams of players playing against each other. For one, coordination and cooperation is generally far more important in team-based game modes.

Even in rather action-oriented shooters such as *Quake*, *Unreal Tournament*, or *Halo*, one can find not only multiplayer and twoteam versions of the classic mutual shoot-out (these game modes are, for instance, called *slayer* and *teamslayer* in *Halo*), but also game modes such as the widespread *capture-the-flag* that require a greater amount of cooperation. In this twoteam-game mode the two teams each try to bring the enemy flag from the enemy base to its own base, and points can often only be scored when the flag of the scoring team is in the base. Another example of a game mode that requires a great amount of cooperation is the bombing run to be found in multiplayer shooters that emphasize tactical aspects, such as *Counter Strike: Source* or *SWAT 4*. In this game mode, the objective of one team of players is to make one or more bombs explode, while the other team tries to disarm them. The necessity of coordinated action and cooperation between several players can be seen as one of the defining elements of multiplayer FPS games, and a central part of the playing experience.

Smith [39] has noted that in team-based game modes not only the opponent team but also the allies of a player can become a problem. "Though team performance is crucial to success, each team member faces some temptation to play selfishly" [39, n.p.]. And even when players try to play as a team, this may still lead to problems because they may not share each other's strategies. In order to better understand these processes, the notion of situation models that has been developed in cognitive science may prove useful. According to Hogan [40], a mental model can be described as the result of two processes, namely the formation of multielement units (which in turn is the result of processes of selection and segmentation of perceived information) and the assignment of relations between these units. Only "[i]f the complex of hierarchically structured units concerns the environment in which we are acting, it is called a 'situation model'" [40, p. 40]. Players form situation models of the game spaces and social spaces of multiplayer FPS games much in the same way that they form situation models of their real-life environments.

In the case of multiplayer FPS games, one can assume that the levels of computer game structure sketched above play an essential role in the models that the players form of the gaming situation as well. While playing, the players will construct models of the game space in which the game takes place. These models will include the position of allies and opponents, as well as the possibilities of interaction with the game space as defined by the ludic structure of the game. Furthermore, the players will construct models referring to the other players as social actors and their mutual social relations, i.e. to the social space of the game. According to Stasser [40], CMC may be defined as a process by which a group of social actors in a given situation negotiates the meaning of the various situations which arise between them. It is indeed the case that a relevant part of teamplay consists of communication that aims at establishing shared situation models among the players in a team. It also is this necessity to communicate that at least partly determines the social structures inside as well as outside of the actual game. But before we discuss these social structures and communicative processes, we need to examine in more detail the various forms of interaction in multiplayer FPS games that are not obviously communicative in nature.

12.3.2 Interaction Forms and Situation Models

Building on *Social Presence Theory*, Manninen [10, 13-15] treats interaction in networked virtual environments. Networked virtual environments are seen "as applications and extensions of virtual reality technologies" [10, p. 385]. Manninen follows Riva's definition of virtual reality as "a mental experience which makes the user believe that 'he is there', that he is present in the virtual world" [42, p. 87]. Riva also stresses the interactive aspect of virtual reality. "Interacting with a virtual environment, the user is no longer a mere observer of that which is happening on a screen, but he 'feels' immersed in that world and can participate in it, in spite of the fact that these worlds are spaces and objects existing only in the memory of the computer and in the user's mind" [42, p. 87]. It can indeed be assumed that a feeling of immersion is evoked not only by the spatial and narrative structure of computer games [43], but also by the ludic as well as the social forms of interaction that occur in multiplayer FPS games [44].

In order to describe rich interaction in networked virtual environments, Manninen has developed a *Rich Interaction Model* and a *Hierarchical Interaction Model*. For this purpose, he mainly refers to examples from "the area of 3D multi-player games" [10, p. 384], i.e. MMORPGs and, more often, multiplayer FPS games. The latest version of his *Rich Interaction Model* [14, 45] entails twelve classes of interaction forms, namely avatar appearance, facial expressions, occulesics, kinesics, gestures, automatic / AI-driven interaction forms, language-based communication, control and coordination, physical contact, environmental details, non-verbal audio, olfactics, and chronemics. These forms are then further divided into subclasses, for instance text-based communication, speech, pre-defined phrases, and sign language in the case of language-based communication.

Manninen's work doubtlessly contributes to our understanding of interaction and communication in multiplayer FPS games. For instance, one of the points made clear by his observations is that spatial interaction, i.e. the spatial behaviour of the avatars inside the game space, is also a form of communication in that it communicates their spatial position to the other players. However, the *Rich Interaction Model* with its many heterogenous classes and subclasses seems to be too complex for describing the communication and interaction processes that occur in multiplayer FPS games. For one, not all of the categories are applicable to multiplayer FPS games (or MMORPGs, for that matter). While language-based communication and physical contact can be seen as central interaction forms in multiplayer FPS games, olfactics are definitely not. Furthermore, it seems to be useful to distinguish between those forms of interaction that occur in the game space as such and those forms of interaction (or communication) that do not manifest themselves on the level of spatial structure. In other words, we propose to distinguish between spatial interaction (which takes place in the game space and can be described referring to the levels of spatial and ludic structure) and language-based interaction (located on the level of social structure and made possible by the communicative devices a particular game offers).

It is generally true that the spatial structure of multiplayer FPS games functions as the environment in which a large part of the interaction takes place. Therefore, interaction forms belonging to classes such as spatial behaviour, physical contact, kinesics, and environmental details are all partly to be located on the level of spatial structure. However, these forms of interaction are also rule-governed. Therefore, they are part of the ludic structure, too. The interaction forms of the spatial behaviour class, for instance, mainly consist of rule-governed movements (ludic structure) of certain objects (spatial structure) that take place in a virtual environment or game space (spatial structure). The interaction forms of the environmental details class mainly consist of rule-governed interactions (ludic structure) between certain objects (spatial structure) and the environment or objects therein (spatial structure). Similar is true for interaction forms belonging to the physical contact class.

One can relate these spatial forms of interaction to the notion that players form situation models while playing. For this purpose, we will refer to Manninen's *Hierarchical Interaction Model* which he intends to be used "[i]n order to enhance the dimensionality of the interaction taxonomy" [10, p. 393]. The model distinguishes between five different levels of complexity of interaction forms.

The lowest of these levels refers to the control of the avatar's motor system, e.g. moving his or her legs and feet.

The second level refers to patterns that consist of combined signals, e.g. the combination of movements necessary to walk.

The third level refers to the direction or purpose of the interaction form, e.g. where the walking movement is aiming at.

The fourth level refers to sub-goals as part of the "goal-oriented and usually generally described interactions" [10, p. 393] of the fifth level, e.g. various waypoints in a complex change of location.

While Manninen does not discuss the model in too much detail, it seems to be quite useful since it allows a distinction of different levels of complexity in the description of interaction (as well as communication).

With regard to the question of situation models, the higher levels of Manninen's model are most important. The actions that take place on the lower levels can be considered as being determined by quite basic forms of knowledge about processes of avatar control that all except the most inexperienced players will normally possess. However, the goals and sub-goals that the higher levels of the Hierarchical Interaction Model refer to are primarily determined by the situation models the players have formed. As Suchman has noted, "[t]o characterize purposeful action as in accord with plans and goals is just to say again that it is purposeful and that *somehow*, in a way not addressed by the characterization itself, we constrain and direct our actions according to the significance that we assign to a particular context" [46, p. 48].

The goals and sub-goals players of multiplayer FPS games form with regard to the interaction that takes place on a game server are determined by the situation models they have constructed. While the main interest of most players will be to win the game, the goals of the various interaction processes that lead to this aim are formed according to continuous re-evaluations of the gaming situation. If the model a player has formed of the gaming situation is not accurate, this may lead to interaction that is unsuccessful with regard to the interests of his or her team, since the player's goals and the team's goals will deviate from each other. Imagine, for instance, a game of *capture-the-flag* in which the avatar of a player has taken the flag from the enemy base and is on its way back to the home base.

The situation model of the avatar's player consists, among other things, of a representation of the game space (spatial structure), the interaction possible within that game space (which is determined by the ludic structure of the game), the position of his or her avatar as well as at least a rough idea of the positions of the other player's avatars. We are talking about a skilled player who is part of a team of skilled players here, so the other members of the player's team will keep the opponent players occupied while our player is running towards the home base. Imagine what happens when, for whatever reason, our player loses orientation, i.e. his or her situation model becomes inaccurate in a small but significant way. Instead of running towards the home base, our player's avatar may be running back towards the enemy base, and our player may only be able to correct his or her inaccurate situation model when the avatar is shot by one of its opponents, who then will return the flag to the enemy base.

Although most cases of inappropriate situation models will probably not be as tragic, our example stresses that one of the main requirements for successful team play is a shared situation model among the players. One can assume that the team of our player might have seen his or her avatar running back towards the enemy base and (probably even successfully) tried to correct the inaccurate situation model by way of communication.

While such communication may take nonverbal forms as well, most of it will usually consist of language-based interaction forms such as text-based chat, speech or pre-defined phrases. These interaction forms are not part of the spatial structure of the game, since their main purpose is to function as communicative devices for the players. They are, however, instrumental in the constitution of a social space and can therefore be located on the level of social structure.

One could argue that the possibility to use communicative devices is part of the game rules and therefore to be seen as part of the ludic structure of the game. The ludic structure, however, mostly refers to the rules that govern the interaction taking place in the game space.

Since language-based communication in multiplayer FPS games is disparate from the spatial structure, it seems sensible to structurally treat it as part of the social structure, though it may play a central role in the models the players construct of the gaming situation.

In the following parts of this chapter, we will analyse in more detail how players use the communicative devices available in multiplayer FPS games and to what end they use them, i.e. what their motivations for communication are. Since especially the latter question requires not only an understanding of the structure of multiplayer FPS games but also at least a rough idea of the social context that surrounds these games, we will begin by examining some research that is of interest in this respect.

12.4 Social Context and Communication Processes

12.4.1 Social Context

One basic distinction to be made with regard to the level of social structure of multiplayer FPS games is that between the social structure that emerges from the interaction of the players in the game and the social context that emerges from the interaction of the players outside of the actual game. The game servers of multiplayer

FPS games "function as virtual social spaces" [12, p. 36] in which the players use certain communicative devices to communicate with each other. In fact, the game server's function as social space is a result of this communication. Furthermore, there are areas outside of the actual game in which communication between players takes place. Every multiplayer shooter is surrounded by a wide variety of websites and discussion forums through which players form social networks and even social groups like clans that are all part of its social context and fulfil various functions for the game.

In describing this social context, we mainly take as our basis the works of Morris, who has conducted a large amount of ethnographic research on multiplayer FPS games as a part of her Ph.D.-project, focusing on the social context of these games [9, 11, 12]. According to Morris, online games are "structuring and mediating communication between large numbers of participants, and spawning subjectivities and social practices within a cultural economy extending beyond the game itself" [12, p. 31]. Players of multiplayer FPS games do not just play, but also engage in various game-related practices such as game development, criticism, commentary, exchange of information, teaching of game skills, file sharing, and social organisation [11, 12]. In short, they participate in various forms of social interaction that constitutes the social context of multiplayer FPS games.

Undertaking ethnographic research in the field of multiplayer FPS games is not without its problems. Players are generally sceptical towards academics, and although the Internet provides a vast amount of information on gamer culture, this information may not always be reliable and needs verification through comparison of various sources. Morris [12] has discussed these issues as well as questions of ethical constraints regarding ethnographic research in some detail. We do not aim at a detailed description of the social context of multiplayer FPS games. Such an attempt would require both an empirical orientation and extensive ethnographic research none of which is intended here. For us, the relevance of the social context lies mainly in its influence on the social structures that are manifested in the various forms of communication in the game and instead of presenting ethnographic research of our own, we will refer to Morris' findings.

It has already been said that every successful multiplayer FPS game is surrounded by a variety of websites and discussion boards that the players use to establish social networks. Quite a large part of the players of multiplayer FPS games belong to hierarchically organized clans, whose members play together in teams and against other clans. Less formally organized social networks may also be formed through acquaintances from real life, knowledge of the same language (other than English, which is generally presupposed in the international FPS gaming community), or shared social or cultural background. Among the various websites devoted to FPS gaming are these that provide gaming news and reviews as well as sites of online leagues for both individuals and clans, and individual clan pages [11]. Morris rightly stresses the fact that this social context of multiplayer FPS games is not something game developers control. "Web pages, discussion forums and chat venues are all run by players. Clans and competitions are organised independently, as are online gaming ladders and the majority of real-life LAN (Local Area Network) meetings" [11, n.p.].

What is especially interesting with regard to our attempt to understand communication in multiplayer FPS games as a form of CMC is the fact that the social interaction surrounding multiplayer FPS games mainly takes place "in game servers and on IRC channels, ICQ chats, discussion boards, mail-lists" [12, p. 33]. Although face-to-face communication and interaction between gamers does occur at LAN-events or during everyday social interaction, most of what constitutes the social context of multiplayer FPS games takes place either inside the game (on game servers) or in other forms of CMC. "Involvement in the online culture, not just through playing the game, but also through web-pages (including discussion forums), mail-lists, Internet Relay Chat (IRC) channels and real-time chat programs, contribute further social influences to the formation of the gaming subject" [9, p. 95]. Hence, in order to appropriately describe the social structures surrounding multiplayer games, one would have to research how the various forms of CMC influence each other and contribute to the formation of a social context that is different from the real-life context of the participants.

As Morris notes, "FPS gamers develop gaming identities which are used across various media" [11, n.p.]. These identities are not the real-life identities of the players, but at least in the case of some players, they are recognizable enough that it is inappropriate to speak of anonymity here. This seems to be an interesting direction for further research, even more so since research on CMC generally emphasizes the fact that there is no guarantee that the self-presentation of interlocutors in CMC is in any way coherent with their real life identities [47]. Without intending to question the validity of this observation, the existence of persistent gaming identities seems to indicate that research should focus on the virtually constructed rather than on the real-life identities of participants in CMC. Although the notion that we perform different roles in different social contexts is not exactly new [48], the phenomenon of persistent CMC identities in gaming contexts has, to my knowledge, not been thoroughly researched yet.

Related to the question of personal identity is the question of group identity. There doubtlessly are different player types in computer games [49] and it is necessary to at least distinguish between clan-players and non-clan-players of multiplayer FPS games. This distinction is also relevant with regard to the question of social norms that govern the communication and interaction processes in multiplayer games. As Morris notes, "[p]layers have developed intricate rules and etiquette governing gameplay and social behaviour, based on fundamental principles of fair play and general social cooperation" [11, n.p.]. While there may be certain social rules that apply to all players (e.g. not to cheat), other rules may be clan specific. Furthermore, clan-players tend to be more professional in their playing style, i.e. tend to focus on playing the game. This also means that certain communicative practices, e.g. talking about non-game-related topics with other players while playing the game, are considered inappropriate more often by clan-players than by non-clan-players. Hence, communication that aims at establishing interpersonal relations may be perceived as a form of miscommunication by more professional players, whereas communication that is task-oriented will generally be perceived as appropriate.

Such an interpretation of communication depends on the situation model a player has constructed of the other players as social actors and the relation between them. Various researchers claim "that the social system should be seen as a network of relationships providing the *space* in which cognitions are elaborated" [18, p. 9]. The reconstruction of the social space as part of the situation model of a player will most likely also include some assumptions about what sort of communication the other players will find appropriate. Hence, the social context of the game as well as the particular social situation on a game server will greatly influence the ways in which players participate in and perceive communication in multiplayer FPS games. These communicative processes are, however, also influenced by the communicative devices that the players can use.

12.4.2 Communicative Devices

In order to communicate, players of multiplayer FPS games use different communicative devices. Which devices they use depends on the player as well as on the game that is played and whether it is played via LAN- or via TCP/IP-connection. When the players are in the same room, as is often the case with games that are played using a LAN-connection, communication does not necessarily have to be computer-mediated since players may use the traditional communicative devices a face-to-face situation provides [50]. However, most multiplayer FPS games allow their players to play games over the Internet. Since players in Internet-based games are generally not near enough to each other to be able to communicate without technical assistance, most if not all multiplayer FPS games that support multiplayer games using a TCP/IP-connection offer their players at least one sort of (tele-) communication device. PC-based FPS games since *Doom* have established the possibility to write text messages to other players (these messages can generally either be addressed to all players or only to the members of the player's team). Since the PC is the predominant platform for multiplayer FPS games, it can be assumed that text-based chat is still the communicative device used most often by the average player [12].

There is, however, another language-based communicative device that has become quite widespread in the last few years. Voice-over-IP programs such as *Teamspeak* allow players to communicate with spoken language, using a headset or comparable equipment. With regard to this development, it is essential to note that players can keep on fighting their opponents while talking. The time that is saved by not having to enter text messages via keyboard can help a player (and his or her team) to win in a fast game such as the multiplayer-shooter. It has also been suggested that the fact that the flow of the game is not continuously ruptured leads to a more immersive gaming experience [50]. Although there are still many players who do not use voice-over-IP programs, they have become quite usual especially among more professional players or clans. Hence, while they are generally not part of the actual structure of the FPS game and our focus lies on the text-based forms of communication that are a part of that structure, the fact that programs such as *Teamspeak* exist and are used by a large number of FPS players has at least to be noted.

Anolli claims that, among the different signalling systems, "language has a prominent position, as it remains the most powerful, flexible and stable communicative device" [30, p.21]. While this is doubtlessly true for communication in computer games as well, one also has to consider non-verbal forms of communication that take place on the levels of spatial and ludic structure. Although the possibilities for non-verbal communication in multiplayer FPS games are quite limited, it does nevertheless occur. Players may gesture with their weapons, showing other team members where they want them to move to. In *Halo*, it is common practice to shoot at the avatar of a team member that is driving one of the various vehicles in order to signal him to wait. This is accepted behaviour since the avatars in *Halo* are protected by shields that prevent them from being injured by a single shot.

Furthermore, there is also a communicative device that is language-based but would hardly be characterized as very flexible. As Manninen has noted, multiplayer FPS games such as *Counter Strike: Source* or *SWAT 4* offer their players the opportunity to communicate using predefined voice-messages, e.g. "Follow me!" or "Need assistance!" However, among the language-based interaction forms in multiplayer FPS games, text-based chat seems to be the most interesting theoretically, since its "rarefied" [42, p. 93] nature makes players develop new ways of using it, for instance by creating forms that can function as substitutes for non-verbal cues.

12.4.3 Language Use

With regard to the use of language in multiplayer FPS games, the influence of the social context of gaming culture has to be emphasized. Most obviously, this applies to the vocabulary used. As Costikyan [51] has noted, there is a rich terminology that is used almost exclusively in certain gaming contexts, e.g. among players of multiplayer FPS games. Here, killing the avatar of another player may be called *fragging*, letting one's avatar jump about the game space in order to avoid being shot may be called *bunny hopping*, and to kill someone's avatar by teleporting into its location may be called *telefragging*. While it should be stressed that rather few players of multiplayer FPS games actually use this terminology, it is true that such genre-specific terminology exists and is used by at least some players. There is, of course, also more and less commonly used vocabulary. While probably just a few players will use expressions such as *low-ping bastard* (a low ping meaning a better Internet connection that leads to faster reaction times in the games), most players of multiplayer FPS games will know that a "*newbie* (or *noob* or *n00b*) is a new player who's just learning the ropes" [51, p. 4]. It may also be noted that calling another player a *noob* is not considered polite behaviour.

Related to this special terminology is another communicative practice peculiar to CMC contexts and often associated with FPS gaming. McKean claims that there exists a "preferred online communication style of online gaming geeks, hacker wannabees, and adolescent chat-room denizens: l33t, pronounced 'leet'" [52, p. 13]. The basic principle that guides the use of *l33t sp34k* (leet-speak) is that certain letters are substituted by numbers or other characters. A is substituted by 4, I by 1, O by 0, T by 7, S by 5 etc. These substitutions may take rather far-fetched forms, for instance when |)\ substitutes R, but we do not want to go into too much detail here. While this special way of writing is indeed sometimes used by players of multiplayer FPS games, it is probably a bit too strong to talk about the "preferred online communication style of online gaming geeks" [52, p. 13]. In fact, like other game specific terminology, it is not used as often as one might think, and even less often used without irony. What is, however, interesting here is that a certain way to use written language occurs not only in the text-based communicative devices of multiplayer FPS games, but across various forms of CMC. In fact, much of what can be observed in the text-based chat in *Halo, Counter Strike: Source, SWAT 4* or similar games can also be observed in other forms of CMC, such as Internet Relay Chat.

One of the phenomena related to CMC-specific vocabulary is the use of abbreviations and acronyms. These are very useful in text-based synchronous CMC, since typing words out takes time and this is generally not something a participant in these forms of CMC will want to do. As Schulze has noted, "[t]he prevalent speed [of Internet Relay Chat, JNT] gives rise to the necessity to formulate and type one's contributions fast and efficiently" [29, p. 71]. In fast-paced games such as the multiplayer FPS, this need to use as little time for typing as possible is even more urgent. Hence, a variety of abbreviations and acronyms can be found in the communication that takes place in these games (cf. table 1).

Furthermore, these time constraints often lead to rather short sentences that tend not to comply with English grammar rules. This can, in some cases, lead to misunderstandings. Such misunderstandings, however, are not of too much interest here, since they basically arise from the mentioned time constraints. As Riva has noted, CMC can be seen as a "rarefied form of conversation" [28, p. 204], or even as a form of miscommunication. Instead of asking where the constraints of the medium lead to misunderstandings, we want to focus on the question of how players try to overcome the miscommunication that seems to be inherent in text-based CMC. One of the most interesting communicative practices with regard to this question is the substitution of non-verbal cues that occurs in Internet Relay Chat [29] as well as in the text-based communication of multiplayer FPS games. Schulze [29] identifies three types of the substitution of cues in Internet Relay Chat, namely the substitution of nonverbal cues, paraverbal cues, and status and presence cues.

Table 1. Abbreviations and acronyms used in multiplayer FPS games

Abbreviation / Acronym	Meaning	Abbreviation / Acronym	Meaning
AFK	Away from keyboard	OMG	Oh my god
CU	See you	SRY	Sorry
G2G	Got to go	TY, TU	Thank you
LOL	Laugh out loud	WTF	What the fuck

Table 2. Emoticons used in multiplayer FPS games

Emoticon	Meaning	Emoticon	Meaning
:), :)), :))), :-), :-)), :-)))	Smiley: humour, irony	: O, :-O	Astonishment
: (, : ((, : (((, :-(, :-((, :-(((	Frowney: sadness, anger	: p, :-p	Tongue out
;), ;-)	Winkey: irony, sarcasm	: D, :-D	Laughing
: /, :-/	Wry face: wry humour	^^^	Laughter

There are various ways that nonverbal cues can be substituted. Participants in Internet Relay Chat may use verbs describing the respective action, where as the verbs (or verbal stems) are embraced by asterisks. Another common way of substituting nonverbal cues is the use of emoticons (cf. Table 2). While descriptions of nonverbal behaviour do not occur as commonly in the text-based chat of multiplayer FPS games as does the use of emoticons, both forms of the substitution of nonverbal cues can be found. With regards to the substitution of paraverbal cues in Internet Relay Chat, Schulze refers to reduplication and the use of upper case, both of which occur frequently in the text-based communication of multiplayer FPS games. "Reduplication of a vowel represents dilatation as it would occur in speech. Reduplication of the exclamation mark also lends special emphasis to a remark" [29, p. 77]. The use of upper case in CMC is generally interpreted as loudness, since it stands out against the rest of the text. It is even the case that some players may consider continuous "shouting" to be impolite.

Finally, Schulze mentions the compensation of status and presence cues. Presence cues are important particularly since "IRC users have to first check out if people listed in a channel are listening and willing to communicate" [29, p. 78]. On a game server, however, the situation is slightly different in this respect. The players of multiplayer FPS games can observe the avatars of the other players that play on a server. Nevertheless, there may be situations quite similar to these in Internet Relay Chat described by Schulze, when it is not possible for an interlocutor "to see whether another (potential) interlocutor whose nick[name, JNT] is listed in a channel is really present at his or her terminal and following the communication on the channel" [29, p. 78]. In this case, players may use the text-based chat to ask whether a player, whose avatar has not been moving for some time, is actually playing. Many players consider killing the avatar of a player who is not actively participating in the game unsporting. This has to do with the fact that the number of kills is generally counted even in game modes that emphasize other ways to score, e.g. *capture-the-flag*, and a high number of kills may be read as indicating a skilled player.

In fact, it can be assumed that the number of kills a player has achieved is a certain compensation for missing status cues, since being a skilled player is at least part of what constitutes high status in the FPS gaming context. There are other compensations for status cues, too. Signalling one's belonging to a clan is one of the most obvious. While there are, of course, more or less prestigious clans, most of them require their members to attach a *clan tag* to their nickname (which than reads something like "[clan]nickname"). Another possible compensation is the nickname itself, at least in the case of persistent gaming identities. It is, however, to be noted that it is not exactly easy to prevent a player from pretending to be a member of a clan or to use the nickname of another player. While such behaviour is, of course, not accepted among gamers, one at least has to consider the possibility of insincere social status cues in CMC. This is also true for cues such as the register and style of the language used by a player. While these features of text-based communication may provide cues to his or her real-life social context, it is perfectly possible that a player using *l33t-sp34k* is actually a professor of information technology pretending to be an "online gaming geek" [52, p. 13].

12.4.4 Communication and Miscommunication

It has become clear that multiplayer FPS games do not posses the same level of social presence that can be found in face-to-face situations. Still, these games offer the opportunity for social-emotional as well as task-oriented communication (a distinction that has already been made in early research on CMC [53, 19]), even when reduced to text-based communicative devices. We have shown that players find ways to substitute the cues text-based chat in multiplayer FPS games is lacking. Hence, while a preference for task-oriented communication can be observed on game servers, this preference may not necessarily be caused by the constraints of a text-based chat system. Rather, it seems to be caused by the communicative situation in which communication on game servers takes place. In the remainder of this chapter we will offer a tentative explanation of why most of the communication in multiplayer FPS games is task-oriented in spite of the fact that the medium makes social-emotionally oriented communication possible. Although we will, again, mainly refer to text-based chat, most of the rather general explanations will also be applicable to voice-over-IP communication.

We have already mentioned that shared goals and shared situation models form an important part of cooperative interaction in team-based game modes. Players do, however, not always share the same situation model. This is equally true for the model that refers to the ludic and the spatial structure as well as for the model that refers to the social structure of the game. Inappropriate cognitive representations of the spatial and ludic structure will prevent a player from successful cooperative interaction in the gaming space. Inappropriate cognitive representation of the social structure or the social space will lead to some interesting forms of miscommunication, or at least to players interpreting certain forms of communication as miscommunication. With regard to these forms of miscommunication, it is essential to understand to what end players communicate as well as what players expect to be the appropriate reasons for communication in multiplayer FPS games.

Quite a substantial body of research exists on miscommunication processes (cf., e.g. [54-56]). While we cannot discuss this research here, we still need a concept of miscommunication that can be used to analyse the communication processes in multiplayer FPS games. For this purpose, we will take as a basis Anolli's *Miscommunication as Chance Theory (MaCHT)* [30] that has been applied to CMC by Riva [28], who notes that "CMC is usually described as an efficient form of *miscommunication*, i.e., a necessarily 'pared down' or, perhaps more accurately, rarefied form of conversation which lacks the rules on which effective interaction depends" [28, p. 204]. We have already discussed the structural aspects of multiplayer FPS games and how they affect the possibilities of communication between their players. Furthermore, it has become clear that players "will try to communicate using any available tool" [28, p. 214], and even develop new ways to use the communicative devices available. What we are interested in now is how players interpret different forms of communication. Here we propose to describe communication and miscommunication from a pragmatic rather than a structural perspective.

Riva claims that the success of CMC "is creating a new psycho-social space that is the fertile ground for social relationships, roles, and a new sense of self" [28, p. 228] and as we have seen, this is the case with regard to multiplayer FPS games. Players with persistent gaming identities interact with one another inside and outside of the various game servers. It does, however, seem that communication outside of game server, i.e. those forms of CMC that can be described as part of the social context of multiplayer FPS games, is more diverse and probably more social-emotionally oriented than communication inside of game servers. This has to do with the structure of multiplayer FPS games as well as with the models players develop of the social situation they are in while playing the game.

It has already been said that players can be categorized in clan-players and non-clan-players. At least broadly similar distinctions would be professional and non-professional players, power-gamers and fun-gamers, or maybe even task-oriented and social-emotionally oriented players. While it is clear that players cannot be appropriately categorized according to such strict binary oppositions, these distinctions may prove useful when understood as opposite ends of a continuum. Clan-players can than be characterized as generally being more professional and task-oriented than non-clan players. Still, there are, of course, very professional and task-oriented players that are not in a clan, just as there is a large number of fun clans, whose members emphasize the social-emotional aspects of communication more strongly.

When discussing miscommunication in multiplayer FPS games from a pragmatic rather than a structural perspective, it is useful to remember that every player maintains a certain situation model of the social situation on a game server. This model consists of a representation of the social structure the player becomes a part of when joining a game, which in turn consists not only of the players as social actors and their mutual interpersonal relations, but also of a set of assumptions as to what sort of communication is appropriate in the gaming situation. Such player expectations regarding the appropriate use of communication may vary considerably among different player types. Hence, the same communicative act may be considered entirely appropriate by one player while another player may interpret it as a form of miscommunication.

With regard to players' evaluations of communicative processes, it is useful to distinguish between different forms of language-based communication. Let us start with the communicative processes referring to the game space of the game. There is the kind of communication that aims at establishing a shared model of the gaming situation, i.e. the levels of spatial and ludic structure, among the members of a team. Such tactical and strategic talk generally fulfils an obvious function, namely to make effective cooperation possible. There may be players that do not actively participate in strategy talk, but this form of communication is considered appropriate by most, if not all players. Then there are forms of communication that refer to the ludic structure of the game as well, but do not fulfil a function with regard to that structure. Such communication has been called "crowing" [50, p. 135] and mainly includes "celebrating one's own achievements, those of another or their misfortune" [50, p. 135]. While an excessive amount of such communication would be considered inappropriate by the more professional players, Morris has noted that such "'[s]mack talk' (inflammatory and often entertaining statements made to an opponent) is a recognised part of FPS gaming culture" [12, p. 39].

With regard to the forms of communication that refer to the social structure or the social context of the game, one can again distinguish between functional forms of communication (e.g. greeting sequences) and forms of *smack talk* (e.g. playful name-calling) that act as "a source of humour within the game" [12, p. 39]. However, while a moderate amount of *smack talk* (which, as we have seen, can refer to the ludic or to the social structure of a game) is generally considered quite appropriate or even entertaining, certain forms of sincere communication referring to the social structure or the social context of the game are not. Here, the notion that players construct situation models that determine the goals of their interaction proves useful. For more professional or task-oriented players, the game is what being on a game server is all about, i.e. in their situation model the aspects connected with the gaming situation are more salient. The communicative processes of less professional players may sometimes be more social-emotionally oriented. For some of them, being on a game server is mainly a social situation. These players will often participate in a lot of social-emotionally oriented communication referring to the social structure and the social context of the game.

Such communicative processes do, however, use a certain amount of space in the small area that displays the text-based chat in multiplayer FPS games. Hence, extensive forms of communication referring to the social structure or the social context of the game are interpreted as a form of miscommunication by more task-oriented players. This is not to say that greeting sequences or the occasional reference to the social context of the game is in any way considered inappropriate. Quite the opposite is true. It does, however, seem that the special structure of multiplayer FPS games emphasizes not only cooperative forms of interaction that require shared goals and situation models, but also rather task-oriented forms of communication. This focus on task-oriented communication is not primarily caused by a low level of social presence. Although there are certain constraints, especially with regard to non-verbal and social status and context cues, the preference for task-oriented communication can be explained with reference to the main goal of most players, which is winning the game. Seen from this perspective, certain forms of communication that would be considered perfectly appropriate in other contexts will be interpreted as miscommunication by a majority of the players. Other forms of communication that may be seen as miscommunication in other contexts are considered as perfectly appropriate, even entertaining communication. Hence, it is clear that a consideration of the communicative situation and the social context is necessary to understand communication in multiplayer FPS games as well as CMC in general.

12.5 Conclusions

We have described multiplayer FPS games as a form of CMC occurring in a situation that makes highly cooperative and goal-oriented interaction necessary. This situation is to a great part determined by the specific structure of these games. Although they are a form of networked virtual environments, it has become clear that a description of computer games not only on the level of spatial structure, but also on the level of ludic and of social structure is necessary to arrive at an appropriate understanding of the situation in which communication occurs in these games. With regard to this understanding, one can distinguish between the game space, in which spatial interaction that is governed by certain game rules takes place between the players (or their avatars), and the social space, that is largely constituted through player's use of certain communicative devices that the games offer. While most of the communication in multiplayer FPS games refers to events in the game space, such games are also part of a rich social context that influences the communicative processes and social interaction between players.

Since multiplayer FPS games are a form of CMC, some of the more general observations on CMC apply to them. Most importantly, they lack certain properties of a face-to-face situation with regard to the social presence offered. Though it is possible for players to communicate with each other using verbal, paraverbal, and nonverbal cues, the latter are very much reduced and genuine paraverbal cues are only made possible through the use of additional software such as *TeamSpeak*. Hence, it could be argued that the CMC that occurs in multiplayer FPS games is a form of miscommunication, since it lacks certain properties that communication in a face-to-face situation normally has. However, players (as well as participants in CMC in general) find substitutes for the cues the communication medium is lacking. This, together with other factors related to the structure and the social context of the games, leads to certain characteristics of language use that are particular to CMC, e.g. the use of specialized vocabulary or the increased use of acronyms.

Finally, we have proposed to focus on the question of how players evaluate communication in multiplayer FPS games. This is necessary because many forms of communication that could be described as miscommunication from a structural perspective are perceived as successful communication by the participants. Furthermore, there are forms of communication that would not necessarily be described as miscommunication from a structural perspective but are perceived as miscommunication by the participants. With relation to this idea, we have described some forms of communication that occur in multiplayer FPS games as well as the different ways in which they may be perceived by different players. We have shown that it is possible to understand large amounts of social-emotionally oriented communication in multiplayer FPS games as a form of miscommunication, since many players will find the use of game servers for extensive social interaction inappropriate.

Most players greet each other when they enter a server and many players know each other's persistent gaming identities, which seems to indicate that players are generally aware of one another as social actors. Still, extensive social interaction is more often to be found in the various other forms of CMC that constitute the social context of multiplayer FPS games. Such an observation, however, does not necessarily mean that the social presence of multiplayer FPS games is low. Rather, it seems to indicate that interaction in these games is influenced by certain norms as part of the social context in which multiplayer FPS games are situated. One of these norms that at least more professional players generally adhere to is represented by the assumption that communication on a game server should generally serve the game. Hence, other forms of communication such as *smack talk* or communication that refers to the social structure or the social context of the game is considered inappropriate when it takes up too much of the space (in the case of text-based chat) that is needed for strategy talk and the like.

Further research should not only focus on the structure of multiplayer FPS games, i.e. the processes of interaction and communication that take place on a game server as well as the situation in which they take place and how the latter influences the former, but also describe the social context of these games in more detail. This would also include the question to what extent the forms of CMC that surround multiplayer FPS games play a role in the communication on game servers and lead to the development of persistent gaming identities. While concepts such as social presence are useful with regard to the question of how the structure of CMC applications influences CMC, it has to be emphasized that CMC is also influenced by the mutual expectations of its participants regarding its appropriate use.

12.6 Acknowledgements

I would like to thank Hannah Birr, Jens Eder and Jörg Schönert for comments on earlier versions of this chapter as well as Joan Schwartz for carefully correcting my English.

12.7 References

[1]   J. Raessens and J. Goldstein, Eds, *Handbook of computer game studies*. Cambridge, Mass: MIT Press, 2005.
[2]   N. Wardrip-Fruin and P. Harrigan, Eds, *FirstPerson: New media as story, performance, and game.* Cambridge, Mass: MIT Press, 2004.
[3]   M. J. P. Wolf and B. Perron, Eds, *The video game theory reader*, New York: Routledge, 2003.
[4]   N. Ducheneaut, R. J. Moore, and E. Nickell, Designing for sociability in massively multiplayer games: An examination of the "third places" of SWG, in *Proceedings of the Other Players Conference*, J. H. Smith and M. Sicart, Eds. Copenhagen: IT University, 2004, n.p. 30. Jan. 2006. Online: http://www.itu.dk/op/proceedings.htm.
[5]   M. Jakobsson and T. L. Taylor, The Sopranos meet EverQuest: Social networking in massively multiplayer online games, in *DAC 2003 Proceedings*, pp. 81-90. 30. Jan. 2006. Online: hypertext.rmit.edu.au/dac/papers/Jakobsson.pdf.
[6]   L. Holin and C.-T- Sun, The 'white-eyed' player culture: Grief play and construction of deviance in MMORPGs,   in   *Digra   2005   Proceedings*,   n.p.   30.   Jan.   2006.   Online: http://www.gamesconference.org/digra2005/papers/5922543c8cba0a282491dbfdfb17.doc.
[7]   J. H. Smith and M. Sicart, Eds, *Proceedings of the Other Players Conference, IT University of Copenhagen, December 6-8 2004*. Copenhagen: IT University, 2004. 30. Jan. 2006. Online: http://www.itu.dk/op/proceedings.htm.
[8]   M. J. P. Wolf, Genre and the video game, in *The medium of the video game*, M. J. P. Wolf, Ed. Austin: University of Texas Press, pp. 113-134, 2001.
[9]   S. Morris, First-person shooters: A game apparatus, in *ScreenPlay: cinema/videogames/interfaces*, G. King and T. Krzywinska, Eds. London: Wallflower Press, pp. 81-97, 2002.
[10]   T. Manninen, Rich interaction in the context of networked virtual environments: Experiences gained from the multi-player games domain, in *People and computers XV: Interaction without frontiers: Joint proceedings of HCI 2001 and IHM 2001*, A. Blanford, J. Vanderdonckt, and P. Gray, Eds. London: Springer-Verlag, pp. 383-398, 2001.
[11]   S. Morris, WADs, Bots and Mods: Multiplayer FPS Games as Co-Creative Media, in *Level Up Conference Proceedings 2003*, n.p. 30. Jan. 2006 . Online: http://www.digra.org/dl/db/05150.21522.
[12]   S. Morris, Shoot First, Ask Questions Later: Ethnographic Research in an Online Computer Gaming Community, *Media International Australia* 110 (2004) 31-41.
[13]   T. Manninen and T. Jujanpää, The hunt for collaborative war gaming - CASE: Battlefield 1942, *Game Studies* 5/1 (2005) n.p. 30. Jan. 2006. Online: http://www.gamestudies.org/0501/manninen_ kujanpaa/.
[14]   T. Manninen, Interaction manifestation in multiplayer-games, in *Being there: Concepts, effect and measurements of user presence in synthetic environments*, G. Riva, F. Davide, and W. A. Ijsselsteijn, Eds. Amsterdam: IOS Press, pp. 295-304, 2003,.
[15]   T. Manninen, Interaction forms and communicative actions in multiplayer games, *Game Studies* 3/1 (2003) n.p. 30. Jan. 2006. Online: http://www.gamestudies.org/0301/manninen/.
[16]   J. E. Short and B. Christie, *The social psychology of telecommunication*. London: Wiley, 1976.
[17]   R. L. Daft and R. H. Lengel, Organizational information requirements, media richness, and structural determinants, *Management Science* 32, pp. 554-571, 1986.
[18]   C. Galimberti and G. Riva, Actors, artifacts and inter-actions: Outline for a social psychology of cyberspace, in *Towards CyberPsychology: Mind, cognition an society in the Internet age*, Amsterdam: IOS Press, pp. 3-18, 2001.
[19]   R. E. Rice and G. Love, Electronic emotion: Socioemotional content in a computer-mediated communication network, *Communication Research* 14, pp. 85-108, 1987.
[20]   S. Kiesler, J. Siegel, and T. W. McGuire, Social psychological aspect of computer-mediated communication, *American Psychologist,* 39, pp. 1123-1134, 1984.
[21]   L. Sproull and S. Kiesler, Reducing social context cues: Electronic mail in organizational communication, *Organisational Behaviour and Human Decision Processes* 37, pp. 157-187, 1987.

[22] M. J. Culnan and M. L. Markus, Information technologies, in *Handbook of organizational communication: An interdisciplinary perspective*, F. M. Jablin, L. L. Putnam, K. H. Roberts, and L. W. Porter, Eds. Newbury Park, CA: Sage, pp. 420-443, 1987.

[23] N. K. Baym, The emergence of community in computer-mediated communication, *CyberSociety: Computer-mediated communication and community*, S. G. Jones, Ed. Thousand Oaks, CA: Sage, pp. 138-163, 1994.

[24] J. B. Walther, Interpersonal effects in computer mediated communication: A relational perspective, *Communication Research* 19, pp. 52-90, 1982.

[25] J. B. Walther and J. K. Burgoon, Relational communication in computer-mediated interaction, *Human Communication Research* 19, pp. 50-88, 1992.

[26] J. B. Walther, Computer-mediated communication: Impersonal, interpersonal, and hyperpersonal interaction, *Communication Research* 23, pp. 3-34. 1992

[27] K. A. Carter, Type me how you feel: Quasi-nonverbal cues in computer-mediated communication, *ETC* 60, pp. 29-39, 2003.

[28] G. Riva, Communication in CMC: Making order out of miscommunication, in *Say not to say: New perspectives on miscommunication*, L. Anolli, R. Ciceri and G. Riva, Eds. Amsterdam: IOS Press, pp. 203-233, 2001.

[29] M. Schulze, Substitution of paraverbal and nonverbal cues in the written medium of IRC, *Dialogue analysis and the mass media: Proceedings of the international conference in Erlangen, April 2-3*, B. Naumann, Ed. Tübingen: Niemeyer, pp. 65-82, 1999.

[30] L. Anolli, MaCHT - Miscommunication as CHance Theory: Towards a unitary theory of communication and miscommunication, in *Say not to say: New perspectives on miscommunication*, L. Anolli, R. Ciceri and G. Riva, Eds. Amsterdam: IOS Press, pp. 3-43, 2001.

[31] S. C. Herring, Introduction, in *Computer-mediated communication: Linguistic, social and cross-cultural perspectives*, S. C. Herring, Ed. Amsterdam/Philadelphia: John Benjamins, pp. 1-10, 1996.

[32] J.-N. Thon, Das Videospiel als Entwicklungsroman des 21. Jahrhunderts?, *Tiefenschärfe* Sommer (2005) 23-27. 30. Jan. 2006. Online: http://www.sign-lang.uni-hamburg.de/Medienprojekt/tiefenschaerfe/pdfe/ts_1-05.pdf.

[33] J.-N. Thon, Der Multiplayer-Shooter als sozialer Raum, to appear in *Tiefenschärfe* Winter (2005).

[34] J.-N. Thon, Schauplätze und Ereignisse. Über Erzähltechniken im Computerspiel des 21. Jahrhunderts, to appear in *Mediale Ordnungen. Erzählen, Archivieren, Beschreiben*, Corinna Müller, Ed. Marburg: Schüren, in preparation.

[35] B. Neitzel, Narrativity in computer games, in *Handbook of computer game studies*, J. Raessens and Jeffrey Goldstein, Eds. Cambridge, Mass: MIT Press, pp. 227-245, 2005.

[36] J. Juul, *Half-Real: Video games between real rules and fictional worlds*. Cambridge, Mass.: MIT Press, 2005.

[37] M. J. P. Wolf, Space in the Video Game, in *The medium of the video game*, M. J. P. Wolf, Ed. Austin: University of Texas Press, pp. 51-76, 2001.

[38] E. Aarseth, S. M. Smedstad, and L. Sunnanå, A multi-dimensional typology of games, in *Level Up Conference Proceedings*, Utrecht: University of Utrecht, 2003, pp. 48-53. 30. Jan. 2006. Online: http://www.digra.org/dl/db/05163.52481.

[39] J. H. Smith, The problem of other players: Ingame cooperation as collective action, in *Digra 2005 Proceedings*, n.p. 30. Jan. 2006. Online: http://www.gamesconference.org/digra2005/papers/599b42f9a8cf4ae206d44bf0d78c.doc.

[40] P. C. Hogan, *Cognitive science, literature, and the arts: A guide for humanists*, New York: Routledge, 2003.

[41] G. Stasser, Pooling unshared information during group discussion, in *Group processes and productivity*, S. Worchell, W. Wood, and J. A. Simpson, Eds. Newbury Park, CA: Sage, pp. 48-67, 1992.

[42] G. Riva, From technology to communication: Psycho-social issues in developing virtual environments, *Journal of Visual Language and Computing* 10, pp. 87-97, 1999.

[43] M.-L. Ryan, *Narrative as virtual reality: Immersion and interactivity in literature and electronic media*, Baltimore: John Hopkins, 2001.

[44] A. McMahan, Immersion, engagement, and presence: A method for analyzing 3-D video games, in *The video game theory reader*, M. J. P. Wolf and B. Perron, Eds. New York: Routledge, pp. 67-86, 2003.

[45] T. Manninen, *Rich interaction model for game and virtual environment design*, Oulu: University Press, 2004. 30. Jan. 2006. Online: http://herkules.oulu.fi/isbn9514272544/.

[46] L. A. Suchman, *Plans and situated actions: The problem of human-machine communication*, Cambridge: University Press, 1987.

[47] G. Riva and C. Galimberti, Computer-mediated communication: Identity and social interaction in an electronic environment, *Genetic, Social and General Psychology Monographs* 124, pp. 434-464, 1998.

[48] S. Stryker and A. Statham, Symbolic interaction and role theory, in *Handbook of social psychology: Volume I: Theory and method*, G. Lindzey and Elliot Aronson, Eds. New York: Random House, pp. 311-378, 1985.

[49] R. Bartle, Hearts, clubs, diamonds, spades: Players who suit MUDs, in *The game design reader: A rules of play anthology*, K. Salen and E. Zimmerman, Eds. Cambridge, Mass.: MIT Press, pp. 754-787, 2006.

[50] J. Halloran, Y. Rogers, and G. Fitzpatrick, From text to talk: Multiplayer games and voiceover IP, in *Level Up Conference Proceedings 2003*, pp. 130-142. 30. Jan. 2006. Online: http://www.digra.org/dl/db/05163.08549.

[51] G. Costikyan, Talk like a gamer, *Verbatim* 27/3, pp. 1-6, 2002.

[52] E. McKean, L33t-sp34k, *Verbatim* 27/1, pp. 13-14, 2002.

[53] S. R. Hiltz, K. Johnson, and M. Turoff, Experiments in group decision-making: Communication process and outcome in face-to-face versus computerized conferences, *Human Communication Research* 13, pp. 225-252, 1986.

[54] H. Parret, Ed., *Pretending to communicate*, Berlin: De Gruyter, 1994.

[55] N. Coupland, H. Giles, and J. M. Wiemann, Eds, *"Miscommunication" and problematic talk*, Newbury Park, CA: Sage, 1991.

[56] L. Anolli, R. Ciceri, and G. Riva, Eds, *Say not to say: New perspectives on miscommunication*, Amsterdam: IOS Press, 2001.

From Communication to Presence
G. Riva et al. (Eds.)
IOS Press, 2006

13 Communication and Experience in Clinical Psychology and Neurorehabilitation: The Use of Virtual Reality Driving Simulators

Brenda K. WIEDERHOLD, Mark D. WIEDERHOLD

Abstract. Virtual reality (VR) driving simulators may be used as an aid to traditional cognitive-behavioral therapy in the treatment of a variety of driving-related disorders. In recent years there has been a heightened interest among researchers and clinicians in using VR technology to address a wide range of driving-related issues. Clinical applications include specific driving phobias, driving phobias related to panic and agoraphobia, and posttraumatic stress disorder (PTSD) as a result of motor vehicle accidents. Other areas of interest include neurorehabilitation for individuals who have sustained various brain injuries, examining the impact of pharmaceuticals while driving, and assessing and predicting driving abilities among teenage and elderly populations. The VR world elicits real reactions that can be modified through therapy to help people overcome disorders and traumas such as these. As with any type of treatment, some limitations exist. However, results thus far have been promising and directions for future research are discussed.

Contents

13.1 Introduction

Virtual driving systems have a variety of applications including (a) clinical applications in psychotherapy for the treatment of specific driving phobia, panic disorder and agoraphobia, and posttraumatic stress disorder (PTSD) for individuals recovering from motor vehicle accidents (MVA's); (b) treatment for neurorehabilitation; (c) testing of pharmaceuticals, and (d) driver training. Furthermore, there are a variety of new and exploratory applications including the assessment of vestibular disorders and examining the effects of road rage. The table below briefly outlines why VR driving assessment protocols outweigh other current assessment protocols (see Table 1).

Table 1. Current driving assessment protocols versus VR driving assessment protocols

Current Driving Assessment Protocols	Limitations	How VR Addresses Limitations
Neuropsychological Tests	▪ Assesses component cognitive skills individually ▪ Questionable ecological validity	▪ Allows assessment of "complex" behaviors, such as driving ▪ Allows assessment of driving skills in "real-life" situations
Computerized Tasks	▪ Simplified graphics ▪ Limited user interaction	▪ Interactive, detailed, "real-life" graphics ▪ Maximum user interaction
Driving Simulators	▪ Variability in level of interaction ▪ Financially inaccessible	▪ Submersive effect allows higher level of interaction ▪ Increased advances in technology allow for a financially achievable system
Behind-the-Wheel Evaluations	▪ Based on subjective measures ▪ Limited driving scenarios due to safety ▪ Non-standardized procedures	▪ Allows for objective recording of all driving measures and behaviors ▪ Easily modifiable environment allows assessment under various conditions ▪ Controlled environment allows for safe evaluation of driving in complex and challenging situations ▪ Allows for standardized assessment across evaluators

13.2 Driving-related Anxiety Disorders

13.2.1 Specific Driving Phobia

Drivers who have been in serious car accidents may develop specific driving phobias. One study found that 15% of car accident victims developed such a phobia [1]. Driving phobias may be so severe that individuals are limited to drive very short distances, or, in some cases they may be unable to drive at all. Patients who present with a fear of driving may be diagnosed with a specific phobia, panic disorder or agoraphobia, or, posttraumatic stress disorder (PTSD) due to a MVA. In addition, as a person avoids driving situations, some of the driving skills previously learned may begin to deteriorate [2].

Emotional processing theory suggests that in order to decrease anxiety one must first elicit the anxiety [2]. However, many patients are unable to imagine a vivid enough scenario to establish an anxiety response. Therefore, many clinicians have taken their patients into the real world (in vivo), in order to assist them in overcoming their fear. Unfortunately, this can put the clinician and patient in an unpredictable, uncontrolled, and often, unsafe situation, with the client exposed to traffic an unfamiliar roads which frequently result in a panic attack or overwhelming anxiety [2]. VR allows treatment to occur in the privacy of the therapist's office, which provides a safe and confidential place in which to begin exposure to the fear situation, with the patient visualizing the fear situation (imaginal exposure) and learning to control anxiety. In this way, driving exposure is achieved systematically and safely for both the patient and therapist. At The Virtual Reality Medical Center (VRMC) VR graded exposure therapy (VRGET) is used to treat driving phobias and is similar to its use with other specific phobias, focusing on gradual exposure and cognitive and behavioral modifications. Tasks of increasing difficulty are assigned to the patient, while the patient's reactions are observed and measured [2, 3].

Early research on VR applications for driving phobias has been promising. Matthews et al. examined individuals' vulnerability to stress during driving by assessing their performance in a driving simulator [4]. It was found that participants who disliked driving (possibly due to their anxiety) had reduced driving control skills, experienced greater mood disturbance while driving, and drove more cautiously. Furthermore, individuals who scored high on aggressive driving were also more prone to errors due to confrontational passing tactics.

Janelle [5] examined the influence of distraction and anxiety on driving abilities during a simulated driving task. Forty-eight women were randomly assigned to one of six groups, each with varying levels of peripheral distraction and anxiety instruction sets. Cognitive anxiety, visual search patterns, performance, and arousal were measured. Results showed that highly anxious participants made more driving errors and displayed a lower driving proficiency than participants in any other group. In addition, they showed a decreased level of concentration, implying a reduced ability to process peripheral information.

Schare et al. examined levels of immersion and emotional reactions to VR driving environments in 17 participants (8 phobic and 9 non-phobic drivers) [6]. Results demonstrated that phobic participants reported higher levels of immersion and higher emotional reactions to the environment. In addition, while subjective ratings of distress levels for the two groups significantly differed, both groups showed similar patterns of change with: 1) an increase in distress from pretest to the first practice course, 2) a decrease from the first practice to the second practice, and 3) an increase from the second practice to the test course. Increases were more prominent for phobic participants, and this pilot study indicated that a VR environment is capable of eliciting subjective anxiety and physiological arousal for both phobic and non-phobic individuals [6].

Additional research conducted by Wiederhold et al. examined the advantages of using wireless communication technology for treating fear of driving [7]. Three case studies, including patients with a fear of driving as part of panic disorder with agoraphobia, PTSD due to a MVA, and fear of driving due to a lack of driving skills all used a cellular telephone to treat patients with a fear of driving. Therapists accompanied patients for in vivo driving sessions once VR exposure (computer simulation) therapy had been performed. The therapist followed the patient in another vehicle, and the patient was allowed to contact the therapist using a cellular phone during periods of increased anxiety. Although in some cases the phones were never used, they provided a "security net" for the patient if needed. While the risks of cellular phone use must be addressed, the ability of patients to contact the therapist with a cell phone was instrumental in overcoming the fear of driving. Therefore, the benefits and cost advantages of increased mobility, reduced dependence on others, and reduced utilization of health care services for patients seem to outweigh the risks associated with cellular phone use [7].

In 2001, Wiederhold et al. examined the physiological responses of 10 patients with a fear of driving using a VR driving simulation (developed and tested at Hanyang University in Seoul, Korea) [2]. Results showed that physiological desensitization, as well as subjective desensitization occurred through the use of physiological feedback and virtual exposure [2]. In comparison, Jang et al. examined the normal physiological response of participants in two different types of virtual environments: driving and flying simulations [8]. There are few studies that have examined the normal physiological response to virtual environments, or reactions to different virtual environments. However, as VR technology continues to attract significant attention, the use of objective measurement tools, such as physiological monitoring, are even more important than ever. In the present study, 11 non-phobic participants were exposed to each virtual world for 15 minutes. Heart rate, skin resistance, and skin temperature were measured and the Presence and Simulator Sickness Questionnaire scores were obtained after each exposure. Results showed that heart rate and skin resistance can be used as objective measures in monitoring the reaction of non-phobic participants to virtual environments [8].

While earlier studies demonstrated that VR is an effective means to evaluate driving deficits among phobic patients, more recent studies show the importance of obtaining physiological measures as well. Physiological measurements significantly aid in the verification of emotional processing [9]. Furthermore, the advantages of measuring anxiety levels via physiological measures include the ability to obtain objective information about a specific patient's physiological response to the stressor, the possibility for therapeutic intervention during various levels of stress, and gauging effectiveness of psychological therapeutic interventions while driving [7].

13.2.2 Panic and Agoraphobia

Individuals who suffer from panic disorder with agoraphobia, or agoraphobia without a history of panic, may experience a fear of driving far from home or on the freeway [10]. Such fears are due to the idea of feeling trapped without the ability to escape and having no help in sight. This type of fear can be treated in VR using the same systems that are used for specific driving phobias or driving-related PTSD. At The Virtual Reality Medical Center in San Diego, CA, patients progress through increasingly difficult driving scenarios (e.g., stuck in a tunnel with cars crowding in behind them) and are taught to employ breathing techniques, thought stopping, and cognitive restructuring techniques while encountering such anxious situations in the virtual world. Between sessions, patients are encouraged to practice tasks as homework assignments in the real world. Eventually, they begin to realize that they can control their reactions to situations, in addition to their interpretations of those situations (i.e., dangerous or not dangerous). Practicing these skills in the virtual world allows patients to generalize their experiences to the real world and they develop a sense of mastery and self-efficacy much more quickly [10].

An additional study set out to use VR in order to treat panic and agoraphobic patients more effectively [11]. In order to accomplish this, it is necessary to determine the physiologic responses of non-phobics when placed in the virtual panic and agoraphobia environments. This study exposed non-phobic participants to virtual panic and agoraphobia worlds. Participants were exposed to four different VR environments (e.g., elevator, supermarket, town square, and beach). Physiologic responses were measured via noninvasive sensors including peripheral skin temperature, heart rate, heart rate variability, respiration, and skin conductance. This study was useful in laying the foundation for future research on treating individuals with panic and agoraphobia using virtual worlds for exposure to fearful situations. Determining how non-phobics respond to VR worlds created for panic and agoraphobia individuals can help to establish a baseline for physiological responses during clinical treatment of those with panic and agoraphobia [11].

Similar to the studies conducted for a specific driving phobia, studies on individuals who suffer from panic disorder with agoraphobia, or agoraphobia without a history of panic have also demonstrated that VR is an effective way to treat [11]. In addition, studies have shown the importance of obtaining physiological measures – not only in those with the disorder, but in individuals without a history of the disorder as well. By knowing the reaction of non-phobic individuals, it is easier to determine what levels of arousal might be realistic to expect from phobic patients. Differences in level of immersion and self-report responses are important as well [11].

13.2.3 Posttraumatic Stress Disorder

MVA's account for over 3 million injuries annually and are one of the most common traumas individuals experience. In any given year, approximately 1% of the U.S. population will be injured in a MVA [12] and approximately 45% of MVA survivors develop PTSD [1]. These individuals may have recurrent flashbacks to the accident, nightmares, avoidance behaviors, and a generalized increase in anxiety. Cognitive-behavioral therapy has been shown to be successful in the treatment of driving-related PTSD [1]. Effective treatments include relaxation training, *in vivo* and imaginal exposure therapy. However, given that in vivo exposure may be impractical and imaginal exposure is non-immersive, the use of VRGET for car accident victims may serve as the most effective method for decreasing the length of treatment and increasing treatment efficacy [3].

One study examined the effectiveness of the combined use of computer generated environments involving driving games (game reality [GR]) and a VR driving environment in exposure therapy for the treatment of driving phobia following a motor vehicle accident [13]. Fourteen participants were exposed to a Virtual Driving Environment (Hanyang University Driving Phobia Environment) and computer driving games (London Racer/Midtown Madness/Rally Championship). Results showed that 50% of participants who were exposed to a combination of VR driving simulation and GR driving tasks became immersed in the driving environments.

Among those participants, significant post-treatment reductions were found on all measures including subjective distress (SUDS), driving anxiety (FDI), posttraumatic stress disorder (CAPS), heart rate rise (HR) and depression (HAM-D) ratings. Subscale analysis of the FDI showed significant reductions on all three subscales including travel distress, travel avoidance and maladaptive driving strategies. These results suggest that VR and GR may play a useful role in the treatment of driving phobia post-accident even when co-morbid conditions such as posttraumatic stress disorder and depression are present.

A second study aimed to investigate if a clinically acceptable immersion/presence rate of 80% or greater could be achieved for driving phobia participants in computer generated environments by modifying external factors in the driving environment [14]. Eleven patients who met the DSM-IV criteria for Specific Driving Phobia (seven of which had an overlapping diagnosis of PTSD), were exposed to a computer-generated driving environment using computer driving games. After undertaking a trial session involving driving through computer environments with graded risk of an accident, 10 of 11 (91%) driving phobic participants met the criteria for immersion/presence in the driving environment enabling progression to VR exposure therapy. These findings suggest that the paradigm adopted in this study might be an effective and relatively inexpensive means of developing driving environments realistic enough to make VR exposure therapy a viable treatment option for driving phobia following a MVA [14].

13.3 Driving for neurorehabilitation

VR driving simulations can also be useful for evaluating the visual-motor skills of individuals recovering from traumatic brain injury, stroke, or other types of physical trauma in order to re-learn driving skills [3]. About 700,000 people have a stroke in the United States annually [15]. Given our modern fast-paced society, a great value is placed on an individual's ability to function independently [16]. However, individuals who sustain brain injuries are often faced with physical and cognitive impairments that hinder their ability to function independently with respect to everyday living. Even more surprising, one-third of the 500,000 people that will survive a stroke each year resume driving without any formal testing, training or counseling [15].

Wald et al. conducted a pilot study in which 28 adults (22 males, 6 females) with a brain injury participated in a standardized driving evaluation, which included VR driving simulator software (DriVR) developed by Imago Systems, Inc. [17]. The DriVR allows playback of the participant's performance, compiles quantitative statistics of the session, and simulates a range of driving routes in a variety of weather conditions, road conditions, and times of day. The system includes head tracking with a head-mounted display (HMD) and tracker, a steering wheel, brake, gas pedal, and graphics of open road scenarios and tall buildings. The system can also be easily adapted for other driving tasks, such as systematic desensitization of those with phobias, PTSD or to teach young drivers. Results of this study showed that DriVR appeared to be a useful adjunctive screening tool for assessing driving performance in participants with brain injury. Moreover, DriVR may be used as a driving rehabilitation tool to retrain driving skill deficits, as well as treating driving fears and avoidance. Future research will need to determine whether the skills mastered from DriVR will generalize to improved driving skills or reduced driving fears in everyday life [17]. One group of researchers developed a VR driving simulator in order to safely evaluate and improve the driving ability of spinal injury patients [18]. Fifteen patients with thoracic or lumbar cord injuries and 10 normal patients participated. Spinal injury participants manipulated the break and accelerator pedal of the simulator by using the hand control device, whereas the normal drivers used foot controls. During the 20 minute simulation, driving data was recorded via computer and five driving skills were measured including average speed, steering stability, centerline violations, traffic signal violations, and driving time in various road conditions such as straight and curved roads. Patients then self-reported level of realism for the driving simulator and the amount that their fear of driving had been reduced. Results showed that type of manipulation method did not seem to influence the relative performance in the VR driving simulator between groups. Furthermore, participants reported an average score of 51.5% for level of realism of the driving simulator and 73% reported that their fear of driving was reduced when driving with their hands. Suggestions for future research include enhancing the realism of driving simulators and increasing the variety of training situations.

In 2003, Kim et al. aimed to identify a driving assessment that would best predict the driving ability of brain injury patients [16]. This study explored the relationship between perceptual, cognitive, and operational variables that form the basis for off-road evaluations. In addition, the authors were interested in determining whether there are basic dimensions that may underlie performance in such evaluations, and to identify the variables that might help refine the methods used for evaluating persons with cerebral injuries. A driving simulator including adaptive hand and foot controls to simulate a real-time driving experience was created. The driving simulator and off-road evaluations composed of psychometric testing that were used in this study are commonly used in rehabilitation settings to assess a person's ability to resume driving after a brain injury.

Recently, Lew et al. evaluated whether driving simulator and road test evaluations could predict long-term driving performance [19]. Eleven patients with moderate to severe traumatic brain injury and 16 healthy subjects participated in this prospective study. At the initial evaluation (Time 1), participants' driving skills were measured during a 30-minute simulator trial using an automated 12-measure Simulator Performance Index (SPI), while a trained observer also rated their performance using a Driving Performance Inventory (DPI). In addition, participants were evaluated on the road by a certified driving evaluator. Ten months later (Time 2), family members observed patients driving for at least three hours over four weeks and rated their performance using the DPI. Results showed that at Time 1, patients were significantly impaired on automated SPI measures including speed and steering control, accidents, and vigilance to a divided-attention task. At Time 2, simulator indices significantly predicted handling of automobile controls, regulation of vehicle speed and direction, higher-order judgment and self-control, as well as a trend level association with car accidents. Automated measures of SPI were more sensitive and accurate than observational measures of simulator skill (DPI) in predicting actual driving performance. Surprisingly, the road test results at Time 1 were not significantly related to driving performance at Time 2. This study showed that simulator-based assessment of patients with brain injuries can provide ecologically valid measures, which may be more sensitive than traditional road tests as predictors of long-term driving performance [19].

Current reports show that a Driving Performance Laboratory has been established at Sharp Memorial Rehabilitation Services in San Diego, CA to evaluate and train patients with stroke and brain injury who want to resume driving [15]. Experts at the Driving Performance Laboratory agree that there are a number of advantages to the driving simulator over the road test. The first advantage is safety because assessment and training of skills and abilities of drivers in hazardous situations can be done in realistic, virtual driving environments without adverse consequences. Second, driving scenarios can be replayed for review and critical analysis by patients and therapists, and third, the simulator may act as a training device to improve driving skills of attention, speed of processing visual information, and situational awareness. Moreover, training sessions can be individually tailored to the specific needs of each patient, encouraging them to practice and make improvements in their specific areas that need improvement [15].

13.4 Testing pharmaceuticals

Driver impairment by medication or illness is an important issue in our society [20]. It is estimated that approximately 30% of all accidents are primarily or secondarily related to driver impairment due to drowsiness, drug consumption or illness [20]. However, the ability to drive is important, especially for depressed patients because it allows mobility and the ability to reestablish social networks that may have been lost. Few studies have examined the effects of antidepressants on driving ability, and those that do exist have primarily been employed in real traffic. However, one study (N = 23 participants; 10 female, 13 male) evaluated a real car-based driving simulator using a motorway test-track to investigate the impact of a single oral dose of sertraline (50 mg) on various cognitive functions related to driving tasks and objective driving performance. Results showed no evidence of drug induced impairment of drivability in the simulator. Until a standardized methodology for evaluating drivability is created, studies such as this one are important and can help to close the gap between driving simulators and driving in real life [20].

As previously mentioned, driver impairment can also be related to illness. One study examined 37 adults with Type I diabetes and their ability to drive in driving simulation tests [21]. Researchers manipulated participants' blood glucose levels by giving them an intravenous insulin solution containing various amounts of sugar (61-72 mg/dl, 50-60 mg/dl, and less than 50 mg/dl). At all three ranges of hypoglycemia, driving performance was found to be significantly impaired. Participants were more likely to swerve, brake inappropriately, and speed in comparison to when their glucose levels were within normal limits. Even more surprising, less than 1/4 of drivers realized that their driving was impaired, while only 1/3 took corrective action by drinking soda or stopping driving, and most did not do so until their glucose levels were below 50 mg/dl. The researchers recommend that Type I diabetes patients have fast-acting glucose- and carbohydrate-rich snacks on hand when they drive or measure their blood sugar before driving.

Drivability is an important and relevant performance parameter in our society [20]. It can be especially important for depressive patients as it means mobility and in many cases, a higher degree of integration with the rest of society. However, there are some limitations regarding drivability related to the unknown drug effects related to driving. Currently, there is no common and reliable method to test drivability.

Furthermore, it is impossible to validate driving tests (on the road) or any other experimental test against the criteria of an accident in real life [20]. It is for this reason that driving simulators are so important, and why realistic virtual driving tests are essential in order to define and measure the potential hazards of drug use while driving.

13.5 Driver training

There are also a variety of non-clinical virtual driving applications, including training new drivers and assessing and retraining older drivers. This type of application could also be applied as a disciplinary treatment for drivers charged with road rage infractions.

13.5.1 Driver Training and Teens

An early study examined young novice drivers and their relationship to high-risk behaviors, traffic accident records and simulator driving performance [22]. Among 198 young male drivers (ages 16-19), this study identified five subtypes of drivers. Clusters one and five showed an increase in high risk behaviors and driving-related aggression and hostility. When placed in a driving simulation task, the drivers in Clusters one and five showed a lower level of skills than the participants in Clusters two through four. These clusters specifically related to ability to handle traffic hazards and to maintain driving ability while having to attend to simultaneous tasks. This study provided a preliminary look at ways to structure training courses for young drivers to help minimize their involvement in automobile crashes. Furthermore, as skill sets in simulated scenarios are increased, their abilities can be transferred and generalized to the real world.

Several years later, The Centers for Disease Control (CDC) funded a study to determine whether training young drivers with a driving simulator would reduce the number of traffic violations and accidents experienced by novice licensed drivers (2002). Two groups participated in this study. The control group attended standard drivers' education and training classes. The experimental group attended standard drivers' education and training classes *and* participated in training utilizing a VR driving simulator. In addition, driving records for both groups were monitored over the next two years.

In particular, one aspect of the cognitive screening protocol evaluated impulsivity, which is being correlated with the two year follow-up data, and related to numbers of fatalities, MVAs, DUIs, moving violations and any other infractions. The study protocol included two phases. Phase I included an introduction to the simulator and minimum performance on a computerized training test that tracks errors such as inappropriate lane changes (going over the white line) and "rolling stops" at stop signs. In Phase II, driving skill development was learned. Teenage participants drove in simulated situations that are often difficult and at times dangerous (e.g., a child running in front of their car – and the computer tracked the errors).

As part of the screening process to enter the study, participants were administered standard personality inventories, a computerized cognitive screening task, and self-report questionnaires concerning perceived self-efficacy. After completion of the study, participants were administered questionnaires to determine level of presence (or immersion) in the VR training simulators and level of simulator sickness, which might have occurred during training. VRMC is in discussions with several physician groups in San Diego to develop a driving simulator that can be used to assess the status of elderly drivers, and to test for early deficits in cognitive function. While this data is still being analyzed, researchers are hopeful that the results of this study will add to the existing literature on teens and driving.

13.5.2 Driver Training and Elderly Individuals

As people age, they often develop difficulties with the demands of driving. Moreover, decrements in cognitive processing speed may limit an individual's ability to handle complex driving situations. Visual processing decrements, including visual processing speed and impaired visual attention skills, have been blamed for the decline in driving skills in older individuals [23]. This can lead to anxiety about driving and insecurity about one's abilities. A driving simulator may allow for a more objective test of such skills in a safe, systematic manner. Interactive simulators, which can simulate various road, traffic, and weather conditions may be used to determine whether these individuals are capable of safe driving, as well as to reassure them that their abilities are still intact. By interacting in an environment that allows for safe assessment and "instant replays", the patient is able to objectively see what their true abilities are. The virtual environment appears to provide a good representation of real world driving skills, and anecdotal reports suggest that patients readily accept weaknesses that are pointed out by simulation tasks [24]. In fact, according to a study funded by the National Institute of Aging and the National Institute on Nursing Research, improvements gained from using a driving simulator and training people to improve their processing speed over ten training sessions led to the successful transfer of real-world driving skills [25]. An early study examined driving performance and simulator sickness in 256 participants as a function of age and gender [26].

Current drivers, between the ages of 60 and 90, participated in this study by using the Atari driving simulator for 20 minutes. Simulator data was collected on 11 variables, eight times per second, while simulator sickness was rated on a 5-point scale at the end of the drive. Results showed that older drivers (70-74 year) drove worse than younger old drivers (60-64 years) on a number of variables including more crossing of the midline, more swerving, more inappropriate braking, more slow driving relative to speed limit, fewer full stops at stop signs, more time to complete left hand turns, and more collisions per miles driven. However, age did not affect speeding, speed variability, maximum break pressure, hesitation at stop signs. Also, in general, gender did not relate to driving performance. Simulator sickness did not affect driving performance and was also not associated with age, although it was significantly worse for females with a history of motion sickness. In a later study, a driving simulator was used to predict future automobile accidents [27]. Data were collected for 38 older subjects who had participated in a driving simulator study three years prior. Both high- and low-risk participants reported that they were still driving. Both types of drivers were also found to have driven similar miles per week, used their seat belt equally as often, and had a similar gender distribution. However, high-risk participants reported having 47 crashes per 1,000,000 miles driven, while low-risk participants reported having 6 crashes per 1,000,000 miles driven. In addition, self-reported ability to drive was unrelated to either crash history or age. Results supported the predictive ability of the driving simulator [27].

13.6 Exploratory Areas

13.6.1 VR as a Diagnostic Tool

The VR driving simulation system developed at Hanyang University is one of the systems currently being used at VRMC to treat patients with driving difficulties related to panic and agoraphobia (see Figures 1 and 2). For example, one case study using this system has been reported in which a 42-year-old female patient suffered from agoraphobia for eight years [7]. When her therapy began, she was unable to drive more than one mile from her home. She also reported being unable to fly or ride in old elevators that she felt were unsafe. After learning anxiety management techniques, she was introduced to a VR world containing a beach scene and an open plaza. Since the scenes did not cause any subjective anxiety and little physiological arousal, the driving scenario was attempted. After four minutes in the environment, the patient became nauseous and the VR session was discontinued.

Figure 1. This driving simulation is used for treating driving phobia as well as driving rehabilitation. Software developed at Hanyang University, Seoul, Korea

She reported feelings similar to motion sickness but no feelings of panic. During her next attempt at VR driving she became nauseous again, this time within two minutes of initiating the VR exposure. The patient was removed from VR and a joint decision was made by both the patient and therapist to discontinue VR treatment. During subsequent sessions, driving was continued in vivo. The patient was subsequently referred to an otolaryngologist and a diagnosis of vestibular disorder was established.

In some cases, patients have been unable to complete VR therapy because of nausea, or "cybersickness" [3]. These patients are referred to an otolaryngologist and the majority of patients who experience cybersickness are diagnosed with a vestibular disorder. Thus, the VR system may also prove useful as a diagnostic tool. Studies have shown that 5% - 42% of patients with panic disorder may have abnormalities in their balance system, compared to up to 5% of healthy controls [3]. There also appears to be a link between subclinical balance abnormalities and the development of agoraphobia [28].

Figure 2. An additional driving simulation used for treating driving phobia as well as driving rehabilitation. Software developed at Hanyang University, Seoul Korea

13.6.2 Road Rage

In the United States, MVA's are the leading cause of accidental death and injury [29]. Moreover, American insurance industry representatives reported that approximately 50% of MVA's involved some type of aggressive driving [30]. Malta et al. compared the physiological responses of self-referred aggressive and non-aggressive drivers [29]. Heart rate, blood pressure, facial muscle activity, and skin resistance were monitored as participants listened to individual vignettes of driving and fear-provoking scenarios, and completed a standard stressor task. Results showed that aggressive drivers, in comparison to controls, exhibited significant increases in muscle tension and blood pressure during the driving vignettes. In addition, the aggressive drivers responded to the fear vignette and mental arithmetic with a lower overall heart rate and electrodermal reactivity, but increased blood pressure and muscle tension. In comparison, controls responded to the fear vignette and mental arithmetic primarily with increased heart rates and decreased skin resistance. It may be that both physiological hyper-arousal and differential responses to stressful stimuli contribute to aggressive driving.

According to research from John Hopkins University in Baltimore, women have more automobile crashes than men [31]. However, men are far more likely than women to have a fatal car crash. It appears that "road rage" behaviors – aggressive driving, speeding, and risk-taking – are concentrated in male drivers, making them three times more likely to have a fatal car crash. Females in the study did have 10%

more collisions per one million miles on the road, but men's additional propensity for drunk driving and distracted driving made them more likely to suffer fatalities [31]. It is troubling that aggressive driving, in one form or another, is responsible for nearly half of all MVA's. Furthermore, aggressive driving behavior usually occurs as a result of heavy traffic, hectic schedules, and pressure and it is unlikely that any of these daily stressors will substantially decrease in any individual's life. That is why virtual driving applications may be a useful treatment; not only as a disciplinary means for drivers charged with aggressive and/or road rage infractions, but even for individuals who want assistance with decreasing their stress levels while on the road.

13.7 Conclusions

There is great interest among researchers and clinicians in using VR technology to address a range of driving-related issues. Clinical applications include specific driving phobias, driving phobias related to agoraphobia, and PTSD as a result of motor vehicle accidents. Other areas include neurorehabilitation, assessing driving ability in teens and elderly populations, and new exploratory areas. Although additional future work is required to standardize VR driving test applications, results thus far show much promise.

13.8 References

[1]   E. B. Blanchard & E.J. Hickling, *After the crash: Assessment and treatment of motor vehicle accident survivors.* Washington, DC: American Psychological Association, 1997.
[2]   B. K. Wiederhold, D. Jang, S. Kim & M. D. Wiederhold, *Using advanced technologies in the treatment of fear of driving.* Proceedings of the 9th Annual Medicine Meets Virtual Reality Conference, Newport Beach, CA, 2001, January.
[3]   B. K. Wiederhold & M. D. Wiederhold, *Virtual Reality Therapy for Anxiety Disorders: Advances in Evaluation and Treatment.* Washington, DC: American Psychological Association, 2005.
[4]   G. Matthews, L. Dorn, T. W. Hoyes, D. R. Davies, A. I. Glendon & R. G. Taylor, *Driver stress and performance on a driving simulator. Human Factors,* 40(1), 136-149, 1998.
[5]   C. M. Janelle, *Change in visual search patterns as an indication of attentional narrowing and distraction during a simulated high-speed driving task under increasing levels of anxiety. Dissertation Abstracts International: Section B: The Sciences and Engineering* 58(7B), 3959, 1998.
[6]   M. L. Schare, J. R. Scardapane, A. L. Berger, & N. Rose, *A virtual reality based anxiety induction procedure with driving phobic participants.* Symposium on the Virtual Reality Applications for Cognitive/Behavioral Assessment and Intervention, Proceedings of the Association for the Advancement of Behavior Therapy Conference, Toronto Canada, 1999 November.
[7]   B. K. Wiederhold, M. D. Wiederhold, D. P. Jang, & S. I. Kim, Use of cellular telephone therapy for fear of driving. *CyberPsychology & Behavior: The Impact of the Internet, Multimedia and Virtual Reality on Behavior and Society,* 3(4), 1031-1039, 2000.
[8]   D. P. Jang, I. Y. Kim, S. W. Nam, B. K. Wiederhold, M. D. Wiederhold, S. I. Kim, Analysis of physiological response to two virtual environments: Driving and flying simulation. *CyberPsychology & Behavior: The Impact of the Internet, Multimedia and Virtual Reality on Behavior and Society,* 5(1), 11-18, 2002.
[9]   B. K. Wiederhold, & M. D. Wiederhold, Lessons learned from 600 virtual reality sessions. *CyberPsychology & Behavior: The Impact of the Internet, Multimedia and Virtual Reality on Behavior and Society,* 3(3), 393-400,2000.
[10]   F. Vincelli, Y. H. Choi, B. K. Wiederhold, S. Bouchard, E. Molinari, & G. Riva, *Cognitive behavioral therapy virtual reality assisted for the treatment of panic disorders with agoraphobia: VR vs. traditional through two case reports.* Proceedings of the 10th Annual Medicine Meets Virtual Reality Conference, Newport Beach, CA, 2002, January.

[11]   K. Moore, B. K. Wiederhold, M. D. Wiederhold & G. Riva, Panic and agoraphobia in a virtual world. *CyberPsychology & Behavior: The Impact of the Internet, Multimedia and Virtual Reality on Behavior and Society, 5*(3), 197-202, 2002.

[12]   T. Buckley, *Traumatic stress and motor vehicle accidents.* Retrieved January 30, 2005 from US Department of Veterans Affairs. National Center for Post Traumatic Stress Disorder, 2005. Available online: www.ncptsd.va.gov/facts/specific/fs_mva.html

[13]   D. G. Walshe, E. J. Lewis, S.I. Kim, K. O'Sullivan, & B. K. Wiederhold, Exploring the use of computer games and virtual reality in exposure therapy for fear of driving following a motor vehicle accident. *CyberPsychology & Behavior: The Impact of the Internet, Multimedia and Virtual Reality on Behavior and Society, 6*(3), 329-334, 2003.

[14]   D. Walshe, E. Lewis, K. O'Sullivan, & S. I. Kim, Virtually driving: Are the driving environments "real enough" for exposure therapy with accident victims? An explorative study. *CyberPsychology & Behavior: The Impact of the Internet, Multimedia and Virtual Reality on Behavior and Society, 8*(6), 532-537, 2005.

[15]   P. Rosen, & P. Raffer, Driver safety evaluation in virtual reality: Patients re-learn to drive. *San Diego Physician*, 25, 2006

[16]   H. Kim, M. Oh, I. Y. Kim, J. H. Lee, B. K. Wiederhold, et al. *Development of a virtual reality system for assessing and training the driving ability of brain injury patients.* Proceedings of the 8th Annual CyberTherapy Conference, San Diego, California, 2003, January.

[17]   J. L. Wald, L. Liu, & S. Reil, Concurrent validity of a virtual reality driving assessment for persons with brain injury. *CyberPsychology & Behavior: The Impact of the Internet, Multimedia and Virtual Reality on Behavior and Society, 3*(4), 643-654, 2000.

[18]   J. H. Ku, D. P. Jang, B. S. Lee, J. H. Lee, I. Y. Kim, & S. I. Kim, Development and validation of virtual driving simulator for the spinal injury patient. *CyberPsychology & Behavior: The Impact of the Internet, Multimedia and Virtual Reality on Behavior and Society, 5*(2), 151-156, 2002.

[19]   H. L. Lew, J. H. Poole, E. H. Lee, D. L. Jaffe, H. C. Huang, & E. Brodd, Predictive validity of driving-simulator assessments following traumatic brain injury: A preliminary study. *Brain Injury, 19*(3), 233-248, 2005.

[20]   R. Mager, S. Brand, T. Senn, O. Stefani, B. Schurmann, M. Spillmann, F. Mueller-Spahn, & A. H. Bullinger, *Driving performance after drug application tested in a real-car based driving simulator.* Proceedings of the First International Conference on Applied Technologies in Medicine and Neuroscience (ATMN). Basel, Switzerland, 2005, June.

[21]   D.J. Cox, L.A. Gonder-Frederick, B.P. Kovatchev, D.M. Julian & W.L. Clarke. Progressive hypoglycemia's impact on driving simulation performance. Occurrence, awareness and correction *Diabetes Care, 23*, 163-170, 2000.

[22]   H. A. Deery, & B. N. Fildes, Young novice driver subtypes: Relationship to high-risk behavior, traffic accident record, and simulator driving performance. *Human Factors, 41*(4), 628-643, 1999.

[23]   C. Owsley, K. Ball, Jr. G. McGwin, M. E. Sloane, D. L. Roenker, M. F. White, et al., Visual processing impairment and risk of motor vehicle crash among older adults. The *Journal of the American Medical Association, 279*(14), 1083-1088, 1998.

[24]   E. Schold-Davis, & J. Watchel, *Interactive driving simulation as a tool for insight development and immersion in a rehabilitation setting.* Proceedings of Envisioning Health, Interactive Technology and the Patient-Practitioner Dialogue, Medicine Meets Virtual Reality Conference, Newport Beach, CA, 2000, January.

[25]   R. A. Clay, Staying in control. *APA Monitor, January 2000,* 32-34, 2000.

[26]   D. J. Cox, B. P. Kovatchev, B. Kiernan, W. Quillian, J. Guerrier & C. George, Evaluation of older driver's performance employing a driving simulator. Manuscript submitted for publication.

[27]   D. J. Cox, P. Taylor & B. Kovatchev, Driving simulation performance predicts future accidents among older drivers. *Journal of the American Geriatrics Society, 47*(3), 381-382, 1999.

[28]   R. G. Jacob, J. M. Furman, J. D. Durrant & S. M. Turner, Panic, agoraphobia, and vestibular dysfunction. *American Journal of Psychiatry, 153*(4), 503-512, 1996.

[29]   L.S. Malta, E. B. Blanchard, B. M. Freidenberg, T. E. Galovski, A. Karl & S. R. Holzapfel, Psychophysiological reactivity of aggressive drivers: An exploratory study. *Applied Psychophysiology and Biofeedback, 26*(2), 95-116, 2001.

[30]   D. S. Snyder, The statement of David S. Snyder, Assistant General Counsel, American Insurance Association, representing advocates for highway and auto safety before the sub-committee on surface transportation, Committee on Transportation and Infrastructure, U.S. House of Representatives, 1997, July 17.

[31]   D.L. Massie, P.E. Green & K.L. Campbell. Crash Involvement Rates by Driver Age and Gender and the Role of Average Annual Mileage. *Accident Analysis and Prevention,* 29 (5), 675-685, 1997.

From Communication to Presence
G. Riva et al. (Eds.)
IOS Press, 2006

14   Learning Communication Skills through *Computer-based* Interactive Simulations

Olivia REALDON, Valentino ZURLONI, Linda CONFALONIERI,
Fabrizia MANTOVANI

Abstract. A learning environment for the training of communicative competence has to consider the complexity of human experience, since it requires a number of cues that are managed *hic et nunc* in the flow of communicative exchange. Therefore, communicative competence has been traditionally considered as a typical face-to-face learning topic. So far, few opportunities exist to learn by experience in an e-learning environment that can combine user's practising and experiencing with an adequate scaffolding structure, giving the learner both the opportunity to fail and the opportunity to give sense to the perspectives selected. Recent work on computer-based interactive simulations and autonomous agents is offering new opportunities for the training of communicative competence in different contexts. Simulation creates a unique environment for developing and executing communication skills. Moreover, the communicative interaction can be developed and enhanced in a realistic, but non-threatening situation. The present chapter aims at analysing how communication skills should be learned through computer-based interactive simulations. First, a definition of communication skills will be indicated considering their involvement in tackling communicative exchanges effectively. Second, an architecture for building interactive simulations will be proposed. In particular, a road map for building e-learning simulations specifically targeted at the training of communication skills will be sketched out, focusing on the development of a narrative structure that should adequately reduplicate the flow of the communicative interaction.

Contents

14.1 Introduction

In general, communication is essentially based on our experience of the world. Many different factors come into play here, since experience is a complex structure, made up at the same time of sensorial and perceptual, cognitive and emotional, inter-subjective and cultural processes, mutually connected with each other. Therefore, communication is influenced and guided by perceptual, cognitive and emotional constraints which control and manage the interaction with reality. Within such perspective, meaning can be seen as the semantic expression of our experience. Meaning entails a remarkable amount of variability in order to fit and express in the right way the continuous flow and the great variety of human experience [1].

A learning environment for the training of communicative competence has to consider the complexity of human experience and the semantic flexibility that enables speakers to use meanings in a pliable way, according to their communicative intentions. Therefore, it should allow trainees to re-define and re-negotiate meanings as happens in the communicative interaction.

As a consequence, the learning of communicative competence should be rooted in experience, since it requires a number of cues that are managed *hic et nunc* in the flow of communicative exchanges. Therefore, communicative competence has been traditionally considered as a typical face-to-face learning topic. However, rooting learning in experience does not mean, in itself, simply doing something. So far, few opportunities exist to learn by experience in an e-learning environment that can combine user's practising and experiencing with an adequate scaffolding structure, giving the learner both the opportunity to fail and the opportunity to give sense to the perspectives selected. Recent work on computer-based interactive simulations and autonomous agents [2-4] is offering new opportunities for the training of communicative competence in different contexts. Modelling the real world, decision making in a simulated environment occurs under pressure, often including conflict, emotional factors, and difficult circumstances. Simulation creates a unique environment for developing and executing decision-making skills. Moreover, the communicative interaction can be developed and enhanced in a realistic, but non-threatening situation. Users can train their communicative style in critical settings through different interactive scenarios that lead their identification and experience in a safe context. The present chapter aims at analysing how communication skills should be learned through computer-based interactive simulations. First, a definition of communication skills will be proposed considering their involvement in tackling communicative exchanges effectively. Second, an architecture for building interactive simulations will be proposed. In particular, a road map for building interactive simulations specifically targeted at the training of communication skills will be sketched out, also focusing on the development of a narrative structure that should adequately reduplicate the flow of the communicative path.

14.2 Defining Communication Skills

The issue of defining communication skills can be suitably addressed by providing a conceptual framework within which communication processes can be analysed and accounted for. Communicative efficacy can be seen as the outcome in the process of mastering communication skills. Hence, the communication competence will be viewed as consisting in the repertoire of communication skills involved in tackling communicative exchanges effectively.

In the following section the basic components that concur in defining and generating communicative exchanges will be highlighted at the same time pointing out how to shape them in an effective way.

14.2.1 The Design of Meaning: Meaning Flexibility, Modal Meaning and Meaning Regularity

Meaning can be viewed as the access to the symbolic domain and it is the way through which individuals become able to communicate each other their internal states of mind [5]. Nonetheless, meaning is a complex matter since, on the one hand, it is endowed with a high flexibility and adaptability to the contingent situations of interlocutors. On the other hand, it shows consistent regularities connected with the need, in any communicative interaction, to expect some kind of stability over time, in order to be graspable and intelligible. In other words, meaning appears to be struggled between contingency and fixedness, with the difficulty to grasp and to confine it into a circumscribed room.

14.2.1.1 Meaning Flexibility

The comprehensive phenomenon of meaning variability can be synthesized in the claim that meaning never repeats itself. A twice-said utterance does not have the same meaning as the first one, since it inevitably arises novel semantic hidden nuances. By definition, a semantic clone is impossible [6]. There are several communicative phenomena implied in the process of generating such variability in the meaning design: among them, we'll focus primarily on the role played by context, since it more suitably applies to the objectives of this contribution.

The basic idea is that the meaning design of a word or an utterance or a facial expression does not depend on a universal, abstract, and fixed semantic system, but is strictly connected with context. No meaning is totally foreseeable or definable *a priori*, since it hinges upon context in a contingent way. Hence, the same message in different contexts may receive a different interpretation. Besides, there may be a basic ambiguity between a given communicative intention by the speaker and the ascription of another intention to him by the interlocutor [1].

This context-dependence of the meaning of any word, of any utterance, of any facial expression implies that it becomes impossible to grasp the comprehensive features of any meaning, since, in speaking and in interpreting the utterances of others we rely on a number of assumptions, taking for granted, in a given communicative exchange, quite a good number of things [7]. Such assumptions are not semantic in their nature, but belong to our knowledge encyclopaedia, since they are derived from our experience of the world, within our culture of reference. Specifically, circumstantial assumptions concern the specific conditions of a given context, the communicative intention of the speaker, as well as the intention ascription by the recipient. People's interpretations of their own and other people's expressions are not necessarily stable or constant over a period of time, but they may change as the context changes. For instance, in the phenomenon called contextual resemanticization, analysed by Violi [8], the speaker can assign specific semantic traits to something that does not possess them of its own, but that obtains them thanks to a specific contingent situation. The phenomenon of contextual resemanticization puts in proper light the great plasticity of meaning, allowing a wide range of opportunities in its use as the result of accurate processes of semantic adjustment. Therefore, one cannot tell which semantic feature in a word, an utterance, or a facial expression depends upon context and which depends upon the text, since they basically contribute in an interdependent way in generating meaning: the former is influenced by the latter in the same moment in which the latter influences the former.

The plasticity and variability of meaning can be considered as posited upon the assumption that meaning is the semantic expression of our experience. That is, meaning does not refer to a fixed and immutable reality, but comes out of the specific interlocutors' point of view (i.e., experience) about reality. Therefore, since communicative exchanges are based on experience (that is a complex structure, simultaneously made of perceptual, cognitive, emotional, and cultural processes, mutually embedded with each other), they will be influenced and guided by perceptual, cognitive and emotional constraints that control and manage our interaction with reality.

Meaning plasticity is hence called for insofar as it enables the expression of the continuous flow and variety of human experience.

14.2.1.2 Meaning Regularity

The semantic variability processes, if assumed at their utmost complexity, make communication virtually impossible, by preventing mutual comprehension. Semantic variability phenomena are indeed compensated and balanced by *semantic stability* processes, which make possible and explain the probabilities of order and regularity in the meaning exchange. So, the meaning design comes to be a quite complex set of patterns in which contingent and momentary components are combined with more enduring and well-grounded ones [6]. Besides, such components of stability are at the base of message intelligibility conditions and of mutual understanding between communicators.

Semantic stability involves some kind of *convention* between interlocutors, because of their sharing the same cultural belonging. As culture is a mediation system which supplies people with a grid of categories, symbols, values, and practices, that enable them to interpret reality, it also provides the learning and the sharing of processes of signification and signalling systems [9]. Such processes are to be considered as the outcome of a long, complex and sometimes hard route to obtain consent and devise conventions between interlocutors (*conventionalisation process*).

A conventionalisation process presupposes the active participation of the communicators, as well as rules, practices, values, and meanings negotiation and sharing, although they may be local and temporary. It ends in working out a set of what Bruner calls *communicative formats* [10,11], each of which is made of a structured sequence of interactive (verbal and non-verbal) exchanges, which allow communicators to reach a joint aim, follow the same procedures, as well as share the meaning of what they are going to say or to do. Many communicative formats show a high and strong regularity structure, such as the greeting exchange, the call for apologies, and the like. These cases can be called *standard* (or *default*) *formats*, and are based on recognising and accepting a shared system of rules and patterns. Usually, words and other communicative signs are "anchored" to a default format that makes their meaning foreseeable and definable.

Specifically, communicative formats swing from *re-production processes* to *production processes*, with an oscillating motion similar to the one proposed by Bourdieu [12,13] for cultural practices. On the one hand, given the nature of re-production processes, communicative formats tend towards repetition and recurrence in an almost stereotypical way, by creating proper "communicative routines" (obviously articulated in sub-routines), and also by establishing a continuity with semantic and communicative past conventions. These recurring and reduplicating processes are at the base of meaning stability and regularity. They are grounded on *context regularity*, as, if it is true that contexts show a great deal of variability and unpredictability, then it is also true that in most cases contexts are structured and provide regular forms to our everyday experience of the world [14]. On this platform, individuals build and share their scripts with reference to specific situations.

Standard context is the context that presents a high routine regularity in the repetition of interactions, sequence of events and communicative exchanges. In such a way, we can assume that *context regularity is equivalent to meaning regularity* [14]. No communicative act, like an utterance, or a facial expression exists without being context related, since it is always indexed in a standard context of use. The meaning of any communicative act is given by the mental representation of standard context regularity. On the other hand, thanks to production processes, communicative formats are neither totally constrained nor completely determined by the past and by context regularity, but they produce variations and deviations as an effect of contingent conditions and novel unpredictable aspects that every communicative situation potentially brings in itself [1].

Context regularity is the outcome of a historical and cultural process, not a logical necessity, since the past neither determines nor constrains the present, although the former steers the latter. In this way, contextual variations may always, in theory and in practice, take place related to *hic et nunc* situations. These variations usually involve a signalling action and a communicative re-adjustment and re-negotiating process between participants.

From this point of view, communicative efficacy is grounded on the ability to tackle, in communicative exchanges, the challenge connected with meaning as a mental and cultural scheme, endowed with a high flexibility and adaptability to the different contingent situations of interlocutors. Such flexibility is grounded on daily experience and, at the same time, allows for meaning to fit the large amount of variability that experience entails. The semantic variability calls for an inferential process, as modal meaning is not an immediate and fully evident datum; rather, it is generated by communicators during their interaction in a dynamic way in the light of the principle of semantic and pragmatic synchrony [1]. At the same time, meaning shows stability over time owing to its conventional nature. As patterned, meaning is coded in some way and follows at least some standard features to be taken by default.

Given this framework, the attainment of communicative efficacy in the sharing and negotiating meaning process seem to be faced with a substantial dilemma: on the one hand, meaning plasticity need to be acknowledged as a basic requirement enabling the fitting and the expression of the continuous flow and variety of human experience.

The effectiveness in communication exchanges hence calls for the ability to co-construe and to set the hedges that define the boundaries of meaning. Language quantifiers, logical connectives, deictic terms, and qualitative adjectives (among others, "that is to say", "more or less", "technically speaking", and so on) make semantic flexibility and gradualness virtually possible, by bringing in light and actually exploiting, within the communicative exchange, the multiple affordances of meaning. On the other hand, the sharing of communicative formats, as rooted in context regularity, provide the necessary requirement for predictability and intelligibility of meaning.

As such, regularity and flexibility define the boundaries within which efficacy can be attained: such a communicative "space" can be seen as the outcome of intertwined paths: relying more on meaning regularity can lead to stiff and over-conventionalised patterns of communication, while indulging in meaning creativity and plasticity can feature communicative exchanges with ambiguity and confusion, eventually preventing reciprocal comprehensibility [14].

14.2.1.3 Meaning as Inferential Outcome and Multimodal Configuration

Since the meaning design is never a fully evident datum, univocally correspondent to an object or an event, it entails the resort to some inferential process by both interlocutors. That is, meaning exhibits an intrinsic opacity insofar as it is the semantic expression of each interlocutor's experience, which does not only generate what is said, but also points out and indexes how to intend what is said. Therefore, words utterances and facial expressions are to be intended as communicative cues from which communicators can proceed to make suitable inferences through logical implication, analogy and similarity processes.

Moreover, as Anolli [1] pointed out, meaning is not connected with a unique and exclusive signalling system, but is generated by the network of semantic and pragmatic connections between different signalling systems. Indeed, besides language, that remains the most flexible and stable communication medium, exclusive to the human species, there are several other communicational devices that participate in the generation of meaning, like the paralinguistic (or supra-segmental), the face and gestures system, the gaze, the proxemic and the aptic, as well as the chronemic. In any communicative exchange, speakers are hence able to arrange a set of different signalling systems to communicate and make public their communicative intention.

Among others, Anolli [14] argued that each of these communicative systems bears its contribution and participates in defining the meaning of a communicative act in an autonomous way. Such multiplicity enhances the freedom degrees of speakers to manifest and calibrate his/her own communicative intentions as related to a specific situation. However, the generative capacity of each signalling system should be connected to produce a global and unitary communicative action, with a more or less high consistency degree.

The process of meaning generation via different signalling systems (multimodality) is ruled out by the so-called *principle of semantic and pragmatic synchrony*, set out by Anolli [14], according to which meaning, whatever it may be, is originated by a non-random combination of different portions of meaning, each of whom produced by a given signalling system. Thus, the meaning of a word, an utterance or a facial expression hinges upon its relations to every piece of meaning arising out of each signalling system within the same totality.

Modal meaning is the standard outcome of the semantic and pragmatic synchrony process, that is, the prevailing and recursive meaning throughout conventionally given situations within a certain cultural community. As Anolli [6] argued, modal meaning is the preferred (or default) one, regularly predominating in a given set of contexts.

While, although, language is subject to explicit and formal learning ever since early stages in individual development, the learning of non verbal communication is substantially implicit and ruled out mainly within interactions between individuals belonging to the same cultural community. As such, non verbal systems are only partially subject to the conventionalisation process and are mainly apt to provide an iconic, spatial and motor representation of reality, rather then a propositional one. Non verbal signalling and signification systems' main function can hence be identified in generating and qualifying interactions, as well as deeply influencing the relationship patterns between the interlocutors. Facial expressions, gaze, gestures, posture and physical distance are comprehensively shaped, together with verbal signs, in order to express and communicate emotions, to qualify the ongoing relationship within a definite context of interaction (for instance, by defining one's role in a dominance-submission relationship), as well as to enhance persuasion processes.

14.2.1.4 Indexicality and Local Management of Meaning

Indexicality refers to the connection between interlocutors, message and context. From this perspective, context consists in an array of constraints put upon a given event or situation. Such constraints basically contribute in defining the meaning of a given utterance or gesture by telling and selecting the perspective for its interpretation. In other words, contextual information is embedded in discursive practices and in the social distribution of knowledge shared within a given cultural community. Rooting in the view on sign as inference advanced by Peirce [15], Anolli [14] states that by indexicality is meant the process through which utterances, gestures, and facial expressions are anchored to their context of use.

   Along this line, indexical (or contextualisation) cues can be identified in all those verbal and non verbal cues that serve a considerable range of functions within the communication process, such as: (a) defining the social identity of the interlocutors (i.e., by selecting social status appropriate expressions); (b) qualifying the utterance in terms of overall positive or negative affective attitude, through the use of quantifiers and superlatives; (c) defining the ongoing social activity (i.e., by employing words whose meaning is related to the knowledge encyclopaedia of specific professions); (d) featuring the epistemic value of the message (i.e., by using adverbs and specific verb modes, like the conditional, or by employing para- and extra-linguistic signals, in order to express one's perspective on the truth content of the utterance, or gesture, or facial expression being acted).

   The appropriate selection of indexical cues turns then out to be a most relevant device in an effective *local management of meaning*, since it calls for the ability to set communicative structures in a pliable way, in order to meet the varying and contingent features of the communication flow. As such, indexical hints can be considered as metapragmatic signs [14], in that they provide the contextual assumptions that give the frame for interpreting the message exchanged. As a consequence, knowledge and training in the use of indexical cues, as anchored to a given cultural (or micro-cultural) community, becomes a necessary requirement in order to enable interlocutors to constantly keep in focus the ongoing communicative exchange, by co-adjusting their verbal and non verbal signals and by selecting the locally most appropriate contextual perspective.

14.2.2 The Intention Design

According to Grice [16], meaning should be considered in a subjective manner as what the speaker means, that is, his/her communicative intention. The interdependency of meaning and intention is a relevant matter to consider in the study of communicative competence. On the one hand, flexibility and regularity of meaning enhance the freedom degrees of speakers in the processes of both intention expression and ascription. On the other hand, intention selection and intention ascription are the requisites for generating, negotiating and modifying meanings. There can't be any communicative exchange without selecting and pursuing specific intentions.

Intention plays a fundamental role in people's communicative exchanges, since it concerns not only the speaker in producing his/her communicative act but also the addressee in recovering and interpreting the meaning of the speaker's message, attributing to it a specific intention. In this way, the communicative exchange is created and governed by a reciprocal game between the communicators: the display and ostension of a given intention by the speaker (*intentionalization process*) and the ascription and attribution of a certain intention to him/her by the addressee (*re-intentionalization process*).

From the speaker's point of view, intention is characterized by an articulated graduation and differentiation within itself. In everyday life, intentionality (as an attitude to produce distinct and specific intentions) is regulated by continuous variations of intensity and precision. This intentional gradability allows communicators to manage the focusing of different communicative acts. Next to plain (common and ordinary) communicative acts, in which the intentional process is almost automatic, there are complex communicative acts (like seductive, ironic or deceptive communication) in which the communicative intention that the communicator conveys to the interlocutor has to be managed by attentive and conscious processes.

In everyday conversation a speaker has to select and choose an intentional layer to convey what he/she has in mind. Since in the production of a communicative act a speaker can only express a part of his/her mental content, the speaker is obliged to follow only one of the different meaning routes he/she has at his/her disposal for conveying what he/she has in mind. Such a choice and continuous gradation of communicative intentions make the communicative act particularly complex, since, on the one hand, it needs a precise cognitive and emotional direction; on the other, it can give rise to communicative uncertainties and difficulties. One intention is usually embedded in another which surpasses and includes the first one. As a consequence, complex communicative acts require the speaker to monitor continuously the efficacy of his intentional effort to reduce such communicative uncertainties. In such circumstances, *explaining* skills can be considered as an attempt to reduce such complexity, identifying and specifying the problem that requires explanation, presenting or eliciting a series of linked statements, and checking that the explanation is understood by the addressee.

In order to succeed, the communicative exchange has to be characterized not only by the producing of a communicative intention in the speaker, but also by its recovery by the addressee. The recovery act involves a precise and conscious activity and the participation of the receiver in the meaning elaboration, since meaning is defined only when the addressee recognizes the speaker's communicative intention [16,17]. However, the idea of recovery as an act of recognizing the source's communicative intention entails an asymmetrical direction, like in a dance where one leads and the other is led [18]. In this sense the speaker appears more significant than the hearer. The former takes a more important position as a source; the latter has only to carry out the recovery as accurately as possible. The more precise the hearer is in this activity, the more suitable he/she is in the communicative exchange and the better he/she does his/her communicative task.

As a consequence, the recovery act appears to be insufficient to explain the interpretation activity of the hearer in relation to the speaker's intention. Therefore, the addressee must attribute a certain intention to the source's communicative act [19]. This intention ascription in the hearer is the "other face" of the intentional stance and is the equivalent of intention production in the speaker. Such a process is characterized by different features: a) it is an autonomous process, carried out only by the addressee; b) it is an active and subjective process, because it depends completely on the addressee's abilities as well as on the perspective he/she chooses to follow.

It is worth remarking that we are faced with an essential condition of communicative interaction, because the speaker and the hearer have different points of view about the same events and objects as topics of communication, even if they share a mutual cognitive background and mutual, culturally defined knowledge. Such a difference in their points of view, that can be radical in some circumstances, involves and presupposes in any case different interpretations and meaning-making in the speaker and the hearer with reference to the same episodes and facts. They possess a different encyclopaedia of knowledge, because they have a different amount of experience in qualitative and quantitative terms. Moreover, they may refer to different beliefs and values systems, as well as be guided by different desires and goals.

In such a perspective it is obvious to expect a plurality of interpretations in the intention attribution from the addressee to the source's message. This plurality is not to be considered as a pathological accident, but it is the standard activity of the addressee. Intention ascription is an open field, and the addressee is allowed a broad space to justify his/her interpretative choice, connected with some cues of the communicative act.

Given the significance and the relevance of his intention ascription, the addressee is as important as the speaker in the communicative exchange. Therefore, intention ascription is a fundamental communicative skill to improve in order to ascribe an intention to the speaker consistently, since it places the addressee and the speaker on the same parithetic level. As a consequence, they share the same responsibility in the construction of the communicative act.

In a standard condition, during the fast flow of communicative exchanges, intention ascription seems to be a default and immediate process, regulated by the *taking-for-granted* principle [20], and rooted in context regularity and in the routine exchanges embedded in meaning stability phenomena. However, the actual intention is often implicit, not directly said by the speaker, but made understandable by means of sufficient leakage cues. In these cases, intention attribution is a significant and subtle communicative task for the addressee. The fundamental questions may be the following: "Why does he tell me such and such a thing? Why does he use this voice intonation?", and the like. We are not interested in limiting our communicative understanding to the apparent, surface intention; we are usually interested in grasping the profound, actual intention of the speaker. If the addressee confines him/herself to taking into consideration only the surface intention, he is quite likely to go wrong sooner or later; in any case, he does not seem a very competent communicator.

It is in such circumstances that emerges the importance of training intention ascription skill to achieve effective communicative competence. The discovering of the actual intention involves a precise, clever inferential process in the trainee. It is an issue of practical reasoning, often based on heuristics and biased by previous patterns of interaction with the interlocutor. Sometimes a few weak clues are sufficient to produce a large inducing process and to reach significant conclusions, which, of course, are not always correct.

To investigate the accuracy of his inferences, the trainee has to search for adding clues from the interlocutor, i.e. re-presenting the perceived essence of the interlocutor's intentions through *reflecting* [21]. Reflection, as a communicative skill, consists of bringing to the surface and expressing in words those states of mind that lie behind the speaker's words [22]. In many professional contexts, it means a restatement of what the client was saying, used to reflect the intention he was expressing, whether or not such intention was directly expressed or only implied [23]. Interpreting back the core message contained in the interlocutor's previous statement enables issues that are vague and confused to be thought through more clearly and objectively [24]. By reflecting, the trainee not only conveys a desire to get to know if his attributions were sufficiently accurate, but also demonstrates to the interlocutor the level of understanding accomplished, despite the fact that the original message may have been inchoate and vague. Moreover, reflecting confirms the speaker in his effort to contribute to the communicative exchange, helping him to express thoughts gradually more clearly and fully. Supported in this way, the speaker is often motivated to continue to explore particular themes more deeply concentrating upon facts, feelings or both, depending upon the content of the reflective statement [25]. From the trainee's point of view, confirmatory responses also serve an important feedback function by indicating accurate understanding of the world of the speaker [26].

14.2.3 Obliquity

The intentionalization and re-intentionalization processes show how the communicative exchange is created and governed by a reciprocal game between the communicators, played hand by hand and move by move [18]. The indefiniteness both in intention production and in intention ascription makes communication seem like an unforeseeable route, not deducible from previous exchanges. On one side, the speaker has the possibility of selecting a certain route of sense instead of another one. It greatly increases the degree of communicative freedom at disposal of the communicator. Therefore, intention plurality and graduation entail an intentional opacity, since in many cases communicative intention, embodied in an utterance or gesture, is shaded and changeable. On the other, intention ascription is indeterminate, since it can take different routes, none of which is either privileged or foreseeable.

Following such considerations, Anolli proposed the MaCHT theory [18], in which many communicative phenomena (such as irony, deception, seduction, and so forth) are considered as chances for communication itself, since they enhances the degrees of freedom available to communicators in their interaction. Communicators have the opportunity to manage their communicative strategy in the best possible way, given the contextual constraints and their respective encyclopaedia of knowledge. These phenomena represent examples of an "oblique" communication with the purpose of optimising interaction with the partner.

The necessity of adopting a type of communication which is "oblique" or indirect is not limited to seductive communication, in which it allows the seducer to combine openness and pleasure whilst allowing him at the same time the reciprocal "disarmament", regarding the content, timing and method involved in the communication. In everyday life there is a great amount of interactive situations that requires different degrees of indirectedness and, in some cases, of ambivalence of the communicative strategies. For instance, irony is a skilful device to assure oneself of many more degrees of freedom than an explicit utterance does [27]. The basic ambiguity of irony allows one to negotiate and re-negotiate the meaning of an ironic comment. Because the ironist is not constrained to undertake responsibility for his/her words and, consequently, he has neither to compromise his/her image nor to lose face [28], the responsibility for the appraisal of ironic value of an utterance moves from the ironist to the addressee. It is up to the latter to recover and attribute an ironic meaning and intention to the utterance of the former. In particular, the ironic sense of a comment is effective when it is not only intenzionalized by the ironist, but also "re-intentionalized" by the addressee. Therefore, oblique communication allows speakers to calibrate the weight of the indirect meaning of their speech. An indirect expression of one's thoughts, desires and feelings cannot only hide one's real intention, but it can also define it and re-draw the limits of social interaction between interlocutors.

As a consequence, a skilled use of irony and humour may serve different communicative functions, and hence prove their importance for the training of communicative competence. It helps to regulate interactions and serves as a social mechanism to facilitate or inhibit the flow of the communicative exchange [29]. For instance, humour assists in maintaining the flow of interaction, filling in pauses in our conversation and sustaining the interest and attention of our conversational partner [30]. In many professional contexts, introducing a topic in a light-hearted way helps the trainee to "search for information", probing indirectly the client's general attitudes and values about an issue and to reveal "touchy" subjects.

14.2.4 Communicative Synchrony and Relationship Management

In communicative exchanges, speaker and interlocutor are at the same level and share the same responsibility; as such, they both participate in that process. As Cohen and Levesque [31] sketched out, "the joint action of dialogue claims that both parties to a dialogue are responsible for sustaining it. Participating in a dialogue requires the conversations to have at least a joint commitment to understand one another". Moreover, a participation framework implies a mutual process of co-constructing and sharing meaning in a continuous stream of communicative exchanges, as shown by Duranti [32].

According to Burgoon [33], when people communicate, they have to "adapt their interaction styles to one another. For example, they may match each other's behavior, synchronize the timing behavior, or behave in opposite ways". Actually, it is well understood in common observations as well as in the scientific field that participants in communicative interaction are usually engaged in a common rhythm. As Cappella [34] pointed out, "co-ordination in social interaction means that people adjust their actions to those of their partners". The notion of interactive co-ordination and mutual adaptation in communication covers a broad range of processes, such as synchrony, mirroring, matching, reciprocity, compensation, convergence as well as divergence. Some of these phenomena have more to do with the temporal co-ordination of the interaction, whereas others focus on the reciprocal adaptation of communicative styles in terms of converging vs. diverging from one's partner's style.

Anolli [18] collected all these processes under the label of *communicative synchrony* as a global and basic property of communication. In fact, communicative attuning and synchrony allow communicators to decline their communicative competence in a practical way for convergence or divergence, and create a broad set of chances for different solutions, ranging from direct and open communication patterns to indirect and cryptic ones.

From a sociological point of view, different scientists have drawn special attention to time patterns in organizing communicative exchanges. The notions of "synchrony of rhythms" proposed by Goffman [35] and "temporal symmetry" advanced by Zerubavel [36] are in this sense. Schutz [37] has widened the concept of a mutual tuning-in relationship as a theoretical extension of the notion of mutual sharing of Cooley [38] and Mead [39]. The "mutual tuning-in relationship" involves, in a particular way, the organization of interaction sequences between partners in a temporal succession.

Within the psychological field, among others scholars, Giles [40], Giles and Powesland [41], and Giles, Coupland, and Coupland [42] deserved attention for their proposal of the Communication Accommodation Theory. According to the CAT, attuning and accommodation strategies consist of a broad set of linguistic and extra-linguistic signals which enable us to adapt our communicative acts to those of our partners, shifting them along a convergent or divergent direction in the sequence of exchanges. In the first case, the communicative styles of the participants become more similar and assume a homogeneous shape; in the second one, the differences become greater, creating a process of schismogenesis. The CAT has been supported by experimental results, since it has been verified that pronunciation [40], speech rate [43], utterances and length of pauses [44], vocal intensity [45, 46], as well as vocal fundamental frequency patterns in childish babbling [47] vary in a sequence of communicative exchanges in conformity with mutual adjustment and attuning.

More recently, Gregory [48], Gregory and Webster [49], and Gregory, Dagan, and Webster [50] have analyzed the accommodation of vocal long-term features, showing that communicators are able to mutually co-ordinate their speech styles in a subtle way, by assuming and maintaining the same specific range of vocal pitch.

The emergence of this synchronized and adapted pattern appears to be of crucial importance in ensuring efficacy and comprehensibility in communication, and in determining the perceived quality of the relationship, effectively managing relational and communicative distance. This topic has been stressed by Grammer [51], and Grammer, Kruck, and Magnusson [52] in investigating the role of communicative synchrony in seduction interaction among people who meet for the first time. In fact, rhythm co-ordination is fundamental in determining the development of interpersonal attraction and a higher degree of satisfaction about the relationship [53]. Patient satisfaction in the physician-patient relationship is also highly related to interactive and communicative synchrony [54]).

Within the perspective here presented communicative efficacy indeed serves and is connected with the basic functions of communication. Besides the facets of effectiveness linked with the propositional function of communication [55,56], which has to do with meaning generation and sharing, the other basic function of communication is the relational one [57]. From this point of view, communication is the psychological dimension through which and by means of which the speaker and the interlocutor's identities are reciprocally defined. In communicating, partners define themselves, the interlocutors and feature the relationship between them. Indeed, for most people, communication takes place within the context of ongoing relationships. As Fogel [58] has illustrated, it is within the context of relationships that individuals develop and grow. Therefore, communication is the basic process through which most patterns of human relationships (from dominance to submission, to conflict) are built upon, can be modified, and can be terminated.

There is a close association between effective communication and relational satisfaction. The relational aspects of communicative efforts are as crucial to effective communication as is the meaning of the message itself, although a sharp dichotomy does not exist: the message transmits relational cues, too [59].

14.3 Developing Effective Simulation Models

Although there is a shared consensus about the affordances interactive simulations can provide, less convergence can be found regarding the architecture they should be built on, especially as far as the training of communication and relational skills is concerned. The aim of the following sections will be to sketch out a road map, theoretically-based and application oriented, aimed at building interactive simulations specifically targeted at the training of communication skills.

First, some basic assumptions regarding the perspective selected for learning in simulations, the multiplicity of specification layers and the expertise resources at issue when developing simulations will be outlined. The topics hence covered will include: (a) identifying a theoretical framework for learning in simulations (expert-novice interaction); (b) defining the specification layers targeted in creating the simulation model; (c) identifying the type of expertise that is required for developing effective simulation models

Second, guidelines for scripting the communicative exchanges will be proposed. We will focus on the development of a narrative structure that should adequately reduplicate the flow of the communicative path.

14.3.1 Basic Distinctions

14.3.1.1 Learning in Simulations: the Expert-novice Interaction

In the light of widely recognized theoretical and empirical evidence [60, 61], learning cannot be considered as a private affair taking place in the mind of the 'learner', this last meant as an isolated pole. Rather, it must be conceived as a social process involving interaction between two or more individuals where knowledge appropriation takes place within and by means of social interaction (concept of distributed knowledge).

Moreover, not only does learning entail interaction, but it also requires *participatory appropriation* [61], in that it involves mutual influence between the learning actors. In other words, learning cannot be conceived as knowledge transmission from an active expert to a passive unskilled learner, but, rather, it may be viewed as an interactive process where expert and novice actively influence each other in an interdependent way: since both take part in such activity (participation is a necessary requisite), the expert influences the novice in the same moment in which the former is influenced by the latter.

The basic idea underlying this approach is that of learning within a community: learning occurs when people participate in shared endeavours with others, with all playing active although sometimes asymmetrical roles in a socio-cultural activity [62]. Such a perspective contrasts with models of learning that are based on one-sided notions of learning – either that it occurs through transmission of knowledge from experts or acquisition of knowledge by novices, with the learners or the others (respectively) in a passive role.

Within this perspective of learning as participation, both experts and novices need to be routinely included in the range of practises of the cultural community they belong to. Hence, simulations can be seen as devices through which knowledge, practices, and perspectives on a specific domain are participated and experienced among novices and experts.

14.3.1.2 Interactive Simulations Specification Layers

Interactive *computer-based* simulations can be viewed as artefacts for learning. As such, they can be featured both as cultural artefacts and as technological artefacts. Following the categorization proposed by Wartofsky [63], in the latter sense they are primary artefacts, that is, materials tools made possible and designed within the technological and graphic affordances thus far available. Moreover, they are secondary artefacts, that is, they consist in mental models and symbols apt to generate different meaning paths. Simulations are therefore built up out of the selection of specific communicative intentions and, at the same time, can be seen as social practices, that is, sequences of organized behaviours and activities which, in order to be participated by expert and novice, need to be suitably scripted and designed. From this point of view, simulations are conventions, insofar as they play a mediation role in the learning process, by shaping it and organizing it (concept of *mediated action*) [64], though not determining it completely: since simulations are cultural artefacts, there is a strong interdependence between simulation-developers, simulation-users and the artefact that mediates the whole learning process.

Therefore, conceptualizing simulations as artefacts for learning entails distinguishing at least between two different layers in their development: (a) the simulation architecture and rationale, that consists in identifying the multiplicity of meaning paths and strategies which can lead to pursue a specific professional goal by mastering specific communication skills (*architecture model specification*) and (b) the simulation design, that consists in the 'visible' output of the architecture simulation (*design model specification*). As will be highlighted further, this contribution will mainly deal with architecture model specification issues.

14.3.1.3 Types of Expertise

In developing the simulation model, both at the architecture specification level and at the design specification level, several types of expertise are involved. Speaking about types of expertise does not imply a one-to-one correspondence with specific expert professionals: rather, the aim is to identify the resources in expertise that are required for anchoring simulations to specific contexts, defining standard regularities and suitable effective deviations from such regularities, in order to manage communicative exchanges effectively.

Conceiving simulations as artefacts gives us the opportunity to identify the expertise domains that need to be taken into account for their development, providing validity and accuracy related to the specific learning goals. First, simulations have to do with conventions resulting from a specific professional culture. Hence, domain specific professionals are needed to identify the relevant cultural practises and the routine sequences of interaction that entail specific communication skills to be managed effectively. Expertise in training communication skills has, moreover, to be connected with identifying the specific shape that practises and the intentional project that directs them, take within the learning path. Finally, being material artefacts, they need to be expertly designed in order to accurately reproduce the perspective architecture behind them. Of course, in the light of the principle of distributed knowledge informing the whole paradigm of learning as participation, none of these types of expertise can be thought of as self sufficient in the process of simulation development, each being, rather, at least, at a minimal level, necessary though never sufficient in itself. More in detail, the types of expertise required in development effort here at issue are: *the professional expertise, the expertise in training communication skills,* and *the technological and designing expertise.*

14.3.1.3.1 Professional Expertise

By professional expertise is meant the expertise on a specific professional domain, in managing and mastering effectively specific interactional and communicative routines, like, e.g., in the banking domain, expertise in mastering cashier-client communicative exchanges, or in the medical domain, expertise in managing patient-physician communicative interaction. As Schank [65] points out, this type of expertise is often linked to those professionals who, given a specific domain, have succeeded in identifying those perspectives that let them negotiate meanings, and manage relationships and emotions effectively. In other words, their experience in meaning generation and strategic mastering of intention expression and intention ascription gives them the opportunity to distinguish between more effective solutions and less effective solutions.

Since experience can be viewed as made up of the perspectives through which meanings are generated, this type of expertise is the requisite for (a) identifying those sequences of action that, in these professional's experience, have generated critical and challenging interactive situations that entail communication skills to be tackled, (b) identifying the communication skills they found most often involved in ruling and acting different strategies, and (c) scaling these communicative solutions according to how they found them to be effective. Of course, being rooted in experience, this type of expertise is intrinsically *domain specific* and cannot be considered as immutable and unchanging, being, rather, subject to re-definition in the light of ongoing cultural (and micro-cultural) adjustments.

From a methodological point of view, robustness, validity and accuracy in the perspectives elaborated by these professionals are deeply influenced by the method employed to gain insights into their experience. Following Schank [65], such perspectives are best identified by asking these professionals to provide *narratives* of their experience, within an interviewing context guided by experts in the training of communication skills. The underlying assumption is that, since this type of expertise roots in experience, it can be properly acquired by relying on the episodic memory, that is by having these experts provide narratives, contextually and temporally grounded, regarding specific events that personally occurred to them, connected with failure, or success, in mastering critical professional situations. The narratives obtained pave the way for communication skills experts to gather the key meanings, structured in sequences of action (scripts), useful for scripting the simulations.

Within this framework, a remarkable affordance in developing interactive computer-based simulations lies in the opportunity to make this type of expertise available to a large number of trainees; as a matter of fact, this highly valuable type of expertise is not only difficult to get via face-to-face formal learning, but it's also highly unlikely to be participated to a large number of potential trainees.

14.3.1.3.2 Expertise in training communication skills

This type of expertise involves the ability to master the declarative – both as episodic and as semantic – knowledge [66] concerning communication skills, so as to be able to teach them effectively. It is connected with bridging the gap between more (or less) effective practises in tackling communicative challenges and the grid of micro- and macro-categories that theoretically map and account for the effectiveness of such practises. Such a map makes possible to identify the specific targets of learning, to operationalize the communication skills at issue into their analytic defining components and to build up a learning path viably designed and structured in order to reach the desired learning goals. From this point of view, this type of expertise is connected with featuring the learning objectives in terms of accuracy and exhaustivity.

The affordances provided by these type of expertise in devising interactive simulations match the underlying assumption that learning is a considerable time- and resource-consuming activity. Given that the narratives supplied by domain professionals have been properly acquired, experts in training communication skills can soundly script the flow of communicative exchanges within which the identified and targeted skills are supposed to come into play. In scripting such flow, meanings are generated and relationships are defined as mental representations of those context regularities highlighted by domain professionals. Moreover, variations in such regularities (and in mastering the skills connected more or less effectively) account for communication paths that sensibly diverge from practises that, from the domain professionals' point of view and experience, turned out to be less effective than others. Nonetheless, since context regularity is the outcome of a cultural process, not a logical necessity, contextual variations not only are needed to reproduce 'natural' communicative exchanges, but also provide the learner with pliable experiential constraints, hence reinforcing the opportunity to fit and express his/her point of view in the scripted though perceived as *hic et nunc* situations.

Therefore, through this type of expertise, the learning path is modelled by taking into account both a grid of theoretically sound categories and the communicative formats provided by expert professionals, nonetheless leaving room for learner's substantial 'deviations' from regularities. As such, a twofold learning strategy is employed: on the one hand, contributions from expert professionals are optimized and give the learner a number of appropriately context-indexed situations and communicatively skilled routes. Learning from imitation and through repetition is therefore possible. On the other hand, by providing significant off-regularity paths, the learner is given the opportunity to face increasingly difficult and demanding communicative exchanges, that can eventually lead to highly inaccurate communicative outcomes. Whatever the path resulting from the learner's choices, successive feedback sessions are needed, as pointed out further, to give sense to the learner's experience.

Therefore, the basic contribution connected with this type of expertise has to do with developing a simulation architecture in which a multiplicity of communication paths, all ecologically sound though different in presumptive efficacy, are identified in order to provide the learner with appropriate experiential constraints that can enhance both a top-down learning path (by facilitating the appropriation of certain communicative formats, rather than others) and a bottom-up learning path (by letting the learner experience and give shape to the communication exchange). To reach this target, besides the scripting of simulations, the development and definition of the sequence of learner's activities need to be worked out within this type of expertise competence, so as to pertinently match learning objectives (i.e., skills and communicative formats appropriation) with sound and specific methods in the education and training of this repertoire of abilities.

14.3.1.3.3 Technological and designing expertise

This type of expertise encompasses a wide array of specific abilities (ranging from computer graphics, 3D animation in virtual environments, computer science informatics) that are necessary in order to accurately reproduce in a "material" artefact the whole simulation architecture, including the design and animation (voice, facial expressions, gestures, and so on) of the characters involved in the scripted communicative exchanges, other than the definition and the visual reproduction of the environment supposed to frame the interaction itself. Since the aim of this contribution has mainly to do with the simulation architecture specification layer, we won't go through the details and relevant implications connected with the technological affordances so far available in this domain. Rather, efforts will be devoted to bringing into light those constraints that, from an architecture layer development, affect and give shape to the designing process of interactive computer-based simulations.

Our basic assumption is that, to enable the user to learn by experience, he must be provided with the opportunity to act communicative exchanges with appropriate contextual information. Nonetheless, context assumptions and indexes cannot be considered as the direct outcome of the physical reproduction of most-similar-to-real communicative exchanges; as Mantovani and Riva [67] point out, from the user's point of view, the criterion of validity for experience in mediated environments does not hinge so much on the comprehensive reproduction of the conditions of physical presence (immersion), but on the development of environments in which actors may share a common ground and interact in an ecological and valid way. Moving back to communication skills training, therefore, it is reasonable to point out that animating bodies and faces of the different characters in interaction taking into account micro-movements (of the brows, of the lips, of the arms, etc.), or designing culture and professionally grounded environments is a design target objective that cannot be faced within a fidelity-based approach to experience in virtual environments [68]. Rather, the designing target objective should be to provide learners with a network of situations and characters that are specifically salient to the skills being trained and to their being indexed to the professional contexts at issue.

Moreover, even considering quite a short communicative exchange (say, two to three minutes long), the range of indexes to be provided to the user encompasses quite a huge number of design choices (modelling the physical outline of the characters, animating them via micro- and macro-expressions, providing temporal coordination to the interaction, defining the environment, and so on), and quite a considerable time (and economical resources) to reproduce them (both in the case of realizing videos with human interlocutors, and in the case of designing 3D embodied characters). A matching between resources to be engaged in design development and priorities connected with the learning target (i.e., the training of communication skills) need then to be reached to enable the use of simulations in a variety of application domains, and not only for research purposes.

Therefore, both from a theoretical view on the constraints to be set in giving validity to the learner's experience, and from an application point of view, one can sustain that priorities in the reproduction of contextual cues need to be set, so as to provide the whole designing process with specific guidelines. For instance, in the simulation design of communicative exchanges, synchronisation between verbal and non verbal signalling systems in each character's animation (by accurately reproducing micro-movements of the face, of gaze, etc., both in each character's expression, and in temporal consistently one with the other over the interaction) can undoubtedly be assumed as far more relevant in comparison with a most accurate reproduction of details in the environment. Hence, expertise in the training of communication skills reasonably need to be combined with design expertise in this process, so as to reproduce exclusively those indexes that, from intention and meaning generation to intention and meaning ascription, suitably anchor the scripted perspectives to a given context.

14.3.2 Scripting the Communicative Exchange

In everyday life, through the interaction with a system people formulate mental models of that system. It helps us to predict the system we confront in our environment. A mental model is one's "personal theory", his own *perspective* on some domain or environment [69]. Such perspective needs not be technically accurate (and often is not), but it must be functional. Perspectives will be constrained by such things as the user's technical background, previous experience with similar systems, and the structure of the human information processing system.

As Norman [70] pointed out, the perspectives people follow to understand social and physical phenomena [71] and to anticipate their behaviour, are characterized by some elements: (a) mental models, and hence perspectives, are incomplete; (b) the ability to "run" them can be severely limited; (c) they are unstable (people can forget details of the system especially when those details have not been utilized for a while); (d) they do not have firm boundaries; (e) they are unscientific, and often include "superstitious" behavior and/or distrust of technology as a factor; (f) they are parsimonious (people often trade off physical action for reduced mental complexity, especially when reduction of complexity can be applied to multiple systems thus avoiding confusion).

As most real systems are non-linear, complex, highly interactive, and their functioning is normally counter-intuitive [72], these perspectives frequently show lack in accuracy and efficacy. Conversely, professional experts operate to see the larger "chunks" (bigger patterns) and to grasp the context (where the important patterns exist in the world), and have a systematic framework (similar to "local" system) to "store" their understanding (deeper knowledge).

In developing the simulation model, communicative exchanges should be scripted as to reduplicate the flow of the communicative path in an adequate narrative structure. In general, such structure entails a *vertical* and a *horizontal dimensions*. Its validity stands in the ability of the expert in modelling different *ad hoc* perspectives of the real system's functioning (*vertical dimension*). The aim is of balancing the coherence of the story against the amount of control afforded the user [73], fixing adequate contextual boundaries and degrees of freedom to user's experience. Starting from such perspectives, experts in training communication skills begin to script each communicative exchange. At each decision point, different choices are scripted in order to let the user experience a particular communicative skill (*horizontal dimension*).

There are two fundamental types of narratives used in computer learning applications: *linear narrative* and *branching narrative*. Linear narrative is a traditional form of narrative in which a sequence of events is narrated from beginning to ending without variation or possibility of a user altering the way in which the story unfolds or ends [74]. Even though the user has a certain degree of control during level play, the only outcome is successful completion of some objective or failure, in which case the user must try again. All users experience the same story and each user will experience the same story during successive sessions.

Conversely, a typical branching narrative offers the user a piece of a story and then asks him to make plot or character decisions. The effects of these decisions may be very small and short-lived, or they may make a huge difference to the story and change everything from that point on. Branching narratives are typically represented as direct graphs in which each node represents a linear, scripted scene followed by a decision point. Arcs between nodes represent decisions that can be made by the users [75]. Even though branching narrative may introduce variability into the experience a user has with a storytelling system, the variability is scripted into the system at design time and is thus limited by the system designer's anticipation of the user's needs or preferences.

In selecting the narrative structure, experts in training communication skills have to fix a level of complexity that is appropriate for the learning objectives and goals of the experience that is being simulated, and makes the simulation experience as easy as possible to understand for the learner. Branching techniques vary from very simple, *bulging tree* structures, where each story segment correspond to a branch, to very complex, open-ended structures, such as what mathematicians call a *complete graph*, in which every decision node is connected to every other node.

Once the narrative structure is fixed, experts begin to script different choices at different decision points. According to Schank [65], more than a great number of choices, the simulation of a system for the training of communication skills requires to communicate that there's not always one right answer. The trainee is invited to learn to use his own judgment rather than rely on someone else's. Throughout the simulation, people should be able to make the same choices they'd make in a real situation. Nevertheless, although assuming that no one of the alternative options should be quite wrong, experts should fix one of them as the best practice, consistently to the targeted skill and to the selected perspectives. Once again, it is a matter of interplay between semantic instability and semantic stability. If semantic instability phenomena are not compensated, completed and balanced by semantic stability processes, the probabilities of order and regularity in meaning exchange would be neither possible nor explainable. Fixing the best practice allows experts to ground the communicative exchange on context regularity, since if it is true that contexts show a great deal of variability and unpredictability, then it is also true that in most cases contexts are structured and regular forms in our everyday experience of the world.

14.4 Conclusions

To sum up, in order to reduplicate the flow of the communicative path, a learning environment for the training of communicative competence has to model the complexity of communicative interaction in a viable way. As we have seen, communicative phenomena appear to move restlessly between contingency and fixedness. On the one hand, they are endowed with a high flexibility and adaptability to the contingent situations of interlocutors. On the other hand, they show consistent regularities connected with the need to expect some kind of stability over time, in order to be graspable and intelligible.

In general, it seems that an open-ended narrative structure should allow the e-learning simulation to fit adequately such complexity of communicative exchanges. An open-ended simulation should present the user with a large number of choices at each turn that lead to an almost infinite number of outcomes. However, from the end-user's point of view, creating a highly complex simulation environment leads often the end-user to confusion, frustration, and disappointment with the experience. From the perspective of experts in training communication skills, the complexity of communicative exchanges is not already reproduced by neither existing algorithms nor predictive models for anticipating communicative boundaries and communicative degrees of freedom. The basic idea is that an effective communicative strategy is not foreseeable a priori, since it requires an articulated path of communicative layers and the control of different degrees of freedom. Moreover, the same strategy may imply different levels of efficacy in different contexts, since it depends on the context in a contingent way. The efficacy of both communication skills managed step by step during the communicative exchange, and the overall communicative strategy is only definable *a posteriori*. As a consequence, the trainee is allowed to compare the perspective he selected and performed with other pre-scripted perspectives. Therefore, scripting different *ad hoc* perspectives is a fundamental requisite for a narrative structure in order to reproduce both the flexibility and regularity of communicative exchanges. An adequate scaffolding structure for the training of communicative competence in an e-learning environment entails fixing both contextual boundaries and degrees of freedom to let the learner the opportunity to give sense to the perspective selected.

14.5 References

[1]   L. Anolli, The detection of the hidden design of meaning, in *The hidden structure of interaction: From neurons to culture patterns*, L. Anolli, S. Duncan, Jr., M. S. Magnusson, and G. Riva, Eds. Amsterdam: IOS Press, pp. 23-50, 2005.

[2]   C. Aldrich, *Simulations and the future of learning: An innovative (and perhaps revolutionary) approach to e-learning*. San Francisco: Jossey-Bass/Pfeiffer, 2003.

[3]   S. Marsella, Pedagogical Soap, *AAAI Fall Symposium Technical Report FS-00-04*. Menlo Park: AAAI Press, 2000.

[4]   A. Paiva, J. Dias, D. Sobral, R. Aylett, P. Sobreperez, S. Woods, C. Zoll, and L. Hall, Caring for agents and agents that care: Building empathic relations with synthetic agents. *Proceedings of the 3rd International Conference on Autonomous Agents and Multiagent Systems*. New York: ACM Press, 2004.

[5]   T. W. Deacon, *The symbolic species: The co-evolution of language and the human brain*. New York: Norton, 1997.

[6]   L. Anolli, Significato modale e comunicazione non verbale, *Giornale Italiano di Psicologia* 3, 453-484, 2003.

[7]   J. Searle, *The rediscovery of the mind*. Cambridge: The MIT press, 1992.

[8]   P. Violi, *Meaning and experience*. Bloomington: Indiana University Press, 2001.

[9]   L. Anolli, *Psicologia della cultura*. Bologna: Il Mulino, 2004.

[10] J. Bruner, *Actual minds, possible worlds*. Cambridge: Harvard University Press, 1986.

[11] J. Bruner, *Acts of meaning*. Cambridge: Harvard University Press. 1990.

[12] P. Bourdieu, *Outline of a theory of practice*. Cambridge: Cambridge University Press, 1977.

[13] P. Bourdieu, *The logic of practice*. Stanford: Stanford University Press, 1990.

[14] L. Anolli, Comunicazione e significato, in *Psicologia della comunicazione*, L. Anolli, Ed. Bologna: Il Mulino, pp. 147-178, 2002

[15] C. S. Peirce, What is a sign?, in *Collected Papers 1931-1935* (vol. 2). Cambridge: Harvard University Press, pp. 297-302, 1984.

[16] H. P. Grice, Logic and Conversation, in *Syntax and semantics* (vol. 3), P. Cole and J. Morgan, Eds. New York: Academic Press, pp. 41-58, 1975.

[17] D. Sperber, and D. Wilson, Relevance: *Communication and cognition*. Oxford: Oxford University Press, 1986.

[18] L. Anolli, MaCHT – Miscommunication as Chance Theory: Towards a unitary theory of communication and miscommunication, in *Say not to say: New perspectives on miscommunication*, L. Anolli, R. Ciceri, and G. Riva, Eds. Amsterdam: IOS Press, pp. 3-42, 2002.

[19] D. C. Dennett, *The intentional stance*. Cambridge: The MIT Press, 1987.

[20] Bach, K., Default reasoning: Jumping to conclusions and knowing when to think twice, *Pacific Philosophical Quarterly* 65, pp. 37-58, 1984.

[21] O. D. W. Hargie, C. Saunders, and D. Dickson, *Social skills in interpersonal communication*. London: Routledge, 1994.

[22] P. Northouse, and L. Northouse, *Health communication: Strategies for health professionals*. Norwalk: Appleton & Lange, 1992.

[23] F. Barnabei, W. Cormier, and L. Nye, Determining the effects of three counselling verbal responses on client verbal behaviour, *British Journal of Social Work* 21, pp. 355-359, 1974.

[24] L. Brammer, *The helping relationship: Process and skills*. Englewood Cliffs: Prentice-Hall, 1993.

[25] P. Hartley, *Interpersonal communication*. London: Routledge, 1993.

[26] D. A. Dickson, Reflecting, in *The handbook of communication skills* (2nd edition), O. D. W. Hargie, Ed. London: Routledge, pp. 159-182, 1997.

[27] L. Anolli, M. G. Infantino., and R. Ciceri, "You're a real genius!": Irony as a miscommunication design, in *Say not to say: New perspectives on miscommunication*, L. Anolli, R. Ciceri, and G. Riva, Eds. Amsterdam: IOS Press, pp. 135-157, 2002.

[28] J. Jorgensen, The functions of sarcastic irony in speech, *Journal of Pragmatics* 26, pp. 613-634, 1996.

[29] J. J. LaGaipa, The effects of humour on the flow of social conversation, in *It's a funny thing, humour*, A. J. Chapman and H. C. Foot, Eds. Oxford: Pergamon, pp. 82-99, 1977.

[30] H. C. Foot, and A. J. Chapman, The social responsiveness of young children in humorous situations, in *Humour and laughter: Theory, research, and applications*, A. J. Chapman and H. C. Foot, Eds. Chichester: John Wiley, pp. 11-36, 1976.

[31] P. R. Cohen, and H. J. Levesque, Preliminaries to a collaborative model of dialogue, *Speech Communication* 15 (4), pp. 265-274, 1994.

[32] A. Duranti, *Linguistic anthropology*. Cambridge: Cambridge University Press, 1997.

[33] J. K. Burgoon, Cross-cultural and intercultural applications of expectancy violations theory, in *Intercultural communication theory* (International and Intercultural Communication Annual, Vol. 19), R. L. Wiseman, Ed. Thousand Oaks: Sage Publications, pp. 194-214, 1995.

[34] J. N. Cappella, Behavioural and judged coordination in adult informal social interaction: Vocal and kinesic indicators, *Journal of Personality and Social Psychology* 72 (1), pp. 119-131, 1997.

[35] E. Goffman, *Interaction ritual: Essay on the face-to-face behaviour*. New York: Doubleday, 1967.

[36] E. Zerubavel, *Hidden rhythms: Schedules and calendars in social life*. Chicago: The University of Chicago Press, 1981.

[37] A. Schutz, *Gesammelte Aufsätze. Volume I: Das Problem der sozialen Wirklichkeit*. Den Haag: Martinus Nijhoff, 1971.

[38] C. H. Cooley, *Social organization*. New York: Pergamon Press, 1920.

[39] G. H. Mead, *Mind, self, and society*. Chicago: University of Chicago Press, 1937.

[40] H. Giles, Accent mobility: A model and some data, *Anthropological Linguistics* 15 (2), pp. 87-105, 1973.

[41] H. Giles, and P. F. Powesland, *Speech style and social evaluation*. London: Academic Press, 1975.

[42] H. Giles, N. Coupland, and J. Coupland, Eds., *Contexts of accommodation: Developments in applied sociolinguistics*. Cambridge: Cambridge University Press, 1991.

[43] J. T. Webb, Interview synchrony. An investigation of two speech rate measures in an automated standardized interview, in *Studies in diadic communication*, A. W. Siegman and B. Pope, Eds. New York: Pergamon, pp. 115-133, 1972.

[44] J. Jaffe, and S. Feldstein, *Rhythms of dialog*. New York: Academic, 1970.

[45] M. Natale, Convergence of mean vocal intensity in dyadic communication as a function of social desirability, *Journal of Personality and Social Psychology* 32, pp. 790-804, 1975b.

[46] M. Natale, Social desirability as related to convergence of temporal speech patterns, *Perceptual and Motor Skills* 40, pp. 827-830, 1975a.

[47] P. Lieberman, *Intonation, perception, and language*. Cambridge: MIT Press, 1970.

[48] S. W. Jr. Gregory, A quantitative analysis of temporal symmetry in microsocial relations, *American Sociological Review* 48, pp. 129-135, 1983.

[49] S. W. Jr. Gregory, and S. A. Webster, A non-verbal signal in voices of interview partners effectively predicts communication accommodation and social status perceptions, *Journal of Personality and Social Psychology* 70 (6), pp. 1231-1240, 1996.

[50] S. W. Jr. Gregory, K. Dagan, and S. Webster, Evaluating the relation of vocal accommodation in conversation partners' fundamental frequencies to perception of communication quality, *Journal of Nonverbal Behavior*,21, pp. 23-43, 1997.

[51] K. Grammer, Human courtship: Biological bases and cognitive processing, in *The sociobiology of sexual and reproductive strategies*, A. Rasa, C. Vogel, and E. Volland, Eds. London: Chapman and Hall, pp. 147-169, 1989.

[52] K. Grammer, K. Kruck, and M. S. Magnusson, The courtship dance: Patterns of nonverbal synchronization in opposite-sex encounters, *Journal of Nonverbal Behavior* 22 (1), pp. 3-29, 1998.

[53] F. Mantovani, Cyber-attraction: The emergence of computer-mediated communication in the development of interpersonal relationships, in *Say not to say: New perspectives on miscommunication*, L. Anolli, R. Ciceri, and G. Riva, Eds. Amsterdam: IOS Press, pp. 229-245, 2002.

[54] T. Koss, and R. Rosenthal, Interactional synchrony, positivity and patient satisfaction in the physician-patient relationship, *Medical Care* 35, pp. 1158-1163, 1997.

[55] L. Anolli, Inquadramento storico e teorico sulla comunicazione, in *Psicologia della comunicazione*, L. Anolli, Ed. Bologna: Il Mulino, pp. 3-32, 2002.

[56] R. Jackendoff, *Language of the mind: Essays on mental representation*. Cambridge: The MIT Press, 1992.

[57] G. Bateson, *Steps to an ecology of mind*. New York: Chandler, 1972.

[58] A. Fogel, *Developing through relationships*. Harvester Wheatsheaf: London, 1993.

[59] M. Burgoon, F. Hunsaker, and E. Dawson, *Human communication* (3rd edition). Sage: London, 1994.

[60] B. Rogoff, *Apprenticeship in thinking: Cognitive development in social context*. New York: Oxford University Press, 1990.

[61] B. Rogoff, *The cultural nature of human development*. New York: Oxford University Press, 2003.

[62] B. Rogoff, Developing understanding of the idea of communities of learners, *Mind, culture, and activity*, 1(4), pp. 209-229, 1994.

[63] M. Wartofsky, *Models: Representation and the scientific understanding*. Dordrecht: Riedel, 1979.

[64] J. V. Wertsch, *Voices of the mind: A sociocultural approach to mediated action*. Cambridge, MA: Harvard University Press.

[65] R. Schank, *Virtual learning: A revolutionary approach to building a highly skilled workforce*. New York: McGraw-Hill, 1997.

[66] E. Tulving, Episodic and semantic memory, in *Organisation of memory*, E. Tulving and W. Donaldson, New York: Academic Press, pp. 381-403, 1972.

[67] G. Mantovani, G. Riva, "Real" presence: How different ontologies generate different criteria for presence, telepresence, and virtual presence, *Presence, Teleoperators, and Virtual Environments* 8, pp 538-548, 1999.

[68] W. A. Ijsselsteijn, and G. Riva, Being there: The experience of presence in mediated environments, in *Being there: Concepts, effects and measurements of user presence in synthetic environments*, G. Riva, F. Davide, and W. A. Ijsselsteijn, Eds. Amsterdam: IOS Press, pp. 4-16, 2003.

[69] D. Gentner, and A.L. Stevens, Eds. *Mental models*. Hillsdale: Lawrence Erlbaum Associates, 1983.

[70] D. Norman, Some observations on mental models, in *Mental Models*, D. Gentner, and A. L. Stevens, Eds. Hillsdale: Lawrence Erlbaum Associates, pp. 7-14, 1983.

[71] J. D. W. Morecroft, and J. D. Sterman, *Modeling for learning organizations*. Portland: Productivity Press, 1994.

[72] R. N. Caine, and G. Caine, *Making connections: teaching and the human brain*. Alexandria: Association for Supervision and Curriculum Development, 1991.

[73] M. O. Riedl, C. J. Saretto, and R. M. Young, Managing interaction between users and agents in a multiagent storytelling environment. *Proceedings of the 2nd International Joint Conference on Autonomous Agents and Multi Agent Systems*, 2003.

[74] M. O. Riedl, and R. M. Young, An intent-driven planner for multi-agent story generation. *Proceedings of the 3rd International Joint Conference on Autonomous Agents and Multi Agent Systems*, 2004.

[75] A. Gordon, M. Van Lent, M. Van Velsen, P. Carpenter, and A. Jhala, Branching storylines in virtual reality environments for leadership development. *Proceedings of the 16th Innovative Applications of AI Conference*, 2004.

From Communication to Presence
G. Riva et al. (Eds.)
IOS Press, 2006
© *2006 The authors. All rights reserved.*

Author Index